Palestinian Religious Terrorism: Hamas and Islamic Jihad

Yonah Alexander

Transnational Publishers, Inc.
Ardsley, New York

Published and distributed by Transnational Publishers, Inc.
410 Saw Mill River Road
Ardsley, NY 10502, USA

Phone: 914-693-5100
Fax: 914-693-4430
E-mail: info@transnationalpubs.com
Web: www.transnationalpubs.com

Library of Congress Cataloging-in-Publication Data

Palestinian religious terrorism : Hamas and Islamic Jihad / by Yonah Alexander.
   p. cm.
Includes bibliographical references.
   ISBN 1-57105-247-X
   1. òHarakat al-Muqåawamah al-Islåamåiyah.   2. òHarakat al-Jihåad al-Islåamåi fåi Filasòtåin.   3. Islam and politics—West Bank.   4. Islam and politics—Gaza Strip.   5. Arab-Israeli conflict.   I. Title.

JQ1830.A98 H373 2002
322.4'2'095694—dc21   2002190388

Manufactured in the United States of America

Table Of Contents

SELECTED DOCUMENTS

SELECTED BIBLIOGRAPHY

Preface

Terrorism—the calculated employment of violence, or the threat of violence by individuals, subnational groups, and state actors to attain political, social, and economic objectives in the violation of law, intended to create an overwhelming fear in a target area larger than the victims attacked or threatened—is as old as civilization itself. Yet unlike their historical counterparts, present-day terrorists have introduced into contemporary life a new scale of violence in terms of conventional and unconventional threats and impact.

The internationalization and brutality of modern terrorism make it clear that we have entered into an Age of Super and Cyber Terrorism with its serious implications to national, regional, and global security concerns. Perhaps the most significant dangers are those relating to the safety, welfare, and rights of ordinary people; the stability of the state system; the health of economic development; the expansion of democracy; and perhaps even the survival of civilization itself.

The academic community—in recognition of its intellectual obligation as well as its moral and practical responsibility to participate in the international effort to arrest the virus of terrorism—has developed in the past four decades multidisciplinary research initiatives focusing on a broad range of issues related to this challenge. For instance, in the aftermath of the February 26, 1993 bombing of the World Trade Center in New York City, the Terrorism Studies Program at The George Washington University organized a research project on the selected Middle East perpetrators. This study grew out of the realization that "if contemporary society is to make terrorism, initiated in the name of supposedly 'higher' ideological and political purposes, a less inviting tactical and strategic tool and a more costly weapon to its precipitators and their nation-state supporters, then it is critical to expand our knowledge of the motivations and capabilities of these groups."[1]

Americans and the international community in general have renewed their interest in terrorism challenges with the emergence of Usama bin Laden's al-Qaida in the 1990s. Clearly, the carnage of September 11, 2001, considered

---

[1] Yonah Alexander, *Middle East Terrorism: Selected Group Profiles* (Washington, D.C.: JINSA, 1994), pp. vi–vii.

as the most spectacular terrorist operation in modern history, has raised a new set of security concerns affecting all civilized nations.

It is against this background that the Inter-University Center for Terrorism Studies (a consortia of academic institutions in over thirty countries), in collaboration with the International Center for Terrorism Studies at the Potomac Institute for Policy Studies, is continuing its research project to increase our understanding of the most notorious contemporary terrorist movements around the world. Two studies have already been published in this series.[2]

The current publication, *Palestinian Religious Terrorism: Hamas and Islamic Jihad*, is designed to provide an easily accessible reference for academics, policymakers, the press, and other interested individuals. The study exposes much of Hamas and Islamic Jihad mystiques and thereby places these organizations in perspective as two of the many challenges facing the international community in its war against terrorism—whether it is waged in the Middle East or elsewhere.

As this study goes to press, U.S. Secretary of State Colin Powell's mission to the Middle East in April 2002 to achieve an Israeli-Palestinian cease-fire to the eighteen months of violence was unsuccessful. Contributing to the failure of his recent efforts as well as to the other diplomatic moves over the years are the activities of both Hamas and Islamic Jihad. These religious-based movements, operating independently, as well as jointly, and at times in collaboration with other Palestinian secular terrorist organizations, are dedicated to murdering noncombatants for the purpose of advancing the cause of establishing a Palestinian theological state that would replace Israel. President George W. Bush asserted repeatedly that "suicide bombers in the name of religion are simple terror" and that "the civilized world must band together to stop this kind of activity if we expect there to be peace and resolution in the Middle East."

It is hoped, therefore, that this publication will advance public understanding of the nature and intensity of the terrorist challenges in the coming months and years.

---

[2]   Yonah Alexander and Michael S. Swetnam, *Usama bin Laden's al-Qaida: Profile of a Terrorist Network* (Ardsley, NY: Transnational Publishers, 2001) and Yonah Alexander, Michael S. Swetnam and Herbert M. Levine, *ETA: Profile of a Terrorist Group* (Ardsley, NY: Transnational Publishers, 2001).

Important contributions were made by Joy Kolin and Alon Lanir (Johns Hopkins University) as well as the research team at the International Center for Terrorism Studies comprised of: Eric Whittington, Kerrie J. Martin, Vivek K. Narayanan, Tyler Richardson, Sean Corcoran, Winter Salembier, and Robert Mellen.

In addition to these researchers, other individuals in the United States and abroad have contributed to this project. We are particularly indebted to the encouragement of Michael S. Swetnam (CEO and Chairman of the Board, Potomac Institute for Policy Studies), and the continuing academic advice of Professor Herbert M. Levine of the Inter-University Center for Terrorism Studies and Professor Edgar H. Brenner of the Inter-University Center for Legal Studies (International Law Institute in Washington, D.C.).

Finally, this volume draws on unclassified information generated over the past two decades from dozens of international seminars and conferences, numerous interviews, media reports, court cases, and field work in the Middle East, Europe, Asia, and Latin America.

Yonah Alexander
April 25, 2002

Hamas—Harakat Al-Muqawama Al-Islamiya

HISTORY

The Islamic Resistance Movement—Hamas—was officially founded in 1988, shortly after the outbreak of the first Palestinian Intifada (Uprising). However, the movement's roots can be traced to the 1940s as an extension of the Muslim Brotherhood. During the first Intifada, the leaders of the Muslim Brotherhood realized that the time was ripe to add a military component to their organization. The group took active measures against Israel, and started to educate the youth against Zionism and the existence of Israel.

A large part of Hamas' success is due to its influence in the Gaza Strip. The socio-economic hardships of refugees in Gaza and the fact that other nationalist parties were not dominant at the time, enabled Hamas to increase its following. The Palestine Liberation Organization's (PLO) center of activity was in Tunisia—outside the Occupied Territories—a factor that contributed to the development of local Palestinian leadership. Hamas was also successful in forming a social system, providing an alternative to the PLO.

In August 1988, Hamas published the Islamic Covenant—its ideological doctrine. The Covenant challenges both Israel and the PLO and claims that Hamas is the sole legitimate representative of the Palestinian people. Hamas' participation in street violence during the Intifada contributed to that organization's central role in the uprising and increased its popularity and growth.

After the Gulf War in 1991, Hamas became the leading terrorist entity in the Occupied Territories, and had become the second most powerful group, after Fatah, headed by Yasser Arafat. The same year Ziccaria Walid Akhel established Izz al-Din al-Qassam Battalions, which kidnapped and executed suspected collaborators with Israel.

The deportation of 415 Hamas and Islamic Jihad activists from Israel by the Itzhak Rabin government in 1992 marked a changing point in Hamas' policies. Hamas decided to adopt Hizballah terrorist methods by using car bombs and suicide bombers in addition to kidnappings against Israeli civilians and military personnel.

The 1993 Oslo Accords and the signing of the Declaration of Principles between Israel and the Palestinian Authority (PA) changed Hamas' strategic situation. First, the agreement put an end to the Intifida, which allowed Hamas to grow as a local alternative to the PLO. Second, the PLO's agreement to curtail violence in the Territories threatened Hamas' military abilities and freedom of action. Despite the changing situation, the Hamas leadership decided to continue the Jihad (holy war) against Israel, while still preserving unity within the Palestinian ranks. Hamas escalated the violence through suicide bombings, which thwarted the peace process and at times threatened to completely stop it.

Since the establishment of the PA in 1994, Hamas' civic activities have focused on the following areas: in the short term, to maintain a strong opposition to the PA; and in the long term, to create a possible alternative to it. The PA views Hamas as a serious challenge to its power.

In an attempt to limit the organization's activity following the February-March 1996 terrorism attacks on Israeli civilians, the PA took steps against Hamas' financial base by closing down several charitable organizations and confiscating funds and equipment. These actions, along with Israel's crackdown on the Islamic movement in Um al-Fahem and Nazareth (two cities in Israel), significantly hindered Hamas' activities and financial resources.

Hamas maintains charitable institutions in Jerusalem, the West Bank, the Gaza Strip, the United States, Saudi Arabia, the Gulf States, Iran and other locations. Those networks focus on providing aid to the families of terrorists who committed suicide bombings, or to prisoners and their families. It also provides funding for Hamas' military operations.

The outbreak of the second Intifada in September 2000 was seen by Hamas as a strategic opportunity to continue the resistance to Israel's occupation. Hamas leaders stated that the Intifada "crystallized and boosted" Palestinian national unity. Hamas calls for continuing the Jihad and resistance against Israel in all forms. From September 2000 to March 2002, Hamas took responsibility for approximately forty suicide bombing incidents against Israeli citizens, taking the lives of over 400 individuals.

IDEOLOGY

The ideology of Hamas is based primarily on the mainstream of the Muslim Brotherhood movement in Egypt, which was founded in 1928 by Hassan al-Banna. It combines both religious principles and pan-Arab ideas, along with Palestinian national aspirations. Hamas added religious meaning to Palestinian nationalism, hence confronting the PLO's secular national ideology with an Islamic nationalist agenda. In the *Islamic Covenant*, published by Hamas in August 1988, Hamas defined itself as the "Palestinian branch of the Muslim Brotherhood."

Hamas' central goal is the establishment of an Islamic state in all of Palestine, i.e., Israel and the Occupied Territories. Jihad is the only means to redeem all of Palestine. It is the duty of all Muslims to participate in this Jihad, not just Palestinian Muslims.

Since its establishment, Hamas has aimed at creating a civic-religious infrastructure that deals with the following issues: aid to the poor, education, health, and religion. Building this foundation has been the goal of the organization since its founding in the Occupied Territories. This network is the main source of Hamas' power in the West Bank and especially in the Gaza Strip, and is used to recruit and deploy suicide bombers.

Since his release from an Israeli prison in 1997, Hamas spiritual leader Sheik Ahmad Isma'il Yassin has issued several conflicting messages regarding his willingness to negotiate with Israel and the PA. In an October 1997 interview, Yassin said that he does not rule out having peaceful relations with the Jews. In January 1998, however, he completely ruled out Israel's right to exist. Since the second Intifada, Hamas has renounced any negotiations with Israel and calls on all Palestinians to continue resistance by any means at any time and any place.

OBJECTIVES

Hamas' objectives include:

A commitment to Islam as a way of life.

- Destruction of the "Zionist Entity." According to the movement, the only solution to the Arab-Israeli conflict is the fighting of a Jihad against Israel.
- Creation of a Palestinian Arab state replacing Israel. The movement contends that all of Israel is located on Islamic sacred land. Any concessions that would leave part of the land in Israel's hands constitute treason to the Palestinian-Arab cause, and signify religious heresy.
- Synthesis of Pan-Islamic religious ideals and Palestinian nationalism.
- Violent opposition to the Israeli-Palestinian peace process.

ORGANIZATIONAL STRUCTURE

The Hamas command network was formed in 1993–94 as part of the group's reorganization in the West Bank and Gaza Strip. It includes three divisions:

- Public—Muslim Brotherhood members who are active in Palestinian-Arab institutions and politics.
- Underground Network—Highly dedicated members that organize demonstrations, transfer funds, and carry out intelligence missions.
- Military Wing—The Qassam Brigades make up the militant wing of Hamas. These armed squads target Israeli civilians and soldiers, as well as Palestinian collaborators. Militant members, called "Striking Arms," target Israelis, and a second underground unit, called the "Islamic Police," attacks Palestinians.

The leadership, membership, and funding techniques of Hamas are also part of its organizational structure.

Leadership

Prominent religious leaders of the Hamas have formed the Association of Religious Sages of Palestine (*Rabitat "Ulama" Filastin*), which serves as a kind of supreme religious body that grants legitimacy to the movement's activities.

Sheikh Ahmad Isma`il Yassin
Founder and spiritual leader of the Hamas. Yassin headed the Hamas until his arrest by Israel in May 1989. He was responsible for a large part of the group's activities, such as writing leaflets, engaging in financial affairs, organizing liaison with radical Islamic elements abroad, and supervising terrorist activities. He established a broad organizational network directing the movement during the Intifada.

Yassin was released on October 1, 1997, in a deal between Jordan and Israel in exchange for the extradition of two Israeli agents arrested in Jordan following a failed assassination attempt in Amman on Khalid Misha'al, chairman of Hamas' Political Bureau.

Musa Mohammed Abu Marzuq
Head of Hamas Political Bureau, and liaison to such groups as Popular Front for the Liberation of Palestine (PFLP) and Democratic Front for the

Liberation of Palestine (DFLP). Due to the Israeli-Jordanian peace agreement in May 1995, Abu Marzuq was ordered to leave Jordan by June 1, 1995. He has been involved in planning Hamas terrorist attacks within Israel. These include the April 1994 bombings in Afula and Hadera. He was arrested in New York on July 25, 1995. Israel asked for his extradition, and an American judge decided in May 1996 that he can be expelled for trial in Israel. Eventually, Abu Marzuq was expelled to Jordan in May 1997. Currently, he resides in Syria where he continues to activate the organization's military operations.

Emad Al Alami
Member of Hamas Political Bureau and chairman of the Hamas interior committee, representative of the organization in Syria.

Khalid Misha'al
Head of Hamas Political Bureau. He has been a member of the Political Bureau since it was established. He was elected as chairman of the Bureau in 1996. He escaped an assassination attempt on his life by Israeli Mossad agents on September 25, 1997, in Amman. Sheikh Ahmad Yassin was released from an Israeli jail as a result of this unsuccessful attempt.

Muhammad Def
A top Hamas activist in Khan Yunis refugee camp. Responsible for the deaths of dozens of Israelis. One of the most wanted men on Israel's list.

Mohammed Nazzal
Member of Hamas Political Bureau and chief representative of the movement's office in Jordan since 1992.

Ibrahim Ghousheh
Head spokesman for Hamas since 1992 and a member of the Hamas Political Bureau.

Dr. Abdel Aziz Rantisi
Hamas spokesman in Gaza. Arrested by Israeli authorities and remained under administrative arrest until mid-1997.

Jamal Mansour
A Hamas leader in the West Bank. Killed in an Israeli helicopter attack on July 31, 2001.

Salah Shihada

Sheikh Salah Shihada was the founder of the first military apparatus of the Hamas, known as "Palestinian Mujahidoun," which was accused of forming military cells, carrying weapons, and attacking Israeli military targets.

Yahya Ayyash

Nickname: "The Engineer." Was responsible for planning many suicide bombings against Israeli soldiers and civilians. Leader of Izz al-Din al-Qassam Brigades. He was killed in Bet Lahia, north of the Gaza Strip, on January 5, 1996, by a small explosive planted in a mobile phone he used occasionally.

Emad Aqel

Leader of Izz al-Din al-Qassam Brigades in Gaza. He was killed by Israeli forces on November 24, 1993.

Membership

Active Operational: Hamas operative fighters are estimated between 750 and 1,200. Some of the members that were exposed and arrested by Israeli authorities include:

Mazen Malaze

Key Hamas activist in the Ramallah region.

Majdi Tabas

Hamas activist in Ramallah.

Fatahallah Abu Srur

Hamas activist in Bethlehem.

Tariq Akash

Hamas activist in Jerusalem.

Ahad Nahshe

Hamas activist in Ramallah.

Raed Abu Dahar

Hamas activist in Ramallah.

Top Hamas Members on Israel's Wanted List

Iman Helawah
Hamas activist in Nablus. Responsible for the Dolphinarium attack in Tel-Aviv in June, 2001.

Keis Adwan Abu-Jabel
Hamas activist in Jenin. Responsible for the Sbarro attack in Jerusalem on August 9, 2001, and other operations.

Nasser Nazal
Hamas activist in Qalqilya. Responsible for the Dolphinarium attack and other operations.

Abas Sayid
Head of Hamas military infrastructure in Tulkarem. Responsible for the "Sharon" shopping mall attack in Netanya on May 18th, 2001.

Nidal Kalak
Hamas activist in Tulkarem.

Ahnas Abu-Alba
Hamas activist in Qaliqilya. Involved in many attacks, including the Dolphinarium operation.

Jaser Smaro
Hamas activist in Nablus. Responsible for the Dolphinarium attack.

Nasim Abu-Ros
Hamas activist in Nablus. Responsible for the Dolphinarium attack.

Salim Hijah
Hamas activist in Nablus.

Muhamad Khalili
Hamas activist in Nablus.

Taher Nasser
Hamas activist in Atsira Shmaliya.

Muhnad Taher
Hamas activist in Nablus.

Jamel Abd-Al Hijah
Hamas activist in Jenin.

Abdallah Jamel
Hamas activist in Beit Rima. Responsible for the Sbarro attack on August 9, 2001, and other operations.

Balal Barghuti/Othman
Hamas activist in Beit Rima.

Imad Sharif
Hamas activist in Betoniya.

Ahmad Abu Taha
Hamas activist in Ramallah.

Hisham Sharbati
Hamas activist in Hebron.

Sa'ad Arabid
Hamas activist in Gaza.

Muhammad Sinwar
Hamas activist in Khan Yunis.

Nafaz Sabin-Daraj
Hamas activist in Gaza.

A'hed B'shiti
Hamas activist in Rafah.

Adnan Al-Ghul
Hamas activist in Gaza.

Supporters

Tens of thousands in the Middle East and beyond. Hamas claims support of 40 percent of the population in the Occupied Territories, although this number is considered greatly inflated. The number is most likely closer to 20 percent at most. However, while PLO support is decreasing, support for Hamas among the general Palestinian population is on the rise.

Funding

Hamas raises funds from several sources to finance its social and military activities. Donations and membership dues are collected from activists and supporters in the West Bank and Gaza Strip. Fundraising is conducted in both Arab and Islamic countries, in addition to Palestinian communities throughout the world. Reports have indicated that Hamas received direct and indirect financial aid from Arab and Muslim states, such as Saudi Arabia, Iran, Jordan, Yemen, Turkey and the Gulf states.

Hamas has diversified its holdings and sources of funding to avoid a concentration of influence. In 1993, Iran reportedly gave Hamas $15 million, apparently as a result of a deal made between them to fight the peace treaty reached between Israel and the PLO.

Estimating the amount of money reaching Hamas is quite difficult. However, a rough estimate places its funding at several tens of millions of dollars per year.

Sources of funding abroad include:

- Official sources: the government of Iran contributes approximately $3 million per year for Hamas activities.
- Four main Hamas charity funds in the West:
  - *Great Britain:* The Palestine Relief and Development Fund—Interpal
  - *United States:* The Holy Land Foundation for Relief and Development. In December 2001, the United States froze the assets of the Holy Land Foundation for Relief and Development. President George W. Bush stated that the foundation's money is "used by Hamas in schools to indoctrinate children to become suicide bombers . . . and to recruit suicide bombers and support their families." According to a U.S. official, the United States froze the assets of the Al Aqsa International Bank and the Beit El-Mal Holdings Company, which were believed to be linked to Hamas.
  - *Germany:* The Al-Aqsa Foundation (with branches in Belgium and Holland).
  - *France:* Comité de Bienfaisance et Solidarité avec la Palestine.
- Funding from other Islamic organizations:
  - Nongovernmental charitable organizations in the Gulf states.

- Islamic aid agencies in the West, i.e., Muslim Aid and the Islamic Relief Agency.
- The Muslim Brotherhood—In the late 1980s, the Brotherhood established the Muslim Aid Committee to the Palestinian Nation in order to aid Hamas.

• Independent sources of funding in the Territories:
- A limited portion of Hamas funding comes from a small number of profitable economic ventures, such as sewing/weaving centers and cattle farms.
- A broad network of charities *(Jamayath Hiriya)* and committees *(Lejan Zakath)* also operate in the Occupied Territories. Hamas uses these institutions, which together with the mosques and worker unions, serve as a cover to the organization's activities.
- Pro-Hamas Islamists collect charity *(zedath)*, obligatory by Islam, through these local committees. This network of charity is a means of channeling funds into the region. The charities assist the Hamas transfer funds through their financial and administrative infrastructures.

• Fundraising in Israel:
- The Islamic movement in Israel acts as a channel for transferring money from charitable foundations in the West to Hamas operatives. Since Israel closed two central bodies—Islamic Aid (in 1995) and the Committee for Aid to Orphans and Prisoners (in November 1996)—the use of this channel has decreased rapidly. Most of Hamas' foundations have representatives in the Territories and operate under an umbrella organization established in 1995. However, later that year, Hamas was able to resume its activities due to the PA's easing of financial restrictions.

AREAS OF OPERATION

The Occupied Territories (Gaza Strip and the West Bank) and East Jerusalem are Hamas' primary centers of activity. The organization also has offices in Amman, where the public relations infrastructure is based. Hamas allegedly has elaborate command structures in both Great Britain and the United States where fundraising and operational planning are performed. Fundraising is centered in Chicago, New York City, New Jersey, Virginia, Washington, D.C., Detroit, Kansas City, and other areas. Hamas is also known to have representation in cities throughout Europe. Some members are known to be trained at a farm outside Khartoum, Sudan. Hamas' official web site (*www.palestine-info.net*) is maintained and operated from Florida.

Two U.S.-based organizations provide political support to the Hamas. One of them is the Islamic Association for Palestine, and the other is the Holy Land Foundation for Relief and Development. These organizations have offices in Texas, Illinois, and New Jersey.

Several U.S.-based "charity" organizations, such as the Islamic Committee for Palestine and the World and Islam Studies Enterprise, are directly connected to the Palestinian Islamic Jihad (PIJ). These so-called charities conduct fundraising activities for the Hamas and the PIJ as well as smuggle members of those organizations into the United States.

HEADQUARTERS

The Sheikh Radwan district of Gaza City is the main command headquarters for the organization. Some of Hamas' financial headquarters are based outside the West Bank and Gaza Strip. A fundraising and policymaking network is located in the United States, as are many of the personnel commanding these efforts. In addition, the Hamas has centers of recruitment and organization in Syria.

Hamas' military infrastructure in the West Bank region is run directly from the organization's headquarters in Syria and Jordan. These offices recruit mostly electronics and chemistry students in their twenties. These students are recruited during their studies and undergo military training. Following their training, the students are sent to the field in order to establish military cells and carry out bombings and suicide attacks.

TACTICS AND CAPABILITIES

Most of the work of Hamas focuses on strengthening its hold on the Palestinian population. The movement has established projects such as dispensing charitable funds to assist the poor, schools and colleges, and clinics and hospitals that provide service free of charge for those in need. Its communal activities cover all areas of life, while promoting a "return to the faith," i.e., a life according to Islamic mores. Hamas' educational process begins in elementary school, continuing through high school. Hamas recruits and trains its members from among youth movements, and has strong support among university students. Hamas leaders and clerics use their mosques not only to transmit religious values but also to incite opposition to the occupation and encourage support for the paramilitary groups.

In addition to engaging in "social welfare" activities, Hamas operates a security apparatus that functions as the organization's emissary in three main units. The first collects intelligence among the Palestinian population concerning those suspected of collaboration, and either investigates and punishes them or "brings them back to the fold of Islam" by using them to gather intelligence or to commit acts of terrorism. The second body monitors society in order to stop immoral activity that violates the Islamic code, such as drug use, prostitution, and profiteering. The third apparatus, the Izz al-Din al-Qassam squads, are in charge of the military operations of the organization. Qassam squads tactics include suicide bombings, mortar attacks, drive-by shootings, kidnappings, assassinations, protests, strikes, agitation, and demonstrations. Qassam squads are recruited and trained from impoverished neighborhoods and refugee camps, and operate in 2–3 men cells. These operatives are usually in their twenties or thirties. Weapons are hidden in mosques and the homes of sympathizers.

TARGETS

Targets are Israeli civilians, security-service personnel, soldiers, and Palestinian collaborators. Targets also include Israel Defense Forces (IDF) installations in the West Bank and Gaza Strip, as well as Israeli civilian and military vehicles. Since December 1993, Hamas has targeted Israeli settlers in addition to Israeli soldiers.

HAMAS TIMELINE

February 1989
Kidnapping and murder of Avi Sasportas—an IDF soldier.

May 1989
Kidnapping and murder of Ilan Sa'adon—an IDF soldier.

July 1990
A Canadian tourist, Marnie Kimelman, was killed by a bomb on a Tel Aviv beach.

December 1990
Murder of three aluminum workers in Jaffa.

October 1991
Two IDF soldiers, Master Sargent Aaron Agmon Klijami and Sergeant Shmuel Michaeli were run over and killed by a terrorist who deliberately drove his vehicle into a queue of soldiers at a hitchhiking station at the Tel Hashomer army base. Eleven other soldiers were injured.

May 1992
May 17th, David Cohen, from Moshav Te'asshur was shot and killed by the Izz al-Din al-Qassam Brigades in Bet Lehe'ya, in the Gaza Strip. On the 24th, a fifteen-year-old girl from Bat Yam, Helena Rapp, was stabbed to death by a Hamas activist. The murderer was apprehended on the spot. On the 27th, Shimon Barr, the rabbi of the Darom Village, in Gush Katif, was stabbed to death. The murderer was apprehended. He was part of the Izz al-Din al-Qassam group.

June 1992
June 22nd, a policeman and an Israeli civilian were injured by shots that were fired from a speeding car at a police building in the Rimal district of Gaza by fugitives belonging to the Izz al-Din al-Qassam squad. June 25th, two Israeli civilians were stabbed to death in a packing-house near the Saja'i'a neighborhood in the Gaza District. The murders were perpetrated by the Izz al-Din al-Qassam squad. The same day a resident of Ma'ale Levona was injured while travelling with his family to Jerusalem by an axe-wielding assailant from the village of Sanjiel. The assailant was shot and apprehended.

September 1992
September 18th, Alon Caravani, IDF soldier, was kidnapped by members of the Izz al-Din al-Qassam Brigades. They gave the hitch-hiking soldier a lift in their car. He was stabbed, and then thrown from the vehicle. On the 22nd, a border policeman, Avinoam Peretz, was shot and killed at Shoefat junction, French Hill, Jerusalem. The murderer claimed that he was recruited by the Izz al-Din al-Qassam squads.

October 1992
October 21st, shots were fired from a speeding car at an IDF vehicle at the southern entrance to Hebron. An IDF soldier and a woman officer were

injured. Izz al-Din al-Qassam took credit for the attack. On the 25th, shots were again fired from a speeding car at an IDF observation post near the Cave of the Patriarchs in Hebron. One IDF reserve soldier was killed and another soldier wounded. The Izz al-Din al-Qassam squad took credit for the attack.

November 1992
Izz al-Din al-Qassam activists planned a car-bomb attack in a heavily populated area in the center of the country. The car was detected in Or Yehuda and, after pursuing the car, it was stopped and the bomb was defused. Two of the terrorists in the car were apprehended and admitted affiliation with the Izz al-Din al-Qassam squad.

December 1992
December 7th, shots were fired from a speeding car at an IDF vehicle on patrol on the Gaza bypass road, near Saja'i'a junction. The three IDF reserve soldiers in the vehicle were killed. The Izz al-Din al-Qassam squad took credit for the attack. On the 12th, shots were fired at an army jeep in Hebron. An IDF reserve soldier was killed and two others injured, one of them critically. The Izz al-Din al-Qassam squad took credit for the attack.

On the 13th, a border policeman, Nissim Toledano, was kidnapped in Lod on his way from his home. A group of fugitives from the Izz al-Din al-Qassam squad took credit for the incident. They demanded the release of Hamas leader Sheikh Ahmad Yassin from prison. Nissim Toledano's body was later found near Jerusalem.

September 1993
Yigal Vaknin was stabbed to death in an orchard near his trailer home, close to the village of Basra. A squad of the Hamas' Izz al-Din al-Qassam claimed responsibility for the attack.

October 1993
Two IDF soldiers were killed by an Izz al-Din al-Qassam squad. The two entered a Subaru with Israeli license plates outside a Jewish settlement in the Gaza Strip, whose passengers were apparently terrorists disguised as Israelis. Following a brief struggle, the soldiers were shot at close range and killed. Hamas publicly claimed responsibility for the attack.

November 1993
Efraim Ayubi of Kfar Darom was shot to death by terrorists near Hebron. Hamas publicly claimed responsibility for the murder.

December 1993
December 1st, Shalva Ozana, age 23, and Yitzhak Weinstock, age 19, were shot to death by terrorists from a moving vehicle, while parked on the side of the road to Ramallah because of engine trouble. Weinstock died of his wounds the following morning. Izz al-Din al-Qassam claimed responsibility for the attack, stating that it was carried out in retaliation for the killing by Israeli forces of Imad Akel, a wanted Hamas leader in Gaza. December 6th, Mordechai Lapid and his son Shalom Lapid, age 19, were shot to death by terrorists near Hebron. Hamas publicly claimed responsibility for the attack. On the 23rd, Eliahu Levin and Meir Mendelovitch were killed by shots fired at their car from a passing vehicle in the Ramallah area. Hamas claimed responsibility. On the 24th, Lieut. Col. Meir Mintz, commander of the IDF special forces in the Gaza area, was shot and killed by terrorists in an ambush on his jeep at the T-junction in Gaza. The Izz al-Din al-Qassam squads publicly claimed responsibility for the attack.

January 1994
Grigory Ivanov was stabbed to death by a terrorist in the industrial zone at the Erez junction, near the Gaza Strip. Hamas claimed responsibility for the attack.

February 1994
February 13th, Noam Cohen, member of the General Security Service, was shot and killed in an ambush on his car. Two of his colleagues who were also in the vehicle suffered moderate injuries. Hamas claimed responsibility for the attack. On the 19th, Zipora Sasson, resident of Ariel and five months pregnant, was killed in an ambush in which shots were fired at her car. The terrorists were members of Hamas.

April 1994
April 6th, seven civilians were killed in a car-bomb attack on a bus in the center of Afula. Hamas claimed responsibility for the attack. Ahuva Cohen Onalla, wounded in the attack, died of her wounds on April 25. April 7th, Yishai Gadassi, age 32 of Kvutzat Yavne, was shot and killed at a hitchhiking post at the Ashdod junction by a member of Hamas. The terrorist was killed by bystanders at the scene. On the 13th another suicide bombing on a bus in Hedera kills four civilians and one soldier. Hamas claimed responsibility for the attack.

May 1994
Staff Sgt. Moshe Bukra, 30, and Cpl. Erez Ben-Baruch, 24, were shot dead by Hamas terrorists at a roadblock one kilometer south of the Erez checkpoint in the Gaza Strip.

July 1994
Lt. Guy Ovadia, 23, of Kibbutz Yotvata, was fatally wounded in an ambush near Rafiah. Hamas took responsibility for the attack, saying it was "a response to the massacre at the Erez checkpoint."

August 1994
Ron Soval, 18, was shot to death in an ambush near Kissufim junction in the Gaza Strip on the 14th. Hamas claimed responsibility.

October 1994
Ma'ayan Levy, 19, a soldier, and Samir Mugrabi, 35, were killed in a terrorist attack in the Nahalat Shiva section of downtown Jerusalem on the 9th. Hamas claimed responsibility for the attack. Cpl. Nahson Wachsman, 20, who had been kidnapped by the Hamas, was murdered by his captors on the 14th. In addition, Capt. Nir Poraz, 23, was killed in the course of the unsuccessful IDF rescue operation to obtain his release.

Twenty-one Israelis and one Dutch national were killed in a suicide bombing attack on the No. 5 bus on Dizengoff Street in Tel Aviv on the 19th.

November 1994
Sgt.-Maj. Gil Dadon, 26, was killed at the army post at Netzarim junction by shots fired from a passing car on the 19th. Hamas claimed responsibility.

January 1995
Two consecutive bombs exploded at the Beit Lid junction near Netanya on the 22nd, killing eighteen soldiers and one civilian. The Islamic Jihad claimed responsibility for the attack. This was a joint operation by the Hamas and Islamic Jihad.

July 1995
Six Israeli civilians were killed in a suicide bomb attack on a bus in Ramat Gan on the 24th.

August 1995
Rivka Cohen, 26, Hannah Naeh, 56, Joan Davenney, 46, and Police Chief

Superintendent Noam Eisenman, 35, were killed in a suicide bombing of a Jerusalem bus on the 21st.

January 1996
Two soldiers were killed on the 16th when terrorists fired on their car on the Hebron-Jerusalem road. An Israeli soldier was stabbed to death on the 30th at the liaison office in an army camp south of Jenin.

February 1996
Sgt. Hofit Ayyash, 20, was killed in an explosion set off by a suicide bomber at a hitchhiking post outside Ashklon on the 25th. Hamas claimed responsibility for the attack.

Seventeen civilians and nine soldiers were killed in a suicide bombing on bus No. 18 near the Central Bus Station in Jerusalem on the 25th. Hamas claimed responsibility for the attack.

March 1996
Sixteen civilians and three soldiers were killed in a suicide bombing of bus No. 18 on Jaffa Road in Jerusalem on the 3rd.

Twelve civilians and one soldier were killed on the 4th when a suicide bomber detonated a 20-kilogram nail bomb outside Dizengoff Center in Tel Aviv.

Michal Avrahami, 32, Yael Gilad, 32, and Anat Winter-Rosen, 32, were killed when a suicide bomber detonated a bomb on the terrace of a Tel Aviv café on the 21st. Forty-eight people were wounded.

June 1996
Two soldiers and one civilian were killed on the 26th as they were ambushed along the Jordan River north of Jericho by terrorists who infiltrated from Jordan.

April 1997
The body of IDF Staff-Sgt. Sharon Edri, missing for seven months, was found buried near the West Bank village of Kfar Tzurif on the 10th. Edri had been kidnapped and murdered by a Hamas terrorist cell in September 1996 while hitchhiking to his home in Moshav Zanoah.

July 1997
Sixteen people were killed and 178 wounded in two consecutive suicide bombings in the Mahane Yehuda market in Jerusalem on the 30th. The

Izz-al-Din al-Qassam Brigades, the military wing of the Hamas, claimed responsibility for the attack.

September 1997
Seven people (including three suicide bombers) were killed and 181 wounded in three suicide bombings on the Ben-Yehuda pedestrian mall in Jerusalem on the 4th. The Izz-al-Din al-Qassam Brigades claimed responsibility for the attack.

July 1998
A devastating car bombing on Jerusalem's main street was narrowly averted when a van loaded with explosives failed to explode on the 19th. A policeman managed to extinguish the fire with a hand-held fire extinguisher. The driver, a Palestinian, was rushed to the hospital in critical condition.

August 1998
In the West Bank settlement of Yitzhar, two civilians were shot and killed on the 5th while patrolling the settlement's borders. The two men, Harel Bin-Nun, 18, and Shlomo Leibman, 24, were ambushed at a place where the settlement's gravel patrol-road descends into a wadi. Rabbi Shlomo Raanan was stabbed to death by a Hamas terrorist in his home in Tel Rumeiyde on the 20th. The attacker entered the house through a window and escaped after throwing a Molotov cocktail that set fire to the house.

A small bomb placed in a garbage dumpster near Allenby Street exploded during the morning rush hour, injuring fourteen people on the 27th. One woman was seriously injured, and two moderately. The other ten suffered light injuries.

September 1998
An IDF soldier was injured when a bomb exploded in a bus station near the Hebrew University in Jerusalem on the 24th.

Fourteen IDF soldiers and eleven Palestinians were wounded when a terrorist hurled two grenades at a border police jeep in Hebron on the 30th. The patrol shot the attacker in the leg and pursued him into the Palestinian-controlled part of Hebron, but he managed to escape.

October 1998
Thirteen soldiers and five Palestinians were injured in a grenade attack in Hebron on the 1st. A Palestinian from the H-1 area threw two grenades at the soldiers. One exploded close to where they were standing, injuring

several Palestinian bystanders, soldiers, and border policemen. The second hit two cars parked on a sidewalk and injured nearby Palestinians. Two border policemen and one soldier suffered moderate injuries, while ten others were only slightly hurt. Five Palestinians were taken to Hebron hospitals. The soldiers gave chase to the assailant, and one of them opened fire and apparently hit him in the leg. However, he managed to escape back into the H-1 area.

One man was killed and another critically wounded in a terrorist attack while swimming in a spring in the Jerusalem Hills on the 13th. The attack took place near Jerusalem. The victims were apparently ambushed by two men who opened fire on them at close range and then escaped in a car belonging to one of the victims.

A Hamas member hurled two grenades into a crowd at the Central Bus Station before running from the scene on the 19th. At least fifty-nine people were wounded in the rush-hour attack. Most of the injured were slightly or moderately wounded, though two were seriously hurt. The attacker was overwhelmed by several bystanders, who turned him over to a civil guard policeman.

A Hamas suicide bomber targeted a school bus carrying children from the community of Kfar Darom to a regional school near the Gush Katif Junction on the 29th. The bus, escorted by army jeeps, was transporting children. A suicide bomber driving an explosives-laden vehicle attempted to collide head-on with the bus. The driver of the leading jeep moved to block the suspicious car from reaching the bus, and the bomber detonated the explosives near the jeep. At least one person in the jeep was killed, along with the suicide bomber. Two passengers of the jeep were seriously injured. Six people, including three teenagers and three children, sustained slight-to-moderate injuries.

August 1999

Six people were wounded when a driver steered into a crowd twice at a bus stop in central Israel on the 10th. The attack occurred as a group of soldiers and civilians waited for the bus at the Nahshon junction. Witnesses say that a red Fiat Uno suddenly veered onto the sidewalk and into the crowd, hitting two Israeli women soldiers. The car then sped off toward Masmiah junction. Five minutes later, the driver returned and attempted to run over the wounded women and several soldiers who were giving first aid. In the second attack four others were injured. The attack ended when police shot and killed the assailant.

September 1999

Three Israeli Arabs, believed connected to the Hamas movement, were killed on the 5th as they were trying to carry out two separate car bombings in Haifa and Tiberias. A woman in Tiberias was seriously injured, while three others were slightly injured.

October 1999

Five Israeli civilians were injured in an ambush on a bus on a Saturday night near the Tarkumiyah Checkpoint on the 31st. The bus was en route from Kiryat Arba, near Hebron, to Jerusalem. According to witnesses, the shots were fired by terrorists sitting in a parked car between the villages of Idna and Adora near Hebron, about a kilometer away from the Tarkumiyah checkpost. It is believed that the perpetrators fled into the nearby autonomous areas. Hamas is believed to be responsible for the attack.

November 1999

Three pipe bombs exploded at a busy intersection in Netanya on the 7th. The bombs were placed near a trashcan in the center of town and timed to detonate during the morning rush hour. A fourth pipe bomb, which was defused by police sappers, was apparently intended to explode when rescue workers arrived on the scene. Twenty-seven people were hospitalized with light to moderate injuries. One woman was seriously injured. Hamas claimed responsibility for the attack.

September 2000

An IDF soldier was killed and another wounded when roadside bombs detonated near the settlement of Netzarim in the Gaza Strip on the 28th. The soldiers were part of a military escort for a civilian convoy. Hamas is believed to be responsible for the attack.

November 2000

A car packed with explosives blew up on a side street near Jerusalem's main outdoor market on the 2nd, killing a man and a woman and injuring ten bystanders. One of those killed in the bombing was Ayelet Levy, the daughter of former cabinet minister Yitzhak Levi. Hamas is believed to be responsible for the attack.

Three people were killed and eight were injured by gunfire on the 13th. Sarah Leisha, a forty-two year-old mother of five, was killed when the car in which she was riding came under attack near the town of Ofra, north of the Palestinian-ruled city of Ramallah. Several minutes later, the gunmen opened fire with automatic weapons from a passing car at a bus carrying IDF personnel. Two soldiers, ages 18 and 19, were killed and eight injured, two seriously. Hamas is believed to be responsible for the attacks.

A powerful bomb blast struck a school bus carrying Jewish children in the Gaza Strip on the 20th. Two people, a man and a woman, were killed and twelve were injured, among them five children. The school bus was deliberately targeted, since the bomb was detonated after a military jeep escorting the bus had already passed. Hamas is believed to be responsible for the attack.

A car bomb detonated next to a crowded bus in the northern Israeli town of Hadera during the evening rush hour on the 22nd. Two people, a man and a young woman, were killed and about fifty-five were injured, five of them seriously. Hamas is believed to be responsible for the attack.

December 2000
A Palestinian suicide bomber blew himself up on the 22nd at a roadside café in the Jordan Valley, killing himself and seriously wounding three people. An Israeli television reporter at the scene said that the remains of an explosives belt, similar to those used by the Hamas suicide bombers in previous attacks, were found in the wreckage of the café.

January 2001
Twenty people were slightly injured when a car bomb exploded near a busy intersection in Netanya on the 1st. Hamas is suspected for the attack.

The body of a thirty-two year-old resident of Kfar Yam in Gush Katif was found near the Kfar Yam hothouses on the 14th. He was working with his Palestinian employees, who are suspected of involvement in the killing. Two groups have claimed responsibility for the murder, one affiliated with al-Fatah and the other with Hamas.

February 2001
Four people were injured on the 8th as a car bomb exploded in Jerusalem's ultra-orthodox Mea She'arim neighborhood. The Popular Palestinian Resistance Forces claimed responsibility for the attack. Israeli security forces claim that this organization may be a cover for Hamas or the Islamic Jihad.

March 2001
Two men were killed, including the suicide bomber, and nine were injured on the 1st as a taxi minivan exploded near Mei Ami junction in Northern Israel. The attack has been linked to the Hamas.

A suicide bomber killed himself and three other people in Netanya on the 3rd. The bombing injured more than sixty people, several of them seriously. Police said the bomber unsuccessfully tried to board a bus, then blew himself up as he mingled with a crowd crossing an intersection in one of the busiest parts of the town. The bomb went off early Sunday in the main commercial center of the city. Hamas is believed to be responsible for the attack.

One person was killed and twenty-eight injured as a suicide bomber targeted a bus in Jerusalem's French Hill junction on the 27th. Hamas claimed responsibility for the attack.

A suicide bomber blew himself up near a bus stop frequented by pupils on the 28th. Two teenagers were killed and four others were injured. Izz-al-Din al-Qassam claimed responsibility for the blast.

April 2001
A car bomb blew up close to a school bus travelling near the West Bank city of Nablus on the 20th. There were no injuries in the attack. The body of the suicide bomber was found in the car. Hamas claimed responsibility for the attack.

A suicide bomber detonated a bomb he was carrying near a group of people waiting at a bus stop on the corner of Weizman and Tchernichovsky streets in Kfar Saba near Tel Aviv on the 22nd, killing himself and an Israeli doctor while wounding sixty others. Hamas claimed responsibility for the blast. The attack was one of three attacks in three days, but was the only one that caused an Israeli fatality.

May 2001
A suicide bomber blew himself up on the 18th at the entrance to a shopping mall in Netanya, killing himself along with five others. The dead included three women and two men. Over seventy others were injured, some of them seriously. Hamas claimed responsibility for the attack, saying it was responding to the killing of five Palestinian police officers earlier in the week.

A truck carrying explosives tried to ram an Israeli military outpost at Netzarim Junction in the Gaza Strip on the 25th. IDF officials said no Israelis were injured in the attack. Soldiers fired on the approaching vehicle, which exploded before reaching the target. The apparent suicide bomber, Hussein Nasser, was the only person killed. Hamas claimed responsibility for the attack, saying it was timed to coincide with the first anniversary of Israel's pullout from southern Lebanon.

On the 29th, two soldiers were wounded, one slightly and the other moderately, in an attack in which one bomber blew himself up and the second was killed by IDF fire as he threw grenades at the military outpost. The militant Izz al-Din al-Qassam faction claimed responsibility for the attack.

June 2001

A Palestinian suicide bomber detonated an explosives belt amid a crowd of youngsters outside Tel Aviv's Dolphinarium, near a beachfront nightclub on the 1st, killing twenty-one (including himself) and injuring more than 120. At least two militant Palestinian groups—the PIJ and Hamas—have claimed responsibility for the blast.

Two Israeli soldiers were killed on the 22nd when a Palestinian suicide bomber lured them toward his booby-trapped jeep with Israeli number-plates, then triggered a massive explosion. When the soldiers got out of their armored car and approached the jeep, the bomber detonated his explosives, killing two soldiers and slightly wounding a third. Israeli forces responded with tanks and heavy machine-gun fire, injuring three Palestinians, two moderately and one slightly, Palestinian officials said. Hamas claimed responsibility for the attack.

July 2001

Three Hamas operatives were killed on the 16th when Israeli helicopters fired three air-to-surface missiles at a Hamas safe house in Bethlehem. Israeli security sources said that senior Hamas operatives Omar Sa'ada and Taha Aruj were killed in the attack. A Palestinian suicide bomber was killed in a car-bombing attack near the Kissufim crossing point in the southern Gaza Strip on the 9th. The bomb exploded without hitting any other vehicles, and caused no other casualties. Hamas claimed responsibility for the attack. Six Hamas members, including senior operative Jamal Mansour, were killed in Nablus on the 31st by an Israeli Air Force (IAF) strike.

August 2001

Israeli helicopters fired on the car of a leading Hamas member who was carrying a carload of explosives on the 5th. Evidence indicates that those explosives were meant to have reached two Hamas suicide bombers who planned to carry out attacks in Israel. A suicide bomber blew himself up in a Sbarro's Restaurant on the corner of Jaffa Road and King George Street in Jerusalem. Fifteen Israelis were killed in the attack, and about 130 others were injured. Hamas and Islamic Jihad both claimed responsibility for the attack. Israel responded by taking control of the PA's unofficial foreign ministry, the Orient House, in East Jerusalem. Israel also launched an F-16 missile attack on a Palestinian police building near Ramallah. No injuries were reported in the attack. On the 23rd, two IAF helicopters fired missiles at two cars of senior Hamas members. The two Hamas members managed to escape from the cars uninjured.

September 2001

On September 9, three terror attacks killed five Israelis and wounded over 100. It included one of the first suicide bombings conducted by an Arab Israeli citizen. In the town of Nahariya, Muhammad Saker Habshi, 55, from the village of Abu Snan and a Hamas recruit, blew himself up at the Nahariya train station while waiting for a Tel Aviv train to disembark. Three Israelis were killed and ninety-four wounded in that incident. In addition, earlier that day, in the West Bank, two Israelis were killed and three wounded when a car fired shots at a van carrying Israeli teachers to work south of Adam junction. Islamic Jihad claimed responsibility for the attack. Later that day, south of Nahariya, thirteen Israelis were injured when a Palestinian suicide bomber prematurely detonated his bomb after spotting a police car behind his car. In retaliation, IDF helicopters hit the Fatah offices in Ramallah and El Bireh in four missile attacks.

On September 11, the IDF surrounded the town of Jenin, which has been a base for suicide attacks on Israel. Nine Palestinians were killed in the operation.

Three Israeli soldiers were wounded when a bomb exploded on the 26th in an IDF outpost inside the Gaza Strip. Hamas has taken responsibility for the attack.

The U.S. Treasury Department froze a Texas Internet service provider InfoCom Corp. bank account on the 28th. Investigators considered it to be at least partly owned by the family of a Hamas official.

October 2001

Israel's General Security Service (GSS, also known as the Shin Bet) arrested more than twenty Hamas terrorists in the West Bank. The GSS claimed that the men arrested were part of a large and widespread terrorist infrastructure, taking orders directly from Hamas headquarters in Syria.

Two Israelis were killed and thirteen others were wounded as Palestinian gunmen entered the Jewish settlement of Elei Sinai in northern Gaza on the 2nd and opened fire. Hamas has taken responsibility for the attack.

Two Palestinians were killed and twenty others were wounded when the Palestinian police tried to disperse a pro-bin-Laden demonstration organized by the Hamas in the Islamic University in Gaza City on the 8th.

Hamas denounced the U.S. offensive in Afghanistan as "pure terrorism against an innocent people when there was no proof they were involved in the September 11 attacks" on the 8th. A senior official of that organization in the West Bank city of Ramallah released that statement. He added, "It is a form of collective punishment that should be condemned by all international laws. We are pained over what happens to the Afghani people, like they feel pain for our suffering."

Two mid-level Hamas activists were killed on the 15th. The first, Abdel Rahman Hamad, was killed at his home in Kalkilya by Israeli sniper fire; the second, Ahmed Marshoud Hassan Mohammed, was killed by an explosion of unclear origin.

Ayman Halaweh, a master bomb maker in the Hamas military wing of Izz al-Din al-Qassam, was killed in an explosion on the 22nd. Palestinians blamed Israel for the killing.

Eleven militants suspected to be involved in the assassination of Israeli Tourism minister Zeevi were arrested in an IDF raid of the West Bank village of Beit Rima on the 24th. Among those arrested were members of the Hamas.

Three Palestinians were killed as they tried to infiltrate the Jewish settlement of Dugit in Gaza on the 26th. The Izz al-Din al-Qassam Brigades claimed responsibility.

November 2001
The United States added twenty-two terrorist groups to a list of organizations subject to stringent financial sanctions on the 3rd. Palestinian groups, such as Hamas, the PIJ, Hizballah, and the PFLP, were included on the new list.

Two people were killed and forty others injured when a Palestinian terrorist opened fire on a municipal bus in northern Jerusalem on the 4th. Both Hamas and the PIJ took responsibility for the attack.

Mahmoud Abu Hanoud, head of the military wing of Hamas in the West Bank, was killed on the 24th by an Israeli helicopter attack.

One Israeli was killed and three others were wounded in a shooting attack when a Palestinian gunman opened fire on a convoy traveling near the Gush Katif junction in Gaza on the 27th. Hamas claimed responsibility for the attack.

December 2001

At least ten people were killed and 180 others were wounded when two suicide bombers detonated their explosives at different places along Jerusalem's pedestrian mall on the 1st. Some twenty minutes later, as rescue and emergency forces worked to evacuate the wounded, a car bomb exploded about 40 meters away, on nearby Rav Kook Street. No injuries were reported from the car bomb blast. Hamas and PIJ took responsibility for the attack.

At least fourteen people were killed and more than sixty others were injured when a suicide bomber blew himself up in a bus stop in Haifa's Halissa neighborhood on the 2nd. Hamas claimed responsibility for the attack.

The Bush administration froze on the 4th the U.S. assets of a Texas-based Islamic foundation that calls itself a charity, saying the organization acts as a front to finance the militant wing of the Palestinian group Hamas.

Ten people were killed and thirty others were injured when three terrorists attacked a bus and several passenger cars with a roadside bomb, anti-tank grenades, and light arms fire near the Jewish settlement of Emmanuel in the West Bank on the 12th. Fatah and Hamas both claimed responsibility for the attack.

Hamas announced a temporary halt to suicide bombings and mortar shelling within Israel on the 22nd.

January 2002

Four Israeli soldiers and two Palestinians died in a firefight on the 9th when Palestinian gunmen attacked an Israeli army post near the convergence of the borders of Israel, Gaza, and Egypt. Hamas claimed responsibility for the attack.

Two people were lightly wounded on the 31st in a series of attacks by Hamas in the Gaza Strip. Two Hamas activists were killed in an exchange of fire with IDF and Border Patrol troops in the area.

February 2002

Three people were killed and two others were injured when a terrorist infiltrated Moshav Hamra in the Jordan Valley on the 7th. Hamas has taken responsibility for the attack.

Two Israeli soldiers were killed and four others wounded when Palestinian terrorists started shooting near IDF Southern Command headquarters in the center of Beersheba's Old City on the 11th. Hamas claimed responsibility for the attack.

During the same day, Palestinian terrorists fired two Kassam-2 rockets at Israel for the first time. All were aimed at different parts of the Negev. Israeli security experts believe the Hamas may be behind the attacks.

Three Israeli crewmen were killed and a fourth suffered light wounds when their Merkava tank set off a powerful mine near the Netzarim junction on the 15th. Hamas and the Fatah both claimed responsibility for the attack.

March 2002

A 16-month-old baby was moderately wounded by shrapnel on the 5th when one of two Kassam-2 rockets fired by Palestinians in Beit Hanoun hit a residential neighborhood of the Israeli town of Sderot in Southern Israel. Hamas claimed responsibility for the attack.

Eleven people were killed and fifty-two were wounded on the 9th when a suicide bomber blew himself up at the popular Moment Café in downtown Jerusalem. The Al Aqsa Martyrs Brigades of the Fatah and the military wing of Hamas, Izz al-Din al-Qassam, both claimed responsibility for the attack.

Five Israeli teens were killed and twenty-three others wounded on the 9th when a Palestinian terrorist infiltrated the settlement of Atzmona in the Gaza Strip. Hamas claimed responsibility for the attack.

March 27th, a suicide bomber killed at least 25 people and injured 172 at the Park Hotel in Netanya at the start of the Jewish religious holiday of Passover. At least 48 of the injured were described as "severely wounded." Hamas took responsibility for the bombing.

March 31st, twenty-five people were killed and forty were wounded when a suicide bomber detonated a bomb at a busy restaurant in Haifa. The Islamic militant group Hamas said it carried out the attack to avenge Israel's incursion into the West Bank town of Ramallah.

April 2002

April 7th, the IDF stated it killed six Hamas terrorists, including Kayes Adwan, the man behind the Netanya Seder Massacre, which killed twenty-five.

Eight people were killed and fourteen were wounded when a commuter bus was blown apart near Haifa on the 10th. Hamas and the Islamic Jihad Palestine claimed responsibility for the attack.

Akram al-Atrash, head of Izz al-Din al-Qassam was killed on April 11th during an exchange of gunfire with soldiers in Dura, southwest of Hebron. Atrash, 24, was responsible for the murders of two Israeli civilians, Rina Didovsky and Eliahu Ben-Ami, in December 2000 when terrorists in a car fired on their van near Kiryat Arba.

Palestinian Islamic Jihad— Harakat Al-Jihad Al-Islami Al Filastini

ALSO KNOWN AS

PIJ, Islamic Jihad Palestine, Islamic Jihad-Palestine Faction, Islamic Holy War

IDEOLOGY AND OBJECTIVES

- The destruction of the State of Israel through violent means is the prime objective of the Islamic Jihad. The Islamic Jihad rejects any peaceful settlement with Israel.
- The overthrow of Arab governments that do not uphold Islamic law.
- Harsh criticism of the PLO because of its involvement in the peace process with Israel which, according to the PIJ, contradicts the continuation of the Palestinian uprising and its further escalation.

The Palestinian Islamic Jihad (PIJ) Fathi Shqaqi faction has in recent years become the most prominent Palestinian terrorist group to adopt the Islamic Jihad ideology. It views Israel, the "Zionist Jewish entity," as the main enemy of Muslims and as a target for destruction. Thus, it calls for an Islamic armed struggle in order to liberate all of Palestine. The desired tactic, according to the faction, is the use of guerrilla groups, led by a revolutionary vanguard, that carry out terrorist attacks aimed at weakening Israel. PIJ militants see themselves as people who lay the groundwork for the day when the great Islamic Arabic army will be able to destroy Israel in a military confrontation. The faction launched some of the deadliest terrorist suicide attacks carried out in Israel from 1995–2002.

HISTORY

Palestinian students in Egypt who had split from the Muslim Brotherhood in the Gaza Strip founded the PIJ in 1979–80. The founders were influenced by the Islamic revolution in Iran and also by the radicalization and militancy of student organizations in Egypt.

The three founders—Fathi Shqaqi, 'Abd al-Aziz 'Odeh, and Bashir Musa— were concerned that the Muslim Brotherhood movement was neglecting the Palestinian question and the establishment of a Palestinian state; hence, they proposed an alternative ideology, which became the basis for the new organization. Their central claim is that the unity of the Islamic world is not a precondition to the liberation of Palestine, but that the liberation was a key to the unification of the Islamic world. Jihad by Islamic groups will liberate Palestine and reconstruct a greater and unified Islamic state.

This group of students had close ties with radical Islamic Egyptian student groups, some of whom were involved in Sadat's assassination in 1981. As a result, the Palestinian radicals were exiled from Egypt and established the PIJ in the Gaza Strip.

The PIJ evolved as an umbrella organization comprised of several fundamentalist Muslim groups. These factions operate separately but share an allegiance to the Islamic regime in Iran and its goal of putting the region under Islamic law. PIJ has been characterized as one of the most radical and violent Islamic organizations in the Middle East.

PIJ attempted to capitalize on the popular Palestinian Arab Intifada soon after it erupted in December 1987. It was the first radical organization to issue a call for general strikes. The attempt to lead the popular violent movement ended in failure after the arrest and subsequent deportation in 1988 of its leaders and the arrest of their replacements in Gaza in mid-1988. A number of reports state that the Islamic Jihad is used by the Syrian intelligence agencies to carry out terrorist operations. Items in the Lebanese news media have linked PIJ to the Lebanon-based and Iranian-backed Hizballah. It is believed that the organization has coordinated training exercises and terrorist attacks with the Hizballah. While Hizballah has not traditionally been known to operate in the Gaza Strip, splinter groups with ties to it may have coordinated an operation with the PIJ in April 1992 in which an Israeli military convoy was attacked there.

PIJ has maintained a more radical position than that of Hamas, but has also been willing to negotiate with the PLO. Nevertheless, one of the PIJ leaders stated in January 1993 that it would be possible for the group to join the PLO. The PLO would have to undergo a fundamental transformation in its ideological and strategic policies before the PIJ could conceivably join it. However, it refused to do so when Israel deported more than 100 of its members, along with several hundred Hamas activists, to southern Lebanon in December 1992.

Following the 1993 Oslo Accords between Israel and the PLO, Fathi Shqaqi expanded the organizational political connections, and the PIJ became a member of the new Syrian-influenced Rejection Front—a coalition of terror groups opposed to the Israeli-PLO accord signed in September 1993.

The PIJ and Hamas were considered rivals in the Gaza Strip until after the foundation of the Palestinian Authority (PA) in 1994. Since then, there has been operational cooperation between the two organizations in carrying out terror attacks such as the one in Beit-Lyd in February 1995, or in coordinating simultaneous terrorist attacks. (Shqaqi's death in 1995 undermined the PIJ's position, and Hamas no longer sees the PIJ as a threatening rival.)

A Western news report stated in mid-May 1994 that the PIJ (led by Fathi Shqaqi) announced its intentions to change tactics to avoid conflict with the Palestinian police force that began providing security in the Gaza Strip. According to the report, Shqaqi advised that this group was still determined to "bring down" the accord between Israel and the PLO, but was rethinking its strategy and would attempt to wield its influence in a more political slant. Nevertheless, the PIJ said (via a fax sent to international news agencies on May 23, 1994) that in defiance of the Palestinian police in the Gaza Strip and Jericho, it would not disarm. The PIJ statement said, "We tell you we will not give up our weapons or stop our Jihad, our path to freedom, greatness and honor, our path to paradise."

Israeli agents are alleged to have assassinated Shqaqi in October 1995 in Malta. His successor is Dr. Ramadan Abdallah Shalah, who resided in Florida for several years and moved to Damascus at the beginning of 1996. However, his personality did not allow him to exhort the same influence over the organization's position and activity as Shqaqi.

The group has been active politically in the West Bank, and especially in the Gaza Strip. Following the Hamas' switch to the strategy of suicide terrorist bombings in the late 1980s, the two groups developed some operational cooperation in carrying out attacks. The strong support of the United States for Israel has made the United States a target of the PIJ, as well. In July 2000, the PIJ threatened to attack U.S. interests if the American Embassy is moved to Jerusalem from Tel Aviv.

Since the outbreak of the second Intifida, in September 2000, the PIJ has been collaborating with Hamas on a number of suicide bombings. In April 2002, during Operation Defensive Wall, Israel's latest attempt to break down Palestinian terrorist networks in the West Bank and the Gaza Strip, new light was shed on the connection between the PA and Palestinian religious terrorist groups, such as the PIJ and Hamas. The IDF discovered documents revealing cooperation between the PA and both the Hamas and PIJ movements. The cooperation includes executing large-scale suicide attacks in Israel. An example is the PIJ suicide bombing in Afula on November 27, 2001. The PA General Intelligence apparatus provided the PIJ with early warnings regarding the PA's intentions to act against Israel, and supplying the PIJ with arms.

MEMBERSHIP

The PIJ's support base is smaller then that of Hamas. Unlike Hamas, which runs schools, hospitals, and other social organizations, the PIJ has no real social or political role.

The organizational and operational strength of the PIJ (including sympathizers, supporters, leaders, and hard-core operatives) in the West Bank and Gaza Strip is unknown. The number of active members, including hard-core operatives, appears to be considerably smaller than it was in the early to mid-1980s in these areas.

The PIJ recruits young Arabs by means of religious indoctrination, and bases its terror strategy on the willingness of its followers to be suicide bombers.

PIJ's support base in southern Lebanon has grown due to Israel's concerted effort to curb PIJ activities in the territories. It is difficult to ascertain the extent of support in southern Lebanon, but a credible base of operations has been established in this area since 1988. Israel had actively sought to apprehend and deport the organization's leadership and known operatives, including the deportation of the group's pre-1988 Gaza-based leadership. Second to Hamas in popularity among Islamic groups in the West Bank and Gaza Strip, the PIJ has had a level of support among the general Palestinian Arab population that has been relatively steady over the last several years.

Some PIJ Members Who Were Arrested by Israel

Mohammed Wail Abed Tsiam—PIJ activist in Ramallah

Hasin Elias Hasin Rabiya—PIJ activist in Beit Einan

A Hakim Masalma—Head of PIJ in Ramallah

Mohammed Tualbe—PIJ activist in Ramallah

Mohammed Tualbeh "Nursi"—PIJ activist in Jenin

Juma Abdullah Khalil Jhaya—PIJ activist from Kfar Naama

Mohammed Jabar Mohi Adin Abeda—PIJ activist from Kfar Naama

Amajad Mahmoud Yusuf Dar Dig—PIJ activist from Kfar Naama

A Raziq Azat Anim Daragma—PIJ activist from Tubas

Top PIJ Members on Israel's Wanted List

Ali Saadi—PIJ activist in Jenin. Responsible for the shooting attack at Bakoat junction.

Thabet Mardawi—PIJ activist in Arabeh. Involved in planning the Sheluhut bombing.

Abd-El Khalim—PIJ activist in Arabeh. Responsible for the Hadera attack.

Mahmud Kalibi—PIJ activist in Arabeh.

Mahmud Tawnlbe/Nursi—PIJ activist in Arabeh. Responsible for the attacks in Binyamina and in Kiryat Motzkin.

Mahmud Zatnie—PIJ activist in Rafah.

Shaker Ja'bari—PIJ activist in Gaza.

Hisam Dib—PIJ activist in Mashru Beit Lahiya.

Bashir Dabash—PIJ activist in Mashru.

Nabil Shrihi—PIJ activist in Neseirat.

LEADERSHIP

Dr. Fathi 'Abd al-'Aziz Shqaqi

Founder of the PIJ. Born in the Gaza Strip in January 1951. Shqaqi became active in the ranks of the Muslim Brotherhood in Egypt, where he studied medicine at Zaqaziq University. In 1974, he left the organization due to ideological disputes. In 1980, Shqaqi returned to Gaza and began to organize a political group. Its members were mostly students who were expelled from Egypt. Shqaqi was the leader of the PIJ until the Israeli security forces in Malta assassinated him in 1995.

Dr. Ramadan 'Abdallah Shalah

Dr. Ramadan 'Abdallah Shalah, born in the Saja'iyah refugee camp in the Gaza Strip, was one of the first extremists within the PIJ and was close to Fathi Shqaqi. He went to London for his studies and later was appointed head of PIJ's office there. From there he handled PIJ's military, propaganda, and information activity in the West Bank and the Gaza Strip.

In 1990, he went to the United States to teach Middle East Studies at the South Florida University in Tampa, were he became director of the World and Islam Studies Enterprise (WISE), a think tank on Muslim religious and political issues affiliated with the PIJ. After Shqaqi's killing in October 1995, Abdallah Shalah became the head of the PIJ faction. Today, he resides in Syria where he continues to direct operational, political, and propaganda activities of PIJ.

Ziad Nakhalah

Deputy head of the PIJ, second only to Shalah. He resides in Syria where he assists in directing the operational, political, and propaganda activities of PIJ.

Sheikh Abdallah al-Shami

A Senior official of the PIJ in the Gaza Strip. He was arrested several times by the PA in response to various criticisms he expressed against Arafat and the PA.

Sheikh Jaber 'Ammar

Sheikh Jaber 'Ammar, was sentenced to life in prison for terrorist activity in the early 1970s. He was the first to form a group of Islamic extremists inside an Israeli prison. 'Ammar was released in 1983 and went to Egypt, but was exiled by the Egyptian authorities. At Present he continues his terrorist and subversive activities against Israel and Egypt from Sudan.

SOURCES OF SUPPORT

PIJ is believed to have received financial, organizational, and operational assistance (including arms, training, intelligence information, and safe haven) from Iran, Iraq, Sudan, and Syria. The type or level of assistance that each country provides is difficult to determine. Reports state that Iran provides the majority of operational support for the organization. Fathi Shqaqi lived in Damascus, and his faction shares a training base with Hizballah in the Syrian-controlled northern Bekaa Valley of Lebanon. In April 1993, Shqaqi told reporters that the PIJ had been receiving assistance from Iran since 1987. The Islamic government of Sudan continues to be of assistance to the organization. It was reported that the PIJ has, in the past, received arms, logistical assistance (including communication networks), and training from the PLO and its Force 17 elite unit.

In April 2002, the Israeli government discovered documents depicting the money flow from the PIJ's office in Lebanon to fund suicide bombings in Israel. One of the documents traces money transfers from Dr. Ramadan Shalah, the PIJ General Secretary operating from Damascus, to PIJ terrorist activities in the PA areas. The money was transferred to Bassam Al Saadi, a senior PIJ activist in Jenin. Al Saadi allocated these funds to the terrorists and the families of suicide bombers.

The documents also reveal widespread corruption within the PIJ. Over $127,000 that was sent through Dr. Shalah "disappeared" before it could be donated to the families of those killed and arrested. In addition, Haj Ali Safuri, the commander of the military-security arm of the PIJ, did not receive $31,000 promised to him as a remainder of expenses incurred by the suicide attack in Afula in November 2001.

HEADQUARTERS

Small cells are dispersed throughout the West Bank and Gaza Strip along with a number of policymaking and logistics operations in southern Lebanon.

AREAS OF OPERATION

The group has offices in Beirut, Damascus, Tehran, and Khartoum, but its activity is focused in Lebanon, where there are several dozens of Palestinian members. It has some influence in the Gaza Strip, mainly in the Islamic University.

In addition to its activities in the Middle East, the PIJ has set up web sites within the industrialized world. Its two primary web sites are registered and hosted in Houston, Texas, and in Toronto, Canada.

Several U.S.-based "charity" organizations, such as the Islamic Committee for Palestine, and the World and Islam Studies Enterprise, are directly connected to Islamic Jihad. These so-called charities conduct fundraising activities for the Hamas and the PIJ as well as smuggle members of those organizations into the United States.

TACTICS

Individual or small group killings (especially by stabbing and bombing), popular agitation and incitement to violence (especially through mass demonstrations), and suicide attacks.

TARGETS

Israeli civilians, security service personnel, soldiers, and Palestinian collaborators. Targets have also included IDF installations in the West Bank and Gaza, and Israeli civilian and military vehicles. The PIJ traditionally tries to carry out attacks against Israeli targets on the anniversary of its murdered leader, Fathi Shqaqi.

TIMELINE

July 1983
A PIJ member stabbed to death an Israeli student in Hebron in the West Bank on the 7th.

February 1986
PIJ Secretary General Dr. Fathi Abd al-Aziz Shqaqi was arrested by Israeli security forces.

October 1986
Three grenades were thrown at participants in a military ceremony in Jerusalem on the 15th. One person was killed and 70 were injured.

August 1987
A commander of the military police in the Gaza Strip was shot in his car by a member of PIJ's Sqaqi faction.

September 1987
Abed al-Aziz Odeh was arrested by Israeli security forces.

1988
Abed al-Aziz Odeh and Fathi Shqaqi were deported to southern Lebanon.

May 1988
PIJ leaders Odeh and Shqaqi's two principal replacements in Gaza were

arrested by Israel. PIJ's leadership and ability to issue proclamations were severely hindered by the arrest.

May 1989
PIJ members murdered two elderly Israelis at a bus stop in Jerusalem on the 3rd.

July 1989
The PIJ claimed responsibility for an attack on a bus on the Tel Aviv-Jerusalem highway, in which sixteen people were killed and twenty-five were injured. One U.S. citizen was killed and seven other U.S. citizens were injured in the July 6 incident.

February 1990
PIJ and a group calling itself the Organization for the Defense of the Oppressed in Egypt's Prisons claimed responsibility for killing nine Israeli tourists and two Egyptian security men, and injuring twenty tourists on an Egyptian bus. The attack occurred near Ismailia, Egypt, on the 4th.

May 1990
The PJI was responsible for the bombing of a Jerusalem market, killing one Israeli and injuring nine others.

October 1990
The PIJ claimed responsibility for three Israelis killed in Jerusalem.

November 1990
One Israeli soldier was killed in an attack on an IDF post near the Allenby Bridge in the Jordan Valley. The terrorist, identified as a member of the PIJ faction Beit al-Muquades, crossed the Jordan River from Jordan.

February 1991
The PIJ claimed responsibility for two small explosions inside the American Express office in Cairo.

May 1991
A PIJ faction claimed responsibility for a lone attacker who wounded three Israelis in Jerusalem on the 18th.

October 1991
PIJ and the Popular Front for the Liberation of Palestine (PFLP) claimed

responsibility for killing two Israelis and wounding at least six, five of whom were children, on a bus north of Jerusalem two days before the opening of the Madrid Arab-Israeli peace conference.

March 1992
A suspected PIJ member stabbed and killed an Israeli student and a Palestinian man who was trying to protect her. Seventeen other students were slightly injured in this incident in the Israeli city of Jaffa.

April 1992
PIJ claimed responsibility for the April 27 killing of an Israeli in Tel Aviv.

October 1992
The Fathi Shqaqi faction of the PIJ claimed responsibility for a roadside bomb explosion in Israel that killed an Israeli woman and injured eight others.

December 1992
A PIJ leader shot one Israeli border policeman to death and wounded three others before dying of his wounds during a clash in the northern West Bank village of Anza.

January 1993
PIJ claimed responsibility for stabbing and wounding four people at the central bus station in Tel Aviv. The assailant was shot to death by a witness of the attack.

March 1993
On the 1st, a Palestinian from the Gaza Strip stabbed and killed two Israelis and injured eight others in Tel Aviv. Fathi Shqaqi claimed that the man (who was arrested) was a PIJ activist operating on behalf of the organization.

August 1993
August 2nd, an armed Palestinian Arab believed to be a member of the PIJ hijacked a bus belonging to the United Nations Relief and Works Agency in the Gaza Strip and rammed two Israeli cars. One Israeli was killed and five others were injured (two critically) in the attack.

The PIJ claimed responsibility for killing an Israeli guard in the West Bank on the 22nd.

September 1993
The PIJ and Hamas took responsibility for an attack in which two gunmen opened fire on an Israeli army patrol in Gaza City in the Gaza Strip. Three Israeli soldiers were killed. The gunmen escaped with the soldiers' weapons.

October 1993
The PIJ claimed responsibility for the murder of two Israeli hikers in a national park in the Judean Desert. The PFLP also claimed responsibility.

November 1993
A single operative stabbed and wounded an Israeli on the 12th. He was in the Gaza Strip to pick up Palestinian workers.

A single operative stabbed an Israeli soldier to death on the 17th.

On the 22nd, an alleged member of PIJ attempted to drive a stolen garbage truck into an army vehicle filled with Israeli soldiers in the Gaza Strip. The man was shot and killed.

December 1993
An IDF reserve soldier was shot and killed by a terrorist attempting to board a bus at the Holon junction. The PIJ claimed responsibility.

Israeli troops shot and killed two wanted members of the PIJ at the Rafah refugee camp in the Gaza Strip on the 13th. A third PIJ member was wounded and captured in the camp.

January 1994
The PIJ killed an Israeli soldier on a Jerusalem bus.

February 1994
The Shqaqi faction claimed responsibility for the murder of Israeli taxi driver, Ilan Sudri.

April 1994
The PIJ claimed responsibility for shooting at the Gaza City IDF headquarters. Two Israeli soldiers were wounded in the attack on the 16th.

May 1994
A PIJ member wanted since the February 1993 attack on two Israelis in the Gaza Strip, was killed by Israeli soldiers in the West Bank village of Tafuah near Hebron on the 22nd.

On the 26th, an IDF soldier was slightly wounded when Palestinian terrorists fired at the vehicle in which he was riding near the town of Rafah in the Gaza Strip. The PIJ claimed responsibility for the attack, stating that it was in response to the May 21 abduction in Lebanon of Mustafa Dirani by the IDF.

The PIJ claimed responsibility for a drive-by shooting in Gaza on the 27th. Two Israeli soldiers were killed. Hamas also claimed responsibility for the attack.

July 1994
An IDF patrol came under attack in Gush Katif in the southern Gaza Strip. One soldier was wounded from the gunfire. A PIJ leaflet, which stated that the ambush was in retaliation for violent incidents at Gaza's Erez checkpoint earlier in the week, was found at the scene.

The PIJ claimed responsibility for a drive-by shooting in Gaza on the 7th. Two IDF soldiers were wounded.

The PIJ claimed responsibility for the killing of Yarom and Hannah Sakuri in the Israeli town of Kiryat Netafim on the 8th. PIJ called the attack "a present" for PLO leader Yasser Arafat for the PLO's agreements with Israel.

November 1994
On the 11th, a suicide bomber on a booby-trapped bicycle blew himself up near an IDF checkpoint at the Netzarim Junction in the Gaza Strip. The attack left three dead and six injured. The PIJ claimed responsibility.

January 1995
Two suicide bombers set off their explosives on the 22nd at a bus stop where dozens of soldiers were waiting for rides. The first bomb exploded in the midst of a crowd of soldiers; the second was detonated as bystanders crowded together in an attempt to assist the wounded. Eighteen soldiers and one civilian were killed in the two blasts. The PIJ took responsibility for the attack.

April 1995
On the 9th, two suicide attacks were carried out within a few hours of each other—one in Netzarim and the other in Kfar-Darom. In the first attack a suicide bomber crashed an explosive-rigged van into an Israeli bus, killing a U.S. citizen and eight Israelis. Over thirty others were injured. In the second attack, a suicide bomber detonated a car bomb in the midst of a convoy of cars, injuring twelve people. The PIJ Shqaqi Faction claimed responsibility for the attacks.

June 1995
A PIJ activist detonated an explosives-laden car near an IDF vehicle on the 25th, injuring three soldiers.

March 1996
On the 4th, a suicide bomber detonated an explosive device outside the Dizengoff Center, Tel Aviv's largest shopping mall, killing thirteen people and injuring seventy-five, including a number of U.S. citizens. Both Hamas and the PIJ claimed responsibility for the bombing.

November 1998
Two PIJ terrorists were killed and more than twenty bystanders were injured in a failed terrorist attack in the Mahane Yehuda market in Jerusalem on the 6th. The blast occurred at 9:45 in the morning when the market was filled with weekend shoppers. Witnesses said that a red Fiat car drove into the crowded market and exploded. The PIJ took responsibility for the attack.

November 2000
A car packed with explosives blew up in a side street near Jerusalem's main outdoor market on the 2nd, killing a man and a woman and injuring ten others. In a statement faxed to the media, the PIJ claimed responsibility for the bombing in Jerusalem. Hamas spokesman Mohammad a-Zahar praised the attack.

December 2000
A Palestinian Islamic cleric jailed in the United States on secret evidence was to be released on the 12th. Mazen al-Najjar, 43, was arrested on May 19, 1997, for overstaying his student visa. Pending deportation, he was held without bond as a security risk. Although no formal charges were ever brought against him, the U.S. Immigration and Naturalization Service presented classified evidence, which it said supported allegations that al-Najjar transferred funds to the PIJ.

March 2001
Seven people were injured in a car bomb explosion in Jerusalem's East Talpiot industrial zone on the 27th. The PIJ took responsibility for the attack.

May 2001
A car bomb explosion on the 25th in the Israeli city of Hadera killed the two bombers and injured some 40 people. The PIJ claimed responsibility for the attack.

Two car bombs exploded on the 27th in downtown Jerusalem about nine hours and a hundred meters apart. In the first incident, a car bomb detonated shortly after midnight in a street filled with nightclubs and discos. No one was injured, although the street was packed with young people. In a fax sent to Reuters, the PIJ had claimed responsibility for the attack.

A car bomb was placed at the entrance to a high school in Netanya on the 30th. Witnesses said that the bombers had attempted to infiltrate the explosives-laden vehicle into the schoolyard, but were deterred by the presence of an armed guard at the school. In the end, the bomb was placed adjacent to a bus stop and detonated several minutes after a school bus, taking on children, pulled out of the station. The PIJ claimed responsibility for the bombing.

June 2001
A Palestinian suicide bomber detonated an explosives belt amid a crowd of youngsters outside a beachfront nightclub on the 2nd, killing at least 20 and injuring more than 120. At least two militant Palestinian groups—the PIJ and Hamas—claimed responsibility for the blast.

July 2001
On the 3rd, Palestinian gunmen shot two Israelis. An Israeli civilian was shot and killed at point-blank range near the Arab village of Baka al Gharbieh in northern Israel. A second Israeli motorist was shot and seriously wounded by Palestinian gunmen in northern Samaria, near the Palestinian city of Nablus. Security forces believe that the PIJ may have been behind the attacks.

On the 16th of July, a suicide bomber blew himself up at a railway station in the town of Binyamina, killing himself and two soldiers. Three people were seriously wounded and a dozen were slightly injured by shrapnel. The PIJ took responsibility for the attack.

August 2001
Fifteen people, including six children, were killed and more then 130 others were wounded when a suicide bomber detonated explosives at a pizza restaurant in the center of Jerusalem on the 9th. The PIJ and Hamas both took responsibility for the attack.

Twenty-one people were injured on the 12th when a suicide bomber blew himself up in a restaurant in the northern Israeli city of Kiryat Motzkin, a suburb of Haifa. The PIJ took responsibility for the attack.

September 2001

Two people were killed and three injured on the 9th when Palestinians attacked a minivan carrying school children and kindergarten teachers to work near the Adam junction. The PIJ took responsibility for the attack.

On the same day, thirty-one people were reported injured when a suicide bomber detonated a large bomb at a busy train station in the northern Israeli town of Nahariya. Hamas, Hizballah, and the PIJ all claimed responsibility for the attack. However, Israeli sources said that it is far more likely that the PIJ, which has links to Hizballah, carried out the attack.

October 2001

Eleven militants suspected of being involved in the assassination of Israeli tourism minister Zeevi were arrested in an IDF raid of the West Bank village of Beit Rima on the 24th. Among those arrested were members of the PIJ.

Four people were killed and twenty-eight were wounded when a Palestinian gunman opened fire in the northern Israeli city of Hadera on the 29th. In a separate incident, one person sitting in his car outside a kibbutz in the Hadera area was shot dead by a Palestinian terrorist firing from a passing car. The PIJ took responsibility for the attack.

November 2001

The United States added twenty-two terrorist groups to a list of organizations subject to stringent financial sanctions on the 3rd. Palestinian groups, such as Hamas, PIJ, Hizballah, and the PFLP, were included on the new list.

Two people were killed and forty others injured when a Palestinian terrorist opened fire on a municipal bus in northern Jerusalem on the 4th. Both Hamas and the PIJ took responsibility for the attack.

Two civilians were killed and at least fifty others were wounded when Palestinian terrorists opened fire near the central bus station in the northern Israeli city of Afula on the 27th. PIJ and the Al-Aqsa Brigades of the Fatah claimed responsibility for the attack.

Three people were killed and nine others were wounded when a suicide bomber detonated explosives on a bus near an IDF training camp near Hadera in northern Israel on the 29th. The PIJ and the Al-Aqsa Brigades of the Fatah took responsibility for the attack.

December 2001

At least 10 people were killed and 180 others were wounded when two suicide bombers detonated their explosives at different places along Jerusalem's pedestrian mall on the 1st. Some twenty minutes later, as rescue and emergency forces worked to evacuate the wounded, a car bomb exploded about forty meters away, nearby on Rav Kook Street. No injuries were reported from the car bomb blast. Hamas and the PIJ took responsibility for the attack.

A Palestinian suicide bomber blew himself up prematurely outside the David's Citadel (formerly the Hilton) Hotel on King David Street in Jerusalem on the 6th. Six Israelis were injured from the blast. The PIJ took responsibility for the attack.

January 2002
One person was killed and more then 125 others were injured when a female Palestinian suicide bomber wearing explosives strapped to her waist blew herself up in downtown Jerusalem on the 28th. Israeli security sources said from the quantity of explosives found, it appears the work of Hamas or Islamic Jihad.

March 2002
One person was killed and 18 others were injured when a suicide bomber blew himself up on a Tel Aviv-bound bus picking up passengers at the central bus station in Afula in northern Israel on the 5th. The PIJ took responsibility for the attack.

Seven people were killed and dozens injured when a suicide bomber detonated a powerful bomb on a bus in northern Israel on the 20th. The bombing occurred on an intercity bus en route from Tel Aviv to Nazareth. The PIJ took responsibility for the attack.

April 2002
Eight people were killed and 14 were wounded when a commuter bus was blown apart near Haifa on the 10th. Hamas and the PIJ claimed responsibility for the attack.

Selected Documents

The Charter of the Hamas

The Charter of Allah:
The Platform of the Islamic
Resistance Movement (Hamas)

In the Name of Allah, the Merciful, the Compassionate

You are the best community that has been raised up for mankind.

Ye enjoin right conduct and forbid indecency; and ye believe in Allah. And if the People of the Scripture had believed, it had been better for them. Some of them are believers; but most of them are evil-doers.

They will not harm you save a trifling hurt, and if they fight against you they will turn and flee. And afterward they will not be helped.

> *Ignominy shall be their portion wheresoever they are found save [where they grasp] a rope from Allah and a rope from man. They have incurred anger from their Lord, and wretchedness is laid upon them. That is because they used to disbelieve the revelations of Allah, and slew the Prophets wrongfully. That is because they were rebellious and used to transgress.* Surat Al-Imran (III), verses 109–111

Israel will rise and will remain erect until Islam eliminates it as it had eliminated its predecessors.

The Islamic World is burning. It is incumbent upon each one of us to pour some water, little as it may be, with a view of extinguishing as much of the fire as he can, without awaiting action by the others.

INTRODUCTION

Grace to Allah, whose help we seek, whose forgiveness we beseech, whose guidance we implore and on whom we rely. We pray and bid peace upon the Messenger of Allah, his family, his companions, his followers and those who spread his message and followed his tradition; they will last as long as there exist Heaven and Earth.

O, people! In the midst of misadventure, from the depth of suffering, from the believing hearts and purified arms; aware of our duty and in response to the decree of Allah, we direct our call, we rally together and join each other. We educate in the path of Allah and we make our firm determination prevail so as to take its proper role in life, to overcome all difficulties and to cross all hurdles. Hence our permanent state of preparedness and our readiness to sacrifice our souls and dearest [possessions] in the path of Allah.

Thus, our nucleus has formed which chartered its way in the tempestuous ocean of creeds and hopes, desires and wishes, dangers and difficulties, setbacks and challenges, both internal and external.

When the thought matured, the seed grew and the plant took root in the land of reality, detached from temporary emotion and unwelcome haste, the Islamic Resistance Movement erupted in order to play its role in the path of its Lord. In so doing, it joined its hands with those of all Jihad fighters for the purpose of liberating Palestine. The souls of its Jihad fighters will encounter those of all Jihad fighters who have sacrificed their lives in the land of Palestine since it was conquered by the Companion of the Prophet, be Allah's prayer and peace upon him, and until this very day. This is the Charter of the Islamic Resistance (Hamas) which will reveal its face, unveil its identity, state its position, clarify its purpose, discuss its hopes, call for support to its cause and reinforcement, and for joining its ranks. For our struggle against the Jews is extremely wide-ranging and grave, so much so that it will need all the loyal efforts we can wield, to be followed by further steps and reinforced by successive battalions from the multifarious Arab and Islamic world, until the enemies are defeated and Allah's victory prevails. Thus we shall perceive them approaching in the horizon, and this will be known before long:

> *"Allah has decreed: Lo! I very shall conquer, I and my messenger, lo! Allah is strong, almighty.:"*

PART I—KNOWING THE MOVEMENT

The Ideological Aspects

Article One

The Islamic Resistance Movement draws its guidelines from Islam; derives from it its thinking, interpretations and views about existence, life and humanity; refers back to it for its conduct; and is inspired by it in whatever step it takes.

The Link between Hamas and the Association of Muslim Brothers

Article Two

The Islamic Resistance Movement is one of the wings of the Muslim Brothers in Palestine. The Muslim Brotherhood Movement is a world organization, the largest Islamic Movement in the modern era. It is characterized by a profound understanding, by precise notions and by a complete comprehensiveness of all concepts of Islam in all domains of life: views and beliefs, politics and economics, education and society, jurisprudence and rule, indoctrination and teaching, the arts and publications, the hidden and the evident, and all the other domains of life.

Structure and Essence

Article Three

The basic structure of the Islamic Resistance Movement consists of Muslims who are devoted to Allah and worship Him verily [as it is written]: "I have created Man and Devil for the purpose of their worship" [of Allah]. Those Muslims are cognizant of their duty towards themselves, their families and country and they have been relying on Allah for all that. They have raised the banner of Jihad in the face of the oppressors in order to extricate the country and the people from the [oppressors'] desecration, filth and evil.

Article Four

The Movement welcomes all Muslims who share its beliefs and thinking, commit themselves to its course of action, keep its secrets and aspire to join its ranks in order to carry out their duty.

Allah will reward them.

Dimensions of Time and Space of the Hamas

Article Five

As the Movement adopts Islam as its way of life, its time dimension extends back as far as the birth of the Islamic Message and of the Righteous Ancestor. Its ultimate goal is Islam, the Prophet its model, the Qur'an its Constitution. Its special dimension extends wherever on earth there are Muslims, who adopt Islam as their way of life; thus, it penetrates to the deepest reaches of the land and to the highest spheres of Heavens.

Peculiarity and Independence

Article Six

The Islamic Resistance Movement is a distinct Palestinian Movement which owes its loyalty to Allah, derives from Islam its way of life and strives to raise the banner of Allah over every inch of Palestine. Only under the shadow of Islam could the members of all regions coexist in safety and security for their lives, properties and rights. In the absence of Islam, conflict arises, oppression reigns, corruption is rampant and struggles and wars prevail. Allah had inspired the Muslim poet, Muhammad Iqbal, when he said:

When the Faith wanes, there is no security. There is no this-worldliness for those who have no faith. Those who wish to live their life without religion have made annihilation the equivalent of life.

The Universality of Hamas

Article Seven

By virtue of the distribution of Muslims, who pursue the cause of the Hamas, all over the globe, and strive for its victory, for the reinforcement of its positions and for the encouragement of its Jihad, the Movement is a universal one. It is apt to be that due to the clarity of its thinking, the nobility of its purpose and the loftiness of its objectives.

It is in this light that the Movement has to be regarded, evaluated and acknowledged. Whoever denigrates its worth, or avoids supporting it, or is so blind as to dismiss its role, is challenging Fate itself. Whoever closes his eyes from seeing the facts, whether intentionally or not, will wake up to find himself overtaken by events, and will find no excuses to justify his position. Priority is reserved to the early comers.

Oppressing those who are closest to you, is more of an agony to the soul than the impact of an Indian sword.

> *And unto thee have we revealed the Scripture with the truth, confirming whatever scripture was before it, and a watcher over it. So judge between them by that which Allah hath revealed, and follow not their desires away from the truth which has come unto thee. For each we have appointed a divine law and a traced-out way. Had Allah willed, He could have made you one community. But that He may try you by that which he has given you [He has made you as you are]. So vie with one another in good works. Unto Allah, you will all return. He will then inform you of that wherein you differ.*

Hamas is one of the links in the Chain of Jihad in the confrontation with the Zionist invasion. It links up with the setting out of the Martyr Izz a-din al-Qassam and his brothers in the Muslim Brotherhood who fought the Holy War in 1936; it further relates to another link of the Palestinian Jihad and the Jihad and efforts of the Muslim Brothers during the 1948 War, and to the Jihad operations of the Muslim Brothers in 1968 and thereafter.

But even if the links have become distant from each other, and even if the obstacles erected by those who revolve in the Zionist orbit, aiming at obstructing the road before the Jihad fighters, have rendered the pursuance of Jihad impossible; nevertheless, the Hamas has been looking forward to implement Allah's promise whatever time it might take. The prophet, prayer and peace be upon him, said:

> *The time will not come until Muslims will fight the Jews (and kill them); until the Jews hide behind rocks and trees, which will cry: O Muslim! There is a Jew hiding behind me, come on and kill him! This will not apply to the Gharqad, which is a Jewish tree (cited by Bukhari and Muslim).*

The Slogan of the Hamas

Article Eight

Allah is its goal, the Prophet its model, the Qur'an its Constitution, Jihad its path and death for the case of Allah its most sublime belief.

PART II—OBJECTIVES

Motives and Objectives

Article Nine

Hamas finds itself at a period of time when Islam has waned away from the reality of life. For this reason, the checks and balances have been upset, concepts have become confused, and values have been transformed; evil has prevailed, oppression and obscurity have reigned; cowards have turned tigers, homelands have been usurped, people have been uprooted and are wandering all over the globe. The state of truth has disappeared and was replaced by the state of evil. Nothing has remained in its right place, for when Islam is removed from the scene, everything changes. These are the motives.

As to the objectives: discarding the evil, crushing it and defeating it, so that truth may prevail, homelands revert [to their owners], calls for prayer be heard from their mosques, announcing the reinstitution of the Muslim state. Thus, people and things will revert to their true place.

Article Ten

The Islamic Resistance Movement, while breaking its own path, will do its utmost to constitute at the same time a support to the weak, a defense to all the oppressed. It will spare no effort to implement the truth and abolish evil, in speech and in fact, both here and in any other location where it can reach out and exert influence.

PART III—STRATEGIES AND METHODS

The Strategy of Hamas: Palestine is an Islamic Waqf

Article Eleven

The Islamic Resistance Movement believes that the land of Palestine has been an Islamic Waqf throughout the generations and until the Day of Resurrection, no one can renounce it or part of it, or abandon it or part of it. No Arab country nor the aggregate of all Arab countries, and no Arab King or President nor all of them in the aggregate, have that right, nor has that right any organization or the aggregate of all organizations, be they Palestinian or Arab, because Palestine is an Islamic Waqf throughout all generations and to the Day of Resurrection. Who can presume to speak for all Islamic Generations to the Day of Resurrection? This is the status [of the land] in Islamic Shari'a, and it is similar to all lands conquered by Islam by force, and made thereby Waqf lands upon their conquest, for all generations of Muslims until the Day of Resurrection. This [norm] has prevailed since the commanders of the Muslim armies completed the conquest of Syria and Iraq, and they asked the Caliph of Muslims, 'Umar Ibn al-Khattab, for his view of the conquered land, whether it should be partitioned between the troops or left in the possession of its population, or otherwise. Following discussions and consultations between the Caliph of Islam, 'Umar Ibn al-Khattab, and the Companions of the Messenger of Allah, be peace and prayer upon him, they decided that the land should remain in the hands of its owners to benefit from it and from its wealth; but the control of the land and the land itself ought to be endowed as a Waqf [in perpetuity] for all generations of Muslims until the Day of Resurrection. The ownership of the land by its owners is only one of usufruct, and this Waqf will endure as long as Heaven and earth last. Any demarche in violation of this law of Islam, with regard to Palestine, is baseless and reflects on its perpetrators.

Hamas in Palestine: Its Views on Homeland and Nationalism

Article Twelve

Hamas regards Nationalism (Wataniyya) as part and parcel of the religious faith. Nothing is loftier or deeper in Nationalism than waging Jihad against the enemy and confronting him when he sets foot on the land of the Muslims.

And this becomes an individual duty binding on every Muslim man and woman; a woman must go out and fight the enemy even without her husband's authorization, and a slave without his masters' permission.

This [principle] does not exist under any other regime, and it is a truth not to be questioned. While other nationalisms consist of material, human and territorial considerations, the nationality of Hamas also carries, in addition to all those, the all important divine factors which lend to it its spirit and life; so much so that it connects with the origin of the spirit and the source of life and raises in the skies of the Homeland the Banner of the Lord, thus inexorably connecting earth with Heaven.

When Moses came and threw his baton, sorcery and sorcerers became futile.

Peaceful Solutions, [Peace] Initiatives and International Conferences

Article Thirteen

[Peace] initiatives, the so-called peaceful solutions, and the international conferences to resolve the Palestinian problem, are all contrary to the beliefs of the Islamic Resistance Movement. For renouncing any part of Palestine means renouncing part of the religion; the nationalism of the Islamic Resistance Movement is part of its faith, the movement educates its members to adhere to its principles and to raise the banner of Allah over their homeland as they fight their Jihad: "Allah is the all-powerful, but most people are not aware."

From time to time a clamoring is voiced, to hold an International Conference in search for a solution to the problem. Some accept the idea, others reject it, for one reason or another, demanding the implementation of this or that condition, as a prerequisite for agreeing to convene the Conference or for participating in it. But the Islamic Resistance Movement, which is aware of the [prospective] parties to this conference, and of their past and present positions towards the problems of the Muslims, does not believe that those conferences are capable of responding to demands, or of restoring rights or doing justice to the oppressed.

Those conferences are no more than a means to appoint the nonbelievers as arbitrators in the lands of Islam. Since when did the Unbelievers do justice to the Believers?

And the Jews will not be pleased with thee, nor will the Christians, till thou follow their creed. 'Say: Lo! the guidance of Allah [himself] is the Guidance. And if you should follow their desires after the knowledge which has come unto thee, then you would have from Allah no protecting friend nor helper. Sura 2 (the Cow), verse 120

There is no solution to the Palestinian problem except by Jihad. The initiatives, proposals and International Conferences are but a waste of time, an exercise in futility. The Palestinian people are too noble to have their future, their right and their destiny submitted to a vain game. As the hadith has it:

The people of Syria are Allah's whip on this land; He takes revenge by their intermediary from whoever he wished among his worshipers. The Hypocrites among them are forbidden from vanquishing the true believers, and they will die in anxiety and sorrow. (Told by Tabarani, who is traceable in ascending order of traditionaries to Muhammad, and by Ahmed whose chain of transmission is incomplete. But it is bound to be a true hadith, for both story tellers are reliable. Allah knows best.)

The Three Circles

Article Fourteen

The problem of the liberation of Palestine relates to three circles: the Palestinian, the Arab and the Islamic. Each one of these circles has a role to play in the struggle against Zionism and it has duties to fulfill. It would be an enormous mistake and an abysmal act of ignorance to disregard anyone of these circles.

For Palestine is an Islamic land where the First Qibla and the third holiest site are located. That is also the place whence the Prophet, be Allah's prayer and peace upon him, ascended to heavens.

Glorified be He who carried His servant by night from the Inviolable Place of worship to the Far Distant Place of Worship, the neighborhood whereof we have blessed, that we might show him of our tokens! Lo! He, only He, is the Hearer, the Seer. Sura XVII (al-Isra'), verse 1

In consequence of this state of affairs, the liberation of that land is an individual duty binding on all Muslims everywhere. This is the base on which all Muslims have to regard the problem; this has to be understood by all Muslims. When the problem is dealt with on this basis, where the full potential of the three circles is mobilized, then the current circumstances will change and the day of liberation will come closer.

> *You are more awful as a fear in their bosoms than Allah. That is because they are a folk who understand not.* Sura LIX, (Al-Hashr, the Exile), verse 13

The Jihad for the Liberation of Palestine is an Individual Obligation

Article Fifteen

When our enemies usurp some Islamic lands, Jihad becomes a duty binding on all Muslims. In order to face the usurpation of Palestine by the Jews, we have no escape from raising the banner of Jihad. This would require the propagation of Islamic consciousness among the masses on all local, Arab and Islamic levels. We must spread the spirit of Jihad among the [Islamic] Umma, clash with the enemies and join the ranks of the Jihad fighters.

The 'ulama as well as educators and teachers, publicity and media men as well as the masses of the educated, and especially the youth and the elders of the Islamic Movements, must participate in this raising of consciousness. There is no escape from introducing fundamental changes in educational curricula in order to cleanse them from all vestiges of the ideological invasion which has been brought about by orientalists and missionaries.

That invasion had begun overtaking this area following the defeat of the Crusader armies by Salah a-Din el Ayyubi. The Crusaders had understood that they had no way to vanquish the Muslims unless they prepared the grounds for that with an ideological invasion which would confuse the thinking of Muslims, revile their heritage, discredit their ideals, to be followed by a military invasion. That was to be in preparation for the Imperialist invasion, as in fact [General] Allenby acknowledged it upon his entry to Jerusalem: "Now, the Crusades are over." General Gouraud stood on the tomb of Salah a-Din and declared: "We have returned, O Salah-a-Din!" Imperialism has been instrumental in boosting the ideological invasion and deepening its roots, and it is still pursuing this goal. All this had paved the way to the loss of Palestine. We must imprint on the minds of generations of Muslims that the Palestinian problem is a religious one, to be dealt with on this premise. It includes Islamic holy sites such as the Aqsa Mosque, which is inexorably linked to the Holy Mosque as long as the Heaven and earth will exist, to the journey of the Messenger of Allah, be Allah's peace and blessing upon him, to it, and to his ascension from it.

> *Dwelling one day in the Path of Allah is better than the entire world and everything that exists in it. The place of the whip of one among you in Paradise is better than the entire world and everything that exists in it. [God's] worshiper's going and coming in the Path of Allah is better than the entire world and everything that exists in it.* (Told by Bukhari, Muslim Tirmidhi and Ibn Maja)

> *I swear by that who holds in His Hands the Soul of Muhammad! I indeed wish to go to war for the sake of Allah! I will assault and kill, assault and kill, assault and kill.* (told by Bukhari and Muslim).

Article Sixteen

We must accord the Islamic [young] generations in our area, an Islamic education based on the implementation of religious precepts, on the conscientious study of the Book of Allah; on the Study of the Prophetic Tradition, on the study of Islamic history and heritage from its reliable sources, under the guidance of experts and scientists, and on singling out the paths which constitute for the Muslims sound concepts of thinking and faith. It is also necessary to study conscientiously the enemy and its material and human potential; to detect its weak and strong spots, and to recognize the powers that support it and stand by it. At the same time, we must be aware of current events, follow the news and study the analyses and commentaries on it, together with drawing plans for the present and the future and examining every phenomenon, so that every Muslim, fighting Jihad, could live out his era aware of his objective, his goals, his way and the things happening round him.

> *O my dear son! Lo! though it be but the weight of a grain of mustard-seed, and though it be in a rock, or in the heavens, or in the earth, Allah will bring it forth. Lo! Allah is subtle. Aware. O my*

dear son! Establish worship and enjoin kindness and forbid inequity, and persevere, whatever may befall thee. Lo! that is of the steadfast heart of things. Turn not thy cheek in scorn toward folk, nor walk with pertness in the land. Lo! Allah loves not braggarts and boasters. Sura XXXI (Luqman), verses 16-18

The Role of Muslim Women

Article Seventeen

The Muslim women have a no lesser role than that of men in the war of liberation; they manufacture men and play a great role in guiding and educating the [new] generation. The enemies have understood that role, therefore they realize that if they can guide and educate [the Muslim women] in a way that would distance them from Islam, they would have won that war. Therefore, you can see them making consistent efforts [in that direction] by way of publicity and movies, curricula of education and culture, using as their intermediaries their craftsmen who are part of the various Zionist Organizations which take on all sorts of names and shapes such as: the Freemasons, Rotary Clubs, gangs of spies and the like. All of them are nests of saboteurs and sabotage.

Those Zionist organizations control vast material resources, which enable them to fulfill their mission amidst societies, with a view of implementing Zionist goals and sowing the concepts that can be of use to the enemy. Those organizations operate [in a situation] where Islam is absent from the arena and alienated from its people. Thus, the Muslims must fulfill their duty in confronting the schemes of those saboteurs. When Islam will retake possession of [the means to] guide the life [of the Muslims], it will wipe out those organizations which are the enemy of humanity and Islam.

Article Eighteen

The women in the house and the family of Jihad fighters, whether they are mothers or sisters, carry out the most important duty of caring for the home and raising the children upon the moral concepts and values which derive from Islam; and of educating their sons to observe the religious injunctions in preparation for the duty of Jihad awaiting them. Therefore, we must pay attention to the schools and curricula upon which Muslim girls are educated, so as to make them righteous mothers, who are conscious of their duties in the war of liberation. They must be fully capable of being aware and of grasping the ways to manage their households. Economy and avoiding waste in household expenditures are prerequisites to our ability to pursue our cause in the difficult circumstances surrounding us. Therefore let them remember at all times that money saved is equivalent to blood, which must be made to run in the veins in order to ensure the continuity of life of our young and old.

> *Lo, men who surrender unto Allah, and women who surrender and men who believe and women who believe, and men who obey and women who obey, and men who speak the truth and women who speak the truth and men who persevere (in righteousness) and women who persevere and men who are humble and women who are humble, and men who give alms and women who give alms, and men who fast and women who fast, and men who guard their modesty and women who guard [their modesty], and men who remember Allah much and women who remember Allah has prepared for them forgiveness and a vast reward.* Sura 33 (Al-Ahzab, the Clans), verse 35

The Role of Islamic Art in the War of Liberation

Article Nineteen

Art has rules and criteria by which one can know whether it is Islamic or Jahiliyya art. The problems of Islamic liberation underlie the need for Islamic art which could lift the spirit, and instead of making one party triumph over the other, would lift up all parties in harmony and balance.

Man is a strange and miraculous being, made out of a handful of clay and a breath of soul; Islamic art is to address man on this basis, while Jahili art addresses the body and makes the element of clay paramount. So, books, articles, publications, religious exhortations, epistles, songs, poems, hymns, plays, and the like, if they possess the characteristics of Islamic art, have the requisites of ideological mobilization, of a continuous nurturing in the pursuance of the journey, and of relaxing the soul. The road is long and the suffering is great and the spirits are weary; it is Islamic art which renews the activity, revives the movement and arouses lofty concepts and sound planning. The soul cannot thrive, unless it knows how to contrive, unless it can transit from one situation to another. All this is a serious matter, no jesting. For the umma fighting its Jihad knows no jesting.

Social Solidarity

Article Twenty

Islamic society is one of solidarity. The Messenger of Allah, be Allah's prayer and peace upon him, said:

> *What a wonderful tribe were the Ash'aris! When they were over-taxed, either in their location or during their journeys, they would collect all their possessions, and then would divide them equally among themselves.*

This is the Islamic spirit which ought to prevail in any Muslim society. A society which confronts a vicious, Nazi-like enemy, who does not differentiate between man and woman, elder and young ought to be the first to adorn itself with this Islamic spirit. Our enemy pursues the style of collective punishment of usurping people's countries and properties, of pursuing them into their exiles and places of assembly. It has resorted to breaking bones, opening fire on women and children and the old, with or without reason, and to setting up detention camps where thousands upon thousands are interned in inhuman conditions. In addition, it destroys houses, renders children orphans and issues oppressive judgements against thousands of young people who spend the best years of their youth in the darkness of prisons. The Nazism of the Jews does not skip women and children, it scares everyone. They make war against people's livelihood, plunder their moneys and threaten their honor. In their horrible actions they mistreat people like the most horrendous war criminals.

Exiling people from their country is another way of killing them. As we face this misconduct, we have no escape from establishing social solidarity among the people, from confronting the enemy as one solid body, so that if one organ is hurt the rest of the body will respond with alertness and fervor.

Article Twenty-One

Social solidarity consists of extending help to all the needy, both materially and morally, or assisting in the execution of certain actions. It is incumbent upon the members of the Hamas to look after the interests of the masses the way they would look after their own interests. They must spare no effort in the implementation and maintenance of those interests, and they must avoid playing with anything that might effect the future generations or cause damage to their society. For the masses are of them and for them, their strength is [ultimately] theirs and their future is theirs. The members of Hamas must share with the people its joys and sorrows, and adopt the demands of the people and anything likely to fulfill its interests and theirs. When this spirit reigns, congeniality will deepen, cooperation and compassion will prevail, unity will firm up, and the ranks will be strengthened in the confrontation with the enemy.

The Powers which Support the Enemy

Article Twenty-Two

The enemies have been scheming for a long time, and they have consolidated their schemes, in order to achieve what they have achieved. They took advantage of key elements in unfolding events, and accumulated a huge and influential material wealth which they put to the service of implementing their dream. This wealth [permitted them to] take over control of the world media such as news agencies, the press, publication houses, broadcasting and the like. [They also used this] wealth to stir revolutions in various parts of the globe in order to fulfill their interests and pick the fruits. They stood behind the French and the Communist Revolutions and behind most of the revolutions we hear about here and there. They also used the money to establish clandestine organizations which are spreading around the world, in order to destroy societies and carry out Zionist interests. Such organizations are: the Freemasons, Rotary Clubs, Lions Clubs, B'nai B'rith and the like. All of them are destructive spying organizations. They also used the money to take over control of the Imperialist states and made them colonize many countries in order to exploit the wealth of those countries and spread their corruption therein.

As regards local and world wars, it has come to pass and no one objects, that they stood behind World War I, so as to wipe out the Islamic Caliphate.

They collected material gains and took control of many sources of wealth. They obtained the Balfour Declaration and established the League of Nations in order to rule the world by means of that organization. They also stood behind World War II, where they collected immense benefits from trading with war materials and prepared for the establishment of their state. They inspired the establishment of the United Nations and the Security Council to replace the League of Nations, in order to rule the world by their intermediary. There was no war that broke out anywhere without their fingerprints on it:

> . . . *As often as they light a fire for war, Allah extinguishes it. Their efforts are for corruption in the land and Allah loves not corrupters.*
> Sura V (Al-Ma'ida—the Tablespread), verse 64

The forces of Imperialism in both the Capitalist West and the Communist East support the enemy with all their might, in material and human terms, taking turns between themselves. When Islam appears, all the forces of Unbelief unite to confront it, because the Community of Unbelief is one.

> *Oh ye who believe! Take not for intimates others than your own folk, who would spare no pain to ruin you. Hatred is revealed by [the utterance of] their mouth, but that which their breasts hide is greater. We have made plain for you the revelations if you will understand.* Sura III, (Al-Imran), verse 118

It is not in vain that the verse ends with God's saying: "If you will understand."

PART IV

Our Position Vis-a-Vis the Islamic Movements

Article Twenty-Three

The Hamas views the other Islamic movements with respect and appreciation. Even when it differs from them in one aspect or another or on one concept or another, it agrees with them in other aspects and concepts. It reads those movements as included in the framework of striving [for the sake of Allah], as long as they hold sound intentions and abide by their devotion to Allah, and as along as their conduct remains within the perimeter of the Islamic circle. All the fighters of Jihad have their reward.

The Hamas regards those movements as its stock holders and asks Allah for guidance and integrity of conduct for all. It shall not fail to continue to raise the banner of unity and to exert efforts in order to implement it, [based] upon the [Holy] Book and the [Prophet's] Tradition.

> *And hold fast, all of you together, to the cable of Allah, do not separate. And remember Allah's favor unto you how ye were enemies and He made friendship between your hearts so that ye became as brothers by His grace; and (how) ye were upon the brink of an abyss of fire, and He did save you from it. Thus Allah makes clear His revelations unto you, that happily ye may be guided.* Sura III (Al-'Imran), verse 102

Article Twenty-Four

Hamas will not permit the slandering and defamation of individuals and groups, for the Believers are not slanderers and cursers. However, despite the need to differentiate between that and the positions and modes of conduct adopted by individuals and groups whenever the Hamas detects faulty positions and modes of conduct, it has the right to point to the mistake, to denigrate it, to act for spelling out the truth and for adopting it realistically in the context of a given problem. Wisdom is roaming around, and the Believer ought to grasp it wherever he can find it.

> *Allah loves not the utterance of harsh speech save by one who has been wronged. Allah is ever Hearer, Knower. If you do good openly or keep it secret, or give evil, lo! Allah is forgiving, powerful.* Sura IV (Women), verses 147–148

The National (wataniyya) Movements in the Palestinian Arena

Article Twenty-Five

[Hamas] reciprocated its respect to them, appreciates their condition and the factors surrounding them and influencing them, and supports them firmly as long as they do not owe their loyalty to the Communist East or to the Crusader West. We reiterate to every one who is part of them or sympathizes with them that the Hamas is a movement of Jihad, or morality and consciousness in its concept of life. It moves forward with the others, abhors opportunism, and only wishes well to individuals and groups. It does not aspire to material gains, or to personal fame, nor does it solicit remuneration from the people. It sets out relying on its own material resources, and what is available to it, [as it is said] "afford them the power you can avail yourself of." [All that] in order to carry out its duty, to gain Allah's favor; it has no ambition other than that.

All the nationalist streams, operating in the Palestinian arena for the sake of the liberation of Palestine, may rest assured that they will definitely and resolutely get support and assistance, in speech and in action, at the present and in the future, [because Hamas aspires] to unite, not to divide; to safeguard, not to squander; to bring together, not to fragment. It values every kind word, every devoted effort and every commendable endeavor. It closes the door before marginal quarrels, it does not heed rumors and biased statements, and it is aware of the right of self-defense.

Anything that runs counter or contradicts this orientation is trumped up by the enemies or by those who run in their orbit in order to create confusion, to divide our ranks or to divert to marginal things.

> *O ye who believe! If an evil-liver bring you tidings, verify it, lest ye smite some folk in ignorance and afterward repent of what ye did.*
> Sura XLIX (al Hujurat, the Private Apartments), verse 6

Article Twenty-Six

The Hamas, while it views positively the Palestinian National Movements which do not owe their loyalty to the East or to the West, does not refrain from debating unfolding events regarding the Palestinian problem, on the local and international scenes.

These debates are realistic and expose the extent to which [these developments] go along with, or contradict, national interests as viewed from the Islamic vantage point.

The Palestine Liberation Organization

Article Twenty-Seven

The PLO is among the closest to the Hamas, for it constitutes a father, a brother, a relative, a friend. Can a Muslim turn away from his father, his brother, his relative or his friend? Our homeland is one, our calamity is one, our destiny is one and our enemy is common to both of us. Under the influence of the circumstances which surrounded the founding of the PLO, and the ideological invasion which has swept the Arab world since the rout of the Crusades, and which has been reinforced by Orientalism and the Christian Mission, the PLO has adopted the idea of a Secular State, and so we think of it. Secular thought is diametrically opposed to religious thought. Thought is the basis for positions, for modes of conduct and for resolutions. Therefore, in spite of our appreciation for the PLO and its possible transformation in the future, and despite the fact that we do not denigrate its role in the Arab-Israeli conflict, we cannot substitute it for the Islamic nature of Palestine by adopting secular thought. For the Islamic nature of Palestine is part of our religion, and anyone who neglects his religion is bound to lose.

> *And who forsakes the religion of Abraham, save him who befools himself?* Sura II (Al-Baqra—the Co), verse 130

When the PLO adopts Islam as the guideline for life, then we shall become its soldiers, the fuel of its fire which will burn the enemies. And until that happens, and we pray to Allah that it will happen soon, the position of the Hamas towards the PLO is one of a son towards his father, a brother towards his brother, and a relative towards his relative who suffers the other's pain when a thorn hits him, who supports the other in the confrontation with the enemies and who wishes him divine guidance and integrity of conduct.

Your brother, your brother! Whoever has no brother, is like a fighter who runs to the battle without weapons. A cousin for man is like the best wing, and no falcon can take off without wings.

Article Twenty-Eight

The Zionist invasion is a mischievous one. It does not hesitate to take any road, or to pursue all despicable and repulsive means to fulfill its desires. It relies to a great extent, for its meddling and spying activities, on the clandestine organizations which it has established, such as the Freemasons, Rotary Clubs, Lions, and other spying associations. All those secret organizations, some which are overt, act for the interests of Zionism and under its directions, strive to demolish societies, to destroy values, to wreck answerableness, to totter virtues and to wipe out Islam. It stands behind the diffusion of drugs and toxics of all kinds in order to facilitate its control and expansion.

The Arab states surrounding Israel are required to open their borders to the Jihad fighters, the sons of the Arab and Islamic peoples, to enable them to play their role and to join their efforts to those of their brothers among the Muslim Brothers in Palestine.

The other Arab and Islamic states are required, at the very least, to facilitate the movement of the Jihad fighters from and to them. We cannot fail to remind every Muslim that when the Jews occupied Holy Jerusalem in 1967 and stood at the doorstep of the Blessed Aqsa Mosque, they shouted with joy:

> *Muhammad is dead, he left daughters behind.*

Israel, by virtue of its being Jewish and of having a Jewish population, defies Islam and the Muslims.

> *Let the eyes of the cowards not fall asleep.*

National and Religious Associations, Institutions, the Intelligentsia, and the Arab and Islamic Worlds

Article Twenty-Nine

Hamas hopes that those Associations will stand by it on all levels, will support it, adopt its positions, boost its activities and moves and encourage support for it, so as to render the Islamic peoples its backers and helpers, and its strategic depth in all human and material domains as well as in information, in time and space. Among other things, they hold solidarity meetings, issue explanatory publications, supportive articles and tendentious leaflets to make the masses aware of the Palestinian issue, the problems it faces and of the plans to resolve them; and to mobilize the Islamic peoples ideologically, educationally and culturally in order to fulfill their role in the crucial war of liberation, as they had played their role in the defeat of the Crusades and in the rout of the Tartars and had saved human civilization. How all that is dear to Allah!

> *Allah has decreed: Lo! I verily shall conquer, I and my messengers. Lo! Allah is strong, Almighty.* Sura LVIII (Al-Mujadilah), verse 21

Article Thirty

Men of letters, members of the intelligentsia, media people, preachers, teachers and educators and all different sectors in the Arab and Islamic world, are all called upon to play their role and to carry out their duty in view of the wickedness of the Zionist invasion, of its penetration into many countries, and its control over material means and the media, with all the ramifications thereof in most countries of the world.

Jihad means not only carrying arms and denigrating the enemies. Uttering positive words, writing good articles and useful books, and lending support and assistance, all that too is Jihad in the path of Allah, as long as intentions are sincere to make Allah's banner supreme.

> *Those who prepare for a raid in the path of Allah are considered as if they participated themselves in the raid. Those who successfully rear a raider in their home, are considered as if they participated themselves in the raid.* (Told by Bukhari, Muslim, Abu Dawud and Tirmidhi)

The Members of Other Religions

The Hamas is a Humane Movement

Article Thirty-One

Hamas is a humane movement, which cares for human rights and is committed to the tolerance inherent in Islam as regards attitudes towards other religions. It is only hostile to those who are hostile towards it, or stand in its way in order to disturb its moves or to frustrate its efforts.

Under the shadow of Islam it is possible for the members of the three religions: Islam, Christianity and Judaism to coexist in safety and security. Safety and security can only prevail under the shadow of Islam, and recent and ancient history is the best witness to that effect. The members of other religions must desist from struggling against Islam over sovereignty in this region. For if they were to gain the upper hand, fighting, torture and uprooting would follow; they would be fed up with each other, to say nothing of members of other religions. The past and the present are full of evidence to that effect.

They will not fight you in body safe in fortified villages or from behind wells. Their adversity among themselves is very great. Ye think of them as a whole whereas their hearts are diverse. That is because they are a folk who have no sense. Sura 59 (al-Hashr, the Exile), verse 14

Islam accords his rights to everyone who has rights and averts aggression against the rights of others. The Nazi Zionist practices against our people will not last the lifetime of their invasion, for "states built upon oppression last only one hour, states based upon justice will last until the hour of Resurrection."

Allah forbids you not those who warred not against you on account of religion and drove you not out from your houses, that you should show them kindness and deal justly with them. Lo! Allah loves the just dealers. Sura 60 (Al-Mumtahana), verse 8

The Attempts to Isolate the Palestinian People

Article Thirty-Two

World Zionism and Imperialist forces have been attempting, with smart moves and considered planning, to push the Arab countries, one after another, out of the circle of conflict with Zionism, in order, ultimately, to isolate the Palestinian People.

Egypt has already been cast out of the conflict, to a very great extent through the treacherous Camp David Accords, and she has been trying to drag other countries into similar agreements in order to push them out of the circle of conflict.

Hamas is calling upon the Arab and Islamic peoples to act seriously and tirelessly in order to frustrate that dreadful scheme and to make the masses aware of the danger of coping out of the circle of struggle with Zionism. Today it is Palestine and tomorrow it may be another country or other countries. For Zionist scheming has no end, and after Palestine they will covet expansion from the Nile to the Euphrates. Only when they have completed digesting the area on which they will have laid their hand, they will look forward to more expansion, etc. Their scheme has been laid out in the Protocols of the Elders of Zion, and their present [conduct] is the best proof of what is said there.

Leaving the circle of conflict with Israel is a major act of treason and it will bring curse on its perpetrators.

> *Who so on that day turns his back to them, unless maneuvering for*
> *battle or intent to join a company, he truly has incurred wrath*
> *from Allah, and his habitation will be hell, a hapless journey's end.*
> Sura 8 (al-Anfal—Spoils of War), verse 16

We have no escape from pooling together all the forces and energies to face this despicable Nazi-Tatar invasion. Otherwise we shall witness the loss of [our] countries, the uprooting of their inhabitants, the spreading of corruption on earth and the destruction of all religious values. Let everyone realize that he is accountable to Allah.

> *Whoever does a speck of good will bear [the consequences] and who-*
> *ever does a speck of evil will see [the consequences].*

Within the circle of the conflict with world Zionism, the Hamas regards itself the spearhead and the avant-garde. It joins its efforts to all those who are active on the Palestinian scene, but more steps need to be taken by the Arab and Islamic peoples and Islamic associations throughout the Arab and Islamic world in order to make possible the next round with the Jews, the merchants of war.

> *We have cast among them enmity and hatred till the day of*
> *Resurrection. As often as they light a fire for war, Allah extinguishes*
> *it. Their effort is for corruption in the land, and Allah loves not cor-*
> *rupters.* Sura V (Al-Ma'idah—the Table spread), verse 64

Article Thirty-Three

The Hamas sets out from these general concepts which are consistent and in accordance with the rules of the universe, and gushes forth in the river of Fate in its confrontation and Jihad waging against the enemies, in defense of the Muslim human being, of Islamic Civilization and of the Islamic Holy Places, primarily the Blessed Aqsa Mosque. This, for the purpose of calling upon the Arab and Islamic peoples as well as their governments, popular and official associations, to fear Allah in their attitude towards and dealings with Hamas, and to be, in accordance with Allah's will, its supporters and partisans who extend assistance to it and provide it with reinforcement after reinforcement, until the Decree of Allah is fulfilled, the ranks are over-swollen, Jihad fighters join other Jihad fighters, and all this accumulation sets out from everywhere in the Islamic world, obeying the call of duty, and intoning "Come on, join Jihad!" This call will tear apart the clouds in the skies and it will continue to ring until liberation is completed, the invaders are vanquished and Allah's victory sets in.

Verily Allah helps one who helps Him. Lo! Allah is strong, Almighty.
Sura XXII (Pilgrimage), verse 40

PART V—THE TESTIMONY OF HISTORY

Confronting Aggressors Throughout History

Article Thirty-Four

Palestine is the navel of earth, the convergence of continents, the object of greed for the greedy, since the dawn of history. The Prophet, may Allah's prayer and peace be upon him, points out to that fact in his noble hadith in which he implored his venerable Companion, Ma'adh ibn Jabl, saying:

> *O Ma'adh, Allah is going to grant you victory over Syria after me, from Al-Arish to the Euphrates, while its men, women, and female slaves will be dwelling there until the Day of Resurrection. Those of you who chose [to dwell in one of the plains of Syria or Palestine will be in a state of Jihad to the Day of Resurrection.*

The greedy have coveted Palestine more than once and they raided it with armies in order to fulfill their covetousness.

Multitudes of Crusades descended on it, carrying their faith with them and waving their Cross. They were able to defeat the Muslims for a long time, and the Muslims were not able to redeem it until their sought the protection of their religious banner; then, they unified their forces, sang the praise of their God and set out for Jihad under the Command of Saladin al-Ayyubi, for the duration of nearly two decades, and then the obvious conquest took place when the Crusaders were defeated and Palestine was liberated.

> *Say (O Muhammad) unto those who disbelieve: ye shall be overcome and gathered unto Hell, an evil resting place.* Sura III (Al-Imran), verse 12

This is the only way to liberation, there is no doubt in the testimony of history. That is one of the rules of the universe and one of the laws of existence. Only iron can blunt iron, only the true faith of Islam can vanquish their false and falsified faith. Faith can only be fought by faith. Ultimately, victory is reserved to the truth, and truth is victorious.

> *And verily Our word went forth of old unto Our Bordmen sent [to warn]. That they verily would be helped. And that Our host, they verily would be the victors. Sura 38 (Al-saffat), verses 171-3*

Article Thirty-Five

Hamas takes a serious look at the defeat of the Crusades at the hand of Saladin the Ayyubid and the rescue of Palestine from their domination; at the defeat of the Tatars at Ein Jalut where their spine was broken by Qutuz and Al-Dhahir Baibars, and the Arab world was rescued from the sweep of the Tatars which ruined all aspects of human civilization. Hamas has learned from these lessons and examples, that the current Zionist invasion had been preceded by a Crusader invasion from the West; and another one, the Tatars, from the East. And exactly as the Muslims had faced those invasions and planned their removal and defeat, they are able to face the Zionist invasion and defeat it. This will not be difficult for Allah if our intentions are pure and our determination is sincere; if the Muslims draw useful lessons from the experiences of the past, and extricate themselves for the vestiges of the [western] ideological onslaught; and if they follow the traditions of Islam.

EPILOGUE

The Hamas are Soldiers

Article Thirty-Six

The Hamas, while breaking its path, reiterates time and again to all members of our people and the Arab and Islamic peoples, that it does not seek fame for itself nor material gains, or social status.

Nor is it directed against any one member of our people in order to compete with him or replace him. There is nothing of that at all.

It will never set out against any Muslims or against the non-Muslims who make peace with it, here or anywhere else. It will only be of help to all associations and organizations which act against the Zionist enemy and those who revolve in its orbit.

Hamas posits Islam as a way of life, it is its faith and its yardstick for judging. Whoever posits Islam as a way of life, anywhere, and regardless of whether it is an organization, a state, or any other group, Hamas are its soldiers, nothing else.

We implore Allah to guide us, to guide through us and to decide between us and our folk with truth.

> *Our Lord! Decide with truth between us and our folk, for Thou are the best of those who make decisions.* Sura VII (Al-A'raf—the Heights), verse 89

Our last call is: Thanks to Allah, the Lord of the Universe.

> From Rafael Yisraeli, in Y. Alexander and H. Foxman, eds., **The 1988-1989 Annual on Terrorism** (The Netherlands: Kluwer Academic Publishers)

Hamas Communiqués
and Political Statements

Hamas Communiqués and Political Statements

22 January 2002

In the name of Allah the most Gracious the most Merciful

Zionist terrorism has crossed all red lines and we swear by Allah to revenge

The terrorist Jewish killers, who are known for spreading mischief, have continued their series of savage massacres on the land of Islamic Palestine. The latest of which was the savage bloodbath that targeted the four martyrs in Nablus:

Martyr Yousef Al-Sourkaji
Martyr Nasim Abul Roos
Martyr Karim Mafarje
Martyr Jasser Samaro

This carnage opens the door wide open for a ferocious war that would target Zionist gangs everywhere and by all means and how true is Allah's promise: *"but if ye revert (to your sins) We shall revert (to Our punishments) . . ."*
"And soon will the unjust assailants know what vicissitudes their affairs will take!"

The Islamic Resistance Movement
Hamas—Palestine
Tuesday 9/11/1422H
22/1/2002AD

12 January 2002

In the name of Allah the most Gracious the most Merciful

Zionist crime in Rafah will not go unpunished

Palestinian smuggling of arms does not justify this crime

The Zionist occupiers have committed a new savage crime that could be only carried out by people stripped of all human values at a time when the world is claiming to be at war with terrorism. The Zionists demolished 73 houses and displaced 150 families in Rafah justifying their crime by saying it was to prevent Palestinians from smuggling arms and in retaliation to the Palestinian attempt to smuggle a shipload of arms.

We condemn this blind terrorism and affirm the following:

1. This cruel terrorist act would not go unpunished and we affirm our full right in defending and protecting our people in face of Zionist terrorism *"And soon will the unjust assailants know what vicissitudes their affairs will take!"*

2. We ask the Arab governments and peoples to strengthen our people's steadfastness through compensating any damage inflicted as a result of occupation practices. We appeal to the Arab League secretary general Mr. Amre Mousa to initiate steps to actualize this measure so as to foil the Zionist schemes aimed at forcing the immigration of our people through exercising various forms of pressures on them.

3. We denounce the American support of Zionist terrorism as voiced by secretary of state Collin Powell when he told reporters, "Israel was retaliating to the arms smuggling incident." He added "the large part of the military operations in the past 24 hours was meant to destroy means of smuggling arms via south of Gaza Strip" then opined "it is a defensive measure." We ask the Palestinian Authority not to depend much on America as an honest mediator.

4. We affirm our people's full rights in resisting occupation and their right of acquiring arms to confront and eject Zionist occupation. The Zionist enemy is spending billions each year for the sake of accumulating the most advanced weapons to impose its occupation by force.

5. The PA's embarrassment due to the shipload of arms was not due to the fact that our Palestinian people did not have the right to acquire arms for the sake of resisting occupation but due to Oslo, which

stripped the Palestinian people from this right along with several other legitimate rights. Consequently, we request the PA to rescind Oslo and return to the Palestinian people's option namely resistance.

And it is a Jihad until victory or martyrdom

The Islamic Resistance Movement
Hamas-Palestine
Saturday 28th Shawwal 1422H
12/1/2002AD

8 January 2002

In the name of Allah the most Gracious the most Merciful

Statement by the Islamic Resistance Movement—Hamas

On the intelligence apparatus' attempt to assassinate a Movement's cadre

The Islamic Resistance Movement, Hamas, views with absolute seriousness the sinful crime perpetrated on Tuesday 8/1/2002–24th Shawwal 1422 at the hands of the intelligence apparatus elements in Gaza. The crime targeted life of paramedic Ahmed Labad, one of the Hamas cadres, while entering the Shati clinic, run by UNRWA, where he works. His car was encircled from both sides and bullets were randomly and madly fired at him. The intelligence men chased him inside the clinic, his place of work, with indiscriminate fire hitting him in his hip and wounding the clinic's doctor Bassam Al-Qutati in his neck in addition to injuring Mona Ranteesi, 16, and Shaima Ukaila, 9, while on their way to their school.

The Islamic Resistance Movement, Hamas, condemns this savage crime and affirms the following:

1. The Hamas Movement considers the assassination attempt of one of its cadres as a serious attempt that targets dragging the Palestinian street into civil war.

2. Hamas holds the intelligence apparatus in Gaza responsible for this criminal act and does not exempt the Zionist entity from responsi-

bility for inciting others to strike the Islamic Movement and to ignite internal strife.

3.   We ask all honorable persons to immediately interfere to end this conspiracy that targets breaking up our people's unity and ending their brave intifada.

4.   The Hamas Movement affirms its legitimate right in resisting occupation. This crime along with the security apparatuses' prosecution of Hamas cadres would not deter the Movement from proceeding in its Jihad march until liberation of all Palestinian soil.

And it is a Jihad until either victory or martyrdom

The Islamic Resistance Movement
Hamas-Palestine
24th Shawwal 1422H
Tuesday 8/1/2002AD

27 December 2001

In the name of Allah the most Gracious the most Merciful

Statement on Peres-Qrei negotiations

And the continuous Zionist aggression on our people

There are two important developments in the Palestinian arena these days first the recent declaration of a secret negotiations channel between Shimon Peres and Ahmed Qrei. The Palestinian Authority later added Yasser Abed Rabbo to its negotiating team, adopted the talks and officially endorsed them despite their meager and serious content. The discussions focus on establishing a mini (Palestinian) state on 42% of the West Bank and Gaza Strip lands, which is the same area the PA is currently controlling, in return for halting the intifada and resistance. The negotiations further envisage postponing final status talks on major issues to a later stage between the Palestinian state and the Zionist entity, which point to the dangerous destiny awaiting future of our cause and our people's rights under such negotiations and accompanying policies. Those negotiations further endanger future and fate of Al-Quds, right of return, borders of the state while ignoring future of Jewish settlements!

The second development is the continuation of Zionist aggression on our people despite Yasser Arafat's address on the eve of the Eid, which came to meet "Israeli" and American demands. The Zionist enemy shelled Rafah in the past three days and stormed Tamun, Azun, Jenin, Khalil and Shuweika (near Tulkarm). The shelling was accompanied by murders, abductions, detentions and destruction of houses. Those developments are ongoing amidst PA's insistence not to retaliate regardless of Sharon's practices. The PA is also insisting on comprehensive calm and ceasefire at the pretext of stripping Sharon of any excuses and exposing his intentions before America and the world as if Sharon was in need of any excuses to go ahead with his aggression or in need of more testing or experimenting!

Those grave developments reveal the PA's real intentions namely to extricate itself from the intifada and resistance situation and proceed to the negotiations on whatever basis available even if it was contrary to our people's aspirations and to the new political ceiling reached thanks to the intifada and resistance and their great accomplishments over the past 15 months.

It is true that the PA was subject to huge pressures and threats by Sharon and the Americans but such pressures do not justify gambling our people's rights and future of the Palestine cause in return for PA's safety. The well being of the country and Al-Quds is above the safety of individuals or leaderships.

In the light of such circumstances and serious developments, we in the Islamic Resistance Movement, Hamas, would like to affirm the following:

1. we refuse any concessions or an end to the intifada and resistance program. We insist on the importance of sticking to both and progressing in them in their capacity as our people's genuine option in rebelling the aggression, ensuring self-defense and accomplishing rights and goals.

2. we condemn the return to the negotiating channels and security meetings with the Zionist enemy. Our people's rights, national unity and intifada are the victims at those meetings and negotiations. Our people and their Mujahid factions strongly reject any solution that would prune Palestinian rights in lands, Quds and holy shrines.

3. we call on our Palestinian people' masses and national and Islamic factions to boost national unity and escalate intifada and resistance against occupation. We call on them to pressure the PA to revoke its meas-

ures concerning the arrests and closures of scores of our people's national institutions that always assisted them in their steadfastness vis-à-vis Zionist siege, starvation and aggression.

In conclusion, we affirm to our people and Ummah's masses that the Islamic Resistance Movement, Hamas, along with all struggling and Mujahid forces would remain God willing the protecting shield of our people and would remain insisting on our people's rights and goals and would continue resisting occupation until it leaves our holy land Insha'allah.

Allaho Akbar and victory to the Mujahideen

The Islamic Resistance Movement-Hamas
12th Shawwal 1422H
27th December 2001AD

23 December 2001

In the name of Allah the most Gracious the most Merciful

"Think not that Allah doth not heed the deeds of those who do wrong. He but giveth them respite against a Day when the eyes will fixedly stare in horror."

The Islamic Resistance Movement—
Hamas, condemns the assault on a Palestinian journalist

The Islamic Resistance Movement, Hamas, strongly denounces the sinful aggression on freedom of expression and clear conscience in carrying events on the land of Gaza. Three of those trying to ignite strife in our striving Palestinian street beat up Seiful Deen Shahin, Jazeera space channel's correspondent in the Gaza Strip, who is known for his integrity in reporting the bloody events that led to the fall of many martyrs and wounded.

The Hamas Movement condemns this wicked crime and congratulates the journalist Seiful Deen for this testimony on his honesty and considers that bitter incident as a medal of honor in his record.

The Hamas Movement asks the Palestinian Authority to disclose circumstances of this crime, names of those involved in it and its motives the soonest.

Allah is above all and the oppressors will be one day punished.

And it is a Jihad until either victory or martyrdom

The Islamic Resistance Movement
Hamas-Palestine
Sunday 8th Shawwal 1422H
23/12/2001AD

21 December 2001

In the name of Allah the most Gracious the most Merciful

Communiqué by Qassam Brigades

"Jihad is ongoing till the Day of Judgment"

In response to our brothers in the political leadership's call, and for the sake of our people's interests, protecting and preserving our people's national unity, especially in the light of the latest Authority measures and their repercussions, we declare in the Qassam Brigades that we will suspend our martyrdom operations and mortar shelling in occupied Palestine 1948 only and on temporary basis.

We affirm that such a suspension is linked to the Zionist enemy's stoppage of the policy of assassination and aggression against our people's civilians. Whenever the enemy ignores that condition, we in the Qassam Brigades would no longer abide by such a suspension and consider that stoppage as null and void.

"An eye for an eye and a tooth for a tooth"

Our Mujahid Brigades will always live up to our people and Ummah's hopes in them.

And it is a Jihad until either victory or martyrdom

Qassam Brigades
Al-Quds-Palestine
Friday 6th Shawwal 1422H
21/12/2001AD

21 December 2001

In the name of Allah the most Gracious the most Merciful

Communiqué by the Islamic Resistance Movement—Hamas

On the suspension of martyrdom operations in the occupied lands

All praises to Allah and peace be upon His messenger, family, companions and his followers,

To our Mujahid Palestinian people and our Arab and Islamic Ummah

Assalamu Alaikum wa Rahmatullahi wa Barakatuh

For the sake of preserving our Palestinian people's unity and maintaining their Jihad march towards freedom and independence, despite our full knowledge of the Zionist enemy's intentions to wipe out our people's determination and impose humiliation on them through repressive measures and aggressive policies, and responding to people of wisdom who wish to foil the occupiers' plan of hitting the unity of our ranks and based on our historic responsibility at this sensitive stage of our people's history, we declare suspension of martyrdom operations in the 1948 occupied territories and a stoppage of mortar firing until further notice.

We affirm that all Hamas cadres especially the Qassam Brigades should abide by this matter until Allah ordains whatever He wills.

It is a Jihad until either victory or martyrdom

The Islamic Resistance Movement
Hamas-Palestine
Friday 21/12/2001AD
6th Shawwal 1422H

17 December 2001

In the name of Allah the most Gracious the most Merciful

"Think not of those who are slain in Allah's Way as dead. Nay, they live, finding their sustenance in the Presence of their Lord;"

Hamas pledges to avenge its martyr hero

The Mujahid Yacoub Fathi Edkaydek

Inhabitants of the city of Khalil woke up to a new crime perpetrated by Zionist occupation. A special Zionist army unit stormed at dawn today the house of Mujahid martyr Yacoub Fathi Edkeydek, which is located in an area under Palestinian Authority control. The unit, backed by scores of heavily armed soldiers, fired at the Mujahid's head and chest in front of his mother, wife and family in cold blood in a preplanned assassination operation.

The liquidation falls in line with the series of assassinations launched by the racist Sharon government against leaderships and cadres of the Palestinian people. This operation also fell in line with the ferocious campaign waged by the American administration with the aim of outlawing Palestinian resistance factions and persecuting them.

Martyr Fathi Edkeydek is one of Hamas' field activists who was arrested for several years in Zionist occupation jails and was also detained in PA prisons. He was a model of heroism, courage and challenge where he displayed steadfastness and heroic challenge during detention especially in interrogation cells. He also played a distinctive role in the social work related to affairs of prisoners and detainees as well as showing strict abidance by Islamic behavior ever since his early childhood.

The racist Sharon government's programmed assassination comes only few hours after Palestinian chairman Yasser Arafat's speech in which he stressed the importance that all Palestinian forces and resistance factions should abide by the ceasefire and not launch martyrdom operations at a time when the terrorist Sharon government was still pursuing the cruelest form of murder and annihilation campaigns against all sect4ors of the Palestinian people.

We in the Islamic Resistance Movement, Hamas, while bidding farewell to a dear martyr and field commander would like to affirm the following:

- It is clear that our backs are still targeted as the PA asserts the concept of one authority, which could not provide protection for the Palestinian people nor for itself. This calls on us to protect ourselves from occupation crimes and liquidations.

- The Zionist entity is insisting on its racist colonialist policy and has never ceased spreading more pain, panic and death in lines of the Palestinians at a time when it was claiming to pursue so-called peace, which only led to more murders.

- We in the Islamic Resistance Movement, Hamas, refuse the PA's silence while watching the Zionist occupation troops storming its areas and killing the Palestinian people's honorable figures without doing a thing. At the same time this Authority is actively prosecuting and arresting Mujahideen, throwing them into jails and closing Islamic institutions in all areas of the occupied homeland.

- We vow to relatives of the martyr, his mother, father, wife, children and brothers that we will remain faithful to our pledges. We promise our martyr, our relatives and people to continue along the same path that of Jihad and resistance and to revenge for the martyr hero despite difficulty of the road.

"And soon will the unjust assailants know what vicissitudes their affairs will take!"

And it is a Jihad until either victory or martyrdom

The Islamic Resistance Movement
Hamas-Palestine
Monday 17/12/2001AD
2nd Shawwal 1422H

17 December 2001

In the name of Allah the most Gracious the most Merciful

Islamic Resistance Movement (Hamas) communiqué

Commenting on chairman Arafat's speech

The Islamic Resistance Movement, Hamas, views with absolute seriousness chairman Arafat's address to the Palestinian people on the occasion of Eidul Fitr due to the following reasons:

- Demanding the Palestinian people and their resistance factions to halt resistance and Jihad even if the Zionist enemy continued its assassinations and massacres of the Palestinians. Such a demand opens the door wide open for mass murderer Sharon to continue his annihilation campaign of the Palestinian people with Palestinian protection.

- Allowing occupation to continue in its aggression against our Palestinian people while preventing the Palestinians from defending themselves is an unacceptable oppressive equation.

- Considering the heroic martyrdom operations that achieved a kind of balance of deterrence and represented the only Palestinian weapon to attain national rights as terrorist operations gained Sharon legitimacy that he was in dire need to launch a rabid war against our Mujahid Palestinian people. It further dealt a blow to our Palestinian people's struggle over the past decade and constituted a new dangerous retreat in face of Zionist blackmail of the Palestinian Authority.

- Depriving the Palestinian people from their right of self-defense and describing it as terrorism, which should have rather been used to describe occupation, was in violation of all laws and norms that allowed peoples the right of self-defense.

- Outlawing Palestinian resistance after considering it as an act of terrorism granted legality to occupation because it stripped Palestinian resistance of legitimacy.

- Insisting on prosecution of Mujahid Palestinian factions threatens unity of the Palestinian lines and achieves the Zionists' repeated and declared target of igniting a civil war in the Palestinian street.

- Closing charitable institutions that effectively contributed in bolstering our Palestinian people's steadfastness in face of the Zionist gang's policies of siege and starvation in a bid to liquidate the Palestine cause and existence would no doubt share in subduing the Palestinian people and accepting the Zionist humiliating dictates.

- Pending hopes on false American promises and adopting destined stands based on such promises posed as a serious threat to the fate of our Palestine cause.

The Islamic Resistance Movement outlines such warnings before the Palestinian people and appeals to all Palestinian national and Islamic forces to declare their stands in absolute integrity for now there is no room for courtesy or partisan rivalry at the expense of our Palestinian people's legitimate rights, just cause and rightful struggle. We also beseech all forces to stand united in the resistance trench before the disaster befalls all at which regret would be of no use. We also urge the Arab and Islamic Ummah to extend support to our legitimate struggle, to back our people's steadfastness in their crucial battle and to break away from American hegemony by refusing all projects aimed at liquidating our Palestine cause.

We are confident that victory will be on our side in the end but we must continue with our Jihad and legitimate resistance and Allah will be along our side and will never make our work go in vain.

The Islamic Resistance Movement
Hamas-Palestine
Monday 17/12/2001AD
2nd Shawwal 1422H

12 December 2001

In the name of Allah the most Gracious the most Merciful

"Fight them, and Allah will punish them by your hands, cover them with shame, help you (to victory) over them, heal the breasts of Believers,"

Qassam epic on the Furqan (Badr battle) anniversary and black day on "Israel"

Six Jihad operations and war of busses renewed to avenge for Abu Hannoud

All praises to Allah and peace be upon commander of the Mujahidden and his family and companions . . .

Badr is renewed as the Mujahideen wore the clothes of the Sahaba . . . Hamza, Saad and Muthana are back to teach the occupiers lessons in heroism. The butcher Sharon believed that his assassinations would wipe out and end resistance and would defeat our giant Brigades. He dared to assassinate and murder but he was disappointed. Who will stop the stormy winds? Who will silence the roaring bullets? Who will face the blazing bombs? For our soldiers will attack, from the fields, from the mountains and valleys of Palestine, from Nablus, Jenin, Gaza, Al-Quds, from all areas of Palestine. The butcher Sharon will pay the price for his foolishness and tyranny 100 Zionists as a first batch of revenge for martyr Mahmoud Abu Hannoud and all martyrs of our people Insha'allah.

Our heroic Palestinian people:

The revenge operations started on the land of Gaza then Affula and later firing incidents took place at settlements in the West Bank (in Jordan Valley). Today "Israel" was covered with hell after the revenge battles started in Al-Quds, Gaza, Yaffa, the Valley and Jenin and Zionist remains were scattered everywhere. Last night two lions of the Qassam Brigades the heroes Nabil Amre Halabiya and Osama Mohammed Eid ignited three qualitative explosions that rocked the heart of Al-Quds inflicting scores of dead and wounded. Later on Gaza woke up to bullets of two other Qassam lions (Jihad Al-Masri and Massalama Al-Araj) that led to the death of a settler and the wounding of several others. The Mujahideen then fired a number of projectiles at Zionist settlements. In the Jordan Valley the Qassam lions blasted an explosive device in a Zionist bus that was totally burnt and filmed on videotape. The city of Jenin also shared in the Qassam grand operations where a Zionist settler was killed near the settlement of Qadmim. This afternoon our cavalier Maher Mohiudeen Hobeisha, 23, from the Nablus city blew himself up to open hell for Zionists. He exploded a Zionist double-decker in Haifa. Death haunted Zionists from various spots, burning scores and even hundreds of them, destroying and killing more than twenty Zionists and wounding hundreds according to the enemy's own reports.

Our Mujahid people:

Sharon and his gang were afraid to death from our hero Abu Hannoud whose operations brought shame on them. They breathed a sigh of relief after committing their crime and hateful joy was drawn on their dirty faces as they drank champagne to rejoice and boasted their crime over the media. But time has come for those rats to return to their holes after the Qassam lions showed up anew to teach the occupiers a lesson of heroism and sacrifice. The Zionist occupiers' alleged security did not protect them from the lions. Furthermore, neither the Zionists' planes would protect them from the freedom fighters' anger nor their tanks would protect them from the Mujahideen bombs. And we will continue along the path God willing.

Allahu Akbar wa Lillah El-Hamd

Qassam Brigades
Commander Abu Hannoud groups
Sunday 17th Ramadan 1422H
2/12/2001

4 December 2001

In the name of Allah the most Gracious the most Merciful

More steadfastness and national unity required in face of the Zionist shelling and aggression

Our Palestinian lands are witnessing since Monday night a fierce Zionist aggression that covered our cities and villages in Gaza and the West Bank. The aggression targeted our people as well as Palestinian Authority premises and security forces in Gaza, Ramallah, Jenin, Khan Younis, Tulkarm and Nablus. The result was destruction of numerous headquarters and the fall of many martyrs and wounded.

This aggression affirms the terrorist nature of the Zionist entity, which the whole world should realize as our people had already realized. It is a nature that only understands the language of force and resistance.

We condemn the American administration's biased stand in favor of this Zionist aggression, which exposes the mistake and falsity of betting on neutrality or seriousness of the American stand or pending any hopes on it. We thus affirm that our Palestinian people today clearly understand role of this administration and the mission of its envoys who came to halt the intifada and quell the resistance. The Palestinian people would not allow implementation of that scheme, which the USA is trying to carry out under the pressure of the Zionist aggression and terrorist war machine.

Those events prove that the Palestinian people are all targeted, whether the PA or the resistance. Our fate as a Palestinian people is to remain united in the resistance, confrontation and intifada trench against that enemy, which targets the whole lot of us. Our people's sole option is the intifada and resistance program, which is the sole road God willing capable of liberating our land and our holy shrines and deterring Zionist aggression and terrorism against our Palestinian people.

We urge all national and Islamic factions along with their resistance brigades to escalate resistance and Jihad operations in defense of our lands, people and institutions. We also call on the PA to retaliate to that aggression by releasing detainees and joining our Palestinian people's national option of resistance. We affirm that escalation of resistance and ending the policy of arrests would boost our people's national unity, which is one of the most important weapons in confrontation of the Zionist aggression.

And it is a Jihad until either victory or martyrdom

The Islamic Resistance Movement
Hamas-Palestine
4/12/2001

25 November 2001

In the name of Allah the most Gracious the most Merciful

"Among the Believers are men who have been true to their Covenant with Allah: of them some have completed their vow (to the extreme), and some (still) wait: but they have never changed (their determination) in the least"

The Mujahid commander Mahmoud Abu Hannoud will remain the symbol of the Ummah's greatness with its sacrifices and victories and the killers' dream will be in vain

To our Palestinian Mujahid people, our people in the diaspora and stead-fast camps, our angry and struggling masses, our Mujahid youths, our stead-fast people, our brave children, our persevering women, our esteemed Sheikhs and our glorified Arab and Islamic Ummah.

To all honorable and loyal people who refused to heed the American cease-fire calls and refused to accept the enemy's dictates and refused to be humil-iated in their own lands. To our heroic Mujahideen, free strugglers and brave fighters in all parts of our occupied homeland and in the diaspora.

To all of you the Islamic Resistance Movement, Hamas, bears with pride, patience and steadfastness the glad tidings of the martyrdom of its martyr hero Mahmoud Abu Hannoud, commander of the Qassam Brigades in the West Bank districts and his brothers the Mujahideen . . . the heroes . . . the brothers Ayman and Ma'moon Hashayka whose pure blood inspired resist-ance in the masses from the Ocean to the Gulf and who renewed hope and strength in those masses along the road of Jihad and resistance.

The people took to the streets bidding them farewell and renewing alle-giance to resistance and support to the Mujahid Brigades from which Yehya Ayyash, Emad Akl, Mohiuddin Al-Sharif and other heroic Mujahideen who cleaned the hearts and cleared the vision of the Ummah graduated.

Hence, Mahmoud did not die but rather his martyrdom breathed life in a situation almost killed by initiatives and understandings. Palestine knows that the man who was chasing martyrdom as the Zionist occupation authorities were chasing him was inevitably meeting his fate. However, the loss was great and painful despite its inevitability. Nonetheless, congratulations should be extended for the martyrdom, Allah's satisfaction and paradise and congratu-lations for meeting Mohammed, peace be upon him, and his companions.

Our Palestinian people . . . our Arab and Islamic Ummah:

Our Mujahid hero Mahmoud Abu Hannoud left this world heading for the upper site in paradise after spending the best ever years in life and after his name was added to the list of heroes of this Ummah and after he became a symbol and a model. Cunning minds and sinful hands that assassinated the Mujahid hero Mahmoud Abu Hannoud were the same that planned for liquidating the Mujahideen leaders such as the martyr Dr. Abdullah Azam on 24th November 1989 and the martyr hero Emad Akl on 24th November 1993 within framework of a spiteful Zionist-Crusade scheme to liquidate Islamic propagators and to abort the phenomenon of Islamic renaissance that posed as a nightmare for oppressive regimes, the Zionist entity and the hateful crusade countries.

History is repeating itself; regimes are allying anew to uproot Islam and Muslims under the cover of "combating terrorism." Even if America were true in its intentions and calls against terrorism, it should have set the Zionist entity at the top of the list of terrorism. It should have fought that entity for representing the cruelest form of occupation and terrorism and it should have backed the Palestinian people (victim of Zionist terrorism) who are fighting to liberate national lands and to win freedom and independence after ejecting Israeli occupation. It should not justify Zionist aggression that assassinate and murder heroic Mujahideen and Palestinian civilians. It was not strange that the Zionists and Crusaders would lead the ferocious campaign against Islam and Muslims.

This savage crime was perpetrated with all cowardice and meanness as a reception to the American delegation that arrived at the pretext of defusing tensions in the region. The American administration did not react in the least in face of such a crime, which affirmed its blatant bias in favor of Zionist terrorism. Hence, accepting American initiatives and offering concessions just to please it is a very serious matter. We urge the Palestinian Authority to declare rejection of all oppressive American initiatives and not to abide by what contradicts our people's rights, ambitions and determination.

Our patient Palestinian people:

Our martyr hero has paid the price of pride and dignity after performing his duty in full towards his religion, country and people. Mahmoud was not only a person who chose the road of dignity and pride but he was also a prominent model of a Palestinian generation. Through representing that generation, Mahmoud gained his value as a Mujahid and a commander who dedicated his life to produce a glorious record in various areas of the country. He remained loyal to his creed and never got bored or stopped by the lie of the so-called "de facto situation" or "prevailing circumstances" but rather topped the list of honorable combatants who attack enemy fortresses and who spread panic and death in lines of its soldiers and herds of settlers.

We in the Islamic Resistance Movement, Hamas, mourn today one of our most prominent commanders and affirm that such a savage crime would not weaken us or halt our Jihad march or check our Brigades' advance towards uprooting the usurping Zionist entity from our holy land. Let Sharon and his frightened army know that they will pay dearly for assassinating our heroes. We tell him not to rejoice much or smile for long because we will smash the fake joy that filled his black, hateful heart. And we will wipe out the fascist smile off his face. We will attack them with unvanquished soldiers who are used to Jihad as a way of life and who yearn for death as their way to martyrdom.

24 Nov. 2001

In the name of Allah the most Gracious the most Merciful

"Say: "Can you expect for us (any fate) other than one of two glorious things (martyrdom or victory)? But we can expect for you either that Allah will send His punishment from Himself, or by our hands. So wait (expectant); we too will wait with you.""

Blood of martyr commander Abu Hannoud says: Resistance is our option . . .

Our heroic Palestinian people: a star has fallen from the skies of Palestine but its splinters would burn the heart of Zionists. Who will stop the burning sea waves after him? Who will deter the angered (avenging) heroes? Who will dare halt the blood-painted revenge? Who will stop the roaring lions? The Qassam Brigades will make out of Zionists charred wood.

The martyr commander was the knight that annoyed occupation; its soldiers and settlers in all areas of Palestine and his students have learnt from him the arts of combat and graduated from his school with distinction. They realize that the time has come now to play their role and teach the Zionists unforgettable lessons so that they would know that if a knight had fallen a group of cavaliers would show up after him. Our people enjoy solid spirit and will remain, with Allah's fate, spreading fear in hearts of the Zionists . . . **"How many of the Prophets fought (in Allah's way), and with them (fought) large bands of godly men? But they never lost heart if they met with disaster in Allah's way, nor did they weaken (in will) nor give in. And Allah loves those who are firm and steadfast."**

Our patient Palestinian people: the heinous crime perpetrated by the Zionist terrorist leaders in assassinating commander of the Qassam Brigades the martyr Mujahid hero Mahmoud Abu Hannoud and his brothers Ayman and Ma'moon Hashayka will not pass unpunished. God willing, they will regret the very hour in which they decided to assassinate those heroes. Our patience has gone out of limits and that arrogant enemy had bypassed all bounds taking cover behind the international community and depending on the state of Arab weakness. The enemy was also hiding behind the so-called ceasefire that did not serve as a cover for anyone. It is committing one massacre after the other against our heroes, children, elderly and women. It is thus imperative that our people should not heed false promises voiced by the biggest patron of terrorism nor the suspicious calls for calming down the situation voiced by arrogant countries. Those countries are quick to denounce any of our Mujahideen's operations against the Zionist enemy, charging our people and intifada with terrorism but they are totally silent while viewing our children's scattered remains in the roads leading to their schools.

Our Mujahid Palestinian people: we in the Islamic Resistance Movement, Hamas, bear with pride and glory the glad tidings of the martyrdom of commander Mahmoud Abu Hannoud and his brothers, a thing that they have always yearned for after he and his brothers managed to survive the enemy's various assassination and arrest attempts for years. We vow before Allah to remain faithful to blood of the martyr and all martyrs of our people and we will remain insisting on resistance until end and ejection of occupation from our lands sacrificing our souls and blood as cheap price along that road.

And it is a Jihad until either victory or martyrdom

Wallaho Akbar wa Lillah El-Hamd

The Islamic Resistance Movement-Hamas
Nablus-Palestine
24/11/2001AD

13 November 2001

In the name of Allah the most Gracious the most Merciful

Islamic Resistance Movement (Hamas) statement

On reported political settlement prepared by Sharon and Peres

Schemes and conspiracies against steadfastness and Jihad and struggle march of our people did not stop ever since our Mujahid people launched their blessed intifada more than a year ago. Our Palestinian masses rejected all those plots because they only served the Zionist enemy and its interests.

Today the Zionist enemy tables a new political plan prepared by both Peres and Sharon based on a disarmed Palestinian state that would be established in stages: "Gaza first" the borders of which guaranteed by America. Such a state would coordinate its policies in advance with the Zionist entity. The plan proposes leaving the situation in Al-Quds as is and denying the refugees' right of return while protecting the "Israeli" security borders topped by establishment of a vast buffer zone in Jordan Valley and a narrow strip to the west of Gaza.

We in the Islamic Resistance Movement Hamas consider that leaking this plan at this particular time targets the following:

1. wiping out the intifada and resistance and pushing the Palestinian Authority into arresting all those resisting occupation.

2. lowering the aspirations of the PA through tabling the "Gaza first" plan. It would also make the PA accept retaining the Jewish settlements, canceling refugees' right of return and retaining Al-Quds situation as is in addition to accepting the security strip in the Valley.

3. the plan proposes a self-rule with the prevailing conditions under the name of a state. It is a disarmed state, a state without borders, its borders guaranteed by another country, a state without sovereignty for its airspace is open for others, and it is an enclave within the Zionist entity.

4. the plan preempts Arab pressure or criticism of the international alliance led by America against the Muslims.

5. the plan evades the question of the refugees and falsifies history through equating those coming from America to usurp Palestine with those who were expelled from their own country to live as refugees

away from it.

6.   the plan preempts any international initiative especially at the UN General Assembly's session that might not meet the "Israeli" goals.

7.   the plan puts America in the "Israeli" square.

The Islamic Resistance Movement Hamas views with absolute seriousness this malicious plan that falls in line with the Zionist tactics aimed at aborting the intifada and wiping out resistance. It further aims at shifting the struggle into the Palestinian arena, liquidating the Palestine cause and then the Palestinian presence in the West Bank and the Gaza Strip. Based on our keenness on unity of Palestinian ranks, preservation of our legitimate right in continuing resistance until ejection of occupation and stabilizing the Palestinian people on their lands, we appeal to all to reject that plan and not to heed Sharon and Peres' political and tactical bubbles and to continue resistance as the sole option to restore usurped rights and maintain our Palestinian people's right in their homeland within its historic borders.

Wallaho Akbar wa Lillah El-Hamd

The Islamic Resistance Movement
Hamas-Palestine
nformation Bureau
27th Shaaban 1422H
13th November 2001AD

3 November 2001

In the name of Allah the most Gracious the most Merciful

Statement on the American offensive against the Islamic Resistance Movement, putting it on the list of terrorist organizations and considering the Palestinian intifada as terrorism that should be combated

Ever since the Zionist occupation of our Palestinian lands the USA displayed hostility against the Palestinian people, their resistance of occupation and their aspirations for freedom. The USA also displayed absolute bias in favor of the Zionist entity and covered up for its terrorist practices against our people including the use of veto to block any resolution that would condemn such practices.

And here again the USA is declaring anew its obvious tilt through declaring resistance movements in Palestine, including the Islamic Resistance Movement—Hamas, as terrorist organizations. The decision meant that the USA would adopt against them a number of procedures not only denying them entry to that country but also arresting all those supporting and sympathizing with those organizations, trying them and deporting them. The USA considers our people's resistance and glorious intifada as terrorism that must be combated.

The Islamic Resistance Movement, Hamas, believes that the American declaration at this particular time reflected the USA's total and unlimited backing to the usurping Zionist entity that is practicing the cruelest forms of terrorism. The decision further provides legitimate cover for all Zionist practices against our people. Hamas would like to assert here that it never viewed America as a friendly or a just country for it is the one supplying the Zionist enemy with all tools of murder and destruction of our people. The USA is also keen on maintaining the Zionist entity the strongest military power in the region and assists that entity with the use of veto along with financial backing and moral support.

The Islamic Resistance Movement, Hamas, considers both America and the Zionist entity as two terrorist states that practice international terrorism against the Muslim peoples of Afghanistan and Palestine.

Such a bleak image of the American administration and the Zionist entity gives us additional momentum to persist along the road of Jihad and resistance depending first and foremost on almighty Allah then on the determination and steadfastness of our people and our Arab and Islamic Nation. We will persevere along that road until we attain our legitimate and full rights and until we free our lands from the usurping occupation, which has no future in the region and which will be ultimately defeated Insha'allah.

". . . and they say, "When will that be?" Say,
"May be it will be quite soon!"

Wallahu Akbar wa Lillah Al-Hamd

The Islamic Resistance Movement-Hamas
Information Bureau
Saturday 18th Sha'aban 1422H
3rd November 2001AD

24 October 2001

In the name of Allah the most Gracious the most Merciful

Massacre in Beit Reema . . . where is al-Mo'tasem?!

Our Arab and Islamic Nation:

A new massacre is committed by the Zionsit enemy this time in Beit Reema village, Ramallah district, scores of martyrs and wounded have fallen in the streets, squares and olive orchards of that village. The enemy has prevented paramedics from carrying away the bodies of martyrs or extending assistance to the wounded and has even fired at the doctors and medical teams. Such acts have been taking place today and last night in Beit Reema while scores of martyrs were falling in Tulkarm, Qalqilya and Bethlehem.

Our Arab and Islamic masses:

Our Mujahid, patient and steadfast people in Beit Reema and in the entire land of Palestine are asking today what is our Nation waiting for? What is our Nation's reaction while witnessing its sons in the holy land murdered, slaughtered and their houses and villages demolished and destroyed? Is such silence towards this pogrom permissible among brothers and holders of the same religion? Will Arab dignity and chivalry accept continuation of that silence? What is the Nation waiting for, if such daily shed blood did not make it act?

We ask the Nation's leaders and governments to shoulder their historic responsibility towards the Zionist enemy's massacres of our people. We urge them to embark on an urgent initiative and practical steps to save and defend our people and check the Zionist aggressions. We call on them to exercise real and serious pressure on the American administration to halt the enemy's massacre and end its protection of Sharon and his terrorist government.

We affirm that our people and Mujahid forces would remain loyal to their pledge of persisting in Jihad and resistance, defending their lands and holy shrines and remaining patient and steadfast for the sake of Allah. We also invite our Nations' masses to rescue their brothers in Palestine and beseech them to commence practical steps to end that carnage and check its possible spread into other areas.

Our Mujahid and patient people:

Our enemy is only deterred by force and only steadfastness and confrontation would halt its aggression. In such difficult moments, we call on all our people's forces and factions especially the resistance brigades in the Qassam, Aqsa Martyrs, Martyr Abu Ali Mustafa, Quds and elements of the Palestinian Authority police and national security to unite their efforts in confrontation of the Zionist enemy that is launching an open war. We urge them to retaliate to the atrocities in an open confrontation that would target all of its leaderships, soldiers and settlers in away that reaches the depth of its security.

> *"So lose not heart, nor fall into despair: for ye must gain mastery if ye are true in Faith."*

And it is a Jihad until either victory or martyrdom

The Islamic Resistance Movement
Hamas-Palestine
Wednesday 7th Sha'aban 1422H
24/10/2001AD

21 October 2001

In the name of Allah the most Gracious the most Merciful

Yes to our national unity and armed resistance

No to cowardice and capitulation

Our Mujahid people:

Our people everywhere, our people in Tulkarm, Qalqilya, Ramallah, Jenin, Bethlehem, Beit Jala and in all areas of Palestine . . . may Allah be with you while facing the biggest terrorist force on Earth. You are facing it with bare chests, flesh and blood while declaring that you would not be eliminated and that with Jihad, patience and sacrifices you will survive forever since you are backed by right and determination. You will continue to survive with the grace of Allah until victory and liberation.

Our proud, Mujahid people:

Here the enemy is storming cities, killing scores of our people, arresting and kidnapping hundreds while his war minister arrogantly declares that he will not withdraw from the cities that his army stormed. He was thus affirming that such practices were our enemy's sole program in dealing with our people. The best proof is that the enemy's arrests and assassinations had covered all those included in the list of wanted persons that was handed to the Palestinian Authority during the security coordination meetings.

We affirm that the whole world is called upon to condemn our enemy's crimes namely the siege, murder, assassinations and detentions and should immediately and practically act to put an end to those crimes. We also declare that our Jihad would continue until ejection of occupation, that our people's resistance would not be deterred by such aggressions and that our people's steadfastness would not be shaken by those aggressions regardless of the murder and destruction tools used.

Our Mujahid people:

Despite that outrageous aggression, the shelling, destruction and storming and despite the fall of scores of martyrs and hundreds of wounded we are surprised to hear discordant voices speaking about a ceasefire. They even call for not confronting the aggression as if they were asking our people to allow the enemy to slaughter them the way it wished hoping to satisfy our enemy or please the American administration, which declares on each and every occasion its backing to our enemy and protects it at international forums.

Our people have the right to ask: which party would benefit from such calls? Is it in the interest of the Palestinian people to remain arms-folded while being slaughtered? Why are some parties so keen to satisfy the American administration and woo terrorist Sharon endangering the lives of our people for the sake of reaching that goal?

Our proud people:

In such circumstances and at a time when we are in dire need of unity of ranks and national unity, the Palestinian Authority issues a very serious decision <u>outlawing all military wings of our national and Islamic factions</u>. This entails prosecution of all Mujahideen in a treacherous stab in the back of our people's Mujahideen who are united over the resistance option.

We denounce that decision and urge the PA to rescind it and request its support of the Mujahideen along with safeguarding them and supplying them with necessary arms. We also affirm the importance of ending all forms of security coordination and meetings with the enemy and warn the PA of the dangerous repercussions of its continued tampering with our people's unity and the national forces and factions' united stand in resisting occupation.

We ask all Palestinian forces especially the resistance brigades and our sons in the police and national security to shoulder their responsibility in defending their people, cities and villages. We urge them to unite in face of the aggression and to reject any procedure that might infringe on national unity or aid our enemy in achieving its mean aims. Let all of you carry the slogan: *"Truly Allah loves those who fight in His Cause in battle array, as if they were a solid cemented structure."*

And it is a Jihad until either victory or martyrdom

The Islamic Resistance Movement
Hamas-Palestine
21/10/2001

19 October 2001

In the name of Allah the most Gracious the most Merciful

Assassinations and arrests

Will not stop our people's Jihad, resistance and intifada

Our Mujahid people

O' you who have chosen Jihad, resistance and intifada as the road towards restoring rights have clearly said to the whole world that the Palestinian rights could not be bargained over or relinquished. O' you who have proven that the Palestinian people despite a year of intifada that was full of wounds and pains were still capable and prepared to offer more sacrifices. The Palestinians are always capable of creating new methods of confronting the enemy. The Palestinians affirmed through the operation that targeted one of the symbols of Zionist terrorism (Rahba'am Ze'evi) that all the enemy's security measures could not protect it or its occupation.

If the entire Palestinian people, with their various trends and forces, have expressed strong support of the heroic operation launched by Martyr Abu Ali Mustafa Brigades. They even expressed satisfaction to see the enemy have a taste of the suffering that it has been subjecting us to by killing our leaders, symbols [of our struggle] and Mujahideen. However, the Palestinian Authority regretfully disappointed the Palestinian people by arresting leaders and cadres of the Popular Front for the Liberation of Palestine ignoring the feelings of its people. It should have been, instead, busy with defending its people against the Zionist enemy's crimes in the past few days when the enemy assassinated a number of resistance cadres, murdered Palestinian women and children and reoccupied Palestinian towns.

We condemn the arrests of our brothers in the PFLP and all previous arrests that included cadres in Hamas and Jihad Movements. We also urge the PA to immediately release all detainees and halt all security and other meetings with the enemy. We further ask the PA not to tamper with national unity to serve the interests of our enemy and the patron of its terrorism, the American administration.

We also affirm our solidarity and extend our warmest condolences to our brothers in the Aqsa Martyrs Brigades who lost a group of Mujahideen especially martyr Atef Obayat. We urge the PA to prosecute agents and severely punish all those involved in this crime. We also call on the Qassam Brigades and military wings of all factions to retaliate to the enemy's crimes and continue their Jihad program asserting our rejection of the so called ceasefire. Our people's option, which won national consensus, was that of resistance and persistence of the intifada. Our people and their Jihad and struggling factions will not be terrorized by Zionist threats and will not be deceived by American promises and will continue in their steadfastness and resistance until ejection of occupation and liberation of our lands and holy places God willing.

And it is a Jihad until either victory or martyrdom

The Islamic Resistance Movement
Hamas-Palestine
19/10/2001

15 October 2001

In the name of Allah the most Gracious the most Merciful

Zionist enemy requests ceasefire while proceeding with terrorist policy of assassinating Palestinian cadres and Mujahideen

"How (can there be such a league), seeing that if they get an advantage over you, they respect not in you the ties either of kinship or of covenant?"

Our Mujahid people, who have chosen the road of intifada and resistance and shunned other roads, . . . the Zionist enemy is proceeding in its criminal schemes against our people without heeding anyone or paying attention to the so falsely called ceasefire. The enemy is besieging and storming cities and suburbs and assassinating our heroes in cold blood. It is exercising terrorism without anyone denouncing its deeds. The enemy is exploiting the international circumstances and the world's preoccupation with the American-led war against Muslims in Afghanistan to carry out its terrorist crimes against this persevering people.

Yesterday the Zionist terrorist forces assassinated the Mujahid hero Abdul Rahman Hammad in Qalqilya district and today they assassinated another hero of our people and one of the cadres of the Islamic Resistance Movement, Hamas, the Mujahid hero Ahmed Hassan Mohammed Marshood. The Mujahid had spent seven years in occupation jails for resisting Zionist occupation and for being a member in the Qassam Brigades. He was released by the end of 1999 only to continue to follow up concerns of the Palestinian detainees. He had lived with them and served them within the prison then served them outside it through his work in the ministry of prisoners' affairs.

The cowardly assassination operation was carried out while Marshood was heading to his work at the office of the prisoners' affairs ministry in the city of Nablus where a booby-trapped car, parking in front of the office, exploded when he was passing near it, which affirms that the operation was engineered by occupation and its agents.

Our Mujahid Palestinian people

The Zionist enemy's continuous policy of terrorism against our people should not be met on the part our Palestinian people with raising the white flag, surrendering to the de facto situation and abiding by the ceasefire, which made the Zionist enemy go to extremes in its terrorist crimes.

Our Palestinian people will not let the blood of their martyrs go in vain, neither will they waste sacrifices or accomplishments of the intifada and resistance. Our people have the right to defend themselves and to resist the usurping occupiers with all available strength.

It is high time for our people and lions of resistance, brigades and factions of our people, to go on the offensive and to retaliate to the crimes of the Zionist enemy with the language that it only understands.

Allahu Akbar wa Lillahi Al-Hamad

And it is a Jihad until either victory or martyrdom

The Islamic Resistance Movement
Hamas-Palestine
15/10/2001

14 October 2001

In the name of Allah the most Gracious the most Merciful

Qassam Brigades Obituary

Mujahid hero / Abdul Rahman Hammad

May Allah have mercy on his soul

"Among the Believers are men who have been true to their Covenant with Allah: of them some have completed their vow (to the extreme), and some (still) wait: but they have never changed (their determination) in the least."

The Qassam Brigades bid farewell to its martyr, the martyr of the land of Isra' Mujahid Abdul Rahman Mohammed Saeed Hammad, 32, with pride. He was assassinated in Qalqilya by Zionist criminals this morning Sunday 14/10/2001 after long years of struggle for the freedom of his people and Nation. He suffered a lot as a result including deportation, arrest and persecution by the enemy forces and their agents but without giving up his determination until he won martyrdom and Allah's satisfaction.

This new crime affirms that the enemy was continuing its policy of assassination and murder of our people despite the ceasefire declarations. It also proves that Jihad, resistance and revenge only will deter the enemy. We, in the Qassam Brigades, affirm that our people have the right to defend themselves and confirm our Brigades' right to retaliate painfully. The enemy will pay the price for his crimes against our Mujahideen and people. The Qassam Heroes will avenge for the Qalqilya martyr and Assaira Shamaliya martyr Mujahid Hani Rawajbe and all martyrs of our people who shed their blood in defense of Al-Quds and Palestine.

We vow to our martyr and all martyrs of our people to continue along the road of Jihad and resistance in self-defense and in defense of the people, lands and holy shrines until liberation and ejection of the usurping occupiers from our lands.

> *"And Allah hath full power and control over His affairs;*
> *but most among mankind know it not."*

And it is a Jihad until either victory or martyrdom

Qassam Brigades
Al-Quds-Palestine
27th Rajab 1422H
14/10/2001AD

3 October 2001

In the name of Allah the most Gracious the most Merciful

"Glory to (Allah) Who did take His servant for a Journey by
night from the Sacred Mosque to the Aqsa (Farthest) Mosque,
whose precincts We did bless . . ."

Appeal

Terrorist Sharon and his government are exploiting the explosions in America and its repercussions on the international arena and the World's preoccupation with that to give a green light for a terrorist group to lay down the foundation stone of the alleged temple near the Maghareba gate, one of the gates of the holy Aqsa Mosque.

We, in the Islamic Resistance Movement, Hamas, consider that act a flagrant encroachment on one of the shrines holy to a billion and a half Muslims all over the world. Faced by such a situation, we cannot stand arms folded and will use all available means to preserve our lands and sanctities. We appeal to leaders of the Nation not to preoccupy themselves with the Bush campaign and to give priority to the Arabs and Muslims' prime cause that of Palestine and its throbbing heart the holy Aqsa Mosque.

We also urge leaders and peoples of the Arab and Muslim Nation to adopt a serious and responsible stand in support of the Aqsa Mosque and the people of Palestine. We also call on our people to break all terrorist, Zionist barriers and obstacles and head to the Aqsa Mosque tomorrow Thursday to protect the Isra' site of our prophet, peace be upon him, and prevent the Zionist terrorists from proceeding with their crime.

We pledge to our people and Nation to remain along the road of intifada, resistance and Jihad until realizing our full rights Insha'allah.

Allahu Akbar and victory to Islam

Allahu Akbar wa Lillah Al-Hamad

The Islamic Resistance Movement
Hamas-Palestine
Wednesday 16th Rajab 1422H
3rd October 2001AD

28 September 2001

In the name of Allah the most Gracious the mot Merciful

Islamic Resistance Movement (Hamas) Communiqué

On the first annual anniversary of the Aqsa intifada

When the intifada broke out this same day last year in defense of the holy Aqsa Mosque against the provocative visit of terrorist Sharon, the most optimistic observers estimated that it would continue for a few days or weeks. However, a whole year has elapsed and our people's intifada is still persisting with the grace of Allah then with the steadfastness and determination of our struggling people that sacrificed all for the sake of their country. This is the spirit with which the executors of martyrdom operations carried while penetrating the enemy's fortifications to spread panic in the hearts of the Zionist occupiers of our country day and night in each and every part of our holy land.

Our people have disappointed the capitulatory elements that kept on championing realism slogans, declaring that our people's struggle was over and that we had nothing else left to accept except what the Zionists offer at the begging tables which they falsely call "negotiations"! In return our people did not disappoint their Nation's aspirations but rather during that year, our people continued to surprise the Nation with acts greater than its expectations and healed the breasts of believers who look forward to victory over the aggressors and to ejecting them from our holy land.

Our people have displayed and still are displaying a legendary and astonishing steadfastness and unprecedented determination to regain their right to their national soil and rejection of undermining that right under any pretext despite the unprecedented Zionist continuous terrorist campaign during the reign of both terrorists Barak and Sharon. Those terrorist campaigns employed all means to enforce surrender on our people and factions including live bullets, internationally-banned explosive bullets, depleted uranium, artillery and tank shells and American-made planes such the Apaches and the F-16s and others. Consequently all conspiracies to abort the intifada were foiled due to that people's solid determination and their dependence on Allah first and foremost then on backing of the Arab and Islamic Nation.

Our Mujahid Palestinian people:

On this great occasion, your Movement, the Islamic Resistance Movement (Hamas) affirms the following lessons from the first year of the intifada:

1. The intifada achieved big gains for the Palestine cause and led to important changes in the Arab-Zionist conflict represented by endorsing the resistance program as a strategic option for the Palestinian people and the Arab and Islamic Nation. Such a consequence necessitated perpetuating and developing the intifada in addition to resisting any attempt to halt or abort it before it reaches its aspired goal of cleansing occupation off our lands.

2. The intifada crystallized and boosted Palestinian national unity and pushed forward horizons of joint Palestinian national endeavor along the way to drafting a Palestinian national program based on intifada

and resistance. It was proven in practice that intifada and resistance united our people and that the settlement process and negotiations divided them.

3. The intifada raised the popular interaction at with the uprising as the Nation expressed its huge support to the Palestinian people. The masses were able of compelling the official Arab leaderships to hold an emergency and ordinary summits. Yet, the official Arab stand, which is suffering from American pressures and internal difference, did not succeed so far in living up to the Nation's popular aspirations and demands represented in breaking relations with the Zionists, ending all forms of normalization and opening the borders for the Mujahideen to join their brothers in Palestine.

4. The intifada succeeded in neutralizing the balance of force with the enemy, which was on its side, when compared to the Palestinians and to each Arab country separately. The martyrdom operations and other heroic attacks succeeded in achieving the "balance" with the Zionists who could not withstand great casualties while our people showed growing patience and sacrifice actualizing Allah's words: *"If ye are suffering hardships, they are suffering similar hardships; but ye have hope from Allah, while they have none."* This is the first and basic step that enhances the possibility of the intifada and resistance's success in flushing occupation out of our lands without peace agreements or concessions.

5. The intifada unveiled the real fanatic image of the Zionist society, which elected a man like Sharon to rule with a big percentage of votes in his favor and which still is expressing support to the terrorist government that is formed out of various forces of that society. Hence, the intifada exposed the false peace calls and erased the so-called barrier between the Zionist "left" and "right" or the "doves" and the "hawks". The Zionist society brazenly exposed its image as a society of hawks that only believed in violence to achieve its goals.

6. The absolute American bias in favor of the Zionists and Europe's inability to exercise any effective role in the region showed that we must depend on the Nation's options of Jihad and resistance rather than American or other mediations.

Our Mujahid Palestinian people—our great Nation's masses

The first anniversary of the blessed intifada fell at a time when repercussions of the explosions in the USA were still live where attempts to form an international alliance to combat "terrorism" were still ongoing. The American administration wants to make of our people's intifada an oblation for the success of this alliance. At the same time, the Sharon government is exploiting the world's preoccupation with what happened in America to launch more terrorist attacks against our people. More than twenty Palestinian martyrs fell over the few days that followed the New York and Washington explosions without any international condemnation voiced coping with the magnitude of occupation forces' massacres!

And again the Zionist aggression escalated yesterday against our people in Rafah when occupation forces killed seven martyrs and wounded scores others in less than 24 hours.

We, in the Islamic Resistance Movement (Hamas) congratulate our people over continuation of their Jihad and intifada and salute all those who resist the enemy and its terrorism especially the Mujahideen who are deployed in all areas of our holy land, guarding the country, chasing the Zionist usurpers and defending the Nation's honor and dignity. We pray that Allah would accept all our victims as martyrs, to reward them the best and to aid us in catering for their families and the families of the wounded and the steadfast detainees. We affirm that our people did not and would not forget their sacrifices and would continue to exert utmost efforts to ensure their release from Zionist jails.

We would like here to affirm the following:

1. All forces of our people, backed by our Arab and Islamic Nation, are determined on persisting with and escalating the intifada until eradication of occupation from all of our usurped lands. This was evident in our people's marches and rallies that rejected ceasefire agreements and denounced security coordination with the enemy.

2. We urge the Palestinian Authority to break away from the so called peace process once and for all, adopt the resistance program, refuse all forms of coordination and negotiations and security meetings with the enemy, not to be deceived by American promises or bow to its pressures and reject any ceasefire calls since the intifada and resistance are our people's legitimate rights.

3. We call on the Arab and Islamic countries to shoulder their duty in backing the Palestinian people's steadfastness and Jihad and to stick to their excellent stand in rejecting attempts to label Palestinian resistance as terrorism. Our people's resistance should never be put alongside terrorism in one basket and we as Muslims, Arabs and Palestinians should not pay the price of the New York and Washington explosions.

4.   We ask our people in the diaspora to display more interaction with our people's intifada in the occupied homeland and share with them in the duty of resisting occupation.

Finally, we pray that the second year of the intifada would be full of blessing and that Almighty Allah would expedite victory and liberation for our people. We are confident that our people's resistance would continue as long as occupation continued and that all the enemies and defeatists' cunning schemes to halt the intifada and return our cause backwards to the mirage of humiliating settlements would end up in utter failure Insha'allah.

"So lose not heart, nor fall into despair: for ye must gain mastery if ye are true in Faith. If a wound hath touched you, be sure a similar wound hath touched the others. Such days (of varying fortunes) we give to men and men by turns . . ."

The Islamic Resistance Movement
Hamas-Palestine
Friday 11th Rajab 1422H
28th September 2001AD

18 September 2001

In the name of Allah the most Gracious the most Merciful

Statement on the American and international moves after the New York and Washington explosions and the Zionist blatant incitement

The Zionist enemy was not content with escalation of its aggression and terrorism against the Palestinian people including storming, besieging and starving cities and refugee camps in addition to murder, demolition and destruction, exploiting the world's preoccupation with the explosions in New York and Washington. It even started provoking America and the West against Arabs and Muslims in addition to Palestinian resistance forces. The Zionist entity intentionally and cheaply mixed up the cards in the region and allied with America and the West in fighting the so-called Islamic terrorism at a time when Palestinian blood is being shed daily and profusely as a result of the escalation of Zionist terrorism in Palestine.

Amidst such an atmosphere American diplomacy stepped up efforts to establish the so-called "international alliance against terrorism". It tried to involve the biggest possible number of Arab and Islamic countries to serve as an international cover for a large-scale war that the USA was preparing against Afghanistan and maybe other countries despite the fact that investigations have not yet pinpointed the party responsible for those explosions.

The American administration resorted to paving the way for its coming strikes through its media and statements of its leaders. American president Bush even described that war as a crusade! It is strange to witness a state of fear and panic in the Arab and Islamic region that made a number of those governments, despite their remoteness from what happened, to bow to American dictates and pressures even at the expense of Arab and Islamic interests.

The Islamic Resistance Movement (Hamas) followed up the US-led diplomatic, security and military activities and the accompanying blatant Zionist incitement and the possible repercussions on the conflict with the Zionist entity and would like to assert the following:

1. In the light of the recent spate of explosions in America, the Hamas Movement would like to affirm that it is against violence being committed against innocent civilians anywhere in the world especially that the Palestinian people can understand the suffering more than many nations as victims of constant Zionist terrorism.

2. We urge all countries to direct their potentials and efforts towards fighting the most dangerous terrorism in the world and the most organized and threatening to global peace and security namely Zionist terrorism (state terrorism). Such terrorism is represented in occupying Palestinian lands and practicing the most brutal forms of repression, humiliation and terrorism against the Palestinian people making use of American weapons and political cover.

3. We would like to stress that the Palestinian people's resistance of Zionist occupation is a legitimate one that could never be associated with terrorism. We would also like to warn here of the Zionist enemy's attempt to mix up the cards and rally international backing to strikes against the Palestinian, Arab and Islamic peoples at the pretext of fighting terrorism and to distract the attention away from the Palestinian people's demands for freedom, liberation and independence.

4. The Islamic Resistance Movement, Hamas, asks the free world countries, especially the Arab and Islamic countries, to be ware of the so-called international alliance to fight terrorism along with its consequent measures and dictates. We believe that such an alliance targets labeling Islam, Arabs and Muslims as terrorists in addition to providing legitimacy and an Arab and Islamic cover for an expected American aggression that would realize economic and strategic goals for the USA along its plan of boosting its hegemony on the world. It would also provide Washington with a golden opportunity to get even with a number of countries, forces and groups in the region. Furthermore, it would serve Zionist goals of persecuting Palestinian resistance forces and making use of the emergency situation to liquidate the Palestine cause according to Zionist schemes.

5. The Hamas Movement also asks the Arab and Islamic countries not to extend support or cover to this declared war against Afghanistan or any Arab or Islamic country. This war is not in the interest of our Nation but rather against it. Furthermore, this war will not serve as the solution to the phenomenon of hostility and violence against American interests but would rather boost such a trend and would increase the affected nations and peoples' hatred of American foreign policies.

The Islamic Resistance Movement, Hamas, while engaged in its conflict against the Zionist enemy in the occupied territories, would like to affirm, in such difficult circumstances and in the light of attempts by many parties to win favour with aggressive forces, that the Palestinian people would go ahead in their efforts to liberate their lands and holy places and to win freedom and that they would persist in the intifada and resistance against the terrorist Zionist enemy until ejection of occupation.

"O ye who believe! If ye obey the Unbelievers, they will drive you back on your heels, and ye will turn back (from Faith) to your own loss. Nay, Allah is your protector, and He is the best of helpers."

The Islamic Resistance Movement
Hamas—Palestine
Tuesday 1st Rajab 1422H
18th September 2001AD

20 August 2001

In the name of Allah the most Gracious the most Merciful

To confront Sharon's massacres:

Escalating resistance, serious Arab action and reprisal

And no return to humiliating negotiations

Zionist aggression against our people witnessed a new escalation in the past few days represented in intensifying storming operations of Palestinian cities and the assassination of more intifada activists. The step follows the moral and security defeat that befell the Zionist occupation at the hands of the martyr heroes who blew up the Zionist security theory and proved failure of terrorist Sharon's government in achieving security for Zionist occupiers. Following the Quds and Haifa operations that terrorized the Zionists, Sharon resorted to political steps such as occupying the "Orient House" then followed it with escalation in military aggression that led to the martyrdom of numerous Palestinians. In a single day, yesterday Sunday, six Palestinians were martyred in Rafah, Gaza and Nablus including two small children in a fresh cold-blooded massacre by the occupation army. Such escalation aims at increasing pressures on our people and pushing them to despair in order to abandon resistance against occupation in addition to pressuring the Palestinian Authority to return to effective security coordination and resume policy of detention of Palestinian freedom fighters. The PA actually responded by arresting a number of Hamas cadres at the pretext of having links to the martyrdom operation in Al-Quds. In the light of such Zionist escalation and aggression, the Zionist enemy circulated possibility of resuming political talks with the PA. A number of Arab parties also exerted efforts in a bid to revive the negotiations. Faced by such developments we would like to affirm the following:

1. The escalation of Zionist terrorism and aggression against our people reflects the Zionist occupation and the Sharon government's misery and moral defeat. They are trying to score illusionary victories over the Palestinian people to preserve their existence and cohesion.

2. The Zionist enemy's signs about political negotiations with the PA and readiness to accept a political settlement in addition to activating role of terrorist Peres in the light of continuation and escalation of

repression, terrorism and aggression aims to distract the attentions and to ensure international support for criminal Sharon's policies and terrorism.

3. We affirm the importance of unity of our people on the option of intifada, resistance and steadfastness in its capacity as the sole option capable of ejecting occupation and putting an end to Zionist aggression and terrorism God willing.

4. Returning to discussions on reviving negotiations with the Zionist enemy and resuming the so-called peace process is a stab in the back of the blessed intifada and lets down our people's Jihad, brave resistance and martyrs' blood. Our people did not indulge in this intifada and resistance and did not offer martyrs and sacrifices only to submit to the criminal enemy's demands and return to humiliating negotiation with it. Any step in this direction on the part of any Palestinian or Arab party would be met with anger on the part of our people along with the Arab and Islamic peoples.

5. We affirm that resistance would persist and escalate and that the criminal Zionist enemy would never know sleep or security as long as occupation continued. Our stationed Palestinian people will not take heed of suspicious calls voiced by defeatists to halt resistance or martyrdom operations under weak pretexts. Persistence of occupation and its daily bloodbaths against our people boost the necessity for escalation of resistance and continuation of martyrdom operations.

6. We denounce the state of Arab and Islamic impotency in face of the Zionist aggression. We invite the Arab and Islamic peoples to restore their role in support of their Palestinian brothers. We also urge the Arab and Islamic governments to shoulder their responsibility in resisting aggression and adopt serious practical steps in confrontation of Sharon and his terrorist gang and not to remain captive to losing bets on the American role. It is high time for the Arab and Islamic countries to sever all kinds of relations and contacts with the Zionist enemy and to pressure the American administration through its interests in the region.

The Islamic Resistance Movement
Hamas—Palestine
Monday 1st Jumada Thani 1422H
20/8/2001AD

1 August 2001

In the name of Allah the most Gracious the most Merciful

The change in Zionist aggression necessitates qualitative leap in the struggle

"If then any one transgresses the prohibition against you, transgress ye likewise against him."

Yesterday the enemy committed a new massacre killing eight of our people including two of the political leaders, the martyrs Jamal Mansour and Jamal Salim.

A few days ago other massacres were committed in Fara refugee camp, Khalil, Bethlehem and Gaza strip in which scores of civilians were killed in addition to members of our people's resistance organizations.

Then there was the serious step of storming and desecrating the holy Aqsa Mosque by enemy soldiers and policemen and the attempt to lay down the foundation stone of their alleged temple on the ruins of the Aqsa!!

Our patient, Mujahid Palestinian people:
Our honest Arab and Islamic masses:

This means that Sharon is committing continuous attritional massacres and an all-out war of annihilation . . . this means a serious qualitative change in the aggression that necessitates an important and inevitable leap in the struggle on the part of the Palestinian people and the Arab and Islamic peoples.

Our steadfast people on the land of Palestine:
The inevitable Palestinian change should entail:

1. an open confrontation in each and every part in Palestine using all means.

2. mobilizing all Palestinian combat potentials: the factions, police and all those owning weapons in the Palestinian Authority and among our people.

It is not religiously or nationally acceptable that guns of tens of thousands within the PA remain curbed in face of such Zionist massacres! All Palestinians are targeted, so let all of them participate in the combat and the defense.

3. there should be a serious plan in which all should cooperate to terminate once and for all the dangers of agents who serve as the enemy's eyes and dirty tools.

4. there should be no other alternative to resistance and intifada. All those advocating more contacts with the enemy, a ceasefire and dealing with American and Western attempts to calm down and end the intifada should shut up! All must unite over the resistance program.

Our Arab and Islamic masses everywhere:

It is a shame on Arabs and Muslims to stand idle by vis-à-vis the daily and continuous extermination of an Arab, Islamic people on the land of Isra' wal Mi'rage!

There is no excuse today for the Nation for not shouldering its duty towards Palestine and its people.

Consequently, it is high time for an Arab and Islamic change to take place quickly and seriously. This necessitates among other things:

1. Jihad against the Zionist Jews in this stage is a compulsory duty on all not only the Palestinian people, but rather on each and every Arab and Muslim concerned with the Aqsa, the first Muslim Qibla, and concerned with Al-Quds and Palestine, and concerned with his Palestinian brother who is slaughtered daily and who is fighting alone with modest weapons against an army equipped with a huge military arsenal and supported by all world Jews.

It is no longer acceptable to say that Arabs and Muslims are not capable of launching Jihad! Rather each and every Arab and Muslim is capable of launching Jihad against the Zionist Jews when he is true with himself and really intends to perform this duty.

Don't the Jews fight your brothers and target you all whether in the east or west?

What will Sharon and the Zionist entity's criminals do if they finish off your brothers in Palestine, God forbid?! And will regret be of any use then?

Each and every Arab and Muslim believing in these facts that lie before his very eyes should be content with Allah's permission to defend himself, his brothers and sanctities: *"To those against whom war is made, permission is given (to fight), because they are wronged; and verily, Allah is Most Powerful for their aid."*

2. The Islamic and national movements and factions in our Nation should bear their responsibility in this open and ferocious battle. Otherwise what will they utter before Almighty Allah? What will they tell history and future posterity? What will they say to the convoys of martyrs: the children, women, the old and men?

Why is the Palestinian, Arab, Muslim always the target of murder at the hands of Zionist occupiers? why don't the Zionist Jews be targets as well?

Do not wait for that from the Palestinian people alone, for despite their presence in a big prison and tightening siege around their cities, villages and camps, they fight with all what they can and sacrifice their dearest men, heroes and leaders. It is about time to perform your role and Almighty Allah will ask you about that; and history does not have mercy on anyone. Your life is meaningless without sharing your brothers in Palestine in the duty of Jihad.

"O ye who believe! what is the matter with you, that, when ye are asked to go forth in the Cause of Allah, ye cling heavily to the earth? Do ye prefer the life of this world to the Hereafter? But little is the comfort of this life, as compared with the Hereafter."

O Allah we have said what we have to say so be our witness

The Islamic Resistance Movement
Hamas-Palestine
Wednesday 11th Jumada Awal 1422H
1st August 2001AD

31 July 2001

In the name of Allah the most Gracious the most Merciful

Our condolence will be in retaliation to the Zionist crime

The Islamic Resistance Movement, Hamas, declares to our Mujahid Palestinian people and to our Arab and Islamic Nation, that were grieved over the severe loss of a number of Movement leaders and cadres in Nablus especially by the martyrdom of Sheikh Jamal Salim and Sheikh Jamal Mansour, that due to the seriousness of the matter, the Movement decided that its mourning of the martyrs would be the Qassam Brigades' expected retaliation to the blood of martyrs . . . all martyrs instead of accepting condolences. This includes all areas except Nablus.

"To Allah we belong, and to Him is our return"

Allahu Akbar and victory to our people

The Islamic Resistance Movement
Hamas-Palestine
31/7/2001

31 July 2001

In the name of Allah the most Gracious the most Merciful

New Zionist massacre against our people's leaders and sons

"Think not of those who are slain in Allah's Way as dead. Nay, they live, finding their sustenance in the Presence of their Lord;"

The Islamic Resistance Movement, Hamas, mourns the death of a fine group of our people, cadres and leaders of the Islamic Resistance Movement, Hamas, in Nablus:

The martyr Jamal Salim—one of the Hamas leaders in Nablus and deputy chief of the League of Palestine Ulama

The martyr Jamal Mansour—one of the Hamas leaders in Nablus

The martyr Mohammed Al-Bishawi—journalist

The martyr Fahim Dawabshe—office director

The martyr Othman Qatnani—photographer

The martyr Omar Mansour

The two children the martyrs Bilal and Mohammed

May Allah have mercy on their soul and house them in His Jannah (paradise).

They were martyred Today Tuesday as a result of Zionist cowardly missile shelling of a studies and research center in Nablus.

The new Zionist crime is in continuation of the war of annihilation launched by the government of terrorist Sharon against our unarmed people that included massacres, assassinations, demolition of houses, desecration of holy shrines, siege and starvation.

We in the Hamas Movement declare to the whole world that our martyrs' blood including the blood of two leaders martyr Jamal Salim and martyr Jamal Mansour along with the blood of Fatah Movement martyrs and the blood of all our people's martyrs will not go in vain. Our people and heroic Brigades' reprisal will be painful and violent. We are confident that our people's Jihad factions will shoulder their responsibility and Jihad duty in this fateful stage.

The terrorist Sharon and his cowardly government and arrogant army target all our people young and old, women and men, politicians and Mujahideen. Their war is a comprehensive one that target liquidation of our cause and capitulation of our people.

The treacherous Zionist crime has revealed the reality of the so-called "cease-fire" and that it was merely a call for suicide and allowing the terrorist killers free access to slaughter us. The strong retaliation to the Sharon crimes will be persistence in the intifada, escalation of resistance, unity on Jihad option and complete suspension of the humiliating settlement process.

We appeal to our Arab and Islamic masses to shoulder their duty in backing our people and ending the daily massacres against them. Our people is involved in a war on behalf of the whole Islamic Nation and the Nation is obliged to support and participate in our people's Jihad and resistance and must shoulder alongside our people in burdens of that battle.

Despite the grave loss, we affirm that our patient and steadfast people will not be terrorized by assassinations and massacres and will continue the Jihad, resistance and brave intifada regardless of sacrifices or lapse of time. This is the march of victory and liberation and this is the tax for dignity and pride.

The members and leaders of the Hamas Movement are living martyrs along the road of liberating our lands and sanctities. Our martyrs will go to Jannah God willing and we wish speedy recovery to those wounded; *"To Allah we belong, and to Him is our return"*

Allahu Akbar and victory to our Mujahid people

And death to Sharon and all Zionists

The Islamic Resistance Movement
Hamas-Palestine
Tuesday 11th Jumada Awal 1422H
31st July 2001AD

29 July 2001

In the name of Allah the most Gracious the most Merciful

"Here is a plain statement to men"

The Zionist invaders daily prove their suspicious intentions and their devilish plots against the holy Aqsa Mosque. Here they are today laying down what they consider as the foundation stone of their alleged temple in one of the holy city's suburbs, the Maghareba suburb, which is adjacent to the holy Aqsa Mosque. Their project would only be completed with the demolition of the Aqsa Mosque God forbid.

As for our people in Palestine, they as usual gather in the Aqsa yards from all over Palestine despite the criminal Zionist repression, siege of their cities and villages and barring the majority of them from reaching the holy city of Al-Quds.

The League of Palestine Ulama has issued a statement addressed to the Arab and Islamic Nation denouncing that heinous crime and the flagrant encroachment on Muslims' holy shrines top amongst them, the holy Aqsa Mosque.

The Islamic Resistance Movement, Hamas, also issued a statement describing the Zionist decision as a crime that exposes the Jews' scheme to demolish the Aqsa and urged the Arab and Islamic peoples to express their rejection of that notorious plot.

We, for our part, appeal to the Nation, with its official and popular forces, to rise up in defense of the holy Aqsa Mosque with all possible means.

We also urge you to launch whatever activities possible including popular programs and media campaigns in addition to mobilizing the people's potentials and to act on all official and popular levels to boost efforts aimed at supporting our people's steadfastness in confrontation with the Zionist enemy. We request all material and moral support for them in their defense of the holy Aqsa Mosque and in face of the enemy's cowardly aggression.

Allahu Akbar and honor belongs to Allah and His Messenger, and to the Believers

And it is a Jihad until either victory or martyrdom

The Islamic Resistance Movement-Hamas
Islamic Relations department
8th Jumada Awal 1422H
29th July 2001AD

28 July 2001

In the name of Allah the most Gracious the most Merciful

"Nor will they cease fighting you until they turn you back from your faith if they can."

The Zionist court's ruling allowing the laying down of the foundation stone of the alleged temple reveals the Jews' scheme to demolish the Aqsa

To our Palestinian people . . .
To our Arab and Islamic masses everywhere . . .

The so-called Zionist supreme court of justice yesterday passed a ruling allowing the fanatic Jewish organization that calls itself the temple mount faithful to lay down the foundation stone of the alleged third temple at the Maghareba gate, which is adjacent to the holy Aqsa Mosque.

The ruling coincided with statements for some of their rabbis that describe Arabs as ants and allow the cold-blooded assassination of our Palestinian people.

The ruling also fell in line with the terrorist Sharon government's repressive measures including the siege, starvation, assassination, abduction, demolition of houses, destroying farmland, wrecking premises, mass murders and massacres against our steadfast and unarmed people. The ruling also falls in line with feverish Zionist attempts to judaize the city of Al-Quds, demolish the Aqsa Mosque and erase any Arab-Islamic relics there through excavations and tunnels that were built at the pretext of looking for ancient ruins as a preliminary step to endorse the holy city as a capital of their usurping entity.

Our Palestinian people . . .
Our Arab and Islamic masses . . .

Terrorist Sharon paved the way for his terrorist era with the desecration of the Aqsa plaza, which ignited our people's intifada since that date. The Aqsa intifada and the brave resistance then erupted shaking Zionist security and defeating Sharon's plan. Here he is today completing what he started yesterday believing that our Arab and Islamic nation had lost all valor and determination.

Our Palestinian people, who are daily presenting greatest models in sacrifice and heroism and who are backed by their Arab and Islamic Nation, are capable of teaching the enemy the bitterest of lessons at the hands of the Mujahideen and commandos.

We, in the Islamic Resistance Movement, Hamas, while drawing the attention to the occupation's policies and seriousness of its various institutions' decisions, call for the following:

1. we urge our people with their forces and factions to gather at an early hour tomorrow at the Aqsa Mosque and its yards to resist any attempt to lay down the foundation stone of the alleged temple and to defend the Aqsa with soul and blood.

2. we affirm the importance of unity of the Palestinian people in confrontation of occupation and its dangerous decision and the necessity of breaking all contacts and meetings with that enemy and giving up once and for all any form of security coordination with it. We also call for ending detentions under any political or security pretexts for the sake of serving the enemy or in response to its demands.

3. we invite our Arab and Islamic peoples to express their anger and dismay at the Zionist decision. We urge them to reject it and to condemn the international forces, especially America, which back that enemy, and to pressure the Arab and Islamic governments to adopt an immediate and decisive position against the terrorist Sharon government and his court's oppressive ruling.

4. we call on the Arab and Islamic countries to denounce the Zionist court's ruling and adopt immediate steps to condemn that ruling on the part of the international community. We also request them to announce a comprehensive boycott of the Zionist entity on all political, diplomatic, economic and other levels.

5. we re-affirm our call on the Arab and Islamic countries to endorse a political resolution supporting the resistance program against Zionist occupation and activating supportive programs of our besieged people.

Let Sharon, the Zionist court and all Zionist terrorists, rabbis and fanatics know that the time of their entity's downfall will not be far God willing and that our Mujahid and patient people are capable of foiling their aggressive schemes and defend Al-Quds and the Aqsa and all holy shrines.

Allahu Akbar—and victory to our Mujahid people

"Allah will certainly aid those who aid His (cause); for verily Allah is Full of Strength, Exalted in Might, (able to enforce His Will)."

The Islamic Resistance Movement
Hamas-Palestine
Saturday 8th Jumada Awal 1422H
28th July 2001AD

19 July 2001

Sharon will pay the price and our battle with the Zionists is open

"Will ye not fight people who violated their oaths, plotted to expel the Messenger, and took the aggressive by being the

first (to assault) you? Do ye fear them? Nay, it is Allah Whom ye should more justly fear, if ye believe!"

The Zionist aggression against our unarmed people is still escalating along with the policy of assassination, kidnap, destruction of houses, siege, starvation and massacres, the latest of which being the heinous carnage in Bethlehem that killed four Hamas cadres and wounded several others. Furthermore, the Zionist army has been sending reinforcements to vicinities of Palestinian cities in preparation for storming them amidst expectations of escalation and widening of the Zionist warfare launched by Sharon against our people and Nation.

<u>We, in the Islamic Resistance Movement, Hamas, would like to clarify and affirm the following:</u>

1. the Zionist military build up at entrances of cites and villages and threatening to storm them does not terrorize our people who vowed before Allah to maintain steadfastness, patience and resistance. The people's Jihad forces are capable, with the grace and help of Allah, to confront and repel the Zionist aggression.

2. we call on our people in all cities, villages and refugee camps to get ready and unite their lines adopting all necessary measures to confront the Zionist threats and foil any attack.

3. the enemy's monstrous crime in Bethlehem will not pass unpunished. Sharon and all Zionists will pay a dear price and the reprisal will be a painful one God willing.

4. our people are entitled to resisting the Zionist occupation and retaliate to its arrogance, massacres and aggressions. This is a legitimate right practiced by our people and Jihad factions in any place on the land of Palestine whether in the West Bank or Gaza Strip or the 1948 occupied areas. Faced by an enemy that is occupying our lands and launching a large-scale war against us, we are all entitled to retaliate with an open battle and comprehensive resistance.

5. terrorist Sharon, who has given his army and settlers a free hand to wreak havoc in our lands, killing, destroying and terrorizing, is claiming his abidance by the ceasefire and is spreading deceptive allegations in this regard in world platforms with US support. On the Palestinian level, our people are daily suffering Zionist aggressions, yet certain parties are advocating calming down the situation, condemning martyrdom operations and warning Jihad factions against launching any military operation in 1948 lands in addition to threatening a return

to the policy of arrests and even did that on certain occasions!

6.　　we along with all our people's factions affirm our absolute rejection of the policy of arresting the heroic Mujahideen, who are defending our people. We denounce the Palestinian Authority's security bodies' step of arresting two Hamas cadres in Qalqilya and trying to arrest others in Jenin. We call on the Authority and its security apparatuses to immediately release the detainees and refrain from resuming that policy, which is a big stab in the back of our national unity, at a time when our people are in dire need of mobilizing efforts and potentials in face of the Zionist aggression.

7.　　we fervently appeal to our Arab and Islamic Nation to back our Palestinian people's steadfastness and resistance with all means possible. We urge the Arab leaders and officials in particular to hold an emergency summit meeting in which they would declare general mobilization and supply Palestinian resistance with money and arms. Talking about settlements and peace is a farce and a cover-up for Sharon's aggressive policy, who is no longer waiting for any excuse to continue his terrorism and aggression against our Palestinian people and our Arab and Islamic Nation. It is about time today to end once and for all contacts with Zionists and their criminal symbols such as Peres, Omri Sharon and their likes.

"And soon will the unjust assailants know what
vicissitudes their affairs will take!"

The Islamic Resistance Movement
Hamas-Palestine
Thursday 28th Rabee Thani 1422H
19th July 2001AD

17 July 2001

> *"If then any one transgresses the prohibition against you,*
> *transgress ye likewise against him."*

A new massacre in Bethlehem to be added to the Zionist criminal record

In a new massacre, the Zionist enemy affirmed its ugly face, which had tried to beautify through various means. The new massacre employed two American-made Apache helicopter gunships that raided the West Bank city of Bethlehem on Tuesday afternoon. They fired more than five missiles at two civilian houses in which Palestinian citizens were gathered awaiting the release of one of their detained relatives from the occupation prison of Majeddo. The despicable crime resulted in the martyrdom of:

Omar Saadeh, Mohammed Saadeh, Ishac Saadeh and Taha Al-Urouj in addition to wounding 15 women, children and youth who were present in the two houses.

We, in the Islamic Resistance Movement, Hamas, condemn this savage crime by that criminal enemy whose crimes could not be covered-up. We urge the whole world, especially those who race to condemn the Jihad of our people and their heroic deeds, to denounce that crime and to firmly confront the Zionist terrorist and criminal government led by Sharon and Peres, the butchers of Sabra and Chatilla and Qana, since the crime affirmed that our people were daily facing murder and that all their houses and individuals were targeted.

We proudly bear the tidings of the martyrdom of those four and affirm that Jihad against our enemy will continue. We affirm that the blood of the martyrs of this massacre and all martyrs will not be wasted but Insha'allah will serve as a beacon along the road of Jihad and resistance until liberation of our lands and restoration of our Quds. We affirm that the intifada will persist regardless of sacrifices until realizing our people's goals and aspirations for the sake of which they have sacrificed and are still sacrificing enormously.

We affirm, as history of our Jihad proves, that the enemy will pay the price of its crimes. Let the enemy know that with such a crime it turned all Zionists on our lands into legitimate targets of our Jihad and operations and that the Islamic Resistance Movement, Hamas, and its military wing the Qassam Brigades will violently retaliate *"And soon will the unjust assailants know what vicissitudes their affairs will take!"*

And it is a Jihad until either victory or martyrdom

The Islamic Resistance Movement
Hamas-Palestine
Tuesday 25th Rabee Thani 1422H
17th July 2001AD

19 June 2001

In the name of Allah the most Gracious the most Merciful

Memo on Jordanian authorities insistence on detaining

Brother Ibrahim Ghoushe in Amman Airport

To the esteemed leaders of:
Parties, movements, syndicates and political and public
opinion forums

Assalamu Alaikum wa Rahmatullahi wa Barakatuh

While our Palestinian people's Jihad is ongoing and their brave intifada is approaching its tenth month, the Zionist occupation is still practicing utmost degree of repression and terrorism against our people. This calls on our Arab and Islamic Nation, governments and peoples, to side by our people: defending and supporting their resistance with all means available especially when that resistance was offering one martyr after the other to liberate the holy lands and to defend the Nation and its holy shrines.

At this historic and sensitive stage we were surprised at the Islamic Resistance Movement, Hamas, with the Jordanian authorities' detention of brother Ibrahim Ghoushe at the Amman Airport preventing him in the process from returning to his country from his forced exile in the Qatari capital Doha.

We present you with this memo to explain the surrounding conditions and indications of that denounced Jordanian decision. To explain the situation we would summarize our viewpoint in the following points:

1. The crisis dates back to 21 months ago after an unjustified decision of the government of former premier Abdul Raouf Al-Rawabde clos-

ing down information offices of the Movement and arresting and prosecuting a number of its leaders and sympathizers. The government then decided to deport five of the Hamas Movement's political bureau members from Jordanian territory. The government then attributed its measures to a number of justifications that were neither credible nor realistic. All Jordanian parties, political and syndicate organizations along with the Islamic and national figures in that country rejected the measure in its capacity as contravening to the Jordanian constitution and international law other than harming national Jordanian and pan-Arab interests. The rejection emanated from the conviction that the measure was in response to Zionist and American pressures on the Jordanian government.

2. The Movement did not spare any effort to solve the crisis and its negative repercussions through adopting flexible stands towards all Arab mediation initiatives in a way taking into consideration Jordan's circumstances and interests and at the same time preserving the Movement and the brothers' right of citizenship and duty to work for their country and cause. However, the Jordanian government closed all doors before dialogue, negotiations and rational solutions. It opted to escalating the situation, turning down all initiatives and insisted on its stand of rejecting return of the brothers to Jordan. Thus it led the internal Jordanian situation into an ordeal that the Jordanian government could have been spared other than worsening relations with a sisterly Arab country.

3. The Movement expected a positive change in the Jordanian government's policy with the advent of the new government of Ali Abul Ragheb towards the issue of the deportees especially in the light of our people's intifada and the terrorist Sharon's government's terrorism and repression. Yet the new government chose to follow the path of Rawabde's government in its irrational dealing with the issue at a time when it was keen to maintain strong relations with the government of terrorist Sharon through retaining his embassy open under Jordanian security protection.

4. The brothers the chairman and members of the political bureau's right to Jordanian citizenship and return to their country was guaranteed by the Jordanian constitution and international law. This citizenship is a genuine one since establishment of the Kingdom following the 1951 unity between the east bank and west bank, which fell under Zionist occupation while under Jordanian sovereignty. It is thus a cit-

izenship not to be stripped via a ministerial decision under pressure by enemies of our Nation and their allies.

5.   It is no secret to all the nature of the inter-mingled Jordanian-Palestinian relationship as a result of the historical and geographic character of both countries. Furthermore, the de facto Palestinian political endeavor in Jordan refutes the Jordanian government's pretexts for its measures. Most Palestinian organizations are present in the Jordanian arena while carrying the Jordanian nationality. There are even some members of the Jordanian parliament who are at the same time members in the Palestinian national council and in Palestinian organizations. They occupy political positions in those organizations. There are also ministers in the Palestinian Authority who are still carrying Jordanian citizenship and live with their families in Jordan.

6.   Bargaining with the deported brothers on surrendering either their Jordanian nationality or political role in the Movement is extremely serious and is rejected at the same time. There is no conflict between both matters for working for the Palestine cause via the Hamas Movement or any other organization is a legitimate national duty on each and every Arab and Muslim not speaking about the Palestinian. It is not permissible under any circumstances to deprive the Palestinian and Arab citizens from their natural right of citizenship because they shoulder their duty towards the Nation's central cause and conflict with the Zionist enemy.

7.   Brother Ibrahim Ghoushe's step in exercising his right of returning to his country would have been open for a solution if the Jordanian government had dealt with the matter in a rational way especially when the constitution guarantees him this right of returning to his country whenever he wishes. Yet the Jordanian government violated this right through detaining and depriving him from entry. Nonetheless, the Jordanian government still owns the key to that problem namely by allowing him and his brothers to enter their country and live there among their people and families.

8.   To affirm Hamas Movement's keenness on unity of Arab ranks, it welcomes any constructive effort based on the return of Eng. Ghoushe to his country along with his deported brothers especially when we showed enough flexibility and took into consideration the general interests of Jordan, our cause and our Nation as a whole.

Esteemed leaders of parties, syndicates and organizations:

We table these events and facts before you to put you before your national and pan-Arab responsibilities. We hope that you would shoulder your duty towards this issue. Your support to the deported brothers' right of return to their country to serve their people and cause with all available means would serve as a solid support to resistance and Jihad in Palestine in addition to our Palestinian people and other peoples of our Nation's endeavor for the sake of the Palestine cause. It would further deepen the basic and important Arab role towards Palestine in its capacity as the question of All Arabs and Muslims and in its capacity as the foremost defense line of the Nation and its civilization project in face of the Zionist project.

We pray for your constant support to our people's Jihad and our Nation

The Islamic Resistance Movement
Hamas-Palestine
19/6/2001

14 June 2001

In the name of Allah the most Gracious the most Merciful

Political memo
On our stand towards western and American pressures
To abort our people's intifada and resistance

To our steadfast and Mujahid Palestinian people

To our Arab and Islamic Nation that is watching the occupation's atrocities

To the international community that is hoisting the banners of justice, freedom and human rights

Western, particularly American, efforts are ongoing these days in an attempt to abort our Palestinian people's intifada under the guise of the so-called ceasefire. Western and American emissaries are flowing into the region in feverish efforts to pressure the Palestinian Authority to accept the Zionist dictates and conditions aimed at aborting our Palestinian people's intifada and right to resisting occupation in addition to turning our people's conflict with the Zionist entity into inter-Palestinian fighting.

The Islamic Resistance Movement, Hamas, would like to explain its stand towards those feverish efforts through the following points:

1. Despite the elapse of more than eight months on the occupation repression, under Sharon and earlier Barak's governments against our unarmed Palestinian people and despite the martyrdom of more than 500 and the wounding of more than 25,000 of our unarmed people and the vast destruction caused by the mass destruction weapons and the internationally-banned lethal arms that resulted in destruction of houses, property and plantations yet those efforts did not intensify until our people's intifada and their brave resistance started to drain the usurping enemy. Until fear and confusion were spread in the enemy lines especially after failure of Sharon's aggressive plan to subdue our people and foil their comprehensive popular intifada and restore security to the Zionists.

    This timing and this concentration of pressures on the PA only meant absolute support to Zionist aggression and occupation with all its beastly qualities and inhuman practices. This is refused on the part of our people of all walks of life and affiliations. Our people will not submit but would rather insist more than ever to continue the intifada and escalate resistance against occupation.

2. Such feverish attempts and their proposals under the title of ceasefire are contrary to truth, justice and logic in addition to ignoring the core of our people's cause. They also indicate blatant siding with the brutal occupation's conditions. In this respect we would like to explain the following:

    *   The ceasefire was a false and deceptive slogan for the crisis is not between two warring and neighboring parties so that it would be contained through ceasing hostilities. In fact it is an aggression by a ruthless occupying power against an unarmed people who are liable to the cruelest repressive measures and who are suffering from huge human and material losses. Occupation is the highest degree of terrorism, violence and aggression. The treatment should now focus on halting that aggression and ending occupation. Any other solution would never solve a crisis or lead to peace and stability. Talking about a ceasefire is a real disaster on our people because it would mean ending the intifada

and resistance while retaining and protecting occupation in addition to wasting our people's great sacrifices without any gains and aborting all intifada accomplishments and effects.

- The international pressures that culminated with those of CIA chief George Tenet, on the PA to arrest intifada and resistance heroes and collecting their weapons along with banning any anti-occupation campaigns and resuming security coordination and cooperation (all being Sharon's demands) clearly reflected the open American administration's backing to this government against the PA and our people, who are the oppressed party. It is a biased and condemned stance that is not accepted by our people.

- The Mitchell committee's report was far from truth, oppressed our people and dealt with occupation through selective issues and that is why we along with our people's forces rejected it. The international efforts emanated from that report despite the fact that George Tenet's proposals overlooked the report's point on halting Zionist settlements. Such a fact reveals that the report and the efforts of Tenet and the others, who visited the region at the advice of the American administration, were nothing but an obvious deceptive attempt to abort our Palestinian people's intifada and end their legitimate anti-occupation resistance, which is a matter that cannot be sold to our people.

3. The PA's approval, under the yoke of pressures and fears of international embarrassment, of the Mitchell committee's report, that was turned down by all sectors of our people via statements and massive marches of national and Islamic forces on numerous occasions, had encouraged or lured the international mediators to exercise more pressures on the PA, which is now in a very critical situation. Insinuations of accepting freezing of settlements in return for halting the intifada, based on Mitchell's disastrous equation that aimed at ending our people's intifada and inciting strife in their lines, had increased such pressures. The PA should be courageous enough and loyal to the blood and sacrifices of our people and stick to one demand that is departure of the occupiers from our lands, Quds (Jerusalem) and holy shrines. If the PA insists on this demand we, along with all our people's forces, will be on its side on the basis of continuation of intifada and resistance until ejection of occupation.

The PA today must absorb past lessons and the intifada lesson. It should not deal with initiatives and projects that do not take into account our people's rights in full headed by their unanimity on defeat of occupation. Our people's sole option is continuation of the intifada and resistance of occupation and insistence on its expulsion from our lands. Whoever challenges this fact will be the loser.

4. The international community must duly realize that the Sharon government is one of occupation, aggression, terrorism, strife and instability. This government does not hide its ugly face despite Peres' talented roles or public relations profession. It declares ceasefire yet that government's racist army daily murders our people's women, children and elderly and its intelligence teams assassinate intifada activists and resistance fighters. Its settlers terrorize our people, demolish their houses and uproot their streets before the very eyes of the whole world. This government should not be dealt with in accordance with reason but rather on the basis of an occupation, expansionist and aggressive government. The only solution to spare the region and the world evils of its policies and aggressions is to exercise pressures on it through continuation of the intifada and resistance until it is forced to end occupation of our lands and holy places.

5. We in the Hamas Movement along with all of our people's forces declare the following:

    •   We condemn and reject George Tenet's demands and declare that our people will foil them as they did with previous conspiracies. We also refuse any similar oppressive effort from a superpower or a friendly or sisterly country.

    •   While realizing the international pressures on the PA, we do not agree with its approval on George Tenet's proposals and denounce it. We affirm that such an approval does not bind our people's national and Islamic forces or us. We urge the PA to revoke its stand and to turn down those pressures and proposals that only serve the enemy's interests. We assert that the country, its future and people's rights should not be for bargaining with any party regardless of its tyranny or threats. We underline that our people's rights, interests, sacrifices and national unity should be taken into consideration rather than foreign pressures and the enemy's threats, dictates and security priorities.

    •   We affirm our people's insistence on resisting occupation regardless of circumstances or conditions and announce, with the support of all our people's forces, our persistence in the intifada and resistance program until defeat of occupation.

- We, along with our Mujahid people and various factions, refuse under any pretext the return to the security cooperation and coordination march with occupation along with political and security arrests and disarming the people. Our people will never allow this to happen because that notorious march was a crime against our people, encroached on national unity and wasted all sacrifices and accomplishments over the past months. Terrorist Sharon and his criminal government should know that their efforts and plots to drive wedges amongst our people and to convert the struggle into inter-Palestinian fighting would not succeed God willing. Our people with all its forces are well aware of such plots and are insisting on national unity that was endorsed in the Aqsa intifada. Sharon's conspiracy will reflex on him and our people's Mujahideen and resistance heroes' reprisal would be violent against Zionist occupation. The resistance's retaliation would be stronger whenever the enemy's incitement increased.

6. We laud the Arab and Islamic governments that supported our people's right in persisting in the intifada and resistance until liberation of the lands and holy shrines and we urge all those governments to turn down and foil western and American mediations as long as they were not based on justice and right namely in ridding our people from occupation. We also ask them to clearly include protection and support of the intifada and resistance in their political programs and stands in its capacity not only as a Palestinian interest but also as an Arab and Islamic interest in face of the Zionist danger and ambition. We further invite our Arab and Islamic masses to intensify their activity and programs in solidarity with our people and in support of their intifada and resistance along with rejecting all projects aimed at aborting our people's struggle and legitimate Jihad against occupation.

The Islamic Resistance Movement
Hamas—Palestine
22nd Rabee Awal 1422H
14th June 2001AD

5 June 2001

In the name of Allah the most Gracious the most Merciful

"Fight them, and Allah will punish them by your hands, cover them with shame, help you (to victory) over them, heal the breasts of Believers,"

Sharon is preparing for aggression . . . let us prepare for resistance and confronting the aggression

Our great Palestinian people . . . the people of sacrifice

In the light of recent developments . . . quickening events . . . and after the Zionists experienced the same bitterness they inflicted on us . . . escalation in the Israeli public opinion's demands for revenge . . . background of the Israeli cabinet members . . . the lust for murder and revenge controlling their minds . . . the bloody criminal history of Sharon . . . and his threats to halt the Aqsa intifada . . . and wiping out the dream of liberation and independence in implementation of his promise to safeguard the security of each Israeli individual through forcing submission on the Palestinian people and their forces . . .

In the light of the previously mentioned, Sharon started to prepare his terrorist schemes and mobilized his racist forces in an attempt to storm the Palestinian Authority areas thinking that it would be a picnic for his "invincible" army.

Our heroic people . . . the sons of Qassam, Salahuddin, Al-Wazir and Ayyash . . . your painful blows to that deformed entity had shocked its senile premier Sharon who is not capable of safe thinking and does not benefit from past lessons. His decisions are based on muscles of his arrogant chief of staff. They have forgotten your Qassam Brigades, Aqsa Brigades, Quds Brigades, armed popular resistance . . . you are Ayyash, Abayat and Hamran, your are Said Hoteri, Hamed Abu Hijle, Ibrahim Abdul Karim and Thabet Thabet. You are the ones who caused that enemy's worst nightmares; you love martyrdom as much as the Zionists love life.

Yes, Sharon might be able to enter our areas but could he get out of them? We believe that the Zionists will soon meet their end; their graves will be in our garbage dumps. Hundreds of commandos with explosive belts will chase them along with thousands of throwers of Molotov cocktails and hundreds of hunters of their insect soldiers along with thousands of women and children who pose as the logistic support of the courageous heroes. You Zionist women if you wish to mourn your sons, brothers and husbands and turn the Zionist society into one of only women send the soldiers to us.

Our heroic Palestinian people . . . the Mujahideen and strugglers:

To perform this duty and to be victorious in that war we invite you to the following:

First: on the resistance and confrontation level:

1. Estimate and expect the spots through which the Zionists might enter or storm the PA controlled areas in coordination with the PA apparatuses.
2. Based on the former point: choose strategic positions for the confrontations and deploy in them activists and all those wishing for martyrdom and known for distinctive performance to obstruct advance of the occupation army and to serve as the people and their institutions' protection shields. Commandos would be of benefit in those positions.
3. Ambushes: to be set near to target areas (houses of wanted activists), (premises of organizations) and to deal with foot patrols when they attempt to storm a certain position to arrest or assassinate certain elements.
4. Planting explosive devices along the roads that the occupation troops are expected to pass through that would be blasted via remote control (after taking necessary precautions, accuracy and preparedness).
5. Preparing a big number of Molotov cocktails mixed with sticking materials and gas cylinders.
6. Preparing explosive belts . . . the number to be estimated by experienced elements that would be available for any commando wishing for martyrdom amidst the enemies.
7. Installing barricades to hurdle the occupation army's movement.

Second: on the security level:

1. Monitoring the enemy's moves and collaborators.
2. Requesting officials of sensitive areas to evacuate all precious equipment and to clean their offices from sensitive information.
3. Establishing emergency clinics equipped with necessary needs to treat

the wounded commandos and others in the event the army taking control of hospitals.

Third: on the mobilization and guidance levels:

1. Preparing statements for circulation in the street including the real facts on events and expectations.

2. Field mobilization: leaders and representatives of organizations and factions in the city would shoulder that responsibility after spreading in various affected areas . . . guiding and lifting the moral. It would be a good idea to use unified earphones.

Fourth: on the relief level:

1. Forming a relief committee in each area in the city grouping voluntary doctors, engineers and university professors the soonest.

2. Preparing relief material and securing telephone numbers of owners of tractors and trucks to contact them whenever necessary.

3. Providing medicines and medical equipment for first aid in various areas.

4. Providing certain foodstuffs and stocking them in stores far from expected strikes at the ground floors.

5. Counting the buildings that might be used as shelters in each area to distribute inhabitants of that area on those centers.

6. Publishing guidance publications that would deal with shelling, evacuation procedures, carrying wounded and first aid.

May Allah bless and aid you

The Islamic Resistance Movement
Hamas—Palestine
5/6/2001

4 June 2001

In the name of Allah the most Gracious the most Merciful

"Fight them, and Allah will punish them by your hands, cover them with shame, help you (to victory) over them, heal the breasts of Believers,"

Qassam Brigades by the grace of Allah strikes hard with precision

We carry the glad tidings of the tenth martyr The executor of the qualitative operation The martyr hero / Saeed Hassan Hussein Al-Hoteri

Our Palestinian patient and Mujahid people
Our Arab and Islamic Nation

The tenth martyr the hero Saeed Hassan Hussein Al-Hoteri, 20, approached his target confidently last Friday at 11.30 pm according to the plan. He carried out his qualitative martyrdom operation in the enemy's depth and heart then ascended to heavens to meet the prophets, the truthful and the martyrs in Allah's Jannah (paradise).

The qualitative operation healed the breasts of believers and humiliated Jews and their collaborators. The blast was made using a highly explosive material (Qassam-19), which was developed by Qassam Brigades' experts in their own factories. The enemy experienced its bitterness in the first test in Netanya at the hands of the martyr hero Mahmoud Marmash.

We tell our people and Nation to rest assured that the Brigades' reprisal, by the grace of Allah, would always be a pioneering retaliation in its implementation, quality and effect.

The Qassam Brigades hail our people and brothers the Mujahideen in Jordan who begot such a martyr hero who mastered the state of wait and see as a true Mujahid.

We tell Jews . . . you have to leave or perish . . . for the Qassam promise of ten martyrs had achieved its goals of realizing balance of deterrence and horror with the grace of Allah. Still wait for what is coming is stronger and more bitter.

A salutation to our lions behind bars . . . here are your brothers working with your guidance the way you wished. Soon relief will ensue. Jihad greetings to all honorable Mujahideen of our people in their various positions and a grateful greeting to all martyrs and their relatives and to all those wounded on the land of Aqsa.

And it is a Jihad until either victory or martyrdom

Qassam Brigades
Palestine—Al-Quds
4/6/2001AD

5 June 2001

In the name of Allah the most Gracious the most Merciful

Qassam Brigades have no connection to the joint truce statement

The Qassam Brigades, military wing of the Islamic Resistance Movement, Hamas, affirm the falsehood of the joint truce statement circulated with the signature of both the Qassam Brigades and the Aqsa Martyrs Brigades.

We consider that statement as an intrigue aimed at besmearing our heroic Brigades after the heroic Tel Aviv operation.

We in the Qassam Brigades did not previously issue any joint statement with any other party. Furthermore, such practice is not of our policy.

We are confident that our Mujahid, mindful Palestinian people would not be beguiled by such media deception. They know who spreads such statements and who benefits from them.

The Qassam Brigades vow before Allah then our Palestinian people and Nation to continue resistance, Jihad and strikes deep inside the occupation lines until it evacuates our lands Insha'allah.

Qassam Brigades
5/6/2001

15 May 2001

In the name of Allah the most Gracious the most Merciful

On the anniversary of the usurpation of Palestine

Let the intifada be the springboard towards liberation

Our steadfast people . . . our people everywhere . . .

We remember today the 53rd anniversary of the usurpation of Palestine at the hands of Zionist gangs with the full and direct support of the then British occupation. Those gangs practiced the most brutal massacres against our people to force their immigration out of their lands and property.

The anniversary this year falls at a time when our people are living through a saga of heroism and sacrifice in face of the Zionist enemy's tyranny. Thus they confirm that more than half a century of occupation and repression would not terminate that people's Jihad, resistance and steadfastness. On the contrary, they affirm their insistence on the right of liberating all usurped lands, Al-Quds (Jerusalem) and holy shrines from Zionist occupation. The anniversary further falls at a time when Sharon's savage aggression against our people is escalating daily in an all-out offensive. The latest such attack was the barbaric aerial and sea shelling of the Gaza Strip last night other than the cowardly assassination of five Palestinian policemen earlier yesterday near Ramallah. The savage onslaught also includes the bombardment and explosions in various cities, villages and refugee camps and the killing of innocent children and assassinating intifada and resistance cadres in a feverish attempt on the part of Sharon to break our people's steadfastness and resistance in preparation for imposing his conditions.

In the light of this continuous Zionist escalation, We affirm to our steadfast Mujahid people the following:

1. Failure of the peace settlement process and program in the light of the bitter experience. It has been proven beyond reasonable doubt that the enemy does not respect any pledges or agreements. It has been proven that there is no use from any contacts or meetings with that enemy for it only understood the language of force and resistance. Hence, all forces in the Palestinian arena, that are daily attacked

and murdered, are called upon to decide their options immediately and stick to the resistance program. They should support and develop resistance means with all potentials without heeding any other alternatives or initiatives.

2. Importance of preserving national unity, which was achieved by the grace of Allah and was strengthened in the field along the road of intifada and resistance. We should boost, protect and insist on the intifada in its capacity as our effective tool in this ferocious battle against the enemy. Here we bless the efforts of factions and forces and we bless this great steadfastness, patience and sacrifice of our people in the occupied homeland. We also bless activity of our people in the diaspora calling on them to reflect more such interaction.

3. Despite the big losses in the ranks of our people, yet the party that is really cornered is Sharon, his terrorist government and the Zionist society in general. This is reflected in the enemy soldiers, settlers and street's low moral as a result of their casualties and loss of security and stability and their growing feeling of concern over the present and future of the Zionist entity despite the elapse of more than half a century over their usurpation of Palestine. Consequently, we call on our Mujahid people and struggling forces to be more patient and steadfast over the resistance program for victory is ours and defeat will befall our enemies, which will not be far off Insha'allah. *"O ye who believe! persevere in patience and constancy; vie in such perseverance; strengthen each other; and fear Allah; that ye may prosper"* . *"if ye are suffering hardships, they are suffering similar hardships; but ye have hope from Allah, while they have none."*

Our Arab and Islamic Nation . . .

It goes without saying that the Zionist usurpation of Palestine did not target the Palestinian people only but rather the whole Nation. Hence and as long as Palestine and its holy places are of concern to the whole Nation, based on religious duty and national responsibility, . . . why is this suspicious silence? Why does the Nation leave its people in Palestine face the Zionist carnage and shoulder burdens of the battle alone?

In the light of the aforementioned we urge the Arab and Islamic governments and peoples to do the following:

1. Sense the importance of shouldering their responsibility regarding the grave events taking place on the land of Palestine and present to our

people all forms of political, financial and popular backing in addition to arms and equipment on the basis of participating in the battle in its capacity as the whole Nation's battle. There is no room here for neutrality, mediation, silence or wait and see!!

We praise, in this regard, the Arab and Islamic masses that renewed their interaction with our people's intifada and request more such action. We call on the rest of the Nation's masses to urgently follow their suit.

2.   The Nation has to realize that the era of defeat, which we suffered in the past, has ended with the grace of Allah. The Zionists could no longer dictate on us whatever they wish. The Zionists' defeat in Palestine is practically possible. Their defeat in South Lebanon, the first anniversary of which passes these days, at the hands of the Islamic resistance is a living example. Our people's intifada, resistance and great sacrifices furnish the atmosphere and allow the opportunity before our Nation today to register a new victory, God willing, against this usurping entity.

Our Arab and Islamic peoples . . .

We are standing these days at an important crossing point in our history and before a big responsibility in confrontation with the Zionist project that necessitate uniting the ranks, shouldering the burden of Jihad and resistance and mobilizing potentials requesting first and foremost the help of almighty Allah.

"If ye will aid (the cause of) Allah, He will aid you,
and plant your feet firmly."

Allahu Akbar and victory for our people and Nation

It is a Jihad until either victory or martyrdom

The Islamic Resistance Movement
Hamas—Palestine
Monday 20th Safar 1422H
14th May 2001AD

12 May 2001

In the name of Allah the most Gracious the most Merciful

To the Arab and Islamic governments:

Support our people's intifada and steadfastness in face of Zionist tyranny

Open the way before your peoples to perform their duty in that support

Sharon, the butcher, is continuing with his aggressions against our people and escalating savage destruction, shelling, bombing and assassination of children, women, men and Mujahideen. He continues to challenge our Nation through inviting the Zionists to desecrate the Aqsa Mosque anew. At this time when our wounded Mujahid people are looking forward to the Nation's masses and governments to support them and share in the responsibility of resisting the enemy's crimes, we were surprised with the painful events in Jordan. A peaceful rally and march organized by the Muslim Brotherhood in Jordan in support of our people's intifada on the occasion of the anniversary of the Nakba and the usurpation of Palestine were quelled by force including assaulting some figures, respected personalities.

It is really a feeling of shock coupled with dismay and pain over what happened at a time when we expected the Jordanian and other Arab and Islamic governments to take the initiative of allowing their masses to back our people and their intifada with all available efforts and potentials.

The governments and peoples of the Nation shoulder a historic responsibility towards the serious events that are taking place on the land of Palestine. Standing idle or playing the role of mediators or extending shyly support are not accepted. Such roles do not exempt them from the religious and national duty. They should extend real and serious support to our people with money, political decision, popular and informational interaction and even arms to share with our people the burden of the historic confrontation against the Zionist enemy.

Let those governments know that if our people were defeated, God forbid, and their intifada and resistance were halted, the Zionists would sweep the whole Arab region. Terrorist Sharon would then find the opportunity to carry out his schemes in forcing the immigration of our people and to launch aggressions against Jordan and other neighboring countries to implement the conspiracy of the alternative homeland.

Will you realize O Arabs and Muslims that our people in Palestine are your first line of defense defending both you and your holy places, by siding with our people, you would be defending yourselves and your countries in addition to defending Palestine and its holy shrines?

Salutations to the Muslim Brotherhood and the Islamic Action Front party in Jordan and to the masses, parties and national and Islamic forces. And greetings to the Arab and Islamic masses to which we look forward for more courageous stands.

Allahu Akbar and victory for Palestine and our
Arab and Islamic Nation

The Islamic Resistance Movement
Hamas—Palestine
Saturday 18th Safar 1422H
12th May 2001AD

1 May 2001

In the name of Allah the most Gracious the most Merciful

Booby-trapped cars and blasting civilian houses

Dangerous stage in Zionist aggression against our people

The Zionist criminal mentality invented a new form of terrorism and murder against our unarmed people namely exploding residential buildings full of innocent civilians with the use of booby-trapped cars in each of Gaza and Ramallah killing children, women and men. At the same time Zionist foreign minister Shimon Peres was embarking on his deceptive tours misleading the world into believing that the Zionist entity was heading towards calming down the situation!

Apparently the Zionist interior minister Uzi Landau's threats to perpetrate explosions in a number of Arab capitals especially Damascus and Beirut had already started in cities of the West Bank and Gaza Strip.

Our people's various forces should be on the alert in view of the seriousness of the current stage and be prepared to confront it especially when the enemy was practicing its crimes against our people in a very serious duality run by the terrorists Sharon and Peres. Murder, destruction and escalation on the ground are practiced while deceptive political maneuvers are launched in various capitals to cover up for the enemy's crimes in the field. The goal is one namely to crush the intifada and resistance and to spread despair among our people in the possibility of liberating their lands and restoring their rights in addition to pressuring the Palestinian Authority into returning to the negotiations according to Sharon's conditions.

Confronted by such serious developments, we affirm the following:

1. We call on our Mujahid people along with their forces, factions and brave resistance groups to intensify efforts and mobilize potentials to defend our people and to continue and escalate the intifada in addition to stepping up resistance operations against enemy targets.

2. We urge leaders of our Arab and Islamic Nation to stop dealings and meetings with the Zionist enemy. We beseech them to drop the mediation roles or initiatives and invite them to support our people's intifada and resistance and to provide our people with political protection which a religious and national duty.

3. We ask the PA to suspend all political and security meetings with the criminal Zionist enemy and to refrain from passing resolutions curbing the resistance or dissolving popular resistance committees because our people have the full right to defend themselves with all means.

4. We condemn the PA' return to the policy of political detention and demand the immediate release of Mujahid Dr. Abdul Aziz Ranteesi and the Mujahid hero Mahmoud Abu Hannoud and the rest of the detainees. The natural place for leaders of our people's Jihad is the confrontation arena and not prisons.

In conclusion, we affirm that such explosions would not terrorize our people and that our people, with their factions and masses, reject to go backward. Our people insist on their intifada and resistance until liberation of their lands and ejection of occupation.

May Allah have mercy on our people's martyrs

Allahu Akbar and victory for the Mujahideen

The Islamic Resistance Movement
Hamas—Palestine
Tuesday 7th Safar 1422H
1st May 2001AD

16 April 2001

In the name of Allah the most Gracious the most Merciful

Statement on the Zionist aggression against Syrian military positions in Lebanon

In a serious escalation, the Zionist enemy's warplanes pounded a radar position for the Syrian forces working in Lebanon leading to the martyrdom of three soldiers and the injury of others.

We, in the Islamic Resistance Movement, Hamas, condemn this brutal aggression and warn of the repercussions of such an escalatory aggressive policy of war criminal terrorist Sharon and the possibility of its expansion in more than one direction in the region.

Today's aggression against the Syrian forces comes in continuation of the enemy's arrogance, aggressions and daily massacres against our unarmed people in Palestine. Murder, cold-blooded assassinations, damaging lands, demolishing houses, displacing their inhabitants, besieging cities and starving their inhabitants have turned into a daily practice for Sharon and his terrorist gang.

Zionist arrogance and crimes are covered with absolute backing on the part of the American administration, which gave Sharon a free hand and a green light. This aggression also continues and escalates amidst a meager Arab position that did not live up to the challenge confronting our Nation.

We express our great anger due to the official Arab position that stands idle in face of the enemy's massacres against our people and remains content with betting on the American role and the so-called peace process with the criminal enemy. Some of the Arabs even maintain contacts and meetings with terrorist Sharon at a time when his hands are still smeared with our children's blood. Doesn't that weak Arab stance lure Sharon into persisting in his aggressions and crimes?!

The Zionist danger does not only threaten our Palestinian people but the whole Arab and Islamic Nation. Sharon's threats do not have any limit, he threatens Jordan considering it the alternative homeland (for the Palestinians) and one of his ministers threatens to flatten the High Dam in Egypt with missiles. This is how they treat countries signing peace treaties with them, how would they treat other Arab and Islamic countries?!

We appeal to the Arab and Islamic governments and peoples to defend with pride their dignity, their very existence and destiny. They must shoulder their responsibility in repelling the Zionist aggression and must support and defend our people in Palestine. They should back the steadfast brothers in Syria and Lebanon for the enemy is one, the danger is one and the fate is one. Let the Nation stand united in face of aggression. Let the Nation affirm that it will always remain a Nation of Jihad, steadfastness and challenge . . . for this is the only road to victory and liberation Insha'allah.

*"Truly Allah loves those who fight in His Cause in battle array,
as if they were a solid cemented structure."*

"The Believers, men and women, are protectors, one of another . . ."

**The Islamic Resistance Movement
Hamas—Palestine
Monday 22nd Muharram 1422H
16th April 2001AD**

11 April 2001

In the name of Allah the most Gracious the most Merciful

Zionist criminals demolish houses on its inhabitants

**Our Mujahid Palestinian people . . .
Our Arab and Islamic Nation . . .**

The Zionist enemy is launching a ferocious war using its terrorist war machine against our people. In one of its beastly and dirty offensives, the enemy forces launched a barbaric assault against our steadfast people in Khan Younis refugee camp in the Gaza Strip. They razed around 30 houses to the ground with all their furniture and other contents. They frightened children and women and attacked the camp like wild beasts: shelling, demolishing and destroying whatever was in their way.

This cowardly war unleashed by terrorist Sharon and his terrorist gang against our people, in which he dares to storm areas previously evacuated, points to the enemy's murderous and destructive plans carried out by land, sea and air.

Our Palestinian people, who are resisting, challenging and defending in absolute bravery and who stand united in face of continuous treachery, asks our Arab and Islamic Nation: why this silence and humiliation? Why fly to Washington to seek solutions while our Palestinian people are continuing to sacrifice blood and soul for the sake of Allah and in defense of the Nation's dignity and sanctities that are occupied by the Zionists with complete American support.

We warn the Nation against repercussions of this war, which is escalating against our unarmed people, especially when that enemy was still mobilizing its forces at the outskirts of the Khan Younis refugee camp and along all borders with Palestine occupied in 1948 in a bid to repeat its storming operations and inflict more killing and destruction and to further frighten children, elderly and women.

Let the Nation stand united and let its marches and protests against the usurping occupation hit the streets of all Arab and Muslim lands.

We affirm that our Mujahid people will not be intimidated by this terrorism and that their march will not be halted by those aggressions depending, in this regard, on Allah first then on our glorified people and Nation.

The martyrs in the Khan Younis battle the martyr hero Elias Abu Issa and the martyr hero Hani Abu Rezk along with scores of wounded persons are enough proof of that enemy's savagery. They also affirm that our people will persist along the Jihad and resistance march and will never surrender or bow down except to almighty Allah.

And it is a Jihad until either victory or martyrdom

The Islamic Resistance Movement
Hamas—Palestine
17 Muharram 1422H
11th April 2001AD

11 April 2001

In the name of Allah the most Gracious the most Merciful

Communiqué by the Islamic Resistance Movement (Hamas)

All praises to Allah, the Patron of patient believers, the One Who glorifies believers and humiliates atheists, and peace be upon His Messenger, his companions and followers.

"Think not of those who are slain in Allah's Way as dead. Nay, they live, finding their sustenance in the Presence of their Lord;"

In a qualitative martyrdom operation that smashed the Zionist security barriers despite intensified Zionist security presence the martyr hero:

Fadi Atallah Yousef Amer, 23 years old,
From the city of Qalqilya launched a martyrdom operation that led to the killing and injuring of scores of Zionists near the Israeli military barrier to the west of Qalqilya.

Yes our heroic martyr has left us, but his memory remains live in our hearts, minds and among the people. You have always been a model for the well-behaved Muslim who is enthusiastic for his religion and his country. All those who saw you described you as the living martyr. Your talk was mostly about love of martyrdom and defense of the country. You joined the convoy of martyrs after a march of sacrifice under the banner of your movement Hamas, the banner of right, strength and freedom.

All those who saw you loved you, your brothers, neighbors, mosque goers and colleagues in the open Quds University where you used to study.

Your blood will remain a torch that illuminates the road of dignity, pride and freedom for the coming generations and will remain the fire that burns the enemies and shakes the ground under their feet.

The Resistance Movement mourns with pride and honor its martyr hero Fadi Atallah Yousef Amer and vows before almighty Allah first then before our masses to remain hoisting up high the banner of Jihad and resistance until victory and liberation God willing.

In paradise may your soul rest in peace and we will remain trekking along the same road.

Allahu Akbar and Al-Hamdulilah

Allahu Akbar and victory for Islam

The Islamic Resistance Movement
Hamas
Qalqilya District
11/4/2001

10 April 2001

In the name of Allah the most Gracious the most Merciful

Appeal from our Mujahid people in Palestine to the Arab and Islamic Nation

The Aqsa is appealing to you . . . will anybody respond?!

Our Mujahid Arab and Islamic Nation

The Palestinian people have been persisting in their intifada and Jihad for one hundred and ninety days in defense of the Aqsa and the holy shrines and in defense of the lands and honor using whatever means available whether stones, knives or light weapons that could not be compared in any way to the Zionist enemy's military arsenal. The Palestinian people are confident in Allah's victory and support then in their just cause and right to all of the holy land of Palestine. They declared that the occupying invaders would not desecrate this holy land and that their men would relentlessly fight for liberation and restoration of this land, which is proud for being the destination of prophet Mohammed's (PBUH) *Isra'* (night journey), then his ascension to heaven and for hosting Christ (PBUH) who roamed its streets calling for purifying humanity from hatred and aggression.

Our Mujahid Arab and Islamic Nation

The aggression is escalating against your people in Palestine and the holy shrines in Al-Quds (Jerusalem). The savage shelling of your people, which was continuing for many months, is now escalating in response to their devil the rabbi Ovadia Yossef who called for killing Arabs without hesitation and even pounding them with missiles until they are completely wiped out. The enemy even grouped thousands of Zionists in front of the Buraq Wall today to urge terrorist Sharon to carry out his promise to allow them enter the Aqsa Haram and to expel all Palestinians from the Aqsa and the holy city.

Our Arab and Islamic brothers . . .

Al-Quds the gate to heavens, ascension site of prophets, land of martyrs and land of Ribat (Garrison), calls upon you to turn next Friday 13/4/2001 into a day of distinctive rage against the Zionist aggression on the people, the land and the holy places.

Your people in Palestine, who are continuing to sacrifice their blood and soul for the sake of Allah and in defense of Al-Quds and the Aqsa, appeal to you with Allah's words: *"Go ye forth, (whether equipped) lightly or heavily, and strive and struggle, with your goods and your persons, in the Cause of Allah."* We hope that our Ulama (religious scholars), intellectuals and leaders of public opinion along with parties, and Arab and Islamic forces would be at the forefront of the defenders of Al-Quds and the Aqsa and would take the initiative in supporting the intifada and resistance on the land of Palestine.

Our Nation . . .

Let marches of rage against occupation take to the streets from Tangiers to Jakarta. Let the enemies of Allah, the Zionists, know that this Nation never accepted and will never accept humiliation and that it would never give up its lands and Quds nor leave the people of Palestine alone in the battle. Let the Nation declare that it is like a single body if one of its members complains then the whole body will cater for it and that it will remain loyal to its pledge to Allah to support His religion, sanctities and Mujahideen on the land of Isra' and M'irage.

*"Allah has ordained that He and His Messengers
will be victorious . . ."*

O Allah be a Witness to our statement

And it is a Jihad until victory or martyrdom

The Islamic Resistance Movement
Hamas—Palestine
17 Muharram 1422H
10 April 2001AD

6 April 2001

In the name of Allah the most Gracious the most Merciful

Appeal to the Palestinian people and the Arab and Islamic Nation

The criminal terrorist Sharon provokes the Nation in its religion and desecrates its holy shrines

Our patient Mujahid Palestinian people
Our patient Arab and Islamic Nation

The terrorist mass murderer Sharon, who desecrated the Aqsa on 28/9/2000 and our Palestinian people retaliated with the blessed Aqsa intifada, returned to the same method after becoming prime minister of the Zionist entity. He ordered his security bodies to protect the Zionists' alleged right of visiting the holy Aqsa Mosque and desecrating its honored yards.

The decision fell in line with his criminal plan to quell our people and in a desperate attempt to deprive them of the right of resisting brutal occupation and ejecting them from this holy land. The decision further came at conclusion of the Arab summit in Amman as if it was telling them that the Nation with its leaders and conferences did not have any weight or worth and that it should only submit to Zionist-American demands in pressuring the Palestinian people to cool down and yield to Zionist terrorism and arrogance.

We in the Islamic Resistance Movement, Hamas, in face of such Zionist Sharonic recklessness, arrogance and provocation call on the Mujahid Palestinian people to abort Sharon's aggressive plan through intensifying presence in the holy Aqsa Mosque regardless of circumstances and prevent the Zionist criminals from desecrating the first Muslim Qibla, third of the holiest shrines and the land of Isra' and Mi'rage. We call on the Palestinian people to defend the Aqsa with hearts and souls and we are confident that Allah supports our Jihad and that the evil will one day terminate God wiling and that He is capable of everything *". . . and it was due from Us to aid those who believed."*

We also call on our Arab and Islamic peoples to take the initiative in supporting their religion and sanctities. We urge them to adopt all necessary measures to back our Mujahid people in their resistance of the Zionist aggression and in their insistence on national rights in lands and holy shrines including supplying them with all possible means.

We also ask leaders of the Arab and Islamic countries to side by our people and Nation's rights and support their resistance option. We beseech them to be in harmony with our Arab and Islamic peoples' demands for confronting Sharon and his aggressive schemes. We hope that they would not be deceived by the Zionist-American cunning that calls for dealing with Sharon and responding to his conditions and dictates under the pretext of stability and peace and the pretext of granting his a chance.

We hold the American administration the responsibility of the savage crimes perpetrated by Sharon day and night against our people, lands, holy shrines, children, trees and property. We also hold our brothers in Arab and Islamic leaderships part of the responsibility unless they hurried to defend our Aqsa and rescue our people rather than leaving them alone in face of the Zionist destruction machine. Almighty Allah will in the end bring those leaders to account where no single atom of good or evil is wasted.

As for us in Palestine, the land of Prophecies, Messages and sanctities, we are determined to go ahead along the road of Jihad until victory depending on Allah alone Who is the best of supporters.

O Allah we have voiced that statement O Allah be our Witness

And it is a Jihad until either victory or martyrdom

Allahu Akbar and victory to our people and Nation

The Islamic Resistance Movement
Hamas—Palestine
12 Muharram 1422H
6th April 2001AD

3 April 2001

In the name of Allah the most gracious the most Merciful

Assassinating Mujahid Mohammed Abdel Aal

New cowardly crime by coward people

The coward Zionist enemy, ascertaining its savagery, endorsing its terrorism against our Mujahid people and implementing the cowardly scheme of assassinations, has assassinated Mujahid Mohammed Abdel Aal in the southern city of Rafah. He was one of the Islamic Jihad Movement's Mujahideen and a fighter who worked alongside our people's Mujahideen.

The enemy's persistence in its campaign of liquidation and shelling of cities such as what took place in Bethlehem, Khalil (Hebron), Rafah, Khan Younis and Beit Lahya, and which included the abduction and detention of numerous Palestinians working in the Authority or members of Islamic and national forces, exposes the nature of that cowardly war launched by that damned enemy. The Zionist enemy is preparing for a large-scale war on all levels against our heroic people.

The Islamic Resistance Movement, Hamas, mourns the martyr Mohammed Abdel Aal and affirms its insistence on the road of Jihad and resistance against the enemy and its herds of settlers. It also affirms that the cowardly assassinations, cruel bombardment, kidnapping and arrests will not terrorize our people and will not affect their insistence on Jihad and struggle in face of that enemy. We will confront that offensive via a lengthy march of Jihad and we will humiliate the enemy and spread terror in its usurping entity until Allah's victory is achieved for our people and Nation.

And it is a Jihad until victory or martyrdom

The Islamic Resistance Movement
Hamas—Palestine
9 Muharram 1422AH
3rd April 2001AD

27 March 2001

In the name of Allah the most Gracious the most Merciful

The Islamic resistance Movement

Hamas—Palestine

Memo from the Islamic Resistance Movement (Hamas)
to the Arab summit in Amman—Jordan

To their Majesties and Excellencies

The Kings, Presidents and Emirs of the Arab countries may Allah preserve them

Assalamu Alaikum wa Rahmatullahi wa Barakatuh

We are pleased in the Islamic Resistance Movement (Hamas) to extend our deepest greetings and appreciation and our best wishes for success of your conference in service of the Nation's questions praying that Allah would guide you to what is best for the countries and peoples.

Your Majesties and Excellencies

Your meeting is held amidst critical circumstances and a historic turning point in life of our Arab Nation and Palestinian people, who are still exercising their legitimate right of self defense and struggle against Zionist occupation, equipped with belief, determination and insistence on attaining freedom and liberation offering along the way grave sacrifices and a long queue of martyrs, wounded and detainees.

Faced by such unprecedented steadfastness, the Zionist occupation escalated its aggressive and terrorist practices against our Mujahid people: killing children, women and innocent, assassinating Mujahideen and active cadres, imposing oppressive siege and cutting the West Bank and Gaza Strip into scores of isolated isles that turned the Palestinian citizens' life into utter misery. The occupation adopted siege and starvation as a policy aimed at ending the intifada and subduing the Palestinian people, terminating their will of steadfastness and resistance and increasing their sufferings . . . turning their life into hell. Our people while living through a state of revolt and struggle with all its repercussions and sacrifices look forward to your esteemed summit for a supportive Arab stand that would back their struggle and steadfastness and ease their pains and help them achieve their goals in freedom, liberation and independence.

Your Majesties and Excellencies

This critical and important stage in our Nation's history and conflict with the Zionist enemy calls on us to remind you with the following facts:

The Zionist enemy is a usurping entity ever since Ben Gurion till the terrorist Sharon that only believes in the Zionist ideology based on murder, aggression and expansion. They do not accept peace unless with their own conditions and dictates that serve a certain stage of their expansionist plans. Consequently the American administration's so-called peace only led to endorsing occupation, settlement and judaization of Palestinian lands. All efforts to convince various enemy leaders to meet the minimum demands of the Palestinian Authority had failed especially when the negotiations reached discussions on the final status solution.

The Palestinian people's insistence on their lands and holy places and on resisting occupation with all available means, including all out popular intifada and armed operations, was the thing that shook the Zionist ideology and caused a real crisis for the enemy. It was the obvious reason for the fall of enemy leaders one after the other and the most important thing is that it led the Zionist society to question destiny and future of the Zionist entity. With absolute understanding of the Palestinian and Lebanese situations and their differences in Zionist thinking, yet the Lebanese lesson remains big and meaningful. The resistance, backed by political resoluteness and popular steadfastness, forced the Zionist enemy to withdraw in humiliation from South Lebanon after more than 20 years of occupation without negotiations or political agreement.

A close follow up of the Zionist entity and the internal political conflicts and debates, loss of security and stability even after 50 years of its creation, inability to end our Palestinian people's intifada and resistance despite the great disparity in the balance of power, would reveal the brittle status of that entity and the fact that it has no future in the region. The Zionist entity has even started the stage of retreat and collapse, God willing, after the peak that it had reached. No American-supplied material strength would help it continue its supremacy over all Arab countries or even a single Arab country. Sharon's ascension to power on the basis of providing security after failure of Barak's program, which was based on peace and security, proves that the entity was in a state of confusion. Sharon and his terrorist government members' threats should not scare anyone because they reflect a state of fear and confusion more than a state of confidence.

The American administration, regardless of who is sitting at the White House, has always been biased in favor of the Zionist enemy and committed to its military supremacy over the Arab countries despite the quantity and quality of American interests in the Arab region. The new administration of George Bush had inaugurated its era with bombing Iraq and declaring intention to move its embassy to Al-Quds, giving a down-level priority to the Arab-Zionist conflict. Above all, this administration is asking for a chance to Sharon; thus it is of no use to bet neither on the American stance that is totally biased nor on the hopeless European position.

The new government of Sharon, which reflects the general Zionist mood, is extremely fanatic and bloodthirsty and it is completely anti-peace. The so-called national unity governments in the Zionist entity were historically governments of aggression and war. Terrorist Sharon did not form his government to save peace or meet our people's rights but rather came to end the intifada and quell the resistance with the use of his repressive measures, siege and starvation along with threats leveled in all direction hoping to restore the Zionists' lost security. The presence of Shimon Peres, the butcher of Qana, in that government's foreign portfolio does not change its true nature of extremism and aggression. Hence we hope that Sharon would not be given any new chance, for such hope is out of the question in addition to being a waste of time and a reflection of weakness and hesitation that would lure Sharon into more stringency and blackmail.

The Palestinian people, despite great sufferings and little potentials, have decided to continue along the road of intifada and struggle and determined to remain steadfast as long as it takes in face of occupation until it leaves Palestinian lands and holy places. Such steadfastness, with your support and assistance, will defeat Sharon's schemes God willing, and will turn upside down the balance in the region and furnish the road for a new stage of our Nation's struggle with the enemy in which we will force that enemy to withdraw from our lands by force in a serious march for liberation and restoration of rights Insha'allah.

We affirm that taking the initiative in this conflict is possible and does not require balance of power. The balance of wills with a degree of force and unity of ranks and stands are enough to restore self-confidence and build a steadfastness and resistance strategy instead of the negotiations strategy, which has proven its failure and futility over the past years and even made the enemy increase its dictates as we kept on reiterating that negotiation was our sole strategic option.

It is no doubt that the Palestinian cause is an Arab, Islamic question and even the central issue of the Arab Nation. Consequently, our success in settling this question and restoring our rights necessitate determination, strength, proper planning and daring decisions in addition to activating joint Arab action, bypassing side differences and uniting the ranks and efforts towards the inevitable confrontation that concerns and targets us all.

We look forward to your esteemed summit with hope and expect it to live up to the level of events taking place on the land of Palestine and hope that your resolutions would include the following demands:

Supporting the steadfastness of the Palestinian people and assisting their intifada with money and arms in addition to forming committees for the support of the intifada in all Arab countries in its capacity as the means of foiling Sharon's plots and the transfer conspiracy.

Endorsing legitimacy of the Palestinian people's right of resisting Zionist occupation and backing that struggle by all means until end of occupation.

Insisting on the Palestinian people's rights in full, rejecting the surrendering of any of those rights, topped by the right of return, Palestinian and Islamic rights in Al-Quds (Jerusalem) including its Islamic and Christian shrines. Boosting efforts aimed at stabilizing life of its inhabitants and preserving its Arab and Islamic identity.

Severing all forms of relations with the Zionist enemy and returning to economic boycott of that enemy including the reactivation of its committees.

Allocating an Arab day for solidarity with Al-Quds and the Aqsa intifada.

Solving all pending inter-Arab problems, in a way securing interests of all parties, and lifting the siege on Iraq and refusing to bow to American pressures.

While presenting those practical demands to your esteemed summit, which reflect our people and Nation's aspirations, we pray that Allah will aid and guide you for the sake of our Nation's interest and dignity.

May Allah guide you along the road of right and benevolence

Please accept our deep appreciation and respect

Wassalamu Alaikum wa Rahmatullahi wa Barakatuh

Khaled Mishaal
Political bureau chief

1 February 2001

In the name of Allah the most gracious the most Merciful

Hamas statement commenting on PA officials' calls asking our people in occupied Palestine 1948 to elect criminal Barak

With the approach of the Zionist entity's premiership elections, more calls and appeals are voiced by Palestinian Authority officials on our people in the occupied lands 1948 to vote for the criminal terrorist Barak, leader of the Zionist labor party, and to weaken chances of the criminal terrorist Sharon.

We, in the Islamic Resistance Movement, Hamas, along with all of our Mujahid people denounce such suspicious calls and regret such a low degree of humiliation to the extent of appealing to our people to elect the terrorist butcher Barak who ordered his army and soldiers to launch repressive and terrorist campaigns against our unarmed people in occupied Palestine 1948 killing 13 people and wounding hundreds of others. That same criminal shelled the West Bank and Gaza Strip cities with missiles using choppers and tanks killing more than 400 people and wounding more than 20,000 others in a period of four months. He also dispatched death squads to kill our people's activists and Mujahideen in cold blood. He is still threatening more such crimes and terrorism.

Such stupid and rude calls send a clear message to Barak and Zionist enemy leaders that despite Barak's massacres the votes of our people in the occupied lands 1948 would be cast in his favor and would attempt to save him regardless of what he had done or would do, thus urging him to commit more suppression and to repeat his bloodbaths.

The feverish attempts to salvage Barak from failure further represent a desperate effort to save the so called settlement process, which is already collapsing, and to save those betting on that alternative after our people had affirmed rejection of that option and declared insistence on the intifada, resistance, Jihad and martyrdom as the sole road to grab our rights and liberate our lands and holy shrines.

The Authority's attempt to deceive our people with its claim that the terrorist criminal Barak was better than the terrorist criminal Sharon will end up in failure. Our people no longer confide in the symbols of capitulation and do not need anyone to pinpoint the enemies and butchers. Our people do not differentiate between Sharon, the mass murderer of Sabra and Shatilla, and Barak the mass murderer of the Aqsa intifada. Our people do not fear Sharon's threats and are not deceived by Barak's allegations. Our people's slogan is let Sharon, Barak and all occupiers go to hell and let our lands be purged from their dirt.

We appreciate the stand of our people in 1948 represented in their commitment to boycott the election and not to vote for either of those criminal killers, since such a stance coincides with the national and religious standpoint in addition to our people's higher interests.

The Islamic Resistance Movement
Hamas—Palestine
1 February 2001

23 January 2001

In the name of Allah the most gracious the most Merciful

The holy Aqsa intifada

An intifada to defeat occupation

Communiqué no. (19)

*"O ye who believe! if ye obey the Unbelievers, they will drive
you back on your heels, and ye will turn back (from Faith) to your own
loss. Nay, Allah is your protector, and He is the best of helpers."*

Taba negotiations will not deceive our people
And will not halt resistance or the intifada

Our stationed Palestinian people
Our glorified Arab-Islamic nation

It is not strange that the Zionist enemy would be surprised by severity of
the Mujahideen and fighters' strikes. It is also not strange that Zionist leaders would stand powerless in face of the holy Aqsa intifada. Lessons of history and the present prove that peoples under occupation equipping
themselves with steadfastness, patience and force, who revolt on the basis of
unity and understanding then make of their blood and sacrifices a bridge to
cross to their just goals, eventually realize victory and actualize aspirations.

Our Mujahid people, with the testimony of contemporary history and our
blessed intifada, have proven a great ability to forebear sacrifices and difficulties and to bypass siege, terrorism and starvation. Our people maintained
their faithful pledge with Allah and Nation to persist along the road not
fearing tyranny, conspiracies or attempts to undermine the glorified intifada.

Our Mujahid people . . . our glorified Nation

It is utterly dismaying to witness the feverish racing to the absurd negotiations and keenness on security meetings at a time when our people are
still the target of one of the cruelest Zionist terrorist offensive and the most
savage attacks by Jewish settlers. Such practice includes burning houses,
destroying crops and terrifying civilians in front of the very eyes of the

whole world such as what took place in the Mawasi area of Khan Younis, in Al-Mighraka, Khalil and other Palestinian cities and villages. Moreover, the negotiating process contradicts our people's unanimous concordance on continuation in the struggle and intifada and rejection of all forms of talks or meetings with the Zionist enemy, which we consider as wasting our people's sufferings and blood just for the sake of beautifying the enemy's ugly face while addressing a bad message to the world.

It is surprising that such meetings are quickening as the Palestinian Authority is proposing marathon negotiations in Taba within framework of the document tabled by the outgoing American president Bill Clinton to save terrorist Barak from his ordeal and market him as the best one to make peace in the upcoming Zionist elections. Certain politicians' attempt to support Barak's election chances compared to terrorist Sharon after the former's missile and tanks' bombardment of residential quarters, assassination of Mujahideen and honorable figures and the siege of our people is an encroachment on blood of martyrs, sufferings of the wounded and the deprived. It also serves as a deadly arrow directed at our intifada and people in addition to turning the back to our Arab and Islamic Nation that stands in one trench in backing of our people and their Jihad.

The Islamic Resistance Movement, Hamas, while affirming, at this historical stage, its rejection and condemnation of any agreement or understanding infringing on our legitimate and historic rights in holy Palestine and on the return of our people to their lands and homes, calls for the following:

First: on the Arab and Islamic level:

1. Hamas urges the Arab and Islamic peoples to show more support and solidarity with the Aqsa intifada on the political, informational, material and moral levels and to revive the economic boycott of the Zionist enemy and refuse any form of meeting or coordination with it in addition to declaring rejection of any attempt aimed at liquidating the Palestine cause.

2. On the tenth anniversary of the oppressive siege, Hamas asks the Arab and Islamic countries to break the siege on the Iraqi Muslim people.

3. We appeal to Sheikh of Al-Azhar Dr. Mohammed Tantawi to rescind his invitation to visit Al-Quds and the Aqsa under Zionist occupation since the call contradicts the Fatwa of the Azhar Ulamah (religious scholars) and similar ones by the Nation's Ulamah. Furthermore, the Zionist enemy would exploit such a call to endorse its aggression and

occupation; it would also encourage Zionist arrogance. We believe that any form of support to the intifada and the Aqsa should be displayed in the Nation's backing of our people with arms and elements of steadfastness rather than visiting the Aqsa under occupation.

4. We request all forces, parties and institutions in the Arab and Islamic world to organize activities in support of our people and our Nation's rights in Al-Quds and the holy Aqsa Mosque along with our people's right of return to their lands from which they were forcibly evacuated and to publicize such issues on all occasions.

Second: on the Palestinian level:

1. The Islamic Resistance Movement, Hamas, asks the PA to respond to the popular and factional stand that calls for ending the absurd negotiations with the Zionist enemy and to stop beautifying face of the mass murderer Barak and covering up for his crimes under unacceptable justifications. We affirm that any agreement infringing on our legitimate rights in holy Palestine, in Al-Quds and the Aqsa will be rejected by our people and will not be binding to future generations but rather will carry seeds of its annulment and will not withstand for long regardless of any attempt to beautify or market it.

2. Hamas appeals to the PA not to have pending hopes on the new American administration under president Bush, affirming the importance of depending on Almighty Allah's invincible power then on the potentials of our people and Nation and to deepen our unity in the trench of the intifada and resistance.

3. Hamas urges the PA to firmly deal with the phenomenon of collaborators, stressing the importance of purging our people from their dirt and corruption. Hamas draws the PA's attention to the necessity of dealing with the root of the problem on all levels and with all means in accordance to justice, religious commitment and legal discipline away from suspicion so as to avoid confusion and strife.

4. Hamas denounces security meetings and demands the PA to stop all forms of security coordination with the enemy, which leads to foiling our people's Jihad and intifada in addition to harming our cause and rights. The Movement also calls for releasing all the detained Mujahideen who are still in PA jails in a bid to boost our people's steadfastness in confrontation of the enemy and to defeat occupation.

5. Hamas advocates activating our people's right of return including

holding conferences and rallies in Palestine and in camps in the diaspora to ascertain the right of return and to reject all projects aimed at liquidating that right under any circumstances. We appreciate in this sphere our people's moves in the homeland and the diaspora and their insistence on the right of return and their unanimity on rejecting anything that might reduce or prune that right.

6. Hamas hails our people and the blessed intifada as well as all Mujahideen and strugglers who are striking the enemy at the confrontation lines and in depth. Hamas also salutes the Qassam heroic martyr the hero of the martyrdom operation in Natanya Hamed Abu Hajle and the Qassam Brigades especially their latest operation that targeted a Zionist tank. We call on our people to launch more resistance operations and to activate all forms of economic boycott of Zionist and American products.

7. Hamas affirms its stable stance towards national unity on the basis of resistance and escalation of the intifada. The Movement hails steadfastness of our heroes in jails of the Zionist occupation who are facing the most brutal forms of repression and we affirm to them that our people back them until their freedom is achieved.

Third: activities:

Hamas affirms all activities included in the National-Islamic program and calls for escalating the intifada on Fridays and to offer prayers in the Aqsa Mosque and to station there.

Allahu Akbar wa Lilallah Al-Hamd

And it is a Jihad until either victory or martyrdom

The Islamic Resistance Movement
Hamas—Palestine
28 Shawal 1421H
23 January 2001AD

15 January 2001

In the name of Allah the most gracious the most Merciful

"It is not ye who slew them; it was Allah: when thou threwest,
it was not thy act, but Allah's . . ." (Quran 8/17)

Communiqué by Qassam Brigades (Special Unit 103)
The first reprisal against assassinations

Our Mujahid people:

Here is the war igniting and the worshippers at night and cavaliers in the morning start their march. Here we live up to our pledge and involve "Israel" in a relentless war so that its settlers and rats would pack up and leave Gaza with no return.

Barak wanted war so let him taste its hell. The war will not end until the Zionists wish that the sea would not only swallow Gaza but also Palestine all of Palestine. Thence our Mujahideen would attack them so that their remnants would completely evacuate Nitsarim, Kfar Darum, Gush Qatif, Kiryat Shmoneh, Khalil (Hebron), Tel Aviv, Al-Quds (Jerusalem) and all areas of Palestine. Our battle that we mentioned in former communiqués has started to bear fruit by the grace of Allah.

On this occasion, we would like to convey the glad tidings on our responsibility for the daring operation along the Karni-Nitsarim road today Monday 15/1/2001 at 7:45 am. which led to the complete destruction of two military vehicles as a result of blasting an explosive device planted by our Mujahideen four meters away from the two vehicles leaving them in complete rubble. Our Mujahideen were able to film that operation on videotape.

Our Mujahid people:

This operation retaliates to the Zionist enemy's assassinations against our heroic people the latest of which was the cold-blooded murder of one of our brothers the leaders in the Fatah Movement.

We vow before Allah that we would never rest along the road of Jihad and martyrdom until victory or martyrdom.

Qassam Brigades
Special Unit (103)
Monday 15/1/2001

4 January 2001

In the name of Allah the most gracious the most Merciful

Important communiqué
By the Islamic Resistance Movement (Hamas)

On PA's "conditional!" approval of the American proposals And the Arab follow-up committee's Cairo meeting to discuss them

In a very serious development, the chairman of the Palestinian Authority headed to Washington for talks with American president Clinton in response to the latter's request and pressures to discuss his recent settlement proposals. It was later announced that the Authority chief had given his conditional approval of those proposals. The White House spokesman further declared that the Authority chief had agreed to work for ending what they call violence (i.e. the intifada) and resuming security coordination with the Zionist enemy. For their part, some PA officials said that the Authority's stance vis-à-vis the American paper would be declared during meetings of the Arab follow-up committee that is to be held later today in Cairo.

In the light of such a critical situation, we in the Islamic Resistance Movement, Hamas, affirm the following:

1. Clinton's proposals were in fact Zionist proposals, conditions and speculations that were adopted by Clinton as is and tabled them as American proposals. They do not meet any of our Palestinian people's rights or those of the Arab and Islamic Nation while meeting all enemy demands and ambitions.

2. Those proposals cancel the right of return for more than five million Palestinian refugees who are living in the diaspora and who are sticking to their right of return to their homeland, lands, houses and property for more than fifty years. Accepting the American proposals would be a stab in the back of our people's refugees.

3. Clinton's proposals endorse Jewish and Zionist sovereignty on the Haram Al-Sharif and on parts of it. They give the Jews sovereignty over the area underneath the Haram, which allow continued digging in a way threatening the very existence of the Aqsa. They also give the Jews sovereignty over the Buraq Wall, which Clinton and the Zionist enemy call the (Wailing Wall) while in fact it is part and par-

cel of the holy Aqsa Mosque. The phrase in Clinton's proposals even speaks of controlling the whole western wall, which extends for around half a kilometer inside the Islamic quarters. A dangerous tunnel was opened underneath that wall in 1996 thus boosting the enemy's control on the whole area. The proposals furthermore retain the city of Al-Quds (Jerusalem) under Zionist sovereignty.

4. Clinton's proposals also meet the Zionists' conditions leaving most of the Zionist settlements in the West Bank and Al-Quds as a dagger in the heart of our lands after turning those lands into isolated and severed isles and keeping our people under the mercy of the armed-to-the-teeth herds of settlers.

5. The promised Palestinian state, according to Clinton's proposals, is nothing but a disfigured autonomous enclave. The enemy's army will continue to control borders and crossings through its presence as the basis of international forces that would be deployed along the so-called (Green line) and along the eastern borders with Jordan. The enemy would also retain early warning stations and arms caches in various areas in the West Bank and would be allowed free access into the airspace as part of its army's exercises.

6. The bases of American (Clinton's) proposals are null and void and contradict our people's interests and legitimate rights. Hence there is no meaning for the so-called demands for clarifications regarding those proposals. Consequently the PA's announcement that it will adopt its final decision after meetings of the Arab follow-up ministerial committee is a rejected maneuver. It is only understood as an attempt to win an Arab support under American pressures. A return to negotiations in Washington on the basis of the American proposals is a new absurd step that is rejected by our people.

Faced by those facts, we in the Hamas Movement call for the following:

1. We urge the Arab follow-up committee and all Arab and Islamic countries to declare a clear-cut and frank position rejecting the American proposals in toto. We remind them that our people within and outside the homeland refuse such proposals and stick to their full rights and insist on liberating their lands and expelling the occupiers. Our people are capable, by the grace of Allah, of achieving that through their blessed intifada, escalating resistance and national unity. This dictates on the Arab countries to adopt our people's stand and back their blessed intifada and anti-occupation program in its capacity as the

real and practical option. We affirm that our people are not facing a dilemma but rather the Zionist enemy and the American administration are the ones who are facing a dilemma and we as Palestinians and as an Arab and Islamic Nation are not concerned with saving them.

2. We demand the PA to clearly decide rejecting the American proposals and to end any dealing with them or negotiating over them. It is high time to stop hesitation and maneuvering. The PA should declare such a position during the Arab follow-up committee meetings. It should give more consideration to our Palestinian people and their clear stand in insisting on their rights and demands. The PA should not give any consideration to American pressures nor to Clinton's personal interests or Barak's election interests.

3. We warn against the return of security coordination between the Authority and the Zionist enemy under supervision of American intelligence and the ensuing persecution of our people's Mujahideen and heroes of their intifada or their liquidation. We also warn of any measures that the PA might resort to in a bid to end the intifada and prosecute its heroes in response to American and Zionist demands.

4. The Hamas Movement along with all our people's forces rejects such a serious deterioration in the Palestinian stand and submission to American-Zionist hegemony. We call on our people to stick to their blessed intifada, resistance and steadfastness in confrontation of the enemy and the Zionist aggression on our people and sanctities.

5. We affirm the decisive fact that no Palestinian, Arab or Muslim leader has the right of approving any agreements or treaties that reduce our people's rights in Al-Quds, the Aqsa, the whole land of Palestine, return of refugees, dismantling settlements, liberating our lands and establishing a real sovereign state. Any such agreements would not represent our people or their free will and they would not be binding on us or our people who will tear apart any humiliating agreement through blood of their martyrs and struggle and Jihad of their sons.

"They plot and plan, and Allah too plans, but the best of planners is Allah."

The Islamic Resistance Movement
(Hamas—Palestine)
4 January 2001

26 December 2000

In the name of Allah the most gracious the most Merciful

Our Eid is decorated with revenge

"Among the Believers are men who have been true to their Covenant with Allah: of them some have completed their vow (to the extreme), and some (still) wait: but they have never changed (their determination) in the least" (Quran 33/23)

To our Mujahid people . . . to the freedom loving people on the land of Isra' & Mi'rage . . . to the foreheads that swore not to bow to Zionists . . . to the towering rocks of sacrifice . . . to the resistance gun that never softens . . . we in the Islamic Resistance Movement, Hamas, congratulate our dignified people on the occasion of Eid ul-Fitr. This Eid befalls us while we daily suffer the pain of witnessing funerals of our martyrs so that our smiles are mixed with our tears in a clear united stand towards the steadfastness and resistance option. This people receive the Eid with smiles of resoluteness declaring each day that they will never sway from their pledge and that the blood that runs in the veins of our blessed land of Palestine will continue to throw fire at the Zionists.

Hamas also extends its congratulations to the Christians in the holy lands and outside on the occasion of the New Year.

The holy month of Ramadan has gone after witnessing our determination to continue along the project of holy Jihad and resistance against the sinful Zionist arrogance. The holy Aqsa intifada is steadily progressing along the road of daily distinctive escalation. Thus it affirms the people's strategy of struggle despite all feverish attempts to restore life to the desperate negotiating process via absurd rounds of negotiations in Washington and in a bid to save the Zionist mass murderer Barak from his political ordeal without gaining any national interest in return. Here we affirm anew that such attempts and efforts will not bear fruit in ending the blessed intifada and will not stand in face of our patient people's anger who swore to grab their legitimate rights with pride.

Our Mujahid people . . . our united intifada people . . . sons of Palestine, the site of our prophet's Isra', . . . our people that stick to their Quds and Buraq Wall along with each and every inch of our lands . . . we in the Islamic Resistance Movement, Hamas, affirm the following:

First: on the Arab and Islamic levels:

1. The Islamic Resistance Movement, Hamas, extends its best wishes to our Arab and Islamic peoples on the occasion of the blessed Eid ul-Fitr praying that Allah would accept from all of us our Ta'at and many happy returns of the occasion.

2. Hamas greets and appreciates our Islamic and Arab peoples that expressed their real solidarity with our just cause through the Quds Day activities in the last Friday of Ramadan and we hail their supportive stance of the blessed intifada.

3. Hamas appeals to the beloved Islamic and Arab masses to increase their supportive acts of the blessed intifada and organize various activities in backing of the Palestinian people in face of the invading occupiers.

4. Hamas calls on the Arab and Islamic Nation to adopt the resistance option, support Jihad and to reject normalization and negotiations.

Second: on the internal Palestinian level:

1. The Movement salutes all Mujahideen who insist on the weapons of right, force and freedom and who continue holding their guns declaring continuation of the method of Jihad. All hail to our brothers who won the honor of martyrdom in the battles of honor in defense of the Nation. Our salutations also to our brave detainees who are in the limelight and we specifically point to the lions who are engaged in the battle of empty stomachs since last Tuesday in the central Junaid prison in Nablus and we hold the Palestinian Authority the responsibility of any harm done to any of the on-strike Mujahideen.

2. Hamas highly appreciates the daily popular marches that sweep the streets of Palestine rejecting the defeatist option and proving their rejection of negotiations with the criminal killers. We also cable our best greetings to our masses that expressed their backing to the Movement in its carnival on the anniversary of its outbreak along with that of the earlier intifada in a frank public referendum.

3. Hamas demands an end to all forms of negotiations with the occupiers and warns against going back to an option that was a proven failure in the past days and that the people had rejected on more than one occasion. Hence we declare our refusal to any bargaining on Al-Quds, the Aqsa, the Buraq or the refugees for it is a Quranic issue in which our great Quran had decided and no-one has the right to negotiate. Any agreement falling in this framework does not bind our peo-

ple or us. The Movement warns in this respect against accepting the American proposals that contradict our people's stable interests and rights and only serves Barak and Clinton.

4. Hamas urges the Authority to release all Mujahideen, thinkers and religions scholars from its prisons since there is no reason for their detention and so that they could enjoy Eid with their sons and relatives topped by Dr. Abdul Aziz Ranteesi and Sheikh Mohammed Jamal Natshe.

5. Hamas affirms its pioneering option in activating all forms of confrontation with the Zionist occupiers on each and every inch of our usurped lands in cherished Palestine.

6. Hamas urges our Palestinian masses to visit the families of martyrs, wounded and detainees and to deepen ties with them especially on the days of Eid.

7. Hamas calls on our Palestinian people to maintain real unity, a unity that would unite ranks in face of usurpers for there should be a form of political, economic and social cohesion so that we would remain in support of each other.

8. Hamas beseeches our beloved people in Al-Quds and its surroundings and all those capable of reaching the Aqsa yards to offer Eid prayers at the holy Aqsa Mosque to deny the Jews the joy of evacuating the Mosque from its soldiers.

9. Hamas affirms the activities included in the national and Islamic committees' communiqués in various areas of our beloved Palestine, which would deepen the concept of unity in the goals and means.

Finally, we in the Islamic Resistance Movement, Hamas, vow to preserve Allah's Message, Religion and Quran and to protect sanctities regardless of sacrifices. We pray that this Eid would rekindle the unity over the path of Jihad and resistance on all levels. We pray that the next Eid would witness the liberation of our lands from usurpers' dirt. May Allah accept your prayers and fasting.

Allahu Akbar and victory to our Mujahid people.
Allahu Akbar wa Lilahulhamad.
And many happy returns of the occasion.

The Islamic Resistance Movement
(Hamas—Palestine)
26 December 2000

14 December 2000

In the name of Allah the most gracious the most Merciful

Holy Aqsa intifada . . . an intifada to defeat occupation Communiqué no. (17)

On the anniversary of its outbreak . . . Hamas: resistance until victory

The anniversary of victory in Bader this year coincides with the 13th anniversary of the outbreak of the Islamic Resistance Movement, Hamas, posing as a renewed hope for the upcoming dawn and victory of our people Insha'allah. It further affirms that the Jihad option is the only one capable of formulating that hopeful victory.

Hence, let the holy Aqsa intifada continue and escalate and all hail to those using guns and to the Qassam elements who launch declared and undeclared heroic operations from Khadera to the martyrdom marine operation off Rafah to Kfar Darum to ambushes targeting occupiers all over our homeland. So continue along your path O heroes whether declaring or not declaring your operations and do not be provoked by those who do not know the truth.

A proud salutation to all martyrs of the blessed intifada and to the Qassam martyrs Hamdy Mikdad, Ibrahim Bani Odeh, Awad Silmi and Abbas Iwewi those pure and hidden heroes who taught the Nation the road to sacrifice, those who vanquished the Zionists.

Our stationed Palestinian people . . . the holy Aqsa intifada had entered a new stage through the painful blows against cowardly Zionists and frightened settlers everywhere, which made them lose their minds and sense that their fragile entity was shaken thanks to strikes of the Mujahideen. Hence they lost confidence in their topmost General and his government fell down heralding the fall of their state God willing.

We affirm that efforts exerted for the sake of returning to the negotiating table were but desperate attempts to save the Zionists at the expense of our people's intifada, Jihad and blood of martyrs. The biased American fact-finding committee was one of those desperate attempts. We do not believe it would lead to anything and we believe that in the end it would only serve the Zionists' interests.

Our Mujahid Palestinian people . . . the ferocious Zionist offensive point to the Generals' despair. The savage storming of Khan Younis refugee camp yesterday, the bombing of Beit Jala or the cowardly assassinations against our people's heroes are all indications of the failure of the Zionist Generals. Such attempts would only boost our people's solidity and determination to go ahead along the road of resistance until defeat of occupation. So depend on Allah and be patient for the victory in the end will be for those who fear Allah.

Our Palestinian people . . . **our Arab-Islamic Nation** . . . the Hamas Movement while commemorating its 13th anniversary would like to affirm the following:

First: on the Palestinian level:

1. Hamas urges the Palestinian people to launch more resistance of the occupation soldiers and herds of settlers using all available means.

2. Hamas affirms the importance of applying the Sharia of Allah against the agent Allan Kharyoush who masterminded, along with his Zionist masters, the assassination of the Qassam Brigades' commander Ibrahim Bani Odeh. The Palestinian people would not accept anything less than executing that agent and his like. Hamas further affirms the importance of exposing, prosecuting and trying all collaborators, who are spreading corruption, in their capacity as the most important tools of occupation in perpetrating internal sabotage and committing assassinations.

3. The Movement stresses the necessity of heading to the Aqsa Mosque despite the criminal Zionists' siege and let the last Friday in Ramadan be the day of Al-Quds (Jerusalem) to affirm our protection and catering of the holy Aqsa.

4. The Movement affirms that there is no justification for retaining political detainees in Palestinian Authority jails. This bleeding wound should be stopped by releasing them topped by Dr. Abdul Aziz Ranteesi who started a hunger strike on Sunday 12.12.00. We request our people to display solidarity with him and pressure decision-makers to ensure his release along with other political detainees.

5. We ask our people to maintain visits to families of martyrs, detainees and wounded especially in this holy month.

6. The Movement asserts the importance of maintaining the boycott of Zionist and American goods and setting a certain mechanism to ensure continuation of this matter and abidance of all.

7.   We salute our brothers in Palestine occupied in 1948 and urge those who serve in the occupation army, which killed their families and brothers in all Palestine, to withdraw from this army and return to the embraces of their people who are struggling to get rid of that occupation. The Movement appreciates efforts by certain Druze figures in the Galilee towards that end and call for supporting them in a way that would enhance our national unity and cohesion in face of occupation.

8.   Hamas greets our heroic detainees in Zionist occupation prisons and vows never to forget them or be content until their release. On this occasion we hail our brothers the Mujahideen in Hizbullah and its secretary general Sheikh Hassan Nasrallah for his insistence on releasing all detainees and prisoners in the Zionist occupation prisons.

Second: on the Arab and Islamic levels:

1.   Hamas calls on the Arab and Islamic peoples to retain the state of solidarity with the Palestinian people in a way coping with continuation and escalation of the intifada.

2.   Hamas urges the Arab and Islamic peoples to extend more material and moral aid to our patient people to strengthen their determination and intifada.

3.   Hamas asks all Arab and Islamic peoples to pray on Lailatul Qadr and the last ten days of Ramadan for the victory of our people and defeat of our enemies the Zionists.

Third: activities:

Hamas calls on its members, supporters and all Palestinians to abide by the struggle and Jihad program issued by the national and Islamic committees and affirms importance of continuation of marches of rage especially following the Friday noon congregations and let the grounds turn into fire under the feet of the Zionist occupiers.

Allahu Akbar . . . victory to our Mujahid people

Allahu Akbar . . . wa Lillah Al-Hamd

The Islamic Resistance Movement
(Hamas—Palestine)
14 December 2000

10 December 2000

In the name of Allah the most Gracious the most Merciful

Here is the truth . . . let the world listen

We powerfully strike the enemy . . . and declare it in the opportune moment

Facts speak for themselves and events affirm our role and Jihad . . . we were not absent from the arena of events as liars claimed. We were always ready to perform our role . . . we struck the enemy on the land and at sea and penetrated all military and security blocks. We hoisted our guns and roamed every spot in our homeland but did not declare responsibility for many operations that we had launched since a new stage in our historic confrontation with the Zionist enemy had started that would lose that enemy its mind.

Within that new confrontation, we declare responsibility for the Rafah operation one month after it took place in addition to other heroic attacks but **we reserve the right of declaring responsibility for other operations at the opportune time.**

1.   The Rafah marine operation on Tuesday 7/11/00 in which **Mujahid hero Hamdy Arafat Ensio** was martyred when he blasted a boat loaded with **120 kilograms of TNT** in an Israeli "Dabur" navy vessel at sea destroying it completely and killing all on board. The enemy did not declare number of casualties or losses suffered in the operation.

2.   The heroic remote-controlled Khadera blast on 22/11/00 that led to the death of 21 Israelis and the injury of 65 others.

3.   The heroic Kfar Darum operation on 20/11/00, which was launched with the use of an explosive device similar to the one that martyred hero commander Awad Silmi.

4.   Constant firing operations in Rafah, Khan Younis, Beit Hanun and the West Bank.

We in the Qassam Brigades while bearing the glad tidings of the martyrdom of our hero **Hamdy Arafat Ensio** to the Arab and Islamic Nation and our stationed Palestinian people, we would like to affirm that there is no other road than that of Jihad and no other alternative than that of resistance. We would also like to affirm that we did not and would not give up Jihad and would not drop our arms despite persecutions and siege. The fall of one martyr after the other would not weaken us or stop our Jihad march or prevent our advance towards plucking the Zionist entity off our holy land.

We tell Barak and his panicked army, which we vanquished, that we never fear death as you do and we never love life as much as you do. We tell him that one day you will taste the bitterness of the Qassam swords; we will make you taste death, which you always flee from and teach you the horror that you dread. You will remember our might when you flee in front of our men's determination and when you get entangled in the mud of your blood that would be shed by Palestine freedom fighters and guardians of the Aqsa. In the coming few days you will see for yourself seriousness of our promises and threats.

Good for you the martyrdom Hamdy that you have always worked for and we pledge that we will remain loyal to you and to your brothers until we meet our fate.

Allahu Akbar and Lilallah Al-Hamad

And it is a Jihad (until) victory or martyrdom

The Qassam Brigades
10 December 2000

2 December 2000

In the name of Allah the most Gracious the most Merciful

The holy Aqsa intifada

An intifada to defeat occupation

Communiqué no. (16)

"And slacken not in following up the enemy: if ye are suffering
hardships, they are suffering similar hardships; but ye
have hope from Allah, while they have none . . ."

The holy Aqsa intifada in its third month

Growing force in face of Zionist occupation

Our stationed people:
Our Arab-Islamic Nation:

Months passed by and the blessed month of Ramadan again shone its lights carrying with it great meanings and concepts that form values of Islamic life. It is the month honored by Allah with the descent of the holy Quran in which the link between Heaven and Earth has been achieved through such heavenly constitution that lightened the way for humanity towards a life of virtue and safety.

Ramadan reminds the Ummah of the necessity of returning to its religion and Quran so as to bypass the stage of backwardness, ignorance and tragedies befalling it. Ramadan is a great opportunity to refuel Jihad into this Ummah and the Mujahideen in their continued civilization struggle with enemies of Allah and the Ummah: the Zionists who are spreading corruption on the land of Palestine and destroying human and greenery life. They are committing massacres, shelling houses and killing in cold-blood the brave Palestinians who are facing the Zionist war machine with bare chests that are full of belief and confidence in Allah's victory. Those Palestinians are insistent on continuing the blessed intifada until defeat of occupation, liberation of Al-Quds (Jerusalem) and return of our Palestinian people to the holy land of Palestine from which they were forcibly expelled and displaced in the four corners of the Earth.

Our Mujahid people:

With the advent of the month of victories and conquers and on the eve of the international day for solidarity with the Palestinian people, the holy Aqsa intifada enters its third consecutive month, more solid in confrontation with the Zionist enemy and its terrorist and repressive means. The intifada enters its third month while our patient people are suffering from tightened siege and more terrorism and liquidation of Mujahideen. They are also facing numerous forms of savagery such as destruction of installations and lands, uprooting of trees and blockage of roads. However, such a situation did not weaken the intifada or our people's determination and insistence on persisting along the road of Jihad and struggle and protecting the intifada from any deviations in its capacity as our Mujahid people's option. The intifada continued, despite escalation of Zionist terrorism, its normal development inflicting casualties and losses in lines of the occupation soldiers and settlers and spreading panic in the heart of the Zionist entity. We hail, in this respect, the heroic Khadera operation and all Jihad and armed operations that preceded and followed it.

Our proud people . . . our brave Ummah:

Your Mujahid Islamic Resistance Movement, Hamas, while vowing to go ahead along the road of intifada, resistance and Jihad, it salutes our people, Ummah and convoy of Mujahideen and fighters who stick to their guns and inflict losses in lines of the enemy. Hamas, meanwhile, affirms the following:

First: on the Palestinian level:

1. The Movement affirms the continuation of the holy Aqsa intifada and escalation of resistance against the enemy with all means. It urges the Mujahideen and fighters to direct more painful blows to the enemy and herds of settlers until defeat of occupation and liberation of Al-Quds and the whole of Palestine Insha'allah.

2. The Movement asserts that the cowardly assassination attempts perpetrated by the Zionist enemy among the victims of which were Qassam commander Ibrahim Bani Odeh, who is the holder of an honorable Jihad record in face of enemies to Allah and the Ummah, the five Hamas martyrs in Qalqilya and two strugglers from Fatah Movement along with other revolting Palestinians from various forces and Islamic and national forces would not weaken our determination, belief or solidity in face of the Zionist enemy. The assassinations open the door wide open for confronting and eliminating collaborators and traitors. We call on the Mujahideen and strugglers in addition to all our people to be careful of the enemy and its agents' attempts to unsettle the Palestinian arena via numerous and mean methods.

3. The Movement stresses the importance of preserving national unity and developing it on the basis of Jihad and resistance against the Zionist enemy in addition to protecting such unity in a way ensuring safety of the Palestinian arena and guaranteeing persistence of the blessed intifada. Here we would like to insist on the importance of releasing all our brothers the Mujahideen detained in jails of the Palestinian Authority for our people detest such detention, express its rejection of it and demand an end to that file.

4. The Movement confirms its rejection of returning to the option of negotiating with the enemy. Hamas considers that such an option reneges on our people's will represented in insistence on resistance and intifada and absolute rejection of the oppressive settlement option. Thus Hamas affirms that our people would not accept all tabled initiatives and all secret and open meetings with the enemy, which displays yearning to Oslo and its hateful results.

5. The Movement emphasizes its support to our people who are the target of constant savage shelling in Nablus, Beit Jala, Beit Sahur, Khaleel, Khan Younis and Rafah and calls on the Arab and Islamic Nation to actively move to end such destruction that daily targets our people.

6. The Movement underlines in this holy month the importance of the spirit of fraternity and cohesion among our people in addition to intensifying visits to families of martyrs and wounded and backing workers and others who are harmed by the Zionist policy of terrorism and siege.

Second: on the Arab-Islamic level:

1. Hamas asks the Arab and Islamic Nation to be more active and supportive of our people's brave intifada. The Arab and Islamic peoples should back our people who are facing a war of annihilation in all spheres of life.

2. The Movement greets the Ummah's Ulama for their calls to activate the Arab and Islamic streets especially on Fridays in the holy month of Ramadan in support of their brothers in Palestine. The Movement also appreciates the Fatwa (edict) passed by the Mufti of Egypt and Sheikh (Rector) of Azhar calling on the Ummah to boycott American and Israeli goods. It also appreciates the Fatwa passed by the Kuwaiti house of Fatwa allocating Zakat this year to Jihad and intifada in Palestine. It also appreciates Fatawa (edicts) and courageous stands of Sheikh Yousef Al-Qaradawi in support of Palestinian rights.

3. The Movement urges the Arab countries that hold periodical meetings attended by the Palestinian party not to discuss means of returning to the absurd negotiations, which our people and Ummah had rejected and bypassed through convoys of martyrs and wounded. The Movement affirms the importance of discussing means of supporting and developing the intifada in addition to providing all forms of backing to our people who decided to continue resistance against that arrogant enemy.

Third: the activities:

The Movement seconds all activities called for by the national and Islamic forces in all areas and calls for:

- Considering Fridays in the holy month of Ramadan as days of rage and confrontations against occupation soldiers and herds of settlers.

- Advocates stationing in the Aqsa Mosque, offering prayers in it and hails all those who offered Friday prayers in Al-Quds streets and paths after the Zionists barred their prayers in the blessed Aqsa Mosque.

- The Movement requests intensification of visits to families of martyrs and wounded, consoling them and alleviating their sufferings.

It is a Jihad until victory or martyrdom

Allahu Akbar and Lillah Al-Hamad

The Islamic Resistance Movement
(Hamas—Palestine)
2 December 2000

27 November 2000

In the name of Allah the most Gracious the most Merciful

**The month of Ramadan . . . the month of seeking
Ta'at and closeness to Allah through
Jihad and escalation of resistance**

*"Ramadan is the (month) in which was sent down the Quran,
as a guide to mankind, also Clear (Signs) for guidance and
judgment (between right and wrong . . ." (Quran 2/185)*

The advent of the month of Ramadan has bought with it blessings and tidings breezing anew the spirit of Jihad through remembering past historical memories of great victories of our forefathers in that blessed month during which they recorded heroic epics that changed history and that are still breathing spirit in our Nation hopefully inspiring it to restore lost honor and past glory.

Ramadan this year befalls us while the Nation is witnessing great events taking place on our holy land in which our people trigger anew the Jihad torch irrigating it with blood and remains of martyrs. The events have united our Nation along the road of Jihad and martyrdom to liberate its first Qibla and site of its prophet's Isra'.

Our heroic Palestinian people . . . here you are initiating the month of Jihad and patience with more martyrs and sacrifices, patiently hoping for reward from Allah, here you are teaching the world with your pride and dignity that you are a people who will never die and will not kneel or surrender before their tormentors regardless of plots or treachery. You tell the world that your determination and readiness for death for the sake of Allah breath life into this Nation and restore hopes anew in Allah's promise and victory.

Our Palestinian people . . . a great month has begun so decorate it with your Jihad for the enemies of Allah, the damned Jews, are terrified of its advent. One of their criminals and senior leaders said, "The approach of the month of Ramadan so quickly (this year) is a very serious thing and necessitates exerting big efforts to prevent escalation of the intifada". Another criminal said, "The Barak government should do all what it could to stop the intifada as soon as possible before the Palestinians seek close-ness to Allah through their and our blood in Ramadan!" So disappoint them and persist in your blessed Jihad march and be sure that thus you would be glorified and honored besides receiving double reward from Allah. Hear our dear brothers, who love death as your enemies love life and who yearn for making even with grandsons of monkeys and pigs that desecrated our sanctities, shed our blood and usurped our holy land, hear the glad tidings of prophet Mohammed, peace be upon him, "The stationing for one hour for the sake of Allah is better than praying Qiyam (late night prayers) of Lailatul Qadr at Al-Hajar Al-Aswad (the black stone in the holy Kaaba)". Hear dear brothers, who are confronting enemies in Beitul Maqdes (Jerusalem) and its surroundings at this month where rewards are doubled, hear the glad tidings of prophet Mohammed, peace be upon him, "Lining for one hour in a battle for the sake of Allah is better than praying Qiyam (late night prayers) for sixty nights". Hear dear brothers, who are guard-ing our Aqsa Mosque with bare chests and offering for its sake convoys of martyrs regardless of enemies' schemes and who guard the land of blessed Palestine, hear the glad tidings of prophet Mohammed, peace be upon him, "Shall I tell you about a night that is better than Lailatul Qadr? A sentry who stands on guard in a land of fear, (for) maybe he would not go back to his family."

Our patient people in Palestine congratulations on the advent of the month of Ramadan, and let it be a distinctive month in escalating intifada activities and targeting criminal Jews in all areas of Palestine. And we, in the Islamic Resistance Movement, Hamas, would like to affirm the following:

1. Let next Friday be a day of rage and escalation of resistance against the occupiers . . . and a day of solidarity on the part of Arab and Islamic peoples through marches and activities.

2. We Urge our people to spend more time on worship of Allah through praying at night, reciting holy Quran, organizing group breakfasting, lectures and seminars in mosques and seeking closeness to Allah through fighting Jews and inflicting severe casualties in their lines.

3. We call on our people to head to the Aqsa Mosque, break the military siege around it and offer night prayers there especially on Fridays.

4. We appeal to the rich people to pay their Zakat (alms), to cater for their brothers and to act as one body in face of the enemy's oppressive measures and savage siege.

5. We ask our people to pay special visits to families of martyrs and detainees and to call on the wounded.

Our Arab-Islamic Nation . . . the Islamic Resistance Movement, Hamas, seizes the occasion on the start of the holy month of Ramadan to congratulate the Arab and Islamic peoples and call on them to stick to the meanings of Jihad as crystallized in that great month. We urge them to shoulder their duty towards their stationed brothers on the land of Palestine and unite in their backing with money, arms, Duaa and political stands that reject halting the intifada or returning to negotiations with the enemy. We also ask them to endorse boycotting the Zionist entity and its supportive countries in words and deeds and to start preparing themselves for the coming day of confrontation with that entity. Let the month of Ramadan be the start of spreading public awareness among those peoples on the compulsory duty of Jihad for the sake of liberating Palestine. Let the television and space channels refrain from presenting disgraceful programs that weaken the Nation and distract youths from their fateful issues.

The month of Ramadan is one of generosity and the best of Sadakat (alms) is that given during that month, so let it be for the Mujahideen stationed on the land of Palestine and let worshippers in all mosques pray for the shackled Aqsa Mosque and for the Mujahideen seeking its liberation.

Finally, let all those who extend their hands to the criminal Jews and continue open and secret contacts with them for the sake of terminating our people's intifada, let them know that Allah will foil their work and that our people will never forgive them. Our people will remain an angry volcano ejecting lava over heads of the usurpers depending on the one and only Almighty Allah.

"Allah has promised, to those among you who believe and work righteous deeds, that He will, of a surety, grant them in the land, inheritance (of power), as He granted it to those before them; that He will establish in authority their religion, the one which He has chosen for them; and that He will change (their state), after the fear in which they (lived), to one of security and peace: 'They will worship Me (alone) and not associate aught with Me.' If any do reject Faith after this, they are rebellious and wicked." (Quran 24/55)

The Islamic Resistance Movement
(Hamas—Palestine)
27 November 2000

21 November 2000

In the name of Allah the most Gracious the most Merciful

The holy Aqsa intifada

Communiqué no. (15)

The intifada will persist until end of occupation

"Be sure We shall test you with something of fear and hunger, some loss in goods or lives or the fruits (of your toil), but give glad tidings to those who patiently persevere."

In face of the growing Zionist offensive against our heroic people and criminal Barak unveils a new criminal plan to quell the blessed intifada and at the time when savage shelling with planes and navy vessels targets our stationed people in Gaza Strip, our people display more determination to confront such barbaric attacks. Such aggressions would not deter our people from continuing their intifada and struggle regardless of sacrifice and from going ahead with strikes and daring operations against occupation wherever it was. Here they are the people's Islamic and national forces decide to persist in the holy Aqsa intifada and not to accept any other alternative to freedom and independence after defeating occupation and ending its presence on our blessed Palestinian land. Thousand salutations to the hands that grabbed triggers and directed bullets at the criminal occupiers. Greetings to the stone throwers, to the patient mothers of martyrs and their relatives, to the wounded, to the brave detainees behind bars and their patient families, to the workers, merchants and farmers, to each and every child, aged, woman and young man of our stationed people.

Our Mujahid Palestinian people:

We, in the Islamic Resistance Movement, Hamas, have vowed not to accept any alternative to that of resistance until our people's aspirations in freedom, defeating occupation and ending its presence in our holy lands are actualized. We are convinced in Allah's victory to our people despite all attempts to foil their heroic intifada. Our Palestinian people have known the way and hoisted the gun, which no one could ever break or quell its fire. No one could confiscate stones of our revolting children in face of Zionist occupiers. This is our people's option after the fake peace was exposed and dropped once and for all, God willing. Our people have affirmed their cohesion and unity in support of the resistance option until victory is achieved and occupation is flushed out.

Our stationed Palestinian people . . . our Arab and Islamic Nation:

To achieve our hopes in defeating occupation, liberation and return, the Islamic Resistance Movement would like to affirm the following:

First: on the Palestinian level:

1. Hamas calls on our Palestinian people to holy Aqsa intifada to cope with the new challenges imposed by the arrogant occupier. We urge them to improvise new painful blows to the enemy that would spread panic in lines of its soldiers and settlers.
2. Hamas requests our people not to heed calls for calming the blessed intifada or even insinuating such an inclination. We also ask them to strongly resist rumors trying to weaken, besmear or divert the intifada from its course.
3. The Hamas Movement hails the martyr hero Baha'uldin Sa'eed from the Maghazi refugee camp who launched the heroic operation in the

Kfar Darum settlement, which led to the death of two soldiers and the injury of others. We also salute those who planned the bus explosion yesterday.

4. Hamas asks the heroic Palestinian people to display more solidarity and cooperation. The Movement renews calls for forming popular committees that would look after people's needs and calls for adapting to that distinctive Jihad atmosphere.

5. The Movement affirms the importance of boycotting all Zionist and American goods and resorting instead to national products.

6. Hamas greets the worshippers in the streets of Al-Quds (Jerusalem) and around its walls, who are prevented by occupation authorities from offering prayers in the holy Aqsa Mosque and who affirm Islamism and Arabism of Al-Quds.

7. We urge our generous merchants and cherished doctors to support our people who are besieged in the old quarters of Al-Khaleel (Hebron) and who are living under siege and curfew for the past 40 days.

Second: on the Arab-Islamic level:

1. The Islamic Resistance Movement, Hamas, hails the Islamic resistance heroes in Hizbullah who have launched the heroic Aqsa martyrs operation in the occupied Lebanese area of Shibaa and condemns UN secretary general's biased statements in favor of the Zionist enemy.

2. Hamas calls on our Arab and Islamic masses to escalate activities in support of the holy Aqsa intifada and in support of the Palestinian people's Jihad through organizing demonstrations, marches, rallies, sit-ins, conferences and panels in backing or our people and rights.

3. Hamas appreciates calls by leaders, Ulama (Islamic scholars) and supporters of Islamic Movements along with all national and nationalist forces in the Arab and Islamic arenas for ending all forms of normalization with the usurping Zionist enemy and for boycotting Zionist and American goods. We also ask them to form anti-normalization committees and other committees in support of the intifada.

4. Hamas demands the immediate interference of the international community and human rights institutions to break the siege and lift the curfew imposed on Al-Khaleel for more than 40 days.

Third: the activities:

1. The Islamic Resistance Movement, Hamas, affirms the importance of abiding by activities called for by all Islamic and national committee in all districts of the country.

2. Hamas urges our Mujahid Palestinian people to turn the grounds into burning fires under the feet of the occupiers especially on Friday.

Finally we call on our Palestinian people, while the holy month of Ramadan is approaching . . . the month of Quran, the month of Jihad, victory, patience and repentance, we call on them to get closer to Allah through the Ta'at (obeying His orders), fasting and asking for His forgiveness, for victory comes with patience and with every difficulty there is relief.

Allahu Akbar and all praises to Allah

Allahu Akbar and victory to our Mujahid people

The Islamic Resistance Movement
(Hamas—Palestine)
21 November 2000

12 November 2000

In the name of Allah the most Gracious the most Merciful

An appeal from Sheikh Ahmed Yassin founder of the Islamic Resistance Movement, Hamas, to leaders and peoples of the Arab and Islamic Nation on the occasion of holding the Islamic summit conference in Doha

"An appeal for backing the people of Palestine"

"How should ye not fight for the cause of Allah and of the feeble among men and of the women and the children who are crying: Our Lord! Bring us forth from out this town of which the people are oppressors! Oh, give us from Thy presence some protecting friend! Oh, give us from Thy presence some defender!" (Quran 4/75)

Our Arab, Islamic Nation . . . Our brothers in religion and creed

From the holy land of Palestine, from Beit Al-Makdes and the precincts of Beit Al-Makdes, from the arena of Jihad, resistance and blessed Intifadha, from the heart of the bleeding wounds and ruins, from the screams of orphans, widows and bereaved mothers, from the midst of the continuous columns of martyrs, I send you, our Nation, an appeal to back the people of Palestine. The people of Palestine who are stationed on the cherished land of Palestine, the Mujahid for the sake of liberating it from Jewish usurpers and the defender of the Nation's dignity and sanctities topped by the first Islamic Qibla, third holiest shrine in Islam and Isra' site of prophet Mohammed, peace be upon him.

We call on you our people and brothers on behalf of the children of Palestine who are facing the enemy with their bare chests. We appeal to you in the name of the mothers and wives of martyrs who rejoice each time a martyr is raised up to the heavens. We appeal to you in the name of the wounded who were mercilessly targeted by enemy helicopter gunships, tanks and gunboats. We appeal to you when everything in Palestine has turned into a target for the enemy's fire whether civilians, houses, installations, streets, trees, mosques and places of worship. Everything has been the target of Jewish savagery, terrorism and aggression. The martyrs have exceeded 200 persons, the wounded surpassed 7,000 persons while thousands of culti- vated lands and trees were uprooted, hundreds of houses demolished, insti- tutions paralyzed and the people besieged from all directions.

Day and night your brothers in Palestine are liable to shelling, threatening choppers and settlers' sniper fire. What is going on in Palestine is a war of liquidation and annihilation. A liquidation of Al-Quds (Jerusalem) and the Aqsa, a liquidation of the people and their fighting youth generation and even a liquidation of the whole Palestine cause. Your brothers' blood is cheap in the eyes of the Jews, killers of prophets, and each day your broth- ers walk in funeral processions and receive more wounded and disabled per- sons. Such terrorism did not single out any Palestinian including your brothers stationed in the Palestinian lands occupied in 1948.

Our brothers everywhere . . .

Your brothers and sisters in Palestine face death each and every moment . . . the columns of martyrs do not stop . . . the roaring sounds of guns do not calm down and all bombard your flesh and blood. Fires break out and bod- ies dismembered as a result of the pouring missiles that assassinate our peo- ple in broad daylight.

We wonder how long will such a situation persist? How long will silence continue vis-à-vis such premeditated killing of a whole people? How long will we be content with condemnation statements that do not help in face of liquidating Al-Quds and the Aqsa Mosque in addition to offending all human values and norms? If we wait until America "bestows" on us a fact-finding committee or international protection or restoration of the settlement framework that drowned in our people's blood then the Zionist danger will spread into other areas of Arab and Islamic lands.

Leaders and peoples of the Nation . . .

What you view on TV, despite the horrific scenes, is much less than what is really taking place. Your brothers are besieged in lands and pockets without having arms to defend themselves or to ward off death that is targeting their families and children. If the conscience of the oppressed world had died, then the Arab and Islamic conscience should wake up from its long nap . . . why don't you support your brothers here with arms, money and supplies? Why don't you open the door for Jihad before the Mujahdieen brigades in backing of the people of Palestine and in defense of the Aqsa and the holy shrines and to halt the ongoing carnage? The people of Palestine beseech you and appeals to you, after praying to almighty Allah, for the mothers' screams had reached the farthest point on Earth and Allah had obliged you to extend support *". . . but if they seek help from you in the matter of religion then it is your duty to help (them) . . ."* (Quran 8/72)

The Islamic summit conference currently convening in Qatar is called upon to launch an effective act to save Palestine, its people and Quds in addition to boycotting the enemy and draining its source of arrogance on the lands of Islam and Muslims.

The wound is deep and the hearts are bleeding. No fine-worded statements would be enough, for the time now is for serious and fruitful work for the sake of liberating Palestine and its people and lifting the oppression on them **through the use of force for whatever was taken by force would be only regained by force.**

From the heart of the holy Aqsa Intifadha we hail this Nation, which reacted from the ocean to the ocean, to reflect its backing to the people of Palestine. Such reactions proved that the question of Al-Quds was not solely a Palestinian question but also an Arab and Islamic one. So more support is needed along with protection means to our people for the situation is extremely grave and Al-Quds is in serious danger.

We affirm to you, Muslims everywhere, that we will continue along the road of Jihad and we will not be terrorized by the enemy's might or suppression for its might, God willing, is dying out and its suppression will lose in the end. And we will remain sticking to the land of Palestine from the sea to the river and we will proceed in unity under the banner of Haq (Right) along the road of Jihad and resistance until victory or martyrdom.

"Your Ummah is nothing but one and I am your Lord so worship me."

Allaho Akbar and all praises are to Allah

Your brother Sheikh Ahmed Yassin
Founder of the Islamic Resistance Movement-Hamas
12 November 2000

9 November 2000

In the name of Allah the most Gracious the most Merciful

The Holy Aqsa Intifadha
An Intifadha to defeat occupation
Communiqué no. 14

The Intifadha will persist until Al-Quds is liberated
The Jewish usurpers are enemies to humanity . . .
They are beasts in humanly form

The footage of the child Mohammed Al-Durra was not the first of its kind and will not be the last to expose the degree of hatred and savagery, which the Jewish usurpers harbinger against our people, for such images recur daily at the hands of the enemy soldiers and herds of malicious settlers. We witnessed the child Ahmed Al-Khafsh martyred after a spiteful settler intentionally hit the boy with his car then pursued him to ensure his death. We also witnessed the Jerusalemite young girl Shifa' Al-Hindi losing her eyesight after the enemy soldiers beat her with their rifle butts for refusing to take off her veil. We witnessed the 23 days old infant suffocating from the occupation teargas in Khaleel (Hebron). There are a lot other atrocities against our people and holy shrines for many mosques were shelled, holy books torn and anti-Islamic and anti-prophet statements were written on the walls. The Zionist massacres are ongoing including the bombing of civilian houses with tanks and armored vehicles as martyrs and wounded continue to fall under the very eyes of the whole world, which stands idle by because the victims are Palestinians but the situation would be completely different if occupation soldiers or settlers are touched or captured.

Our Palestinian people . . . our Arab, Islamic Nation . . . we in the Islamic Resistance Movement, Hamas, would like to affirm the following:

First: on the Palestinian level:

1. We call on our Mujahid people to continue the holy Aqsa Intifadha and to escalate their revolt turning it into fire eating up the occupiers. We also ask them not to heed any call for tranquility or an end to the uprising under any pretext. We affirm that this Intifadha is an Intifadha to defeat occupation and not to return to the negotiations option or to improve negotiating conditions. The settlement process, which some of our people are still insisting on, has turned into a dead body and whoever attempts to reinvigorate it would be only deceiving himself and would be only met with a mirage.

2. The meeting that is to take place in Washington with the US president Clinton is nothing but a fresh attempt by the US and the Zionist entity to halt and abort the Intifadha. It will end up in failure similar to the Sharm Al-Sheikh and other open and secret meetings because all those meetings do not cope with our people's aspirations and do not achieve any of their goals. Our people only expect evil from such meetings where the US and the Zionist entity attempt to conspire on blood of martyrs and the Aqsa Intifadha, which will nonetheless persist and no-one will be able to stop it.

3. We urge our people in Nablus to break the siege and curfew imposed on the town of Hawwara for more than 35 days. We ask them to organize a solidarity campaign under the title of "Let the curfew on Hawwara be lifted".

4. We appeal to our brothers in the Fatah Movement to stick to the Intifadha option and not to abide by any directives aimed at ending

the Intifadha or resistance. The Intifadha and resistance unite our people while the negotiations and concessions divide them.

5. We advise our people to be careful of attempts by certain elements to smuggle Zionists goods, especially the rotten ones, into the Palestinian markets benefiting from the prevailing difficult conditions and the exhaustion of foodstuffs and other supplies. Those goods are hazardous to the health of our offsprings.

6. Our people, with all its forces and factions, denounce the Palestinian Authority's insistence to ignore all popular calls and appeals to close down the political detention file and to free all political detainees and Mujahideen. Scores of them are still thrown in PA jails especially in the West Bank. Closure of that file will remain an urgent request for our people in addition to being the first step towards crystallizing national unity.

7. We beseech our people to stand alongside the workers who lost their jobs as a result of the siege. Many of them do not find what to eat or what to feed their children. Let us all stand by them as people, individuals and popular institutions, so that the worker would not alone pay the price of the Intifadha. Let us form voluntary popular committees in each city to cater for the workers and support them.

Second: on the Arab and Islamic levels:

1. We urge the Islamic summit to back our people and support the holy Aqsa Mosque. We call on the conference to be in harmony with stands of the Islamic peoples who demand suspending all forms of relations and normalization with the Zionist enemy, opening the door for Jihad to liberate Al-Quds (Jerusalem) and the sanctities and to prepare the Nation for that day. We call on the summiteers to support struggle in Palestine, recognize its legitimacy, supply it with money and arms, pressure the US to end its unlimited support of Zionist aggression and employ the Arab and Islamic oil weapon in the battle.

2. We appeal to the Arab and Islamic peoples in addition to parties, syndicates and popular bodies everywhere to organize marches and angry protest activities. The wonderful reaction at the first weeks of the Intifadha addressed a clear message to the whole world namely that our Arab and Islamic peoples would not remain hands folded in face of the persisting Zionist bloodbaths. In view of the continuation and

escalation of Zionist aggression, we call for activating popular moves by displaying rage towards such a situation and expressing solidarity with our people and the Aqsa.

3. We urge the Arab and Islamic people to boycott Zionist and American goods in retaliation to the occupation's crimes and the US attempt to conceal them.

Third: the activities: (We affirm the activities included in the national, Islamic follow up committees in various districts in our country) and call on our people's masses to organize the following:

1. Today Thursday 9/11 should witness marches during which photos of martyrs and Palestinian flags decorated with "There is no God but Allah and Mohammed is His Messenger" are hoisted on the anniversary of the passing of more than 40 days on the fall of our first group of martyrs.

2. Tomorrow Friday 10/11, and on each Friday, should be a day of popular rage and massive marches starting from mosques following the Friday noon congregation. There should be heroic confrontations with the enemy soldiers and herds of settlers to affirm continuation of the Intifadha and our people's insistence on Al-Quds and holy shrines in addition to rejecting attempts to abort the Intifadha.

3. Sunday 12/12 should be a day of distinctive escalation, massive demonstrations and confrontations on the inauguration of the Islamic summit to ask the summit to support our people and to resist the Zionist aggression.

4. There should be continuous visits to families of martyrs and wounded to check their conditions and express our people's solidarity with them.

Let the holy Aqsa Intifadha continue . . . an Intifadha to defeat occupation

Allaho Akbar . . . and victory to our people

The Islamic Resistance Movement
(Hamas - Palestine)
9 November 2000

2 November 2000

In the name of Allah the most Gracious the most Merciful

The holy Aqsa Intifadha
The Intifadha to defeat occupation
Communiqué number (13)

Whatever was taken by force would be only regained by force

Our Mujahid Palestinian people are still facing with their bare chests the enemy's missiles and tanks without fearing death or terrorism and offering one martyr after the other as a price for liberation of the Aqsa and Palestine and in defense of the Arab and Islamic Nation's dignity. So more patience and more steadfastness, challenge and pride are required from you: the people of martyrs and sacrifice. Do not heed any calls for halting or aborting your blessed Intifadha and let us continue along the road of Jihad and struggle for whatever was taken by force would be only regained by force. Such a great slogan was the motto under which the child Mohammed Al-Durra has martyred. Thousands greetings are accorded to heroes of the daring operations in Gaza and Al-Quds (Jerusalem) and to more such resistance by our Mujahideen.

Our Palestinian people . . . our Arab, Islamic Nation . . . we in the Islamic Resistance Movement, Hamas, would like to affirm the following:

First: on the Palestinian level:

1. We call on our people's heroes and Mujahideen to chase and target enemy soldiers and herds of settlers and let the daring armed operations escalate using all forms of resistance. Let the throwing youths continue their all-out civilian damage of all enemy interests. Let the ground turn into fire burning the occupiers.

2. We appeal to our people to head in big numbers to the Aqsa Mosque, to pray all five prayers there and to guard it for that would be considered Ribat (stationing) for the cause of Allah.

3. The holy Aqsa Intifadha is an Intifadha to defeat occupation and the blood of martyrs and wounded that was spilt targeted defending the Aqsa and the holy shrines in addition to defeating occupation. Our people will never accept that their sufferings and that blood of their martyrs would be the price for returning to negotiations or just to improve conditions of negotiations. We affirm our absolute rejection of all meetings between the Palestinian Authority and leadership of the criminal enemy the latest of which was Arafat's meeting with the terrorist and mass-murderer of the Qana massacre Peres for the enemy's crimes had proven that there was no way for coexistence between the victim and the culprit.

4. We along with our people criticize statements of Mahmoud Abbas, a PA official, to Al-Shark Al-Awsat newspaper on 31 October in which he said "The Intifadha does not achieve victory and it is of no use." . . . "We do not want to fight Israel for our option is negotiations and we want calm to return gradually" . . . "What happened at the Cairo summit is a great thing and we did not expect more than what happened."

5. We urge the PA anew to close the political detention file and to release the remaining political detainees and Mujahideen in its jails. It is not logical that enemy missiles shell our villages and cities while the PA is still detaining the honorable Mujahideen. It is high time to tear apart security agreements with the enemy and end the PA's abidance by them.

6. We are surprised at the PA's decision to limit training on use of arms to the Fatah elements and limiting carrying arms only to them since such a right should be open to all our people.

7. We affirm the request of the nationalist and Islamic forces to the armed men not to fire bullets in the marches among the demonstrators and amidst residential quarters, which leads to inflicting severe losses in lines of our people as a result of Zionist retaliatory aggressions. We urge the armed brothers to chase and target the enemy away from such places.

8. We appeal to our people to express solidarity with cities and villages besieged by the enemy forces. We ask them to extend what they can including foodstuff to enhance steadfastness of the besieged and to organize popular programs to break that siege.

9.   We urge our people to support the workers who became unemployed as a result of that siege considering their backing as a religious and nationalist duty. The institutions that receive donations should perform their role in compensating the workers so as to boost our people's steadfastness.

Second: on the Arab, Islamic level:

1.   We salute our Arab, Islamic Nation that strongly backed our people's Intifadha and we greet the Arab and Islamic communities especially the Islamic community in the US. We request their continued activities and programs in support of our people and the Aqsa. We ask them to firmly oppose the savage Jewish massacres against our children and our unarmed people. We demand a continuous, long-range program for our battle with the enemy is a lengthy one and the Zionist terrorism and aggression are escalating. Furthermore, the Aqsa Intifadha is ongoing and martyrs are falling daily.

2.   We call on the Arab and Islamic leaders, who will meet in the upcoming Islamic summit conference in Doha, to adopt vigorous stands to back our people's resoluteness, to confront the Zionist aggression and to end all forms of relations and normalization with that enemy. We also urge sisterly Qatar to close down the Zionist trade representation office and we call on both Egypt and Jordan to close the enemy's embassies and expel its ambassadors. We demand from the Nation's leaders to prepare their peoples for Jihad for the sake of liberating the land of Isra' wal Mi'rage. We also ask the Arab and Islamic countries to condemn the stands of the US government and congress, which are blatantly biased in favor of the Zionist aggression.

3.   We beseech the Nation's Ulama (religious scholars) and intellectuals to pursue along their pioneering role, which they started in support of the Aqsa and in encouraging the masses to do the same thing.

4.   We appreciate the brothers in Saudi Arabia and Kuwait for their financial donation to our people and the Intifadha and call on all countries to offer more to boost our people's steadfastness. We stress, meanwhile, that they should ensure that the funds are channeled to families of martyrs and wounded in addition to supporting the Intifadha and defending Al-Quds and the Aqsa.

5. We urge our Nation to donate blood to save the wounded who fall in large numbers each day.

6. We implore the Arab and Islamic peoples to boycott American goods and any party or company dealing with the Zionist enemy. Parties and popular organizations in each country should prepare a "blacklist" including names of companies and persons dealing with the enemy.

Third: the activities:

(We second the activities called for by the Islamic-Nationalist follow up commitee) and call on our people to launch the following activities:

1. Today Thursday 2/11 should be a day of escalation in all areas on the occasion of the anniversary of the ill-famed Balfour Declaration.

2. Tomorrow Friday 3/11 and all coming Fridays should be days of rage and tumultuous demonstrations that would follow Friday noon congregations. They should witness distinctive escalations and confrontations against the enemy's army and settlers.

3. Let Palestinian flags decorated by "There is no God but Allah and Mohammed is His Messenger" be hoisted over the Aqsa Mosque and the honored Dome of the Rock. Let a hero raise such flags each time the enemy soldiers bring them down to affirm our people and Nation's sovereignty over the holy Aqsa Mosque. Let such flags be raised extensively in all marches.

4. Female demonstrations should be organized on Thursday 9/11 with mothers of martyrs and wounded at the forefront to affirm that our people would continue the Intifadha until defeat of occupation.

**Let the holy Aqsa Intifadha continue . . . the
Intifadha to defeat occupation**

Allahu Akbar . . . and victory to our people

**The Islamic Resistance Movement
(Hamas—Palestine)
2 November 2000**

31 October 2000

In the name of Allah the most Gracious the most Merciful

More escalation, confrontations and days of rage

Our people's retaliation to the Zionist aggression

As the blessed Aqsa Intifadha enters its second month, Zionist aggression and terrorism escalated and the enemy's army crimes continued including shelling our unarmed people with tanks, helicopter gunships and missiles. The heavily armed herds of settlers intensified their acts of revenge and murder against our people while the fall of martyrs and wounded continued along the road of Jihad, resistance and steadfastness in defense of the Aqsa, Al-Quds and each and every inch of our holy land.

Thousand greetings to our people's heroes . . . men and youths . . . women and children for their heroic steadfastness and strong challenge to the enemy's army and aggression. We vow to the blood of martyrs and wounded to continue along our path and Jihad until our people's goals are realized in driving the occupation away from our lands and holy shrines.

At the time when the Zionist aggressive savagery continues, we in the Islamic Resistance Movement, Hamas, affirm the following:

1. We call on our Palestinian masses and all Islamic and nationalist forces to forge more cohesion and unity along the road of continuation of the Aqsa Intifadha, to escalate struggle and confrontation against the enemy's army and herds of settlers. We call on them not to heed any pressures or attempts to calm down or halt the Intifadha until its goals of expelling the occupiers are achieved. **We also call on our people to retaliate to the Zionist aggression and terrorism through more escalation, confrontations and days of rage.**

2. We urge all our people, heroes and Mujahideen to chase and target enemy soldiers and settlers in all areas of our occupied Palestinian lands: in Al-Quds (Jerusalem), the West Bank, Gaza Strip and our lands occupied in 1948. Surprise the enemy with your operations and brave resistance with arms, knives, Molotov cocktails and all available resistance tools and forms. We extend our salutation to the heroes who launched the heroic operation in Al-Quds and the martyrdom operation in Gaza.

3. We appreciate the Arab countries that responded to our calls and our people's requests for solidarity with the Aqsa Intifadha and severed relations with the criminal enemy. Meanwhile, we appeal to the other countries, which are still establishing relations with the enemy of our people and Nation and allowing its embassies and representation offices to continue functioning, to immediately sever those relations in retaliation to the enemy's crimes and continued massacres against our families and children and in solidarity with the blessed Aqsa Intifadha.

4. We salute our Arab and Islamic masses that are still reacting in solidarity with our people and that are still organizing programs in support of the Aqsa and in condemnation of the Zionist aggression. We call on those masses and all Arab and Islamic peoples topped by the movements, forces, parties, syndicates, popular and trade unions and students' councils to continue their activities and solidarity with our people in the lengthy and hard battle against the Zionist aggression and occupation. We also appeal to the Arab and Islamic media to continue exposing the Zionist aggression and highlighting our people's sufferings, steadfastness and Jihad. For the battle is ongoing . . . the Intifadha is persisting . . . the Zionist repression and aggression is escalating . . . and the martyrs and wounded are still falling.

The Islamic Resistance Movement
(Hamas—Palestine)
31 October 2000

26 October 2000

In the name of Allah the most Gracious the most Merciful
The holy Aqsa Intifadha
Communiqué no. (12)

The Intifadha will persist . . .
The enemy's missiles and tanks do not terrorize our people

Our Mujahid Palestinian people:
Our Arab and Islamic Nation:

These are the days of Jihad, struggle and steadfastness . . . the days of dignity . . . the days of martyrs and martyrdom . . . the days of Palestinian, Arab and Islamic rage against Zionist aggression and occupation . . . the days of live Arab and Islamic people who assert each and every day that Palestine is the whole Nation's cause and that the Aqsa is a trust on shoulders of all world Muslims who are yearning for Jihad for the sake of its liberation from usurpers' dirt.

The savage Zionist aggression is continuing against our people, the missiles and tanks are shelling our cities and villages every day. Our people face such aggression with relentless steadfastness and insistence on persisting along the road to its final end regardless of obstacles and sacrifices at a time when the Arab summit ended up in resolutions that did not live up to our people and Nation's requests, with due appreciation to the stands of some countries and the Saudi brothers' support to the establishment of two funds in support of Al-Quds (Jerusalem), the Aqsa and families of martyrs and wounded.

The Palestinian Authority returns to security meetings with the Zionist occupiers even before the blood of martyrs dry amidst our people's anger and dismay towards such a step.

Our Palestinian people . . . our Arab and Islamic Nation . . . we, in the Islamic Resistance Movement, Hamas, would like to affirm the following:

First: on the Palestinian level:

1. We affirm persistence of the holy Aqsa Intifadha and its escalation with all possible means for the sake of defeating occupation, protecting Al-Quds and the Aqsa and grabbing our people's stable rights.

2. The siege and curfew imposed by the criminal enemy's forces are still in force for the 28th consecutive day on more than 50,000 of our heroic people in the brave city of Al-Khaleel (Hebron). Thousands of greetings to those heroes and thousands of salutations to our people in that city and the surrounding villages and towns who sent food and other supplies to the besieged. We urge our people to continue supporting the besieged, to organize rallies in solidarity with them and to work for breaking the siege.

3. We hail our steadfast people in all cities, villages and refugee camps who challenged the bombardment and terrorism of the enemy's army

and challenged its herds of armed settlers, thus affirming to the world that our Mujahid people do not fear missiles or tanks.

4. We urge our people to maintain cooperation and to support families of the martyrs and wounded, meet their needs and check their conditions. We also urge them to inspect conditions of families of workers who were forced to stop working due to the enemy's siege against our people. We beseech the rich among our people to donate with money for the assistance extended from other peoples abroad is not enough to meet the Intifadha's requirements and repercussions.

5. We assert unity of our people including all forces and trends in confrontation with the Zionist enemy and in all Intifadha activities. We ask the PA to release all detainees in its jails immediately. It is not logical that those detainees would remain behind bars in accordance with the Authority's security commitments to the enemy at a time when that enemy was bombing our people with missles and suspending the humiliating settlement accords.

6. We denounce the PA's security meetings with Zionist security officers in the West Bank and the Gaza Strip under patronage and supervision of CIA security officers with the aim of aborting the Intifadha. We affirm that our people viewed such meetings with absolute dismay for bypassing blood of martyrs and wounded and ignoring our people's will and stands.

7. We call on the PA chairman to refuse meeting with Clinton since such a meeting and its predecessors in Paris and Sharm Al-Sheikh targeted implementing American and the Jews' demands of aborting the Aqsa Intifadha and returning to security coordination with the enemy in addition to luring the PA into accepting Barak's dictates and conditions.

8. Hamas Movement's keenness on national unity made it forget about the Fatah Movement's elements recent step in Nablus when they pointed their guns at a Hamas leader during one of the marches. However, we demand the Fatah Movement to condemn such an act and punish those responsible.

9. We appeal to our people to indulge in volunteer work and help farmers in harvesting olives especially in the light of Zionist attempts to damage farmlands.

Second: on the Arab and Islamic levels:

1. We greet our Palestinian and Jordanian people who took to the streets in tens of thousands in the "Return March" in Jordan to affirm the right of return for our Palestinian people in the diaspora regardless of the lapse of time and to express solidarity with the Aqsa Intifadha and our people in the occupied homeland. We also condemn the Jordanian security bodies' step of quelling that march and using force to disperse the marchers. We also greet the Arab and Islamic peoples and communities who maintained their campaigns of solidarity with our people and with the Aqsa and appeal to all peoples and forces to continue denouncing the Zionist massacres.

2. Results of the emergency Arab summit were disappointing to hopes of our and the Arab peoples who demanded severance of relations with the Zionist enemy, expulsion of its ambassadors and closure of the Zionist embassies and representation offices. They also called for resolutions in support of our people's Intifadha and Jihad in face of Zionist aggression. We consider that the summit's resolutions do not represent the Arab peoples who expressed dismay over the summit's meager results and strongly affirmed their solidarity with our people, insistence on Al-Quds and the Aqsa and demands for opening the door of Jihad against Jewish occupiers.

3. We appreciate the Arab countries that severed relations with the enemy and closed down the Zionist representation offices. We invite Egypt and Jordan, since today 26/10 falls the anniversary of the ill-famed Wadi Araba agreement, and we ask other countries who retain abhorred ties with the enemy to respond to the masses' demands and sever relations with that enemy, expel its ambassadors and close its embassies, which are in fact espionage and conspiracy dens.

4. We call on the Arab and Islamic media, especially the space channels, to continue in their distinctive role in covering the Aqsa Intifadha, highlighting the enemy's crimes and covering sufferings of our people at the hands of the enemy's gangster army and herds of settlers. We hail all media means that mobilized potentials and programs for the sake of serving the Intifadha and supporting our people.

Third: the activities:

1. Let all Fridays be days of rage and revenge in addition to roaring popular confrontations against the enemy's army and herds of settlers and

let angry marches hit the streets from all mosques following the Friday congregations.

2. We appeal to our people in Al-Quds and Palestine occupied in 1948 along with all those capable of reaching the Aqsa Mosque to head and station there. We beseech them to crowd the Mosque during prayer times to prevent the Jews from approaching it and to affirm our people and Nation's rights in Al-Quds and the Aqsa and to prepare for defending and protecting it with blood and soul.

3. On Sunday 29/10 falls the anniversary of the tripartite aggression on Egypt and the anniversary of the Kufr Qassem massacre. Let it be a day of escalation and confrontation with the enemy and herds of settlers.

4. Allocate next Monday 30/10 as the martyr's day during which our people would visit houses of martyrs' families to honor them, stand by their side and express solidarity with them. Let us visit the cemeteries to recite the Fatiha for the martyrs and let photos of the martyrs be hanged everywhere out of loyalty to them and to pledge continuation along their road.

5. Let next Thursday 2/11 be a day of distinctive and comprehensive escalation on the occasion of the notorious Balfour declaration and let women and children demonstrations be organized on that day to denounce the Balfour declaration and to affirm our people's insistence on their lands and rights.

Allahu Akbar and victory to our Mujahid people

**The Islamic Resistance Movement
(Hamas—Palestine)
26 October 2000**

17 October 2000

In the name of Allah the most Gracious the most Merciful

Hamas rejects Sharm Al-Sheikh resolutions
The PA has to correct the mistake and side by the
People and Nation's demand of struggle
The American stand is biased and is not worth heeding

A responsible source in the Islamic Resistance Movement (Hamas) stated the following on results of the Sharm Al-Sheikh summit:

The results and resolutions of the summit meeting have adequately proved that we, along with our Palestinian people and Nation, were right in refusing such a summit and rejecting participation of the Palestinian Authority and other Arab parties in it. The summit was held for the sake of aborting the blessed popular Intifadha, return of the security coordination between the enemy's government and the PA and the return anew to the absurd negotiating table. The results came as the American administration and the Zionist enemy wished and re-affirmed that the summit's target was not for the interest of our people who offered more than 100 martyrs and more than 4,000 wounded but rather to save the government of Barak and to boost Clinton's administration in the peak of the American elections battle.

As far as the details are concerned the PA demands were bypassed, despite their low tune and concentration on formal procedures, while the Zionist viewpoint was imposed due to American bias and pressures, which had drawn three goals for the summit that were imposed on the Palestinian party and which the summit adopted through its three resolutions.

In the light of what happened we, in the Hamas Movement, declare our stands as following:

1. We declare our rejection of all results of that summit. We consider that our people, including its political forces and nationalist, Islamic figures, were not represented in that summit and hence we and our people would not abide by its resolutions.

2. We affirm that the Aqsa Intifadha did not break out for the sake of partial demands but rather to defeat occupation on our lands and sanctities and to attain our full rights. Occupation is the reason of all evil and our people's sufferings, wounds and pains. We, along with our all forces of our people, are determined to continue the Intifadha until it achieves its goals Allah willing.

3. We condemn and denounce the American flagrant biased stand in favor of the Zionist enemy. We call on the Arab countries in their forthcoming summit conference not to heed the American position or the ill-fated Sharm Al-Sheikh summit. We ask them to side by the Palestinian and Arab-Islamic masses' option that of persisting along the road of struggle and popular intifadha until occupation is defeated.

4. We urge our Palestinian people to continue their blessed Intifadha

and to foil the Sharm Al-Sheikh resolutions in practice. Let all our people's forces unite along the road of all-out confrontation against occupation, for this is the real road of national unity. We appeal to our Arab and Islamic Nation's masses to continue their popular programs in support of the Aqsa Intifadha and to continue demanding their governments to keep in harmony with such an option and reject the Sharm Al-Sheikh resolutions.

5   We ask the PA to side by our people and Nation's choice, which is resistance and popular Intifadha. If the PA had committed a grave mistake through participation in the Sharm Al-Sheikh summit we hope that it would not go farther in its mistake by implementing the ominous summit resolutions or else it will be the loser in the end and out of our people's national consensus.

The Islamic Resistance Movement
(Hamas—Palestine)
Monday 17 October 2000

15 October 2000

In the name of Allah the most Gracious the most Merciful

The holy Aqsa Intifadha
Appeal to support the Aqsa

Angry demonstrations, popular
confrontations and commercial strike

In retaliation to the Jews' attempt to lay down the foundation stone of their alleged temple in the Aqsa Mosque tomorrow Monday and in retaliation to the notorious Sharm Al-Sheikh summit that target aborting the holy Aqsa Intifadha, the Islamic Resistance Movement, Hamas, appeals to our Mujahid people to intensify their presence tomorrow in the Aqsa Mosque's yards. We urged them to resist the attempts to lay down the foundation stone of the alleged temple and defend the Aqsa with souls and blood.

We particularly appeal to our people in Palestinian lands occupied in 1948 to mobilize the biggest possible number of people to foil the enemy's conspiracies and to defend our religion and sanctities.

We also request our people to launch a commercial strike and to take to the streets tomorrow Monday in massive angry demonstrations and popular confrontations with the enemy soldiers and herds of settlers in each and every city, village and refugee camp to declare our people's condemnation and rejection of Palestinian Authority chairman's participation in the Sharm Al-Sheikh summit and to resist the attempts to judaize the Aqsa and build the alleged temple.

The Islamic Resistance Movement
(Hamas—Palestine)
Sunday 15 October 2000

15 October 2000

In the name of Allah the most Gracious the most Merciful

Statement on the Jews' attempt to lay down the foundation stone of the alleged temple tomorrow on the date of the notorious Sharm Al-Sheikh summit

Our Mujahid Palestinian people:
Our Arab, Islamic Nation:

In a fresh hostile and provocative step the Zionist enemy's authorities agreed to build the so-called "Temple Mount" and allowed the laying down of the foundation stone of the alleged temple near the honored Dome of the Rock. The Jewish temple mount trustees' group had purchased more than five tons of marble to use one stone of them as the foundation stone at the construction site and use the rest in building the foundations. The construction will take place tomorrow at the same site under protection of Special Forces of the enemy's army to coincide with the convening of the ill-famed Sharm Al-Sheikh summit between chairman of the Palestinian Authority and the criminal terrorist Barak with the aim of aborting the holy Aqsa Intifadha. It also coincides with the PA chairman's submission to demands of Barak to re-detain Hamas cadres who were freed from PA jails by the masses.

We, in face of such a hostile step, affirm the following:

1. We consider the attempt to lay down the foundation stone of the alleged temple in the Aqsa Mosque as a hostile step to our Palestinian

people and to our Arab, Islamic Nation. We also consider it as a war against our religion and Islamic beliefs in addition to representing a scorn to feelings of more than 1.3 billion Muslims.

2. Such a step follows the enemy government's approval of terrorist Sharon's stroll in the Aqsa plaza in a bid to ascertain Zionist sovereignty over the Aqsa Mosque and falls in line with the continuous rabid campaign to judaize Al-Quds (Jerusalem) and desecrate sanctities.

3. The coinciding of laying down the foundation stone for construction of the alleged temple with the convening of the notorious Sharm Al-Sheikh summit raises the anger and denunciation of our people and Nation towards that summit which would work for foiling our people's Intifadha and frustrating the Nation's masses that are eager to launch Jihad and resistance. It also falls at a time when criminal Barak is continuing his aggression and suppression of our people in addition to his indifference to our Arab, Islamic peoples' feelings through desecrating the Aqsa and allowing the laying down of the foundation stone of the temple under the protection of the enemy's army.

4. We urge our faithful, Mujahid people to head early tomorrow in massive marches and occupy yards of the Aqsa Mosque to repel the attempt of laying the foundation stone of the alleged temple and defend the Aqsa with souls and blood. We particularly appeal to our people in Al-Quds and in Palestinian lands occupied in 1948 to mobilize the biggest possible number of people to foil the enemy's conspiracies and defend our religion and holy shrines. We also call on our people to take to the streets tomorrow in angry demonstrations and confrontations with the enemy soldiers and herds of settlers in each and every city, village and camp to declare our people's condemnation and rejection over the PA chairman's participation in the Sharm Al-Sheikh summit and to resist attempts to judaize the Aqsa and build the alleged temple.

5. We appeal to our Arab and Islamic Nation to continue programs in support of the Aqsa and in solidarity with our people. We ask them to condemn the notorious Sharm Al-Sheikh summit and not to heed whatever it issues since it does not represent our Palestinian people nor our Arab and Islamic peoples.

The Islamic Resistance Movement
(Hamas—Palestine)
Sunday 15 October 2000

14 October 2000

In the name of Allah the most Gracious the most Merciful

The holy Aqsa Intifadha
Communiqué No. (11)
Statement on the PA's approval to attend
The Sharm Al-Sheikh summit with criminal Barak

Our Mujahid Palestinian people:
Our Arab, Islamic Nation:

The Palestinian Authority has surprised our people and Nation with its approval to attend the Sharm Al-Sheikh summit with the criminal terrorist Barak at a time the blood of more than 100 martyrs along with four thousand wounded did not dry yet, those who fell in the holy Aqsa Intifadha in defense of our lands and sanctities. We, in the Islamic Resistance Movement, Hamas, faced by such a serious decision would like to affirm the following:

1. We condemn the PA's approval to attend the Sharm Al-Sheikh summit and consider it a serious indifference towards the blood of martyrs and wounded who shed their blood on the ground of Palestine and the Aqsa. We also consider such a decision as a flagrant disdain of our Mujahid people's feelings who are still resisting occupation and confronting its suppression, tyranny and terrorism. It also represented a scornful act in face of our Arab, Islamic Nations' masses that have reacted and still are reacting with our people's Intifadha in an unprecedented manner.

2. the PA's approval to attend that ill-fated summit came at a time when the enemy soldiers and settlers' crimes were escalating at the orders of Barak. This PA step would frustrate our people's feelings who are eager for Jihad and resistance in addition to our Nation's feelings. It further serves the enemy's goal of quelling the Aqsa Intifadha.

3. The approval to attend that summit without any prior conditions as Barak and Clinton wished points to the extent of dictates and humiliating solutions imposed on the Palestinian party, which had already retreated from its conditions before the convening of the summit so how would it act on the table of dictates!?

4. The holding of that ill-fated summit prior to the date of the Arab

summit certainly means foiling the Arab summit's goals in addition to carrying negative impact on its resolutions.

5.   We affirm the continuation of the Intifadha against the criminal enemy and call on our people to continue the march of Jihad and struggle in defense of our land, rights and sanctities and out of loyalty to blood of martyrs and wounded. We also urge our angry Arab, Islamic masses that supported our people and strongly backed the Aqsa and resistance to continue their role and solidarity with our people and the Aqsa. We request them not to give attention to the Sharm Al-Sheikh summit and whatever it could pass of decisions that do not represent the Palestinian people and do not reflect stands and feelings of the live Arab, Islamic peoples.

6.   We understand the attempt by some PA officials to charge the Hamas Movement with inciting certain events in Gaza Strip as a clear attempt to justify tightening the noose round the Hamas Movement and re-detaining its leaders and cadres who were released by the angry masses. The statements also served as a cover-up for the PA's serious decision to attend that summit and an aborted attempt to preoccupy our people and our Movement in side battles away from our role alongside our people in resisting the criminal enemy.

7.   We call on our brothers in the Fatah Movement to continue their role in the Intifadha and popular confrontations against occupation and not to heed the Sharm Al-Sheikh summit but rather to urge the PA not to participate in it.

The Islamic Resistance Movement
(Hamas—Palestine)
Saturday 15 October 2000

12 October 2000

In the name of Allah the most Gracious the most Merciful

The holy Aqsa Intifadha
Communiqué no. (9)
Our Mujahid people do not fear warplanes, missiles
or the enemy's nuclear arsenal

Popular angry demonstrations continue to sweep Arab and Islamic lands
We call on the leaders of the Nation to declare Jihad
In defense of the Aqsa and our unarmed people

Our proud Palestinian people . . . Our Arab, Islamic Nation:

The Zionist enemy is continuing its crimes and terrorism against our unarmed people using warplanes, tanks and missiles. It unleashed its heavily armed settler gangsters who spread destruction, terrorism and bloodletting in a bid to subdue our people, judaize Al-Quds (Jerusalem) and demolish the Aqsa to build the alleged temple in its place. This wanton enemy believed that the language of terrorism and blind force could force our people into submission in accordance with Zionist conditions and speculations. Here is the enemy with its military hardware encircling our unarmed people and here they are our people, as they have always done, resisting the enemy and its missiles with bare chests, heads high, not terrorized by tanks or missiles. Martyrs fall one after the other in defense of al-Quds, the Aqsa, holy shrines and dignity of the Arab and Islamic Nation.

Our Palestinian people . . . Our Arab and Islamic Nation:

We in the Islamic Resistance Movement (Hamas) would like to announce and affirm the following:

1. The Hamas Movement and its Mujahideen brigades (the Qassam Brigades) will defend the people, lands, honor and sanctities alongside our people. The criminal enemy will not go unpunished for his crimes and will pay dearly and our people's blood will not be wasted.

2. We appeal to our people in the West Bank and the Gaza Strip to hit the streets to defy the Zionist shelling and form a human shield to protect their installations and national institutions. We affirm that our heroic people will defend themselves, their sanctities and dignity until the last Palestinian child God willing and will never bow for other than Allah but rather will withstand and fight and will not be scared by missiles or tanks or all the enemy's nuclear arsenal.

3. We ask the Palestinian Authority at such a critical stage to hurry up and arm our people and anyone capable of using arms to defend our lands and holy shrines.

4. We urge the leaders of our Arab and Islamic Nation to immediately act in support and defense of our people and to prepare for confrontation and war against the arrogant Zionist enemy. Let this enemy understand that our people are not alone in this world but rather backed by their Arab and Islamic Nation that will not let them down and will not let them face death and terrorism alone. This is the time of real work for the sake of defending the Nation's higher interests and this is the time for the Arab and Islamic armies that must move to rescue the Aqsa, Al-Quds and our unarmed people.

5. We appeal to the Arab and Islamic masses that strongly backed our people in the past few days and expressed their anger over Zionist massacres to continue their solidarity with our people and to continue supporting the Aqsa and take to the streets tomorrow Friday and the other days in angry marches and roaring protests to condemn the Zionist aggression and to reflect unity of our Nation and its insistence on its rights and sanctities and to demand from leaders of that Nation to declare Jihad in defense of the Aqsa and to rescue the unarmed Palestinian people.

6. We call on the Arab countries, which established relations with the Zionist enemy, to expel the enemy's ambassadors and representatives and to close down its embassies and representation offices at once in retaliation to the Zionist aggression, which is the least they should do at this particular stage. On this occasion we hail our brothers in Oman Sultanate for their nationalist decision of closing down the Zionist representation office to protest the Zionist aggression against our unarmed people, which came in harmony with the Nation's conscience.

7. We consider the Zionist missiles that bombarded Ramallah and Gaza as the mercy killing the already dead peace process and we ask the PA to declare officially the end of that peace process and to announce that the only option to confront the arrogant enemy is Jihad and resistance and that whatever was taken by force would be only restored by force.

Allahu Akbar and victory to our Mujahid people

**The Islamic Resistance Movement
(Hamas—Palestine)
Thursday 12 October 2000**

8 October 2000

In the name of Allah the most Gracious the most Merciful

The holy Aqsa Intifadha
From Lebanon to Palestine . . .
one people who do not capitulate

Our Mujahid Palestinian people:

From the land of Jihad, sacrifice and liberation Lebanon . . . to the land of resistance, steadfastness and conquer Insha'all Palestine . . . our Palestinian masses marched from the steadfast camps in Lebanon to the northern borders of Palestine to smell the scent of the Aqsa, the country and martyrdom. They affirmed their loyalty to the option of Jihad and struggle and their constant belonging to Palestine and their support to the steadfast and revolting people there. Yet the enemy, whose nature is treachery, would not allow the spirit of Jihad to move from Palestine to our people in the camps and the diaspora. So the enemy's soldiers fired at our unarmed people and two martyrs fell to join the convoy of martyrs those of the Aqsa's Intifadha. The blood of those martyrs and that of the other wounded men thus declared that there would be no surrender to that enemy and that our people in the diaspora, similar to our people at home, reject all forms of humiliated settlements, refuse to erase Palestine from their memory and affirm that Jihad and struggle are the means of returning to their homeland. All hail to our Mujahid Palestinian masses in Lebanon and salutations to the Mujahid people of Lebanon and to the blessed hands that are throwing the enemy with stones.

Our Mujahid Palestinian people . . . Our Arab, Islamic Nation:

We would like here to re-affirm unity of Palestinian blood within and outside the usurped homeland. We would also like to affirm that our brothers in Hizbullah through retaliating to the enemy's bombardment by shelling its military positions and capturing three soldiers, assert the unity of that nation in confrontation against the Zionist enemy and the Nation's insistence on the option of resistance and Jihad. They further prove that our people were not alone in the field but rather that the whole Nation was backing them. We thus greet our brothers in Hizbullah and our Arab, Islamic Nation and we call on our Nation to exert more action against the Zionist enemy.

Our Palestinian people . . . Our Arab, Islamic Nation:

The Islamic Resistance Movement, Hamas, hails the martyrs of our people in south Lebanon and affirms that it would shoulder its duty towards the families of both heroes:

The martyr hero Hassan Hassanain
The martyr hero Shadi Anas

We renew our pledge before Allah then before our people and Nation that we will remain guardians of our wounded and martyrs 's blood and will continue to look after our captives. We affirm that the blood and sufferings will not go unheeded but rather, with the will of Allah, would furnish the road to victory, liberation and dignity.

> *'Allah has decreed: It is I and My messengers who must prevail"*
> *"Allah will certainly aid those who aid His (cause)"*

Allahu Akbar . . . and victory to our people and our Nation

The Islamic Resistance Movement
(Hamas—Palestine)
Sunday 8 October 2000

8 October 2000

In the name of Allah the most Gracious the most Merciful

The holy Aqsa Intifadha
Communiqué No. (8)

Herds of armed settlers backed by enemy soldiers attack our people everywhere

We declare state of maximum alert and formation of popular committees to defend our people and sanctities

Our Mujahid Palestinian people:

The rabid Zionist terrorist campaigns are continuing and escalating against our unarmed people. Thousands of heavily armed herds of settlers attacked last night our unarmed people in the city of Nazareth of occupied Palestine 1948. Two martyrs fell along with scores of wounded. The attacks were backed and protected by the enemy's army. They also attacked our people in the suburbs of Al-Quds (Jerusalem), Hebron and Gaza Strip. Furthermore, they burnt a mosque in Tiberias. At the same time the enemy's government is threatening to wage war against Lebanon and Syria and is mobilizing its army along the Lebanese borders in an attempt to rid itself from the crisis facing this usurping entity due to escalation of our heroic people's Intifadha and the heroes in Hizbullah's kidnap of three enemy soldiers. At such a critical time officials in the Palestinian Authority's security apparatuses declare the formation of a joint security operations room between the PA and each of the Zionist entity and the USA only hours after Barak's threat to the PA of terminating the peace process if the Intifadha and confrontations do not cease! Here our people, after sacrificing the most precious thing they own and still are, have the right to wonder: Why form a joint operations room and what is its mission? Is it formed to escalate the Intifadha, which has become a comprehensive popular demand? Or is it formed to end and abort it in accordance with the American-Zionist parties' demand, which fear its repercussions and reactions on the Palestinian, Arab and Islamic levels?

Our Palestinian people . . . Our Arab, Islamic Nation . . . at this serious stage, we in the Hamas Movement would like to affirm the following:

First: on the Palestinian level:

1. **We declare a state of maximum alert and call on our people and the Hamas cadres and its supporters for general mobilization and urgent participation in popular resistance committees** in all cities, villages, camps, universities and schools so that they would shoulder their national duty in protecting our unarmed people and defend them in face of the enemy soldiers and herds of settlers. We further ask them to organize day and night guarding shifts of our cities, villages, sanctities and properties of our people bearing in mind the good omens of our prophet's Hadith **"Two eyes are not touched by (hell) fire,**

an eye that shed tears out of fear of Allah, and an eye that was
on guard all night for the cause of Allah."

2. We greet our heroic people in the city of Nazareth who are the target of organized terrorism and repression campaigns on the part of
enemy soldiers and herds of settlers. We hail their steadfastness and
bravery in defending themselves. We also salute our people's masses
who responded to the appeals and hit the streets in late hours yesterday to help them and break the siege against them. We highly appreciate our angry masses that took to the streets in Ramallah and Gaza
in solidarity with them and clashed with enemy soldiers.

3. We strongly denounce the new and old security agreements between
the PA and the enemy. We condemn the formation of a joint operations room that would only serve to strike the resistance and abort
the Aqsa Intifadha. We consider that such a step had let down our
Aqsa, our people and the Arab and Islamic peoples that took to the
streets in solidarity with our people and in support of the Aqsa. But
we are content with the fact that our people is well aware with the
truth and we are content with the promise of our prophet, peace be
upon him, to the victorious group in Al-Quds and its precincts who
"would not be harmed by those who differed with them or those who
let them down."

4. We affirm that the prophet Yousef's tombstone that was liberated by
our angry masses in Nablus is an Islamic Waqf and will remain a
mosque at which the five daily prayers will be offered. We will resist
any attempt for the return of the settlers or soldiers, who had turned
it into military barracks and a dagger in the center of the brave city
of Nablus. We urge our people to reconstruct it and offer next Friday's
noon prayers in it.

Second: on the Arab, Islamic level:

1. We salute the heroes of Hizbullah and the Lebanese people who united
with our Palestinian people in Lebanon in confrontation of the enemy.

2. We appeal to leaders of the Nation to perform their duty and responsibility in protecting and helping our people who are threatened by the
gangs of the enemy's army and herds of settlers everywhere. We demand
their backing to our people's steadfastness and adopting the struggle
option including providing weapons to our people to enable them continue their Jihad and to defend themselves and their holy shrines.

3. We call on leaders of Arab and Islamic countries to strongly support Syria and Lebanon in face of the enemy's war threats.

4. We hail our Nation's masses that continued their solidarity campaigns with our people and in support of the Aqsa. We call for more such activity and more serious official stands.

5. We demand the concerned Arab countries to close the enemy's embassies and missions and to sever all forms of relations with the occupying enemy.

Third: the activities:

1. Let our masses escalate confrontations against the Zionist enemy and herds of settlers on Tuesday and Wednesday 10, 11/10 in solidarity with the Nazareth heroes and let the funeral processions of martyrs turn into roaring demonstrations and all-out confrontations against the occupying enemy.

2. We call on our people to boycott the enemy's products and resort to the Palestinian or Arab alternative if found.

3. We advocate organizing special marches for university students and others for school students, their dates to be determined according to the regions.

4. Let Thursday 12/10 be a day for collective fasting for all our people seeking Allah's satisfaction and in solidarity with the families of martyrs and wounded.

5. Let Friday 13/10 be a day of rage and distinctive escalation including tumultuous rallies marching from mosques after the Friday noon prayers in defense of our holy shrines.

6. Organize visits to families of martyrs, wounded and detainees in a show of solidarity with them and to meet their needs.

Allahu Akbar and victory to our Mujahid people

**The Islamic Resistance Movement
(Hamas—Palestine)
Monday 9 October 2000**

7 October 2000

In the name of Allah the most Gracious the most Merciful

The holy Aqsa Intifadha
Statement on the occupation's defeat

At mosque of Yousef's tombstone in Balata

"And in that day believers will rejoice. In Allah's help to victory. He helpeth to victory whom He will. He is the Mighty, the Merciful." (Rum)

All praises are to Allah and peace be upon our prophet Mohammed the leader of Mujahideen and on his family, companions and all those who marched along his path and Jihad till doomsday.

We herald to our Mujahid people today the good omens of defeating Zionist occupation at a dear spot in our precious homeland. The enemy withdrew in humiliation thanks to Allah in the first place then to the heroic resistance and Jihad cohesion expressed by our people ever since the outbreak of the Aqsa Intifadha and finally thanks to the blood of martyrs that poured over the country's lands and holy Aqsa's plaza. On this occasion we would like to affirm the following:

1. This tombstone was known a long time ago as an Islamic mosque that the Jews had no right in it at all whether historically or religiously. The Islamic Waqf documents prove that the tombstone was an Islamic Waqf and a mosque for Muslims and remained so for a long period until the herds of settlers came to plant a dagger in that brave city and convert the tombstone into a military camp through claiming Jewish right in that Islamic Waqf while it is well known that prophet Yousef, peace be upon him had lived, died and buried in Egypt.

2. We call on our people to end the destruction and burning of that Waqf and Islamic mosque. We call on them to preserve, clean and purge it from dirt of the settlers and deal with that event in a civilizational way coping with our Mujahid Palestinian people.

3. We ask the Islamic Awqaf department in Nablus to take the initiative and take control of the mosque, cleaning and purging it in addition to restoring things to normalcy and appoint a servant and an Imam for that mosque to supervise and serve it.

4. We request our people in Nablus district to share in purging that mosque through maintaining the five daily prayers in it, which would bear the real meaning of liberating that Islamic shrine. Let the immortal calls of Allahu Akbar rise high from above that mosque.

5. We urge the Awqaf department and all Muslims in that city to form a committee that would reconstruct that mosque so as to host the five daily prayers and to open a school for memorizing the holy Quran in it.

Finally we call on all Muslims in the city and district of Nablus to offer the next Friday's noon prayers 13/10/2000 at the yards of that Islamic shrine "the tombstone of prophet Yousef."

Allahu Akbar and victory for our Mujahid people

Allahu Akbar and all praises to Allah

**The Islamic Resistance Movement
(Hamas—Palestine)
Saturday 7 October 2000**

7 October 2000

In the name of Allah the most Gracious the most Merciful

The holy Aqsa Intifadha
Communiqué No. (7)

Blood of martyrs hoists the Palestinian flag over the Dome of the Rock

Our Mujahid Palestinian people:

An epical day . . . rare heroism and sacrifice . . . unequaled martyrdom and bravery . . . this was your day . . . day of rage in which you proved that you are worth being the protectors and guardians of the Aqsa. You hoisted up high with your blood the flag of Palestine over the Dome of the Rock . . . and you resisted with bare chests the criminal Barak who is ordering the killing or our people and insist on his program to judaize Al-Quds (Jerusalem) and seize the Aqsa.

You are not alone in the battle for Al-Quds and the Aqsa for the Nation, the whole Nation stands by your side and yearns for the day of Jihad for the sake of liberating Palestine and salvaging the Aqsa. Here it is now (the Nation) reflecting its genuineness through the massive demonstrations in all Arab and Islamic capitals and wherever its communities reside. Yes our Mujahid people, the Aqsa is uniting our people and Nation . . . here they are the Intifadha and struggle uniting us after negotiations and settlements divided our people and Nation. Here they are foiling all illusionary and humiliating peace with the occupying enemy and here they are our people affirming that that there is no way for returning back and warning against any attempt to abort the Aqsa Intifadha or exploiting it to try and breathe spirit into the dead body of the settlement process! That criminal enemy would only submit to the logic of force and resistance. Bargaining over the blood of our martyrs will only lead to more Zionist arrogance, wasting rights, judaizing Al-Quds and expediting the Zionist Jews' attempt to demolish the Aqsa.

Our Palestinian people . . . our Arab, Islamic Nation, on the tenth day of the Aqsa Intifadha we in the Hamas Movement would like to affirm the following:

First: on the Palestinian level:

1. We call on our Mujahid people to continue the Aqsa Intifadha, escalate it and confront enemy soldiers and herds of settlers. We also call for breaking the siege on the Aqsa Mosque by heading for prayers in it especially on the part of our people in Al-Quds and our people in occupied Palestine in 1948.

2. We hail our people for responding to the Aqsa's appeal and their tumultuous demonstrations following the Friday noon prayers in all mosques of Palestine, their confrontation of the enemy soldiers and offering 11 martyrs along with hundreds of wounded. We salute the Mujahid family of Shamlakh who offered their second martyr in the Intifadha.

3. We highly appreciate the initiative of our people who jammed Palestinian hospitals donating blood for their wounded brothers and assisting in treating victims.

4. We urge the Palestinian Authority to release all political detainees and Mujahideen in its prisons to enable them, each from his position, perform their role in that Intifadha and in protecting our people and fighting the enemy. Our people have the right of wondering for whose interests are those freedom fighters and Mujahideen behind bars of PA jails?

5. We ask the PA and its security apparatuses to stop security cooperation with the Zionist enemy and end all kinds of meetings with it.

Second: on the Arab, Islamic level:

1. A thousand greetings from the captive Aqsa and from our Mujahid people and their martyrs to our Arab and Islamic masses that hit the streets in huge demonstrations and rallies along with prayers in mosques for the support of the Aqsa especially in Egypt, Jordan, Syria, Lebanon, Saudi Arabia, Yemen, Iraq, Qatar, United Arab Emirates, Oman sultanate, Kuwait, Sudan, Iran, Morocco, Algeria, Bahrain, Mauritania, Pakistan, Malaysia and Indonesia. We also hail the Arab and Islamic communities and all freedom-loving forces in European countries, America and Russia.

2. We ask for continuation of solidarity and support campaigns with our people and protests against Zionist massacres in all Arab and Islamic capitals.

3. We demand that the forthcoming Arab summit be that of the Aqsa, a summit for Jihad and resistance, a summit for building a real Arab strategy for the sake of defeating the occupiers and purging the Aqsa Mosque, Al-Quds and Palestine from them. We do not want it to be a summit for issuing condemnation communiqués and giving a fresh chance for the humiliating peace process.

4. We call on leaders of the Nation to strengthen steadfastness of our people and bolster their Mujahideen in addition to opening the door for Jihad to liberate Palestine and allowing the angry masses to express their support and solidarity with our people and not to quell them. We denounce the crime of killing one of our people in Jordan as a result of using force and violence to quell the demonstrators.

Third: the activities:

1. Let the coming days be those of confrontations with enemy soldiers and herds of settlers. We advise the throwing arms to develop tools

and means of their revolt and to use all popular resistance methods stones, Molotov, cold arms and pouring oil in roads of enemy vehicles and seeking to inflict biggest possible losses in enemy lines.

2. We call on the youth of the Aqsa Intifadha to start a campaign of writing slogans on walls condemning Zionist massacres and desecration of Al-Quds and the Aqsa, and demanding an immediate halt to negotiations and continuing Jihad and struggle, and hailing the Arab and Islamic peoples who backed our people.

3. Let next Thursday 12/10 be a day of collective fasting for all our people to win Allah's satisfaction and in solidarity with families of the martyrs and wounded.

4. Let next Friday 13/10 be a distinctive day of escalation, and let demonstrations march from mosques following the Friday noon prayers to affirm the Islamism and Arabism of Al-Quds in addition to our right in the Aqsa and all its walls and yards.

5. Organizing visits to families of martyrs and wounded expressing solidarity with them and meeting their needs.

Allahu Akbar and victory to our Mujahid people

The Islamic Resistance Movement
(Hamas—Palestine)
Saturday 7 October 2000

4 October 2000

In the name of Allah the most Gracious the most Merciful

The holy Aqsa's Intifadha—Communiqué No. (6)
"Here is a message to Mankind"

The seventh day of the Aqsa's Intifadha
Meeting criminal Barak is a stab to our people, Al-Quds, Aqsa and martyrs

Our people will continue their Intifadha and heroic resistance to defeat the occupiers

Our proud Palestinian people: Our Arab and Islamic Nation:

Another day passes and our Mujahid people continue their holy Aqsa's Intifadha and a new group of martyrs join their brothers who won the honor of martyrdom for the sake of Allah and for the sake of the Aqsa. Our people has offered more than 60 martyrs and 2,000 wounded so far for the sake of protecting Al-Quds (Jerusalem) and the Aqsa. Our glorified Arab and Islamic masses continue their solidarity campaigns with our people. Our Nation is reflecting its unity as a one Nation and one body, which if one of its organs felt pain the other organs felt with it.

As martyrs fall and the Arab and Islamic cohesion with our people escalates, Clinton seeks to save the criminal Barak and the image of the Zionist entity, which the whole world had witnessed its savagery and terrorism. He arranged a meeting between criminal Barak and chairman of the Palestinian Authority with the aim of aborting the holy Aqsa's Intifadha and paves the way for resuming the humiliating negotiations with the criminal enemy! Any such meetings would mean a flagrant heedlessness of the blood of the martyrs and the wounded and would be met with great anger on the part of our people and enemy.

Our Palestinian people . . . our Arab and Islamic Nation:

On the seventh day of the holy Aqsa's Intifadha, we in the Islamic Resistance Movement, Hamas, affirm the following:

1. We affirm, along with our people, our rejection of any meeting between chairman of the Palestinian Authority and the terrorist Barak, whose hands are smeared with blood of our unarmed people. We consider such a meeting as a stab in the back of the Aqsa's Intifadha and to blood of martyrs.

2. We salute with pride our people's martyrs from the steadfast Palestinian universities especially the National Najah University and the Islamic University in Gaza. We call on students of universities, institutes and schools to escalate confrontations and resistance of the enemy 's army and herds of settlers.

3. We greet all Palestinian, Arab and fair-minded world journalists and media men along with all news agencies and space channels for their big role in exposing the occupation's practices especially through the large-scale coverage of events and giving prominence to Zionist repression and spitefulness against our people and children. We also wish speedy recovery to all wounded journalists and cameramen.

4. We bless the steadfastness of our people in 1948 occupied Palestine and their strong rejection of the Zionist aggression against the Aqsa. We condemn the sinful assassination attempt against Sheikh Ra'ed Salah, head of the Islamic Movement, at the hands of Jewish snipers.

5. **We re-affirm the program of activities included in yesterday's communiqué as follows: today Wednesday and tomorrow Thursday days of escalation and all-out confrontations against enemy soldiers and herds of settlers. Friday should be a day of distinctive confrontations. Let massive demonstrations march from all Palestine mosques in the West Bank, Gaza Strip and areas occupied in 1948.**

6. A thousand salutations to our angry Arab peoples in Egypt, Jordan, Lebanon, Syria, Iraq, Yemen, Oman Sultanate and Sharjah emirate who hit the streets in tumultuous demonstrations in solidarity with our people and in denunciation of the Jews' massacres. We request more solidarity activities with our people and in support of the Aqsa.

Allahu Akbar and victory to our Mujahid people

The Islamic Resistance Movement
(Hamas—Palestine)
Monday 4 October 2000

3 October 2000

In the name of Allah the most Gracious the most Merciful
"Here is a message to Mankind"
The sixth day of the Intifadha
Communiqué No. (5)

"Think not of those who are slain in Allah's Way as dead. Nay, they live, finding their sustenance in the Presence of their Lord;"

Jihad is our way . . . and death for the cause of Allah is our noblest goal

The holy Aqsa's Intifadha unites our people in face of the aggression

We will continue the Intifadha and resistance and we will burn the ground under the feet of the occupiers

Our hero the Mujahid Palestinian people:
Our glorified Arab, Islamic Nation:

The Zionist massacres are ongoing . . . and the criminal nazi occupation army continues to wage its all-out war against our unarmed people using all kinds of weapons: tanks, helicopter gunship, missiles, machineguns and bombs in a bid to terrorize our people and compel them by force to accept continuation of Zionist occupation of Al-Quds (Jerusalem) and Jewish sovereignty over the Aqsa in preparation for establishing the alleged temple in its place. The savage Zionist Jewish crimes are clearly evident in the image of the martyr child Mohammed Jamal Al-Durra who was murdered by the enemy soldiers in cold bold. They did not have mercy on his innocent childhood, hence came the terrifying scene that shook the whole world. On the other hand, our proud people continue to resist the occupation army, the government of criminal Barak and the herds of settlers. The Palestinians continue to defend their lands, holy shrines, Al-Quds, the Aqsa, religion, honor and Arab and Islamic dignity. Our people prove once again that they are a people of heroic deeds and sacrifice, a people of Jihad and martyrdom, a people of martyrs and that their sacrifice for the sake of the Aqsa was boundless.

More than fifty martyrs and 1,500 wounded fell in the Aqsa Intifadha, which broke out in all areas of our occupied Palestinian lands uniting the blood of our people in the West Bank, Gaza Strip and Jerusalem with that of our heroic steadfast people in our occupied Palestinian lands in 1948. The battlefield united our people with all their layers, trends, factions and forces in the holy Aqsa's Intifadha, for the enemy is one . . . the destiny is one . . . and the blood is one.

Our Palestinian people . . . our Arab, Islamic Nation:

On the sixth day of the holy Aqsa's Intifadha, we in the Islamic Resistance Movement, Hamas, affirm the following:

First: on the internal Palestinian level:

1. The Movement stresses unity of the Palestinian people in their continued confrontations and resistance against the Zionist enemy through the holy Aqsa's Intifadha. That uprising that came in retaliation to the savage massacres committed and still are committed by the enemy

in the holy Aqsa's yards and in all occupied Palestinian cities and villages including our occupied lands in 1948. The Movement salutes our martyrs and wounded in various areas of our holy land and hails their families and relatives affirming Hamas' backing to them all.

2. The demand for resignation of the chairman of the Palestinian Authority did not reflect the Movement's stand nor its policy. The Movement affirms that it works for the liberation of our lands, our Quds and our Aqsa with all our people in a liberation march from the usurping enemy and for the sake of the return of our lands and country.

3. We call on our people in the West Bank, Gaza Strip and the 48 areas and in each and every city and village, camp and alley to continue the confrontations and to escalate them against the Zionist enemy and to resist the settlers and defend the Aqsa and guard it with our lives and money and not to allow an end to this Intifadha.

4. We demand the Palestinian Authority to immediately set free all political detainees and Mujahideen in its jails topped by Dr. Abdul Aziz Ranteesi, Dr. Ibrahim Makadme, Sheikh Jamal Mansour, Sheikh Mohammed Jamal Natshe, Mujahid Mahmoud Abu Hannoud and Mujahid Mohammed Daif.

5. We renew our salutation to our heroic steadfast people in occupied Palestine-1948 for their steadfastness, sacrifices and strong rejection of the Jewish conspiracies against the Aqsa and for their blessed Intifadha and for their martyrs and hundreds of wounded.

6. Let the days of Tuesday, Wednesday and Thursday 3,4,5/10 be days of escalation and all-out confrontations with the enemy soldiers and herds of settlers.

7. In response to the appeal by the Nation's scholars and leaders of Islamic Movements, who expressed solidarity and support with our people: let Friday 6/10 be a day of distinctive escalation and clashes. Let tumultuous demonstrations march from all mosques in Palestine to reflect the Palestinian immense anger towards Zionist massacres. We also request from the Friday preachers to allocate the Friday sermon to Al-Quds, the Aqsa and our people and Nation's duty towards them.

8. The Hamas Movement declares that it would shoulder its duty towards all families of the martyrs who fell in the Aqsa's Intifadha through catering for them and ensuring that our people would also cater for them out of our responsibility towards the blood of martyrs and to preserve their families and sons after them.

Second: on the Arab and Islamic levels:

1. We call on our Arab and Islamic masses to intensify their activities in support of Al-Quds and the Aqsa and to express solidarity with our stationed people. Let the masses hit the streets in all Arab and Islamic capitals to reflect their dismay towards the Zionist carnages and to affirm our Nation's insistence on Al-Quds and the Aqsa and its readiness to defend its holy shrines.

2. We ask leaders of the Arab and Islamic countries to shoulder their duty and responsibility towards Al-Quds and the Aqsa and towards our stationed people. We ask them to strengthen their steadfastness and Jihad materially and morally. We ask them to allow freedom of expression to the Arab and Islamic peoples so that they would express their opinions and support their brothers in Palestine. We demand the countries establishing relations with the criminal enemy to sever those relations and expel ambassadors and representatives of that criminal entity who are desecrating Arab lands.

3. The Hamas Movement lauds our Nation's masses that took to the streets in support of the Aqsa especially our people and brothers in Yemen, Jordan, Egypt, Syria and Lebanon. We also hail the Arab and Islamic community in Britain, America and Europe and request more such activities.

4. We call on our Arab and Islamic peoples to contribute in the Aqsa's Intifadha and in the defense of Al-Quds and the sanctities by sharing in the honor of Jihad through donating money to our people and their certified charitable societies.
    "Go forth, light-armed and heavy-armed, and strive with your wealth and your lives in the way of Allah!"

Long live the holy Aqsa's Intifadha

Glory and immortality for our martyrs

Allahu Akbar and victory to our Mujahid people

**The Islamic Resistance Movement
(Hamas—Palestine)
Sunday 3 October 2000**

1 October 2000

In the name of Allah the most Gracious the most Merciful

Communiqué no. (4)

Here is a Message for mankind

Our souls and blood sacrificed for the sake of the Aqsa

Let the Aqsa Intifadha continue and let the confrontations progress and let the ground turn into fire and volcanoes under the feet of the usurpers

Our Mujahid Palestinian people:

"If ye are suffering hardships, they are suffering similar hardships; but ye have hope from Allah, while they have none." In these blessed days . . . the days of Jihad and martyrdom . . . the days of Jihad for the cause of Allah, in defense of His religion and in revenge to Al-Quds (Jerusalem), sancties and the Aqsa . . . and in support of the Arab and Islamic Nation's dignity, the precious Palestinian blood continues to be shed for the sake of the Aqsa . . . in these days you, our people, prove again and ever again that you are the people of sacrifice, martyrs, pride, dignity, patience and steadfastness . . .

All hail to you our people for your Jihad and steadfastness . . . for your Intifadha for the sake of the Aqsa and the sanctities . . . for your strong confrontation in face of Zionist tyranny and aggression . . . and a glorified salutation to the martyrs and the hundreds of wounded who colored with their blood the Aqsa yards and the holy land of Palestine.

Our stationed Palestinian people:

The blessed Aqsa Intifadha will continue and escalate to affirm to the whole world that our people are not tired or weakened and will never succumb to humiliation, repression and occupation and that they are still capable of sacrifice, resistance and confrontation of the Zionist occupation savagery in defense of Al-Quds and the Aqsa.

The Zionist occupation army's confrontation of our unarmed Palestinian masses employing thousands of panicked soldiers who used live bullets, internationally banned bullets along with armored vehicles and Lao missiles to commit brutal war crimes against demonstrations of our people exposes the truth of the illusionary peace with that enemy. It further affirms that coexistence between the victim and the culprit is a big lie for that criminal enemy only understands the language of suppression, terrorism and sacrilegious acts. That enemy wants complete surrender of our people to all its conditions but the blood of our people that was shed everywhere on all parts of our usurped lands revealed reality of that spiteful enemy no matter how much supporters of peace and settlements try to deceive our people and Nation over that fact.

This blessed Intifadha came as a strong response to the crime of the Barak government in collusion with Sharon and his followers against the Aqsa. It also came in retaliation to allowing him to stroll in the Aqsa plaza under the protection of thousands of soldiers and accompanied by a military build up that was not even known during the time the Aqsa was occupied. It also came in response to the enemy's stands in declaring its insistence on sovereignty over Jerusalem and the Aqsa and declarations by its leaders on the intention of constructing their alleged temple in the Aqsa Mosque. Hence came this Intifadha and the bloodletting as a strong message that we will burn the grounds under feet of the usurpers and that any tampering with the Aqsa or desecrating it was out of bounds that if breeched would move our people young and old, women and men, elderly and children and that rivers of blood would be shed and martyrs fall for its sake.

Our Mujahid Palestinian people: our Arab and Islamic Nation:

We in the Islamic Resistance Movement, Hamas, call for the following:

First: on the domestic arena:

1. We call for a general strike tomorrow Monday 2/10/2000 declaring it a day for popular escalation on the anniversary of Salahuddin's liberation of Al-Quds. We also call on our masses to continue the Aqsa Intifadha and escalate confrontations with enemy soldiers and herds of settlers and clash with them in all cities and villages . . . in all camps, alleys and streets of our holy Palestinian lands to protest the savage massacres against our people and the Jews' desecration of the Haram Al-Sharif and to insist on our people's sovereignty over Al-Quds and the Aqsa.

2. We request our people to head for the Aqsa Mosque and stage a 24-hour sit-in to guard and defend it. We urge students to organize continuous group visits to the Aqsa.

3. We call on university students, students' blocs and school pupils to hit the streets in massive demonstrations everywhere to reflect our people's anger and in support of the Aqsa and the holy shrines.

4. We urge the return of using the blessed Intifadha tools such as stones, slingshots, Molotov and cold arms and let our lands turn into a resistance, heroism and Jihad arena.

5. We call for solidarity with families of martyrs and congratulating their relatives. We also plead for visiting the wounded, assisting them and extending to them whatever they need.

6. We call on the Palestinian Authority to immediately withdraw from negotiations with the criminal enemy and to declare suspension of all forms of security coordination with it.

7. We ask the Authority not to end the Aqsa Intifadha or calm down our angered masses as it had done after the tunnel's uprising. We also call on it to observe cohesion with our people and stand by their side in the confrontation against aggression. We also invite the Authority to let the people freely express their stands and defend the sanctities and retaliate to the Jewish aggression.

8. We call on the Authority to release all detained Mujahideen in its jails topped by Mujahid Mahmoud Abu Hannoud and Mujahid Mohammed Daif to be in their proper place alongside the Mujahideen in the confrontation against the enemy.

9. We extend our glorified salutations to the heroic Palestinian policeman who opened his gunfire at the enemy soldiers and condemn the Authority's decision to try him at a time when the occupation entity's leaders and soldiers were committing the most savage crimes against our unarmed people.

10. We greet our people in Palestinian lands occupied in 1948 and hail their blessed backing to their next of kin in addition to their defense of the Aqsa and appraise their holding of different activities to express our people's insistence on their blessed Mosque and their legitimate rights.

Second: on the Arab and Islamic levels:

1. We appeal to our Arab and Islamic Nation's masses to move in support of the Aqsa and in solidarity with our Palestinian people. We beseech them to express their denunciation of the enemy's measures, massacres and desecration of the Aqsa through organizing rallies, carnivals and other activities to support our people. Let the whole world understand that the holy Aqsa Mosque is the property of more than one billion Muslims and that any tampering with it is a red line and a declaration of war against our Nation, its religion and pride.

2. We invite the Arab regimes that maintain any form of relation or normalization with the criminal enemy to end dealings with the enemy and halt all forms of normalization with it and expel its ambassadors and representatives.

3. We ask Arab and Islamic peoples and governments to extend all forms of material, moral and informational support to our people, back its steadfastness and resistance and aid the Mujahideen.

Let the blessed Aqsa Intifadha continue

Let the Palestinian bloodshed continue in defense of Al-Quds and the Aqsa

Let our holy land turn into volcanoes burning the usurpers

**The Islamic Resistance Movement
(Hamas—Palestine)
Sunday 1 October 2000**

29 September 2000

In the name of Allah the most Gracious the most Merciful

Hamas calls for an all-out strike and popular confrontations tomorrow Saturday and for a three-day mourning for the souls of the martyrs

The Islamic Resistance Movement, Hamas, calls on the Palestinian people to conduct an all-out strike tomorrow Saturday to protest the Zionist savage massacre against our unarmed people in the yards of the blessed Aqsa

Mosque. We call on them to confront the enemy's soldiers and settlers to assert our people's rejection of Zionist aggressive ambitions and their rejection to surrender Al-Quds (Jerusalem) and the Aqsa.

We also call on our Mujahid Palestinian people to observe a three days mourning for the souls of the martyrs of the Aqsa carnage.

Allahu Akbar . . . and victory to our Mujahid people

**The Islamic Resistance Movement
(Hamas—Palestine)
Friday 29 September 2000**

29 September 2000

In the name of Allah the most Gracious the most Merciful

New massacre by enemy forces against our unarmed people in the Aqsa plaza

We confront aggression and protect sanctities with our blood and souls

The Zionist occupation forces committed yet another carnage against our unarmed people in the blessed Aqsa Mosque's yards. Another savage crime is added to the record of continuous Zionist terrorism: repression, aggression, bloodletting and desecrating sanctities. Five martyrs and more than 200 wounded fell by gunshots of the occupation soldiers. Precious blood is spilt to color the Aqsa plaza defending and protecting it against spiteful Jewish aggression and guarding it against their greediness and plots.

In this manner the hateful assaults against the Aqsa continue day after day and year after year and massacre after massacre. And the Mujahid Palestinian people young and old, women and men continue to defend their Mosque and repel aggression with bare chests, stones, blood, souls and confident belief in the victory by the grace of Allah against their enemies the Jews.

Our patient Mujahid Palestinian people . . .

our Arab and Islamic Nation:

The blood of our people that was shed today in the Aqsa yards appeals to you to shoulder your responsibility and duty towards Al-Quds (Jerusalem) and the Aqsa. Those believers, who responded to the Hamas call for the defense of the Aqsa, affirm with blood to our people and Nation the following:

1. This is the clear and practical response to the greed of the Jewish occupiers and to the terrorist Sharon's stroll in the Aqsa yards under the protection of the occupation authority. It is the strong retaliation to Barak and his government's greed. Al-Quds was and will remain Palestinian, Arab and Islamic and the Aqsa Mosque, the Muslims' first Qibla and site of the prophet's Isra', will remain under our people and Nation's sovereignty. All attempts to steal or desecrate that Mosque will end in failure and will crash on the rock of our people's steadfastness and Jihad.

2. This (spilt) blood form a clear message to the Palestinian Authority demanding its immediate withdrawal from the humiliating negotiations with the Zionist enemy. That blood further asserts to the Authority our people and Nation's rejection to surrender one inch of Al-Quds or any part of the Aqsa Mosque and that the blood of martyrs will burn any agreements giving up our people's rights, Al-Quds and the Aqsa.

3. We call on the Palestinian Authority to respond to our people and Nation's conscience and return to the people's fold and their real option of Jihad and martyrdom. We call on the Authority to deal with the Zionist enemy in the language that it understands best that of force and resistance, the language of Intifadha and revolution against oppression, aggression and occupation. Rights are not begged but rather grabbed through sacrificing blood and soul for the cause of Allah and in defense of His religion and sanctities.
   "Against them make ready your strength to the utmost of your power, including steeds of war, to strike terror into (the hearts of) the enemies, of Allah and your enemies, . . ." (Quran 8/60)

4. We appeal to leaders and peoples of our Arab and Islamic Nation to support our people, back their Jihad and enhance their steadfastness, to end all forms of relationship or negotiations or normalization with the criminal enemy and to perform their duty and responsibility towards Al-Quds and the Aqsa.

5. We call on our patient Palestinian people to continue resisting the criminal enemy and its aggressive ambitions. We request them to be always on the alert and be prepared to protect Al-Quds and the Aqsa and to foil the enemy's schemes. We finally ask them to insist on our sanctities and on constant readiness to sacrifice for their sake regardless of pains and blood.

Allahu Akbar . . . and victory to our Mujahid people

The Islamic Resistance Movement
(Hamas—Palestine)
Friday 29 September 2000

27 September 2000

In the name of Allah the most Gracious the most Merciful

Statement on terrorist Sharon's declared intention to visit the Haram Al-Sharif

In a fresh provocative step to feelings of our Palestinian people in addition to our Arab and Islamic Nation, terrorist Ariel Sharon announced his intention to tour the Aqsa Mosque along with a number of his followers tomorrow Thursday to assert the Zionist occupation authority's sovereignty over the holy Aqsa Mosque

The step falls in line with continuous Zionist aggressive measures against Jerusalem and the holy Aqsa Mosque. It also falls at a time when capitulation negotiations undergone by the Palestinian Authority with the Zionist enemy were progressing and at a time when Zionist calls are voiced out loud demanding sovereignty over the Haram Al-Sharif in preparation for building the alleged temple.

Our Palestinian people:
Our Arab and Islamic Nation:

The Jews have clearly and unequivocally declared their ambition in continuing occupation of Jerusalem and the holy Aqsa Mosque. It is quite clear that plans to demolish the Aqsa Mosque and build the so-called Jewish temple in its place were no longer the aspirations of limited or extremist groups in the Zionist society, as some believed. The fact is that all Jews believed and shared in such an issue no difference in that matter between the labor party led by Barak, the Likud Bloc led by Sharon or the Temple Mount Trustees organization led by Girshon Solomon.

The Palestinian Authority's continuation in negotiations with the criminal enemy under such acts and ambitions is a serious pointer to the bulk of concessions and bargaining offered by that Authority which dared breach our people's principled stands, holy shrines and religion by accepting to negotiate over the holy Aqsa Mosque and Jerusalem. The Authority has already started to table various solutions and proposals such as offering sovereignty over Jerusalem to all world countries as stated by Qrei and leaving sovereignty over the Haram Al-Sharif to the Security Council in addition to Arafat's declaration on his readiness to surrender the Buraq Wall and the Maghareba alley to the Jews!

Our Mujahid Palestinian People:

We call on our people to head tomorrow Thursday to the holy Aqsa Mosque to confront the terrorist Sharon and prevent him from entering the Mosque and its yards and to check his attempt to desecrate it regardless of sacrifices. Let the masses have a say in rejecting and aborting plans and aggressive ambitions of the Jews and in refusing any agreements or projects that would undermine our people and Nation's rights in Jerusalem, the Aqsa and all sanctities.

"And Allah hath full power over His affairs but most of Mankind do not know . . ."

The Islamic Resistance Movement
(Hamas—Palestine)
Wednesday 27 September 2000

2 September 2000

In the name of Allah the most Gracious the most Merciful

Trial of Mujahid Mahmoud Abu Hannoud
Shameful spot in records of the Palestinian Authority

In a flagrant challenge to feelings of our Palestinian people and feelings of our Arab and Islamic Nation, the Palestinian Authority at a late hour yesterday, Friday night 1/9/2000, staged a summary trial of the Mujahid Mahmoud Abu Hannoud the hero of the northern Osaira battle at the so-called state security court. The court sentenced Abu Hannoud to 12 years behind bars! The "comic" trial took five minutes only!

The charges were: first forming armed cells and supplying them with arms and second establishing an alternative authority to that of the PA! The hero Abu Hannoud's response to those charges was: "I am a Mujahid for the cause of Allah and what I have done was a Jihad against occupying enemies and in defense of my country and people."

Our people as well as our Nation have been surprised over the trial of the hero Abu Hannoud and with the oppressive verdict passed against him. The defense team that was composed of more than a hundred lawyer from within Palestine and others from Egypt and Jordan, who volunteered to defend the Mujahid hero was also surprised by the sentence. The team was not informed with date of the trial or the indictment list but rather the court hearing was arranged under the guise of darkness. To cap the comedy, a police lieutenant who does not have a license to practice law was assigned to defend Abu Hannoud.

We in the Islamic Resistance Movement, Hamas, in the light of the crime of trying Mujahid Abu Hannoud would like to affirm the following:

- We condemn this trial or any other trial against this hero and his likes of the Mujahideen. And we condemn the policy of arresting them for the heroic Mujahideen should be honored and their heroism glorified and not imprisoned and tried.

- This trial against Mujahid Abu Hannoud is a national crime that made light of our people's feelings and convictions. It further shocked the feelings of our Arab and Islamic masses.

- This trial is merely a humiliating submission to demands and conditions of the occupation, which impose on the PA and its security apparatuses protection of occupation and security coordination with the Zionist Mossad and Shabak along with the CIA and persecuting and arresting Mujahideen. This summary trial posed as an immolation offered by the PA on the eve of its upcoming meeting with CIA chief George Tenet and US president Clinton.

- This phony trial and its oppressive verdict affirm our people's conviction that the PA had no justice and affirm absence of integrity and independence at its court and judiciary. This reminds our people of the years of scores of make believe courts and tyrannical verdicts conducted by that Authority over the past few years.

- The trial and the harsh verdicts should be rather passed against the leaders of the Zionist enemy and their herds of soldiers who wreaked havoc in the village of northern Osaira at night. They forced its inhabitants out of their homes at gunpoint, demolished one of the houses and destroyed many apartments, where was the PA's leaders and judges towards that enemy's crime?

- We call on the PA in the name of our people within and outside Palestine and on behalf of the Arab and Islamic masses to cancel that trial and its verdict. We call for the immediate release of Mujahid Abu Hannoud, the termination of such trials and the annulment of their verdicts against him and his colleagues the Mujahideen and other notable figures of our people. Our cause today especially in the light of threats against Al-Quds (Jerusalem) and the Aqsa was in dire need of their Jihad and efforts, which necessitate the immediate release of Mujahid Mohammed Daif and other Mujahideen along with other notable figures such as Dr. Ranteesi, Dr. Makadme, Sheikh Jamal Natshe and Sheikh Jamal Mansour.

- We greet and hail our people in the West Bank and Gaza Strip who expressed solidarity with Mujahid Abu Hannoud and flocked into the village of northern Osaira to support its inhabitants. We also highly appreciate the efforts of the lawyers in the defense team who volunteered to defend the Mujahid Abu Hannoud.

- We urge our people in all cities, villages and Palestinian refugee camps along with political forces, popular bodies, professional syndicates and students to express denunciation of the PA's crime of arresting and trying the Mujahid Abu Hannoud. We ask them to express their anger and dismay by all possible means so as to put an end to the Authority's contempt and challenge of our people's feelings and compel it release him and all his brothers the Mujahideen.

"So lose not heart. Nor fall into despair: for ye must gain mastery if ye are true in Faith." (Quran 3/139)

"O ye who believe! If ye obey the unbelievers, they will drive you back on your heels, and ye will turn back (from Faith) to your own loss." (Quran 3/149)

The Islamic Resistance Movement
(Hamas—Palestine)
Saturday 2 September 2000

27 August 2000

In the name of Allah the most Gracious the most Merciful

"Verily Allah will defend (from ill) those who believe" "That, and also because Allah is He Who makes feeble the plans of the unbelievers."

Heroic battle by Mujhaid Mahmoud Abu Hannoud Against Zionist occupation forces

Our Palestinian people . . . Our Arab and Islamic Nation:

Mujahid Mahmoud Abu Hannoud, one of the commanders of the Qassam Brigades, has indulged in a heroic battle in the brave village of Aseera Shamaliya of Nablus, against a terrorist special unit grouping hundreds of Zionist enemy soldiers backed by five helicopter gun ships and armored vehicles. He was able, all praises to Allah, to kill three enemy soldiers and wound nine others, one of whom sustained serious injuries.

The occupation army's suspicious moves started at 9.50 pm Saturday a few meters away from Abu Hannoud housing complex owned by brother of the wanted Mujhaid Abu Hannoud. Close to that complex there was a house of one of his relatives named Nidhal Daghles Abu Yassin where the occupation authority expected the Mujhaid to be there. The enemy soldiers and snipers occupied surrounding houses and stationed in sensitive spots along with rooftops to tighten their siege.

During that siege and build up the Mujahid Abu Hannoud was not inside the house but rather in its vicinity where he surprised the enemy by opening his machinegun fire at the panicked soldiers.

The occupation troops wounded owner of the house Nidhal Daghles in the chest and feet and he could not get out of the house due to his severe injuries. Two hours later the enemy soldiers stormed the house and dragged Daghles out of it for more than 50 meters. They started torturing him, beating his wounds, to force him provide information on the Mujahid Abu Hannoud.

The night of northern Osaira turned into daylight due to the abundant use of flare bombs fired into its skies that were seen by all those in the Nablus vicinity. Shooting and clashes continued until a late hour.

During that military siege and confrontations between Mujahid Abu Hannoud and the enemy soldiers calls of Allahu Akbar and there is no God but Allah were voiced from the Mosques' loudspeakers along with calls on the inhabitants to break the curfew, which the enemy tried to impose on the village. Calls were also voiced for backing the Mujahid Abu Hannoud in a bid to break the siege against him. Men, women, young and old, rushed to the rescue and clashed with the enemy's confused soldiers.

Enemy soldiers arrested five citizens including Imam of the village's main mosque Sheikh Dhirar Hamadne, 39, who was one of the deportees to Marj Al-Zuhour in South Lebanon eight years ago along with the wounded man Nidhal Daghles and each of Ahmed Khalil, Shaher, Taher and Taiseer Abdullah Odeh.

Mujahid Mahmoud Abu Hannoud was able to flee from the occupation army's siege thanks to Allah and reach Nablus despite the injuries in his shoulder, arm and back and the enemy's chase. In Nablus, Palestinian Authority's security men arrested him and he is still in their custody.

The PA's preventive security apparatus had intensified its efforts in the past few months in search of Mujahid Mahmoud Abu Hannoud and arrested all those believed to have any connections with him. They were pressured into providing any information that could lead to his arrest.

Our Palestinian people . . . our Arab and Islamic Nation:

We, in the Islamic Resistance Movement, Hamas, in the light of that unbalanced heroic battle, which led to the killing of enemy soldiers and lowering their morals, affirm the following:

The failure of more than 300 Zionist armed-to-the-teeth soldiers along with their choppers, reconnaissance planes and advanced hardware in arresting the brave hero Mahmoud Abu Hannoud and the killing of three soldiers and the injury of many others proved the fragility of the theory of the so-called "myth of the invincible Zionist army". The incidents also proved that the resistance option was still capable of inflicting heavy losses in lines of that army and defend the Palestinian people's rights.

The military confrontation that took place in Aseera Shamaliya, in which a Qassam Brigade hero stood fast against the Zionist army, boosted our conviction and our people's confidence that when the will of confronting the occupation was coupled with unshaken belief in our creed and principles then we could defeat the Zionist occupation and force its withdrawal from our occupied lands by the grace of Allah.

This is the lesson that should be well absorbed in this sensitive stage of our cause in the light of the successful experience of the brave resistance in Lebanon, especially after the failure of the settlement option in restoring our rights and lands from the enemy in addition to the humiliating conditions attached to that settlement as evident in the results of the latest Camp David summit.

The occupation troops' savage and barbaric aggression against Aseera Shamaliya, storming and besieging it, clamping a curfew on its inhabitants, demolishing one of the houses and leaving an injured person, who was later arrested, for more than an hour without treatment along with other practices proved anew that Zionist terrorism and aggression were still savagely targeting our people even under the so-called "peace march."

Our people's joyful reaction to the military confrontation, within the occupied homeland and in the diaspora, especially inhabitants of Aseera Shamaliya, revealed that our heroic people were still clearly in favor of the struggle option. It also proved that our people were not hesitant in supporting resistance with all available means despite the attempts to blackout or to forge the will of that people in service of the meager settlement program. Hence, we call for backing the resistance option on the official level and allowing the Arab peoples to support that option so that it would succeed in defeating occupation.

While greeting our people especially inhabitants of the steadfast Aseera Shamaliya, we hold the PA responsible for arresting Mujahid Mahmoud Abu Hannoud. We strongly call on that Authority to free him along with all his brothers the Mujahideen and to stop hurdling the resistance program for the enemy's sake. We affirm that maintaining the detention policy against him and his brothers the Mujahideen was an unforgivable national crime and posed as a challenge to the will of our Palestinian people and the Arab and Islamic Nation, which are in dire need of such heroes to lead the Jihad and struggle in defense of the Aqsa, Al-Quds (Jerusalem) and Palestine. We also warn against any harm done to him or delivering him to the enemy.

We appeal to our Arab and Islamic Nation at this crucial stage in history of the cause, with Al-Quds and the Aqsa being main symbols of that stage, to shoulder its responsibility in confronting the Zionist enemy, its practices and ambitions. We call on it to back our people's rights, support their heroic resistance and bolster their insistence on national soil, Al-Quds and sanctities.

"O ye who believe! Give response to Allah and His Messenger when He calleth you to that which will give you life;"

Long lives Arab Islamic Palestine
All sacrifices for the sake of Al-Quds and the Aqsa

Greetings to the Mujahideen and to all our Palestinian
people especially our people in proud Aseera Shamaliya

Allahu Akbar and victory to our people and our nation

The Islamic Resistance Movement
(Hamas—Palestine)
Sunday 27 August 2000

20 August 2000

In the name of Allah the most Gracious the most Merciful

*"And We decreed for Beni Israel in the Book, that twice would
they do mischief on the earth and be elated with mighty
arrogance (and twice would they be punished)"*

**Our souls and blood will be sacrificed for the Aqsa
31st Anniversary of burning the Aqsa Mosque**

To the Palestinian people:
To the Arab and Islamic Nation:

Ever since the Zionist Dennis Rohan committed his crime on Thursday 21 August 1969 and Zionist Jewish spite against the Aqsa Mosque was growing and hoping to destroy the whole lot of it after the fire destroyed most of Salahuddin pulpit, which was installed after liberating Al-Quds from 90 years of crusade occupation in 1187AD. Incidents are accelerating these days and that acceleration bears dangers against the Aqsa Mosque as the Jewish threats and violation of its sanctity increase and as Jewish elevation daily grows to the extent that it is about to assume power in the strongest state on earth. Furthermore, calls are voiced out loud calling for demolishing the Aqsa and building the alleged temple in its place!

Tomorrow falls The anniversary of that ugly crime to remind Muslims with what happened to their Mosque and the possible destruction that could target it, God forbid, in the event silence towards our enemies' conspiracies persisted. During the recent Camp David summit's discussions, the enemy's premier Ehud Barak demanded the establishment of a Jewish synagogue inside the holy Aqsa Mosque's yards. Furthermore, the so called high rabbinate council in the Zionist entity discussed on Monday 7 August the possibility of establishing that synagogue and decided to postpone the debate and not canceling it!!

In a serious development, members of the "Temple Mount Trustees" accompanied by other fanatic Jews tried to enter the Aqsa Mosque through Bab Al-Maghareba on Thursday 10 August. They marched in tumultuous demonstrations chanting anti-Arab and anti-Muslim slogans. They demanded the construction of their alleged temple in place of the Aqsa Mosque on the anniversary of what they consider the destruction of the two temples, which fell on that same day. They carried the foundation stone of what they called their temple and washed it in Ein Silwan while reiterating, "Bring down the Mosque over their (Muslim) heads"!! Meanwhile, severity of the Jewish rabbis' statements calling for leveling the Aqsa Mosque was increasing in an unprecedented manner. In late last July rabbi Abraham Shabeer, who was the Zionist entity's chief Ashkenazi (Western Jews) rabbi and who is currently the biggest source of Jewish edicts, said in a ceremony organized to lay down the foundation stone of a religious school in the presence of ministers, "There is nothing called the Aqsa Mosque. This is a lie fabricated by the Arabs and they believed themselves. Regretfully some of us also believed them."

He added, "There is no way for deception here for the Temple Mount (The Aqsa Mosque) is the property of the Jews and the Jewish people in their Diaspora. It is not becoming of the state, which represents the Jewish people, to give up this place."

To couple the stand of the chief rabbi of the western Jews, the chief rabbi of the eastern Jews Ovadia Yossef, also the chief rabbi of the Shas party, advocated similar stands. In the past few days he condemned presence of Arabs in Al-Quds describing them as snakes and animals. He even attributed lies to almighty Allah by saying that every day Allah "regrets" that he created the Arabs as written in the Talmud "because they are evil doers and hate Israel."

In line with the accelerating campaigns to judaize the city, mayor of the so-called Jerusalem municipality Ehud Ulmert said on 9 August that "After 33 years of preventing Jews to practice their right of prayers in the Aqsa, today work must be done to actualize that right." Ulmert had recently opened a tunnel connecting the Ma'aleh Adomim settlement to the Hebrew University during which he announced the annexation of that settlement to Al-Quds!

Falling in line with such growing dangers engulfing our captured Mosque, there is the American administration's position topped by the US president's call for moving his country's embassy to Al-Quds. There is also his statement during the Camp David summit in which he affirmed that most Christians in the world believed that the Aqsa Mosque was in fact the Temple Mount, displaying total bias to the Jewish viewpoint in this matter. He was also trying to affect the international public opinion into accepting judaization of Islamic sanctities with the blessing of a superpower.

Our fears, worries and concern over fate of the Aqsa and Al-Quds are doubled with recent Arafat's statements after his return from Camp David in which he openly gave up the Buraq Wall to the Jews claiming they had the right to praying at that wall.

Our Palestinian people . . . our Arab and Islamic Nation:

We in the Islamic Resistance Movement (Hamas) on the anniversary of the burning of the blessed Aqsa Mosque would like to explain and affirm the following:

1. The so-called settlement negotiations with the Zionist enemy are nothing but capitulation talks and an umbrella to give up rights. At present those negotiations are drawing the final episode of the conspiracy against our people and Nation through which most of the blessed Palestinian lands are surrendered along with the Muslims' right of owning Al-Quds. Furthermore, the refugees' right of return is being obliterated. Confronting the various stages of the Camp David con-

spiracy should top the list of duties and responsibilities. Such a stance also necessitates exposing all capitulators regardless of their positions.

2.   We call on the Palestinian Authority to end the capitulation talks with the enemy and return to the people's option that of steadfastness and struggle to grab our rights, protect our sanctities and defeat occupation since the enemy only understands the language of force while that of begging only boosts its arrogance.

3.   We urge the Nation's religious scholars to be at the forefront of the lines in face of the Zionist danger and to spread awareness among the Muslim masses about that enemy's aggressive plots against the Muslims' first Qibla, site of our prophet's ascension to the heavens and third mosque that should be visited in Islam.

4.   We appeal to leaders of intellect, parties, movements, Arab and Islamic forces, popular and syndicate bodies and all civilian institutions to assume their role in resisting the Zionist danger and exposing its dimensions. They should confront challenges equipped with determination and active moves in various arenas including spreading public awareness and organizing popular rallies to reflect the Nation's real stand towards Al-Quds and the Aqsa Mosque. Let the governments and regimes listen to the masses' voices and conscience in face of Clinton and Barak's threats.

5.   We ask leaders of the Arab and Islamic countries along with the Organization of Islamic Conference and the Arab League to shoulder their responsibilities and duties towards Palestine, Al-Quds and the Aqsa Mosque. We ask them to support the steadfastness of our people and their living forces that insist on the Nation's rights and defend its sanctities. We finally ask them to adopt the Jihad and struggle option to seize our rights and prepare our Nation's peoples to live up to the level of struggle and challenge with that hideous enemy.

Let our people head tomorrow Monday to Al-Quds on the anniversary of the big crime to gather and pray at the Aqsa Mosque and let all Muslim masses move in support of its great Mosque, the symbol of their pride, honor and dignity before it is too late and before the Nation bewails the third holiest shrine after the Grand Mosque and the Prophet Mosque. Let all rise up in support of our people's steadfastness in Al-Quds and its surroundings. Let all declare in loud voices their rejection of bargaining on one inch of our pure Quds' soil and let all voice up high calls for ending the comic peace negotiations aimed at surrendering our holy shrines.

Let the whole world know that wiping out, demolishing or attacking the Aqsa Mosque would only be possible over the skulls and remains of the whole Nation.

"So when the time of the second (Jewish) mischief in the holy land comes, we will send against you our worshippers to inflict on you utter defeat and enter the Mosque (of Al-Aqsa) as they had entered it before and to devastate with utter destruction whatever they (the Jews) have built in their elevation."

The Islamic Resistance Movement
(Hamas—Palestine)
Department of Islamic Relations
Sunday 20 August 2000

10 August 2000

In the name of Allah the most Gracious the most Merciful

Important appeal to the Arab

and Islamic Nation: Al-Quds is in danger

We call on our people to head in big numbers tomorrow to offer The Friday prayers at the Aqsa Mosque to assert the Muslims' insistence on their Mosque and their preparedness to defend it

Our Palestinian people . . . our Arab and Islamic Nation

Real and great dangers are threatening the blessed Aqsa Mosque, the Muslims' first Qibla and Isra' site of prophet Mohammed, peace be upon him. The spiteful Jews will not be requite until they achieve their aggressive ambitions in destroying the Aqsa Mosque, wiping it out and building their alleged temple in its place. Their conspiracies and efforts were intensified over the past few days for this purpose. It was evident in the following:

1. The position of the enemy's premier Ehud Barak in the ill-fated Camp David summit and his insistence on maintaining Jewish sovereignty on Al-Quds (Jerusalem) and the blessed Aqsa Mosque.

2. The meeting of the Jewish rabbinate council a few days ago including the chief Rabbis of both the western and the eastern Jews to study a plan for establishment of a jewish synagogue in the Aqsa.

3. Threats by Ovadia Yossef, chief rabbi of the Shas Movement, against the Palestinian and Arabs and his racist remarks against them.

4. Conintuous threats by other rabbis such as the one to erase the Aqsa Mosque and end the Muslims control on it that extended for more than 1,400 years and the threat by Gershon Solomon, chief of the temple mount trustees' movement to demolish the Aqsa Mosque on the anniversary of the destruction of their alleged temple.

We, in the Islamic Resistance Movement, Hamas, call on the Arab and Islamic Nation to decisively confront such dangers, defend the Aqsa Mosque and support the Nation's dignity, sanctities and first Qibla. We also urge our Nation's masses to activate their stands by demanding their leaders to check such attempts, sever all ties with the Zionist enemy, expel enemy ambassadors and open the door for Jihad by training and preparing for protecting Al-Quds and the Aqsa Mosque *"Against them make ready your strength to the utmost of your power, including steeds of war . . ."*

We also call on our patient people to head in big numbers, men, women and children, to offer the Friday noon prayers tomorrow at the blessed Aqsa Mosque to confirm the Muslims' insistence on their mosque and preparedness to defend it and sacrifice souls for its sake.

The Islamic Resistance Movement
(Hamas—Palestine)
Thursday 10 August 2000

7 August 2000

In the name of Allah the most Gracious the most Merciful

Hamas comments on statements
by Jewish rabbi Ovadia Yossef

"Commenting on the statements of Jewish chief rabbi of the ultra orthodox Shas movement Ovadia Yossef in which he described the Palestinians as "snakes" and Arab descendants of Prophet Ismail as "liars, evil doers and

Allah has regretted that He created them,"—Allah is above what they attributed to Him—, an official source in the Hamas Movement said:

Such statements reveal the Jews and the occupying Jewish-Zionist entity's racist nature. They further reveal that that entity was growing in extremism, racism and hatred against all Palestinians, Arabs and Muslims.

Such spiteful declarations are only voiced by abnormal psyches that view all non-Jews with arrogance and hatred in addition to considering other peoples "Guyim" as lesser than Jews who consider themselves the "chosen people of Allah."

Quoting Allah as saying such declaration, Allah is above what they attributed to Him, affirm their lies and distortion of Allah's words as included in the verses *"Of the Jews there are those who displace words from their (right) places."* Those statements are pronounced almost two weeks after conclusion of the ill-fated Camp David summit during which the Jewish-Zionists' plotting against Jerusalem was evident along with their aggressive intentions to demolish the Aqsa Mosque and build in its place their alleged temple. Such statements show how naive are those betting on peace with the usurping Zionist entity and coexistence with that extremist occupying people, whom Allah had portrayed as treacherous and Said they revoked pledges with Him, so will the peace and settlement mongers expect the Jews to respect agreements or pledges with them?!

Our people and Nation's experience with the Jews affirms that the only feasible road against the usurping occupation is that of resistance and Jihad and that the only healing against that cancerous disease is total extermination.

> *"Strongest among men in enmity to the*
> *Believers wilt thou find the Jews and Pagans."*

The Islamic Resistance Movement
(Hamas—Palestine)
Monday 7 August 2000

27 July 2000

In the name of Allah the most Gracious the most Merciful

All conspiracies crash at the gates of Al-Quds

Our people has the right to know the true PA stands towards final status issues

After two weeks of meaningless talks between the Palestinian Authority and the Zionist entity, failure of the ill-fated Camp David summit was declared despite the great efforts and pressures practiced by the American administration on the Palestinian side to reach an agreement ending the state of conflict with the Zionist enemy and coronating Bill Clinton's tenure in office with such an accomplishment.

Our Palestinian people:
Our Arab and Islamic Nation:

We have warned from the beginning against involvement in such a summit and affirmed that its success would be inevitably at the expense of our Palestinian people and our Arab and Islamic Nation. Its success would mean the PA's submission to Zionist-American conditions and its approval of the Zionist settlement speculation towards the final status issues namely those of Al-Quds (Jerusalem), refugees, borders, settlements and others.

Failure of the summit because of Al-Quds and the Zionist enemy's insistence on retaining it under Zionist sovereignty affirms that the arrogant Zionist enemy only accepts the total surrender of our people to its will and greed. It also affirms that there is no difference among leaders of the occupying entity as far as our people and their legitimate rights are concerned. Ehud Barak, who was received with a tumultuous welcome by the PA and deceived persons in lines of our people and Nation, is not different from Benjamin Netanyahu as far as arrogance, extremism and hostility to our people are concerned. Peace, in the concept of those people, means absolute submission and surrender to Zionist hegemony and means giving up our people's rights, Quds and sanctities.

The assertion by all parties that Al-Quds was the reason for the failure and that progress was achieved in all other issues make us wonder about what happened over the refugees' right of return, the borders, the settlements and other basic questions?!

All pointers and information indicate that the PA had offered major concessions in all those issues but remained stringent on the issue of Al-Quds in view of its sensitivity and Arab and Islamic dimensions. For it would be difficult to justify any agreement belittling the Palestinian, Arab and Islamic rights in Al-Quds.

The Camp David negotiations were shrouded in secrecy and ambiguity fearing the leakage of information on concessions to the public opinion so as not to affect attempts to reach an agreement. Now the time has come that our people and Nation should know what did really take place in that infamous summit and the PA's true stands regarding the issues of the refugees' return, dismantling of settlements, borders and the Palestinian state's jurisdictions and sovereignty. The general satisfaction towards failure of that summit because of Al-Quds should not make our people forget their rights and other national stable principles. It is also not acceptable to partition the refugees' right of return under the pretext of giving priority to the refugees in Lebanon, which means that the PA had agreed on a partial return of limited numbers of those refugees as suggested by the Zionists.

Our Palestinian people:
Our Arab and Islamic Nation:

In this serious and crucial stage in history of our Palestine cause, we, in the Islamic Resistance Movement, Hamas, affirm the following:

1. we want the PA to brief our people with all frankness and transparency on the complete story of its stands towards various final status issues and not to deceive our people or play with their feelings.

2. we urge leaders of the Arab and Islamic countries along with the Arab League and the Organization of Islamic Conference to adopt strong and clear positions in support of our Palestinian people's steadfastness, Jihad and legitimate struggle for liberating their lands and defeating occupation. We further ask them to assert their stable stands towards Palestinian rights topped by Al-Quds and the refugees' right of return to their homeland.

3. the negotiations' march with the Zionist enemy, particularly the latest one in Camp David; confirm the correct course of the Hamas Movement and other national forces that reject the settlement process. It also affirms the absurdity of the peace process and negotiations and failure of that method to liberate the lands and restore Al-Quds and our people's other rights. Hence, the PA is called upon to divulge frankly what happened, to withdraw from the negotiations' process

and not to insist on proceeding along that dead-end.

4.   the only way to liberate our lands and holy shrines is that of Jihad and martyrdom in addition to steadfastness and resistance; for rights are grabbed and not begged. Rights are forcibly taken through dear blood and unlimited sacrifices. Our people have proven across history that they were capable of being patient and steadfast and of launching Jihad, struggle and sacrifice for the sake of their sacred cause and blessed lands.

5.   we call on the PA to return to the lines of the people and re-arrange the Palestinian home from within. We ask it to meet with us over a comprehensive Jihad and struggle program, to stop persecution of the Mujahideen and to end security cooperation with the enemy. We also call on it to free hands of the resistance while protecting its back and supporting it, to respect anew the fighting guns and to benefit from lessons of the heroic resistance's victory in South Lebanon and the Lebanese official harmony with it.

Hamas, along with all loyal elements of our people, will remain faithful to its people and cause, loyal to their rights and stable doctrines and a guard of their Quds and Aqsa. Hamas will continue to defend, with its Jihad and blood of its sons, our people's rights in their lands and sanctities. Hamas will also maintain its defense of the refugees and their right of return to their lands and of the heroic detainees and their absolute right in freedom.

Allahu Akbar . . . and victory to our people and Nation

**The Islamic Resistance Movement
(Hamas—Palestine)
Thursday 27 July 2000**

23 July 2000

In the name of Allah the most Gracious the most Merciful

"Glory to (Allah) Who did take His prophet for a journey by night from the Sacred Mosque to the Farthest Mosque whose precincts We did bless."

Urgent statement by Hamas

Palestine and Al-Quds (Jerusalem) are the sole property of the Nation; No one has the right to surrender

The Zionist enemy only understands the language of force

The negotiations and bargains on the rights of our people and their sanctities are continuing in Camp David between the Palestinian Authority and the Zionist entity. The American president Bill Clinton insists on retaining each of Arafat and Barak to continue pressures on the Palestinian party so as to offer more concessions and surrender our people's rights and holy shrines for the sake of attaining an agreement coronating his period in office that is about to terminate.

The negotiations are currently focusing on a number of American proposals over major issues of the final settlement basically emanating from the notorious (Abu Mazen-Beilen) doctrine. The proposals stipulate that the PA would give up Al-Quds to remain under sovereignty of the usurping Zionist entity in return for an administrative self-rule in the old quarters of the city and surrounding suburbs. They further stipulate annexing the settlements of Ma'aleh Adomim and Giva'at Ze'ef to Al-Quds and allowing the Palestinians a safe passage to the Aqsa Mosque, which would be under religious administration only.

In a bid to beautify the agreement, a Palestinian state with separated areas and pruned sovereignty, the borders and authorities of which would be determined by the Zionist enemy, would be declared. It would have no army while the enemy would have the right of using its air space and deploying its army in the Jordan Valley. Meanwhile the West Bank would be linked to the Gaza Strip via a flyover bridge.

As for the Zionist settlements, most of them would remain in their places and annexed to the occupation entity in return for exchanging certain areas. The Zionists would enjoy freedom of movement in the vicinity of those settlements that spread like cancer in all of our occupied lands.

The refugees' right of return to their lands would be dropped and efforts would be made to re-settle them in their diaspora. They would be bribed with sums of money as the occupation entity pledged to accommodate a few number of them within family re-union programs. Only half a million refugees would be accommodated gradually in the Palestinian mini-state over a period of 20 years!

Our Palestinian people . . . Our Arab and Islamic Nation

This is the perilous deal that is being negotiated, a mutilated Palestinian state with no sovereignty, will or dignity. It is in fact a self-rule entity linked to the Zionist regime. A deal that stipulates selling Al-Quds and the holy shrines topped by the Aqsa Mosque in return for running municipal services, health and sewerage along with forsaking the refugees' right of return to their lands leaving them for ever in camps of the diaspora.

What is going on in Camp David is a Zionist-American plot against our people, rights, lands, sanctities and Arab and Islamic dignity.

Al-Quds and Palestine are blessed holy lands and are part and parcel of the Muslims' religion and creed. They host the Aqsa Mosque the Muslims' first Qibla and the site of prophet Mohammed's Isra' (night journey) and the third mosque that Muslim should visit as the prophet, peace be upon him, had said. Muslims across the centuries and generations had colored that blessed soil with their blood to retain it in Muslims' hands.

Any surrendering of Al-Quds or part of it is a surrender of the Arab and Islamic Nation's religion and pride and is a flagrant aggression on our creed and sanctities.

No one could or own the right of giving up Al-Quds. Whoever attempts to do so is reneging on our people and Nation's will, a servant to our enemy, an aggressor on our religion and creed. He would not bind us, our people, Arab and Islamic Nation with a thing and he thus represents only himself.

Our Palestinian people . . . our Arab and Islamic Nation

We, in the Islamic Resistance Movement (Hamas), call for the following:

1. We demand Arafat and the Palestinian Authority to immediately withdraw from the farcical Camp David's conspiracy and return instead to the lines of our people in their steadfastness and resistance of the Zionist enemy and its schemes.

2. We urge our steadfast, Mujahid Palestinian people to reflect their anger regarding the cheap bargaining in Camp David over our people, lands, sanctities and rights with all possible means.

3. We appeal to our Arab and Islamic peoples, parties, Movements, groups, authorities, syndicates, unions and popular forces to reject any concession or capitulation in the land of Palestine, Al-Quds and the Aqsa Mosque. We also invite them to express their stands and raise up high their voices to contribute in foiling the conspiracy targeting

Palestine and Al-Quds. It is a compulsory duty on each and every Muslim all over the world.

4. We ask leaders of the Arab and Islamic Nation along with the Arab League and the Organization of Islamic Conference to confront any concession or surrendering of Palestine or Al-Quds and to pressure the PA to prevent it from responding and submitting to Zionist and American pressures.

We, in the Islamic Resistance Movement (Hamas), along with our Palestinian people and our Arab and Islamic Nation will continue to hold fast to our right in our land, Quds and Sanctities. We will continue our steadfastness and struggle and mobilizing our Nation in confrontation of the Zionist occupation and arrogance. We will grab our rights, lands and holy shrines with our own hands by the grace and help of Allah regardless of the lapse of time for the Zionist enemy does not understand the language of begging and submission, which only increase its aggressiveness and arrogance. It only understand the language of Jihad, resistance and martyrdom, that was the language that led to its blatant defeat in South Lebanon and it will be the language that will defeat it on the land of Palestine. We are confident in Allah's promise of victory.

Allahu Akbar and the aggression is only against the oppressors

Allahu Akbar and victory for our people and Nation

**The Islamic Resistance Movement
(Hamas—Palestine)
Sunday 23 July 2000**

15 July 2000

In the name of Allah the most Gracious the most Merciful

There is no justification for Arab and Islamic silence towards the Camp David conspiracy

The convening of the Camp David summit in the American capital grouping US president Bill Clinton, prime minister of the Zionist enemy Ehud

Barak and head of the Palestinian Authority (PA) Yasser Arafat, leads the Palestine cause to a very serious stage that it never experienced over its history.

No doubt Arafat's Authority is largely responsible for deterioration of the Muslims' central cause. However, this does not mean that Muslims are not involved in that sin if they remain silent towards surrendering the holy land and the first Qibla to grandsons of the monkeys and pigs.

The Ummah has passed through times of weakness during which its enemies such as the crusades, the moguls and others had the upper hand but he Ummah, despite its weakness, never recognized what the usurpers had occupied of Muslim land. The Ummah remained pending hopes on an end to the period of weakness and a return of Jihad to uproot the usurpers. One such example was the Hitteen battle in which the hero Salahuddin was able to wipe out crusade armies and managed to liberate most of Sham areas and restored Al-Quds (Jerusalem) to Islamic sovereignty after a hundred years of crusade occupation. When the Ummah was weak again in face of the moguls, capital of the caliphate rule Baghdad fell in their hands along with other Islamic cities. However, the Ummah did not give up and two other leaders Dhaher Beybars and Qutuz were able to defeat the moguls in the battle of Ein Galout on the land of Palestine.

The Ummah's current weakness, during which those on whom the wrath of Allah is ordained have seized a part of Muslim land that is dear to hearts of all Muslims and established on it their alleged entity, is nonetheless a temporary period. It does not mean that the Ummah should accept solutions endorsing the Zionists' rights on the land of Palestine as the negotiations in Camp David now target. The excuse that the PA represents the Palestinian people and that its decision was theirs is a kind of evasion from responsibility and an unacceptable pretext. Events have proven that Arafat's Authority only represented a limited section of the Palestinians and acted in accordance with personal interests along with American and Zionist pressures that made it ready to give up the Palestinian people's rights in their country and lands. That Authority further served as the persecutor of the living popular forces who are insisting on the Jihad and resistance option. It also worked for corrupting the Palestinian people's moral values and spreading indecency in their lines.

Hence, any agreement concluded by that Authority with the Zionist enemy is null and void for that Authority represents only itself. Our right in our land and sanctities will remain solid regardless of the lapse of time and of heavy sacrifices.

We ask the Muslim Ummah, especially the Islamic movements, groups and parties, to shoulder the responsibility towards that sacred cause. They should all check that Authority's concessions and should warn it against repercussions of capitulation. They should also voice out loud such a stance whether through issuing communiqués, organizing angry demonstrations, torching Zionist flags and condemning the Authority's humiliating stands through speeches and lectures. They further should declare insistence on Al-Quds, with both its western and eastern sectors, as a sacred Islamic city that was and will remain for the Ummah of Isra' not for the killers of prophets. They also should declare their rejection of the American-Zionist conspiracy that is currently being hatched in Camp David and refuse its consequences. They must genuinely support steadfastness of the Palestinian people and their Jihad movements to restore the rights, abort the Zionist project and purge the sanctities from the dirt of Jewish occupation.

That is the least the Ummah should do out of its duty towards Palestine so that Al-Quds would not be judaized, the Aqsa demolished, the Azan silenced, the star of David hoisted over the lands of Palestine and the jews allowed to penetrate all Islamic countries.

"Be not weary and faint-hearted, crying for peace, when ye are the uppermost: for Allah is with you, and will never put you in loss for your (good) deeds." (47/35)

**The Islamic Resistance Movement
(Hamas—Palestine)
Saturday 15 July 2000**

10 July 2000

In the name of Allah the most Gracious the most Merciful

"Here is a message for mankind"

"They plot and plan, and Allah too plans, but the best of planners is Allah"

**The doomed Camp David summit
A serious conspiracy against our people,
rights and sanctities**

A new Camp David is to be held in Washington tomorrow grouping US president Bill Clinton, Zionist enemy's premier Ehud Barak and head of the Palestinian Authority Yasser Arafat.

The summit, held at the invitation and pressure of the American president, aims at achieving an accomplishment namely closing the file of the Palestine cause and reaching a framework agreement for a final peace settlement between the PA and the Zionist enemy's government in a bid to end the struggle in the region before expiry of Clinton's term in office.

The Camp David summit targets concluding a framework agreement on issues of the final status of the occupied Palestinian lands in 1967 while indefinitely postponing any agreement on details of those issues. Such a step would entail new and serious Palestinian concessions that would close the file of the Palestine cause. It would also lead to ending the struggle with the Zionist entity and open the doors wide-open for Zionist penetration of the Arab and Islamic region and normalization of relations. Barak had forestalled this summit by announcing his five Nos clearly pinpointing his government's stands. Those are: no return to the pre 5 June 1967 borders, no division of Al-Quds (Jerusalem), no to the right of return of Palestinian refugees to their homeland, no to dismantling of settlements, no to presence of any other army than the Zionist one in Palestine. As for the PA, it declared its demands of implementing the remaining articles of the transitional stage and its intention to declare the Palestinian state on 13 September.

While the Zionist aggressor heads to that summit armed with those red lines and a public opinion rejecting to grant our people their rights, the PA goes to the summit carrying the illusion of the American role and stripped of any popular support. The PA is rather carrying the burden of quelling the loyal forces and Mujahideen of our people. It goes to the summit with actual readiness to offer dangerous concessions that apparently had been already approved or showed signs of approval during secret rounds of negotiations in Stockholm and others.

The self-rule Authority, realizing that it had already wasted a lot of rights and bypassed basic principles, will seek to cover up any concession via a big deception campaign directed to our people along with the Arab and Islamic Nation. It will attempt to highlight the declaration of the state as the real victory and the most wanted wish or aspiration. Thus it would be ignoring our people's will, hopes and preparedness to sacrifice and it would jump over decades of Jihad and sacrifice.

At this time, the expected results of the Camp David summit will be more serious on our people, cause and rights. The PA now is demanded to present the most important element in the humiliating settlement process, which started in Madrid and Oslo and would only end in total surrender and absolute submission to the Zionist enemy.

Our Palestinian people . . . Our Arab and Islamic Nation

The dangers of the ill-fated Camp David summit on our cause and people, in the event the PA succumbed to American and Zionist pressures, would be represented in the following:

1. The PA's acceptance of the so-called Palestinian state with Zionist and American conditions so that it would be stripped of its will, sovereignty and dignity.

2. Giving up Al-Quds and its sancties leaving the holy city united under Zionist sovereignty and be requited with Alezariye, Abu Dees and a passage to the Aqsa Mosque. Meanwhile, efforts to judaize the holy city would continue along with the Zionist groups' attempts to sacrilege the Aqsa Mosque and destroy it to build the alleged temple in its place.

3. Abandoning the Palestinian refugees' right of return to their lands and country and accepting compensation and resettlement in other countries.

4. Retaining settlements as castles spreading like cancer in all Palestinian lands and keeping the herds of armed settlers as continued threat against our unarmed people.

5. Penetrating the Arab and Islamic region and opening the door for normalization and all forms of official political relations with the Zionist enemy at the pretext that the Palestine cause was settled and the struggle was terminated.

6. Continuing to strike the live popular forces that insist on the option of Jihad and resistance along with increasing security cooperation with the Zionist enemy in pursuing the Mujahideen and protecting occupation.

Our Palestinian people . . . Our Arab and Islamic Nation

We in the Islamic Resistance Movement, Hamas, at this serious stage would like to assert the following:

1. We consider the Camp David summit as a new Zionist-American conspiracy that target terminating our people's stable rights in Palestine, Al-Quds, return of refugees, dismantling of settlements and surrendering the right of establishing a fully sovereign state enjoying full rights in its waters and borders in return for a cartoon state.

2. We condemn the PA's approval to attend that summit of conspiracies and warn it against infringing or giving up our people's rights and inalienable doctrines that are not for bargaining under any circumstances. We affirm that the PA does not represent our people in that case and it would be considered out of their national line if it went ahead with such concessions.

3. Backed by our Palestinian people and the Arab and Islamic Nation, we consider any result of that summit including surrendering of any part of our blessed lands or our people's rights and dignity, as null and void. They would not bind our people or Nation, and we affirm that our people within and outside the homeland did not entrust any party to surrender their rights.

4. The PA's repeated declaration of timings to announce the Palestinian state was a mere deception to market its dangerous concessions and surrender of our people's rights in return for a meager state tailored to fit Zionist standards and specifications.

5. We call on our steadfast and heroic people including their vivid Mujahid powers in the homeland and the diaspora to resist any concessions or relinquishment of our rights. We call on them to express the people's anger and denunciation of the PA's practices and concessions with all possible means. We ask them to abort all plots hatched against our people and escalate popular confrontations against the enemy to shake the ground under the occupiers' feet.

6. We call on leaders of the Arab and Islamic countries to reject any surrendering of Palestinian rights and to practice all possible pressures on chairman of the PA, warning him against the repercussions of capitulation and surrender. We also ask our Arab and Islamic peoples to strongly back our Palestinian people and their Mujahid forces to restore rights and bolster our people's steadfastness, Jihad and resistance in face of the Zionist offensive.

7. Hamas confirms the necessity of forging a solid national unity on the basis of a new national project envisaging unity of the land and people. It further demands adopting Jihad and resistance as the sole road to liberate the lands and defeat the usurping occupation.

"Against them make ready your strength to the utmost of your power, including steeds of war, to strike terror into (the hearts of) the enemies of Allah and your enemies . . ."

The Islamic Resistance Movement
(Hamas—Palestine)
Monday 10 July 2000

24 May 2000

In the name of Allah the most Gracious the most Merciful

". . . How oft, by Allah's will, hath a small force vanquished a big one . . ."

Today Lebanon . . . Tomorrow Palestine
Congratulations to Lebanon and its brave
resistance for their great victory

The Lebanese people along with the Arab and Islamic Nation these days celebrate the resistance's victory over the enemy's army and its quislings in South Lebanon. Here it is, the Zionist enemy, running away from South Lebanon humiliated, panicked and defeated. And here it is the army of agent Lahd collapsing and vanishing completely after the brave Islamic and nationalist Lebanese resistance turned its life, along with that of the occupation, into unbearable hell thanks to heroism and daring operations of the Mujahideen. Lebanon, on the official and popular levels, has adopted and supported the resistance with all its trends, sects and strength. It extended support and backing, it was patient and bore the repercussions, blood . . . pain . . . tears, and here it is now reaping the fruit of its patience, Jihad and stands.

Our Arab and Islamic Nation:

The victories of our people in Lebanon against the Zionist enemy affirm beyond any doubt that Jihad, resistance, blood and sacrifices extract rights. Victory is not granted nor begged. The Lebanese victory emphasizes that the Zionist enemy only understands the language of force and arms and only kneels before steadfast men. The Palestinian people should be fully aware of that lesson and to resume, with its guidance, their Jihad and resistance.

Our Palestinian people
Our Arab and Islamic Nation:

It is really painful that at the time when the Lebanese people and government affirm their cohesion and support to the resistance and achieve their wonderful victories, the Palestinian Authority, on behalf of the occupation, pursues the Mujahideen to arrest them. It also confronts our angry masses and prevents them from engaging the occupation soldiers. The PA is also seeking to abort the latest Palestinian detainees' Intifadha.

The PA thought that through such practices it would please the occupiers and facilitate its humiliating negotiations with them while Barak's arrogance was increasing along with his conditions and dictates on the PA, which finally gives up because it lost all pressure and power cards and stood before the Zionist enemy completely paralyzed and submissive.

Our Palestinian people
Our Arab and Islamic Nation:

We, in the Islamic Resistance Movement, Hamas, and on behalf of the patient, steadfast Palestinian people congratulate the brotherly Lebanese people, government and brave resistance topped by the heroes the Mujahideen of Hizbullah over their great victory and for liberating their lands and forcing out the invading occupiers. We also congratulate Syria and Iran and all those who backed the resistance. Congratulations to our Palestinian people and to our Arab and Islamic nation for this victory. And we pledge to our people and Nation and we vow to all martyrs and steadfast detainees that we will go ahead along the road of Jihad and resistance insisting on our right to all of our lands regardless of the length of that road or its dear sacrifices and no matter how arrogant was the Zionist enemy.

We are confident that the will of our people will be victorious in the end exactly similar to the victory of the Lebanese people's will against Zionist aggression and arrogance.

Allahu Akbar and victory to our people and Nation

The Islamic Resistance Movement
(Hamas—Palestine)
Wednesday 20 Safar 1421H
24 May 2000

16 May 2000

In the name of Allah the most Gracious the most Merciful

The PA commits another crime by arresting

The Mujahid commander Mohammed Daif

We hold it responsible for any harm done to him or any threat to his life

Our detainees in occupation jails are engaged in the battle of empty stomachs against the occupation authority, our people are revolting in various cities, villages and refugee camps in solidarity with our heroic detainees and engaging the enemy troops in bloody confrontations, the Zionist enemy's government is degrading the Palestinian Authority imposing on it humiliating concessions over Al-Quds (Jerusalem), right of return and settlements in the so-called final status talks.

At such a critical stage, the PA committed a sinful crime by arresting the Mujahid hero Mohammed Daif as a sacrifice for the Zionist enemy's government and as a price for the latter's approval to surrender part of the blessed land of Palestine in Abu Dees and Alezariye to the PA. The arrest also came to pave the way for the government of the enemy to announce its approval of the establishment of an illusionary (Palestinian) state that is based on scattered areas of land, with no army or sovereignty on land, air or wealth. The PA is thus performing its role, drawn by the occupation, to strike the resistance, humiliate our people, accept the occupation as a de facto situation and submit to its conditions and dictates.

This crime is yet another chain in a series of similar crimes against heroic Mujahideen of our people especially the Qassam Brigades, some of which included sharing in assassinating the two heroes Eng. Yehya Ayyash and Kamal Keheil and assassinating their brothers heroes Eng. Mohaiuddin Sharif, Adel and Emad Awadallah in addition to scores others of our people's heroes and Mujahideen.

The timing and the attempt to cover up for the crime in addition to attempting to deny it in the media aim at deceiving our people and avoiding their expected angry reaction against that Authority, a matter that would expose its symbols and security officials.

We, in the Islamic Resistance Movement, Hamas, condemn that hideous crime, which reveals treachery, cowardice and villainy. We warn that

Authority of insisting on its crime or of any harm done to our brother the hero or handing him over to the occupation authority and we demand his immediate release along with all other detainees in its jails.

Let the Authority know that by insisting on that crime, it would be fighting its own people and their right of defending their lands and resisting the Zionist occupiers. It would be also turning its back on the Jihad and sacrifices of our people, Ummah, Islam and Arabism.

Let the Authority, along with the occupation; know that our Jihad and resistance against occupation will continue until liberation regardless of obstacles, campaigns or treachery. We are confident that victory is for the believers the Mujahideen and that shame is the fate of all quislings. We are confident that Allah supports us and also our people and all those oppressors will one day realize what a deep pit they had fallen in. And Allah's ordained words will no doubt be prevalent, But most people do not know.

And it is a Jihad until victory or martyrdom

**The Islamic Resistance Movement
(Hamas—Palestine)
Tuesday 12 Safar 1421H
16 May 2000**

15 May 2000

In the name of Allah the most Gracious the most Merciful

On the anniversary of the Nakba and for the sake of detained heroes

The blood of the martyr Samer Ortani fuels Palestinian anger

Palestinian anger against the Zionist enemy and its soldiers and settler herds is escalating in each and every city, village and refugee camp in our occupied Palestinian lands. The popular confrontations are persisting in solidarity with our heroic detainees who waged an open hunger strike. They decided to launch the battle of empty stomachs to force the Zionist enemy to release them.

A hero, a martyr from the Islamic Resistance Movement, Hamas, sacrifices his soul for the cause of Allah and as a price of dignity and freedom; and for the sake of steadfast detainees in Zionist dungeons:

Martyr Samer Ahmed Abdul Karim Ortani

One of Hamas' cadres who fell at the hands of the Zionist enemy troops in steadfast Qalqilya. His cherished blood irrigated the soil of the sacred land of Palestine to fuel the Palestinian anger in face of the usurping occupiers.

Our Mujahid people

Let the popular confrontations in our entire occupied lands rise on the anniversary of the Nakba (disaster) and in solidarity with the heroic detainees. Let us face the occupiers with our bare chests and with stones of our blessed lands. Let the lands turn into fire under the Zionists' feet.

Our Palestinian people . . . our Arab and Muslim Ummah

On the anniversary of the Nakba . . . the anniversary of the declaration of the occupying Zionist entity on our usurped lands, we affirm to our people anew that Palestine, all of Palestine from the (Mediterranean) sea to the river (Jordan) is the sole property of the Palestinian people, the Arab Nation and the Muslim Ummah. It is an Islamic Waqf land that no human being can give up, negotiate or sell in return for a humiliating illusionary peace or as a price for a country with deformed will and sovereignty. On the anniversary of the Nakba, our people affirm their attachment to Al-Quds (Jerusalem) all of Al-Quds . . . the eternal capital of the free and dignified Palestine. Our people also affirm the right of their refugees in the diaspora to return to their lands. On the anniversary of the Nakba, our people affirm that they are a people of Jihad and martyrdom, a people of continuous struggle, a people of the great Intifadha and a people of sacrifices.

Our Palestinian people . . . our Arab and Muslim Ummah

On the anniversary of the Nakba, and in the wake of the escalating popular confrontations in solidarity with the heroic detainees, the Hamas Movement vows to you that it will remain loyal to its people, Ummah, blood of martyrs and to the towering detainees in prison cells. Hamas affirms that it will continue along the road of resistance and Jihad as the sole road for grabbing our rights, protecting our sanctities, liberating our prisoners and defeating the aggressors.

Allahu Akbar and victory for our Mujahid people

**The Islamic Resistance Movement
(Hamas—Palestine)
Monday 11 Safar 1421H
15 May 2000**

15 May 2000

In the name of Allah the most Gracious the most Merciful

Congratulations to our people over the release of The Mujahid leader Salah Shehade

Twelve years in Jail was part of the price that a Mujahid like Sheikh Salah Shehade had paid in sacrifice for his country and cause. Twelve years of struggle along with his colleagues the other detainees in occupation prisons, recording shining pages of heroism and sacrifice for the sake of our land, cause and sanctities.

The Zionist Occupation authority has refused to set free the Mujahid Salah Shehade despite the fact that his prison sentence had expired. It renewed his arrest for more than two years in a way exposing arrogance of occupation, which does not accord any weight to right, and whose entity is founded on aggression, oppression and wrong for 52 years.

Brother Salah Shehade, along with his brothers the Mujahideen in the military wing of Hamas, represented the symbol of Jihad and resistance for our people and Ummah. They represented a symbol of patience and steadfastness, a model in challenging jailers. The operations, which he launched along with his brothers, posed as our people's hope for victory and liberation. His steadfastness in jail was a model of pride and dignity through which he affirmed that the Qassam heroes never bargain over their country, sanctities or dignity of their people and that they sacrifice their souls for the cause of Allah in their battle against occupation. They drew to other detainees the image of a patient believer.

We, in the Islamic Resistance Movement, Hamas, affirm that releasing all heroic detainees will remain our and our people's permanent goal and that we will not rest until the last prisoner of our people is set free.

The coincidental release of Mujahid Salah Shehade with the popular confrontations, the solidarity campaigns with our detainees and resisting occupation soldiers and settler herds strongly affirm that rights are grabbed. It also underscores that releasing heroic detainees is only possible through pressuring the occupation authority and escalating confrontations against it rather than begging (for rights) at the negotiating table.

We regret that the release of Sheikh Salah Shehade fell at a time when the Palestinian Authority is pursuing and arresting Mujahideen in service of Zionist occupation.

Allahu Akbar and victory for our Mujahid people

The Islamic Resistance Movement
(Hamas—Palestine)
Monday 11 Safar 1421H
15 May 2000

14 May 2000

In the name of Allah the most Gracious the most Merciful

On the anniversary of the establishment of the usurping Zionist entity

Let the popular confrontations with the enemy

soldiers and settlers continue in solidarity with the heroic detainees

Nation wide strike in Palestine tomorrow in solidarity with the detainees

The heroic detainees in prisons of the Zionist enemy's jails continue their open hunger strike demanding their release and ending their ordeal after the humiliating peace agreements and negotiations between the Palestinian Authority and the enemy failed to set them free. Their strike was also launched after hopes of most of them in freedom faded away due to their political opposition to the capitulatory agreements concluded with the usurping occupiers.

The heroic detainees have decided to take the matter into their own hands and extract their own thorns, thus they launched the battle of empty stomachs to halt the series of oppression, suppression and torture, which they daily suffer in enemy jails. They also decided to resist attempts to break their will and steadfastness by humiliation, beating, constant provocations, solitary confinement, which lasted for more than three years for some of them, depriving them of seeing their relatives and children and refusing to provide medicine or medical treatment along with bad detention conditions.

We, in the Hamas Movement, affirm our absolute support to all heroic detainees and stress the following:

1. we hail the heroes of our people and their towering symbols in jails. We assert to them that their cause will permanently remain at the top of our priorities and programs. We also affirm that liberating them will remain the noble goal that we will work for along with all our people and Mujahideen. We stress that our people will never forget them regardless of their affiliation and will never forget their sacrifices and Jihad for the sake of their people, cause, nation, Quds and sanctities.

2. our people's Intifadha in various areas of our country against the enemy soldiers and settler herds is but a reflection of the faithfulness of our people, young and aged, women and men, to those heroic detainees. The uprising also points to the status of those heroes, the bright stars in our country's skies and in hearts and conscience of our country and nation's hearts.

3. we call on our Palestinian people in each and every city, village and refugee camp to maintain their supportive campaigns with the detainees and to escalate popular confrontations with the enemy soldiers and settler herds in solidarity with the heroic detainees and to mobilize all efforts for the sake of ensuring their release.

4. we ask the Palestinian Authority to immediately halt its absurd negotiations with the Zionist enemy if it was really serious in adopting the issue of the detainees.

5. we beseech leaders of Arab and Islamic countries along with the Arab League and the Islamic Conference Organization to express solidarity with the detainees of our steadfast people and to adopt their just cause in all international platforms. We appeal to them to organize activities and different programs to spread awareness of their case and shed light on their sufferings in addition to exercising all necessary efforts to guarantee their release.

6. we call on the UN Secretary General Mr. Kofi Annan to exert all efforts possible to liberate our detainees in enemy jails and to halt all forms of repression and violation of human rights and dignity of those detainees at the hands of the occupation authority.

8. we invite our people to launch a commercial strike in all occupied Palestinian lands tomorrow Monday 15 May in solidarity with our heroic detainees and to display popular backing for their release and to declare our people's rejection of the establishment of the usurping Zionist entity on our occupied lands, the anniversary of which falls tomorrow.

As for you, the brave heroes behind bars, towering like the Dome of the Rock, loyal men who made glory for their people and nation . . . we feel with you, all your sufferings and pains, steadfastness and patience, revolution against the jailers, hunger strike. We will remain in your support with all our might until you enjoy freedom, break the shackles of imprisonment and return to your people and families.

Let us all stand united in backing of the detainees to realize their goals of freedom and dignity and let confrontations escalate in all areas against occupation, its soldiers and settlers and let us all stick to the option of steadfastness "If you raise high the word of Allah, He will make you victorious and steadfast."

Allahu Akbar and victory for our Mujahid people

The Islamic Resistance Movement
(Hamas—Palestine)
Sunday 10 Safar 1421H
14 May 2000

21 April 2000

Urgent Appeal To our people and Ummah to back the heroic detainees and adopt their cause. The heroic detainees in enemy jails are persisting in their hunger strike for more than ten days

The heroic detainees in prisons of the Zionist enemy are persisting in their hunger strike, which they started on 10th April to pressure the Zionist entity into releasing them and end their suffering. Their strike is further aimed at protesting their inhuman detention conditions and the daily harassments and suppression, which they are subjected to at the hands of the Zionist prison authorities.

Those heroic detainees, held behind bars, in solitary confinement and in savage torture cellars . . . are the Palestinian people's conscience and their bright stars who have waged Jihad for the sake of their people and Arab and Muslim Ummah. They have struggled in defence of their people and Ummah's dignity, Quds and sanctities. They are now tormented in occupation prisons, aspiring for freedom and an end to their suffering and detention.

More than two thousand detainees are subjected daily to cruel courses of humiliation and oppression in addition to attempts to break their will and steadfastness. They are stripped of their clothes, thrown with gas canisters, beaten and provoked by hateful Zionist jailers other than solitary confinement in dark cells for long periods that lasted for more than three years for many of them.

Our steadfast Palestinian people
Our Arab and Muslim Ummah

This is not all that your sons suffer in Zionist oppressive dungeons, for writing about them takes long pages of pain and anger. Lately the Zionist prison authorities opened a big prison specially for isolating Palestinian captives called Hadarim. A big number of Palestinian detainees were thrown there and not allowed to see their relatives for more than six months while continued solitary confinement penalties continued against prisoners in Beer Sheba and Ashkelon prisons.

The occupation authorities also cancelled a lot of gains and rights extracted by detainees during the past few years through their Jihad, struggle and steadfastness. They were now deprived of seeing their children and prevented from receiving second-degree relatives.

In face of such Zionist inhuman practices that contradict all international laws and norms, to improve their detention conditions, to re-impose their cause that was lost and faded because of the Palestinian Authority's continued concessions and submission to Zionist dictates in various negotiation rounds, and to pressure the Zionist enemy into releasing them, the heroic detainees waged the "war of empty stomachs" and maintained their hunger strike since 10th of this month.

Those heroic detainees' main demand is their release to acquire their right of freedom, until that is attained they demand improving their detention conditions as follows:

1. Halting the prison administration's ferocious offensive and the daily harassment against prisoners.

2. Ending the state of solitary confinement in Beer Sheba and Ashkelon prisons and closing down the Hadarim prison.

3. Granting the detainees their right of ventilation in summer and heating in winter.

4. Allowing the prisoners to study in Arab and foreign universities.

5. Permitting children to visit their fathers along with second-degree relatives.

6. Removing asbestos from windows of their rooms.

7. Taking out a bed from each room to ease pressure within those rooms.

8. Allowing adequate medical care and expediting operations.

Our Palestinian people
Our Arab and Muslim Ummah

We owe those detainees the right of support, and utmost efforts to liberate them, to preserve their dignity and to rid them of the daily torture, which they are subjected to. Thus we call for the following:

1. Organizing activities in solidarity with those detainees such as sit-ins and marches in our Palestinian land and outside it.

2. Allocating the Friday Khutba (sermon) in all mosques to shed light on the issue of those detainees, their sufferings and the inhuman Zionist practices against them.

3. We call on the Palestinian Authority to stop its futile negotiations with the Zionist entity if it was really serious in adopting the case of the detainees.

4. We ask the Arab League and the organization of Islamic Conference to adopt the Palestinian detainees' cause, organize activities in solidarity with them and exert all efforts to maintain their dignity and ensure their release.

5. We call on Arab, Muslim and freedom loving media men to adopt their cause, giving prominence to their suffering and exposing the enemy's repressive measures against them.

6. We ask human rights' organizations and institutions to defend the Palestinian detainees in occupation prisons and to organize a campaign of solidarity with them and to pressure the occupation authorities for the sake of setting them free.

We hereby congratulate the Lebanese resistance and steadfast people over the release of 13 Lebanese Mujahid from Zionist captivity as a result of the unified resistance stance in the Lebanese arena, which is a model to be followed and developed in the Palestinian arena so that all would back and protect the resistance and not turn into a daggers in its back, as some parties do.

We, in the Islamic Resistance Movement (Hamas), vow to our people and our steadfast detainees, that their cause, defending it and attempting to set them free would remain at the topmost of our priorities, and this is the least duty we can do towards those heroes who waged Jihad and struggle for the sake of their people and Ummah's dignity and in defence of their religion and sanctities.

The Islamic Resistance Movement (Hamas—Palestine)
Friday 16th Moharram 1421
21st April 2000

17 April 2000

In the name of God, the Merciful, the Mercy-giving

Statement by Khaled Mishaal Hamas political bureau chief to the Palestinian people and the Arab and Muslim Ummah on the occasion of the Palestinian prisoner's day—17 April

To the Mujahid Palestinian people:

More than two thousands of your faithful sons are still in the Zionist enemy's jails suffering from the worst kind of torture, repression, humiliation and isolation under very difficult circumstances that violate the human dignity and simplest human rights.

They are the best of men, the pioneers who sacrificed themselves for the sake of Allah and devoted their soul and blood for the sake of your freedom and pride. They have sacrificed themselves in defence of Al-Quds (Jerusalem) and the holy blessed land aspiring for the ultimate goal of liberation and building a bright future for us all.

Today is the Palestinian prisoners' day . . . the day of solidarity with them, backing them and activating with their cause with all forms and means until they attain their freedom and force the enemy to halt its inhuman practices against them and set them free.

It is the least duty we should perform towards them, for they have a much greater right . . . for they are the blessed Intifada makers, heroes of the Jihad and martyrdom operations and protectors of the sanctities in Al-Quds, Khalil (Hebron), Nablus and Gaza in addition to all cities, villages and refugee camps in the West Bank and Gaza Strip. They are the ones who drew, with their sacrifices and daringness, the picture of the country and features of the Mujahid people, and hoisted up high the name of our people and cause all over the world.

The most precious things owned by peoples and countries are the human being, land and sanctities. Countries, which respect themselves, and living peoples, are those who preserve the human being's life and dignity as well as defending their lands, doctrines and holy shrines offering in the process the most precious sacrifices. It is not correct at all, especially in our Palestinian matter, to surrender our Palestinian human being's right, freedom and dignity or to fall short towards our principles and sanctities or preoccupy ourselves away from liberating our lands from occupation for the sake of alternate partial gains and decorative rituals.

The prisoner's day is an opportunity to pursue a serious policy in support of our heroic prisoners behind bars, back their rights and stand by their families. We should amend the present situation and re-arrange our priorities to be topped by liberating prisoners and lands and stick to our right to Al-Quds not accepting any alternative to it. We should also stick to our religion, values, principles, and national prerogatives and insist on the refugees' right to return to their homeland.

The prisoner's day urges us to back the detainees in both the enemy jails and those of the Palestinian Authority, which should immediately release all Mujhadeen and detainees if it was serious in reviving that day. It is an outright contradiction to call on the enemy to release Palestinian detainees while your jails are crowded with renowned cadres, Mujahideen and freedom fighters.!! We furthermore warn you against deceiving our prisoners and people by asking for the release of some of them in return for relinquishing great portion of our people's rights in their lands and pride through your meager negotiations with our enemy.

To all our free people

Your brothers the detainees have started a continuous program of struggle and steadfastness in various forms in defence of their dignity and rights demanding their freedom. They have voiced warm appeals asking you to move for their sake. You already responded in various cities, villages and refugee camps so go ahead with your efforts and double them, for the freedom of those detainees and their just demands is not their cause alone but the cause of us all. We are a live Muslim people who can never forget their prisoners, because in short they are the symbols of Jihad, heroism, dignity and pride.

To sons of our Arab and Muslim Ummah

The captives of Palestine in the enemy prisons are asking you for support and appeal to you to save them from Zionist claws. So do not let them down, you owe them the rights of fraternity, Jihad, joint destiny and joint battle.

The prophet, peace be upon him, said, "the believer to the believer is like a building that groups together." He also said, "a Muslim is the brother to (other) Muslim, he does not oppress him nor give up him" and in another narration "Does not let him down"

The U.S.A. and other Western countries back their citizens and followers and seek to rescue their prisoners and detainees even if they were agents and spies or even criminals. The Zionist entity defends all Jews in the world even if they committed crimes against the country they live in and carry its nationality. Here they are now mobilizing the whole world for the sake of the 13 Jews accused of spying in Iran, so why do we belittle our own sons? Why should we be less than other nations? Our Ummah that was known for supporting the weak and the oppressed, regardless of his religion and sent an army for the sake of a woman who called on Mo'tassem in Amoriya to save her, should rather be the spearhead in saving its sons the Mujahideen in Palestine who defend Al-Quds and its surroundings, those who resist the Zionist enemy that targets the whole Ummah and poses a serious danger against it.

As for you our heroic prisoners and detainees

Your people will not let you down and your Movement (Hamas) and all living forces in Palestine and the whole of the Ummah will never let you down and will not forget you until you win your freedom and re-unite with your sons and families God willing.

The pages of glory, heroism and dignity against the Zionist Jews, which each and every Palestinian, Arab and Muslim are proud of, you and the devoted martyrs have made with your blood and sacrifices. Thanks to Allah then to you and to those who march along your path, before or after you, and those who fell as martyrs or those who still wait and never change their position.

> **Mercy and immortality for our faithful martyrs**
> **Freedom and glory to our heroic detainees**
> **Pride and dignity to our steadfast Mujahideen**
> **Allahu Akbar and victory for the Mujahideen**

9 April 2000

In the name of God, the Merciful, the Mercy-giving

New wave of arrests takes place in Jenin and Nablus by PA security apparatus

Commenting on the Palestinian Authority's newest arrests in Jenin and Nablus, a responsible source in the Hamas Movement stated the following:

At a time when the Palestinian Authority is standing helpless in the face of the Zionist enemy and is surrendering to whatever that enemy dictates, it continues the policy of repression, violation of liberties and tightening the noose round our people's rights, freedoms and dignity. That Authority arrested a number of school students in the city of Nablus for preparing a photo exhibition in solidarity with our people's detainees in the jails of the

Zionist enemy on the occasion of the Palestinian detainee's day. The PA also arrested a number of Islamic cadres in the city of Jenin.

Such incessant arrests within the ranks of our people confirm that the PA and its security apparatus are in a state of confusion. These arrests further make clear the PA's annoyance with any activity, even if it is at the level of secondary school students. It is all the more painful that the Authority adds new detainees to the already existing list, at a time when our people are expressing their solidarity with internees in occupation prisons on the anniversary of the Palestinian detainee's day!

That Authority, which neglected the issue of those heroic detainees, surrendered to the enemy conditions regarding them and left them to oblivion and is now trying to repress any activity to revive their case, such as expressing solidarity with them or pressuring the enemy to release them.

The PA's repeated arrests in Jenin and Nablus—even the arrest of students—all add to its long record of suppression of public freedoms and detention of honourable elements opposing its capitulatory policy as far as our people's rights and sanctities are concerned. Those elements object to the PA's corruption, to security cooperation with the enemy's security bodies and to the prosecution and liquidation of the Mujahideen. We recall here what happened to the group of 20 and the security men's assault against a number of Legislative Council members.

Such repressive practices will not prevent our people and their active forces, syndicates and students from persisting in their role in confrontation of the occupation, backing the resistance, maintaining solidarity with the internees, rejecting PA's policies and suppressive practices and exposing its corrupt administration and security apparatuses.

We demand that the PA immediately release all detainees, end political detention and halt its repressive measures. We also call on our people to maintain solidarity with the heroic detainees in the jails of the Zionist enemy and the Palestinian Authority.

Islamic Resistance Movement—Hamas—Palestine

11 March 2000

In the name of God, the Merciful, the Mercy-giving

"And hold fast to God's rope and do not separate"

Declaration concerning
the Arab Foreign Ministers' meeting in Beirut

The Islamic Resistance Movement (Hamas) hails the initiative of the League of Arab States, represented in the meeting of its Foreign Ministers Council, to hold its current session today in the Lebanese capital, Beirut, as a sign of support for the resistance movement and in solidarity with the right of fraternal Lebanon to defend its land and people.

This meeting constitutes an important opportunity to affirm Arab solidarity with the leadership, people, and resistance movement of Lebanon, and the response to Zionist arrogance in its on-going aggression against populated civilian areas of Lebanon, in violation of the international norms and laws that prohibit such actions.

The Arab Foreign Ministers' meeting, backing the resistance movement as it does, is a firm indication that our Arab Nation possesses the will to stand together, solid and steadfast, and that it rejects attempts of the Zionist enemy and its hegemonic backers to separate and overcome the Arab peoples, one by one. This meeting is an important step towards healing the Arab condition in general, bringing it together and uniting its ranks.

The Hamas Movement and with it the Palestinian people, as they hail the Arab foreign ministers' meeting in Beirut, would like to affirm the following points, hoping that they might become a pivot for discussion and counsel:

1.   A reaffirmation of the moral and material support of the Arab states for the Islamic and Patriotic Resistance movement in Lebanon against the Zionist occupation, and in affirmation of the legitimate right of Lebanon to defend its territory, and to regain its sovereignty over it.

2.   A declaration that the Arab states stand at the side of the Palestinian people and their genuine and active support for the resistance program against the Zionist occupation, and in rejection of the attempts of the hegemonic powers to impose a racist colonialist solution on our people and nation, by negating their just and historic rights through the establishment of a feeble form of "self rule." The Lebanese

and Palestinian resistance is the strongest possible language, one that the Zionist enemy can understand and thoroughly reckon with.

3.   A halt to attempts to normalize relations with the Zionist entity that occupies our land and the activation of the declaration of the last Arab summit meeting held in Cairo that called for a halt to normalization.

4.   A transcendence by the Arab governments of their differences, and an affirmation of the fact that they are at one in their aims and in their defiance of external attempts to assert hegemony over them, and a firm declaration rejecting the embargo that the United States has imposed upon Iraq and the Sudan, supporting the right of the peoples to choose their own future.

The Hamas Movement renews its support for any step that helps strengthen the unity of the Arab perspective and it hopes that the declarations of the Arab Foreign Ministers' Council will be up to the level of the current threat, and that they will increase real solidarity and respond to the aspirations of the Arab peoples in defiance of the external danger as represented by expansionist Zionist colonialism and its allied powers.

Islamic Resistance Movement—Hamas—Palestine

10 March 2000

In the name of God, the Merciful, the Mercy-giving

The so-called breakthrough in the Zionist-Palestinian talks, a new deception

Events of the past few days have now yielded the news that the Palestine Authority (PA) and the Zionist enemy have agreed that they will sign an accord on a framework for an agreement on the final status of Palestinian territories by the end of this coming May, and that they will carry out the third part of the second redeployment of Zionist troops this April, instead of by its original deadline of last January 20th. The sides have further agreed that the third redeployment of Zionist troops will be completed after the conclusion of the framework accord, and that the sides will sign an agreement on the final status of the Palestinian territories on 13 September this year.

These news reports thus indicate that the Palestine Authority has yielded to the conditions laid down by Zionist Prime-minister Ehud Barak concerning the talks. In particular, the PA has backed down on its demands concerning the three villages in the Jerusalem area—Abu Dees, al-Ram, and al-'Ayzariya—included in the 6.1 percent of land designated for Zionist redeployment. This capitulation on the part of the PA is the real reason for the recent "breakthrough" in the Palestinian-Zionist negotiations.

The conviction has grown day by day over the course of following each stage of the negotiations between the Palestine Authority and the Zionist enemy that the PA's positions, and its apparent insistence upon them, are meant only to throw dust in our eyes. They are nothing but public-relations stunts aimed at winning over local public opinion, and deceiving the people about the real position of the PA, and about how far they are willing to go in making concessions and squandering the rights of our people and our nation. All the while this show goes on, the rate of Zionist colonization accelerates, topping that of Barak's predecessor Benjamin Netanyahu, particularly as regards Jerusalem, specifically in Jebel Abu Ghunaym and Ras al-'Amoud. In practice, this means that the Palestine Authority looks the other way as the Zionist enemy deepens its actual hold on the land, imposing situations ahead of time that will become part of the final settlement, trampling upon the very essence of the Palestinian cause, and most importantly upon Jerusalem, the right of Palestinian refugees to return to their land, the removal of the Zionist colonies, and other such matters.

Barak's release of several detainees, his opening of the so-called "secure northern corridor," and his payment of some of the funds due to the Palestine Authority, are only an attempt to deceive our people and distract their attention from the reality of the PA's concessions, its dangerous squandering of the rights of Jerusalem and the refugees, its frightful silence over the escalation of Zionist settlement, and its abject submission to Barak time after time, giving him every little thing he wants.

Barak managed his negotiations with the PA with great skill. He made clever use of the different tracks of negotiations—with Syria and with the Palestinians—now starting this track while slowing down the other in order to win new concessions from the Palestine Authority. The PA always feared that starting up negotiations on the Syrian track would lead to the neglect of their own talks with the Zionists.

The Palestine Authorities only deceive themselves with their renewed talk about American guarantees and about their faith in the American stewardship of the negotiations. The US Administration has always emphasized that it can only support and align itself with the Zionist entity. Indeed, what else could be the case as the grip of the Administration grows more and more feeble as the President approaches the end of his term?

We believe in the consciousness of our Palestinian people and their detailed knowledge of the true nature of the Palestine Authority, of its squandering of their land and holy places. We believe that all the means of misinformation and deception employed by the Palestine Authority to cover up the positions it is really taking will never deceive our people. Our people reaffirm every day that they continue to rally around the program of the resistance, as shown all the time by the mass movements rejecting the Oslo agreements and by all the fair elections that take place on our Palestinian lands.

Islamic Resistance Movement—Hamas—Palestine

25 February 2000

In the name of God, the Merciful, the Mercy-giving

The wave of arrests of Mujahideen will only increase the fighters' determination to continue their resistance, and on the threats by the Zionist entity's leadership against the people of Lebanon, its land and children

In a Zionist attempt to raise the morale of its army and citizenry after the painful blows inflicted on them by our people's heroic Mujahideen, and after the series of defeats that the heroic Islamic resistance has inflicted upon the Zionists in south Lebanon, the Occupation Authorities have announced that they are carrying out a campaign of arrests, picking up dozens of Mujahideen members of the Izz al-Din al-Qassam Brigades who have carried out numerous armed operations in recent months, and who, the Zionist authorities believe, planned to blow up a large residential building.

The Zionist enemy's attempt to exaggerate the importance of these arrests, presenting them as a great achievement, will not benefit the Zionist enemy . It will not raise their sunken morale. These arrests are no different from other such campaigns that take place from time to time and to which our people have grown accustomed in the course of their open and continuing struggle against the rapacious Zionist enemy. The Mujahideen have always shown that they are stronger than all forms of repression and tyranny, stronger than the waves of arrests. No such attempts will be able to divert them from their course or shake their resolve to wage a holy struggle and resistance in defense of their land, their country, and what they hold sacred.

The threats against Lebanon, its people and children, that the Zionist enemy's foreign minister made—threats that were affirmed and supported by the terrorist Prime Minister Ehud Barak—show clearly the breakdown and collapse that the Zionist entity and its military staff are experiencing as a result of the defeats they have sustained at the hands of the brave Islamic resistance in south Lebanon. The hysterical terrorist threats against Lebanon and the exaggeration of the achievements of its arrest campaign against heroic Palestinian Mujahideen also expose the Zionists' need to search for victories, even if they be imaginary victories, to hide their own impotence and to raise the morale of their people and their defeated army.

Resistance and opposition to the occupation will remain the firm policy of the Hamas movement and of all sincere members of our people. All the campaigns of repression and arrest will only increase the determination and resolve of our people and our heroes to continue the holy struggle, to attain martyrdom in defense of our land, our Jerusalem, our holy places, and for the liberation of our country . . . all of our country!

Islamic Resistance Movement—Hamas—Palestine

5 February 2000

Statement on the recent meeting between Barak and Arafat and on the resolution of the Central Council on the declaration of a state next September

The latest meeting between the chairman of the Palestinian Authority, Yasir Arafat, and the Prime Minister of the Zionist entity, Ehud Barak, that Took place last Thursday confirms once again the pointlessness of the negotiations on what is called the Palestinian track, and shows up the weakness afflicting the Palestinian negotiators.

Once again Barak is imposing his conditions and dictates on the Palestinian Authority. Barak has decreed redeployment of occupation troops from an area of 6.1% of the West Bank, an area that he has delineated unilaterally. He has refused to include the suburbs of al-Ayzariyah and Abu Dis, near Jerusalem, in the redeployment area. These are the regions that the Palestinian Authority has demanded so that it can declare them a capital of an imaginary Palestinian state, in return for the PA's submission to abandon Jerusalem to remain under Zionist sovereignty, and a capital of the occupation state.

The Palestinian Authority has rejected the maps of areas of redeployment drawn up by the Zionists. It has become customary, however, for the PA to eventually accept the things that it has been rejecting. Its initial rejection and display of firmness are always followed by a breakdown and submission to what the Zionist enemy dictates. This is precisely what happened with the last redeployment that included 5% of the West Bank—an arrangement that was at first rejected, but later, it was accepted.

We have said repeatedly that the Palestinian Authority goes to the negotiations psychologically defeated and feeble, with no source of strength and unable to apply pressure after having given up its sources of strength and isolated itself from our people. It has lorded it over their heads, resorted to all sorts of repression, deprived them of their freedoms and rights, tracked down those who carry on the struggle, opened the prisons and detention centres to honourable citizens and members of the opposition, and shredded national unity. For that reason our people pin none of their hopes upon this Authority. They also expect nothing from such an Authority but more squandering of their rights and the holy places.

The resolution of the PLO's Central Council, issued at its latest meeting a few days ago, came in line with the Authority's approach. Declaring a state has become a tactical matter for the Authority. Many times it has hinted that it was planning such an announcement, only to submit in the end and accept the Zionist and American orders and conditions. The United States and the Zionists want to see the declaration of a Palestinian state postponed until after the conclusion of the final status talks. That way the declaration of a state would come as a cheap reward for liquidating the Palestinian cause and all critical issues, in exchange for a state in name only that conforms to Zionist conditions, that has been stripped of sovereignty, will, and honour.

Such a freakish state has been and always will be acceptable to the Zionist leaders because they consider it to be entirely in the interest of their usurping entity. What our people want is not a declaration of just any kind of state. They want to build a real state that enjoys the basic components of a state on the ground, that exercises its own sovereignty and will on the liberated Palestinian land.

Our people and our nation know that our rights and our land cannot be regained by begging the Zionist enemy. They can only be seized back from that enemy through the steadfastness of our people, through the escalation of their heroic resistance, and through the solidarity of the Arab and Islamic peoples with them, supporting their steadfastness and struggle. The defeat of the enemy forces and puppet militias allied with them in south Lebanon confirms that only resistance can compel this enemy to submit.

Islamic Resistance Movement—Hamas—Palestine

8 December 1999

Zionists are our enemies, Jihad is our way to freedom

Statement issued by the Islamic Resistance Movement (Hamas) on the occasion of the 13th anniversary of the blessed Intifada and the launching of the Hamas Movement

Our Palestinian People,
The people of heroism and sacrifice,

These days coincide with the anniversary of the blessed Intifada (uprising) and the establishment of Hamas while we are standing at a dangerous cross-road: whether to resume the glorious days of resistance for freedom and dignity or to establish the life of humiliation and submission to the ugly occupation under the justification of a final resolution that is dictated by the Occupation State.

Our steadfast People on the Holy Land, martyrs and heroes! be an insurmountable barrier in the face of the conspiracies and challenges and reject all projects of submission and humiliation. You, the people who made the greatest revolution in our contemporary history, the people who drew with their red blood the borders of your homeland, the people who wrote the cleanest record of heroism and sacrifice with the blood of your martyrs, and the people who firmly faced the most impudent enemy known to mankind, have patience and steadfastness.

Our hero People,

How it is great that we observe in these days the anniversary of the blessed Intifada sparked by our Palestinian people making the greatest revolution in the contemporary history of our people. And how it is great that we observe the anniversary of the launching of the Islamic Resistance Movement (Hamas) that carried the injuries of the homeland and advanced towards the time-honoured victory, resisting the enemy with one hand and alleviating the suffering of our people with the other in order to enhance the hopes and create facts to realize God's victory.

Blessed are our People on the anniversary of the Intifada and the launching of Hamas. Salutations to the blessed martyrs, to the hundreds of thousands injured whom their injuries did not deter them from their goal, to the thousands of freedom prisoners in the oppressive jails of the Zionist Occupation, and to our brothers and leaders of our Jihad who have been absented in the jails of the self rule authority, especially our brothers Dr. Abdel Aziz Rantisi, Dr. Ibrahim Maqadma, Jamal Mansour and Mohammad Jamal Natsheh.

Greetings also to the martyrs Yahya Ayyash, Imad Aqel, Kamal Kehail, Muhiel Deen Sharif and the brothers Adel and Imad Awadallah. And greetings to the martyrdom bombers in our country who plant death and horror in the hearts of the Zionists and seed victory and dignity among the Palestinian People and who prove that we are a non-dying people who do not surrender and who are able to extract victory and defeat the enemy: "God has decreed: It is I and My apostles who must prevail."

Our Palestinian People, our Arab and Islamic nations

These two great occasions pass while the self rule authority is still insisting on going ahead with the final status negotiations, which endanger our future in our land, our rights and the history and Jihad of the Palestinian People in favour of the Zionist Enemy. They also come in difficult circumstances while the Zionist Enemy continues to exhibit arrogance against our People and our Nation, supported by the United States.

Therefore, we, in the Islamic Resistance Movement (Hamas), would like to stress the following principles:

1. The aims to which the blessed popular Intifada were launched were to remove the Occupation, liberate the land, clean the holy places, and to build our independent State on the whole soil of our Palestinian homeland. These aims still exist; they did not change or come to an end. Therefore, we are requested to continue our Jihad and resistance until we achieve our goals.

2. We and our Palestinian People reject the idea that the price to be paid for the Oslo accords and the consequent unfair agreements be the sacrifices of our People and our Nation. Therefore, we emphasize our rejection of all humiliating and fragile agreements which ignore the rights of our people to liberate their land, to return to their homeland, to build their own State and to liberate their holy places. We also emphasize that the Intifada and the sacrifices of our People and their national and Islamic forces should not be by any means used to establish the occupier's foothold or to legalize its domination over our land and holy places.

3. We, in the Islamic Resistance Movement (Hamas), on this blessed occasion, warn of the consequences of running after the *fata morgana* of the so-called peace agreements, calling on the self rule authority to promptly stop the final status negotiations and not to mislead the Palestinian People by alleging that it is able to restore some of their rights, which it cannot achieve without relinquishing the historic, religious and national rights in Palestine.

4. We call upon the Palestinian Authority to seize the anniversary of the blessed Intifada to release all of the Palestinian detainees from its jails, to end the corruption within it and not to protect the corruptionists, to stop the confiscation of public freedoms, and to release our People and allow them to protect their rights, unity and Jihad against the Occupation authorities which dominate all of our lands and holy places.

5. We emphasize that the two parts of Jerusalem, the eastern and the western, are a unified Palestinian, Arab and Islamic city and that no one has the right to abandon any part of it. We also do not accept any attempt to abandon our right in Jerusalem and the holy places. Our People will never accept Abu Dis or any other place as an alternative to Jerusalem.

6. We emphasize that our People's right of return to their homeland is a sacred right that cannot be abolished by any agreement or bypassed over time.

7. We call upon all our People in the Occupied land and in Diaspora to protect their unity and enhance their steadfastness and to work jointly to resist the Occupation and not to give a chance to those who want to relinquish our land, holy places and rights.

8. We call upon all Arabs and Muslims to support our People and their steadfastness and Jihad. Again we stress Hamas' policy of its keenness to foster relations with all Arab and Muslim countries and peoples. We also stress Hamas' keenness to protect their security and stability, especially those Arab States that surround Palestine.

9. We stress our keenness to have a special relationship with our dear Jordan and its dear people, who are our people, calling on the Jordanian government to reconsider the arbitrary measures it recently took against Hamas and some of its leaders.

Our Arab and Muslim Nation,

While we in the Islamic Resistance Movement (Hamas) stress—on the anniversary of our movement—on grasping our right to resistance and Jihad until the liberation of the whole national soil, while rejecting all humiliating and fragile agreements that abandoned the rights of our People and which were signed without their will or agreement, we vow before our Palestinian People and our Arab and Islamic Nation that we shall continue the resistance and the Jihad, and we shall not forget our brothers who are imprisoned in the Zionist Enemy's jails and will do our best to free them. Hamas, as you know her, will continue its resistance for liberation and freedom. It will remain a force to serve its people and nation; it does not deviate from its direction; it will remain honest, protecting its nation and the nation's resources; it will remain keen on protecting the security and stability of the Arab and Muslim world because it is aware of the fact that Palestine, as it is a cause for Palestinians, is also a cause for Arabs and Muslims everywhere.

It is a Jihad, a victory or a martyrdom.

Islamic Resistance Movement—Hamas—Palestine

2 December 1999

Statement on the wicked assault against
Dr. Muaweya al-Masri

With deep concern and anger, the Islamic Resistance Movement (Hamas) learned of the assault by gunfire against Dr. Muaweya al-Masri in Nablus of the West Bank, which threatened his life. This cowardly attempt is directly and plainly linked to the statement issued by a number of national figures criticizing the corruption that is widespread among Palestinian Authority circles and its destructive consequences on our Palestinian society, and rejecting the policy of relinquishment and abandonment of our People's rights and land through negotiations with the Zionist Enemy.

While we condemn this crime, we hold the Palestinian Authority responsible for it because of the suppressive spheres it has created and its shriveling reactions, including the threatening of those who signed the statement. We consider this an attempt to terrify and silence those who oppose it and also an attempt to prevent them from exposing facts concerning the conduct of the PA, its corruption and relinquishments.

What the PA did when it gathered its subjects, employees and members of its security bodies to stage ceremonial rallies, when it pushed the Legislative Council to condemn some of its members who signed the statement and when it threatened them in order to protect its reputation reveals that this Authority is fragile and lacks credibility. It also reflects the gap between the Authority and the ambitions of our People and their popular opinion.

While we in Hamas condemn the policy of political assassination in dealing with those who oppose the peace process and who call for reformation, we call upon the PA to reconsider its policies and accounts, to treat the corruption within its ranks and to put an end to the policy of relinquishments instead of insisting on its mistakes.

Islamic Resistance Movement—Hamas—Palestine

24 November 1999

Statement
Deportation of Hamas leaders

The Jordanian government on Sunday, 21 November, implemented another provocative step by deporting four Hamas leaders to Qatar. The leaders, who have been detained in a Jordanian prison, are brothers Khalid Misha'al, head of Hamas political bureau; Ibrahim Ghousheh, spokesman; and Ezzat Risheq and Sami Khater, members of the bureau.

We, in the Islamic Resistance Movement (Hamas), stress that this step is arbitrary and completely rejected. It is a dangerous measure, which violates the human rights and the Jordanian Constitution. The decision made by the Jordanian government to deport the four Hamas leaders from Jordanian territory was made by one party and hence it puts an end to the mediation efforts that have been exerted to resolve this issue in a way that serves the interests of our Arab and Islamic Nation.

We emphasize that the step was not taken with previous arrangement between the Hamas leadership and any other party and was taken without the approval of the deported leaders. Therefore, we call upon the Jordanian government to reconsider its decision and to allow the four leaders to return home to Amman to their families and homeland. This is an arbitrary measure, which reminds us of the expulsions carried out by the Zionist enemy against our people, and does not resolve the crisis between Hamas and the Jordanian government. We, in Hamas, stress our strong rejection of this measure. We will confront it with all peaceful means possible and will continue the efforts to enable our brothers to return home.

Islamic Resistance Movement—Hamas—Palestine

02 November 1999

A new conspiracy at Oslo Summit

On the occasion of the fourth anniversary of Rabin's assassination, Clinton, Arafat and Barak met in Oslo to liquidate what remains of the Palestinian rights by rescheduling the phases of the so-called "final solution," which will be implemented in several years' time. In the interim, the Zionist Enemy will certainly legitimize all facts created by the Oslo accords.

This new summit will not be any different than the previous summits. However, this time it will aim to liquidate the Palestinian Question by resolving the issues slated for the final status negotiations-Jerusalem, the refugees, borders, the State, sovereignty and water.

Our Palestinian People, our Arab and Islamic Nation

During the first Oslo summit, the influential leadership of the PLO marketed the inauspicious Oslo accords as a victory and an achievement, slating it as a vehicle by which Statehood, freedom, independence, well-being, prosperity, security and stability could be reached and as a peace agreement to be celebrated in the White House.

Today, in the second Oslo summit and after six years, our people are experiencing economic hardship; loose security; a proposed State with sovereignty over only 18% of the West Bank; the redeployment—not the withdrawal-of Occupation troops; and dependence on their occupier for their security, politics and economics. They are also at the mercy of the direct negotiations between Arafat and Barak, which are in accordance with the Zionist vision in which the Zionist regime dictates its perspectives regarding the final status.

This summit was held even in the absence of some invitees. It was attended only by an American President who begs for peace in order to enter history, a Chairman of an Authority who begs for the survival of the Oslo accords, and a swindling, arrogant Zionist Prime Minister who imposes his conditions on the other two.

Between the first summit and the second, there have been six lean years; settlements built and others expanded; continued land confiscations; multiple home demolitions; continuous suppression of resistant people by the self-rule Authority and the occupation authorities; continued Judaization of Jerusalem; repeated denials of the rights of our refugees and displaced persons to return to their homes and to pursue self-determination; concerted efforts made to suppress our people's right of Jihad and resistance by hunting down our Mujahideen in cooperation and coordination among the security bodies of the self rule authority, the occupation authorities, the CIA and others; and a rushing by some States in the region towards the building of relations and normalization of ties with the Zionist Enemy hoping to get financial assistance from the United States while at the same time fearing its threats.

Our Arab and Islamic Nation

The summit being held in Oslo today coincides with the anniversary of the inauspicious Balfour Declaration, which promised the Jews a homeland in Palestine. If "Balfour" was the promise, the Oslo agreement would be the real translation of this promise into the practical means necessary for the Zionist regime to procure a legitimacy which is not accepted by our Nation.

While we are reminded that the Zionist gangs succeeded, through their military attacks, to make the Balfour Declaration a reality and an entity, we would like to emphasize that resistance and Jihad are the only ways to break this promise and to destroy this entity. They are also the only ways to liberate our land and build our State. We also call upon the Palestinian Authority to stop the series of relinquishments it had started, to reconsider this approach (which brought disaster to our Cause), and to return to its people and nation to make use of their will of steadfastness. It should, through this bitter experience, recognize that the Zionist Enemy does not seek or want peace, that its expansionistic settlement project will not stop, and that the U.S. Administration is a full partner and colluder working only for the interests of the Zionist Enemy.

Islamic Resistance Movement—Hamas—Palestine

31 October 1999

Statement on Mauritania's promotion of full diplomatic ties with the Zionist Regime

The Islamic Resistance Movement (Hamas) has observed with extreme disapproval and annoyance the decision made by the Mauritanian government to promote to ambassadorial level its diplomatic representation with the Zionist Regime. Mauritania opened a guardianship office in the Zionist State in 1995, an issue that was faced with a wide range of anger and rejection among the Arab and Muslim worlds.

This step by Mauritania is being taken at a time when the Zionist leaders are escalating their arbitrary measures and suppression of our People, their continued occupation of the Palestinian and Arab territories, their denial of the legitimate rights of our People, their expansion of settlement activities, their insisting that Jerusalem is their eternal capital, as well as their rejection of the return of the refugees and their hunting down of our Mujahideen. This step is equivalent to a stab in the backs of our Palestinian People in particular and the Arab and Muslim nations in general. It is also considered a new blow to Arab Unity, which the United States and the Zionist Enemy have been combining their efforts to fragmentize in order to pave the road for the Zionists to dominate the whole Arab region.

Hamas rejects the submission by the Mauritanian authorities to American and Zionist false promises of introducing economic assistance and prosperity to Mauritania. It seems that the Mauritanian authorities have not learned from what happened to other Arab States that signed peace treaties with the usurping Zionist entity and that also falsely believed that these treaties would bring assistance, luxury and prosperity to their countries. On the contrary, they destroyed their economies and increased poverty, unemployment and frustration.

The Zionist Regime took advantage of Mauritania's poverty and its need to build relations with Tel Aviv since 1995 by reaching an agreement with Mauritania to make its desert a dump for Israeli nuclear wastes, which raised fears and concerns by the Mauritanian People and the Magharebi States because of their consequent threats against the people and states of the region.

The recent decision by the Mauritanian authorities is a blatant refusal of Palestinian and Arab rights. It is also a show of support for the Occupation, which was rejected and condemned by the Mauritanian Muslim People.

We call upon the Arab States to pressure the Mauritanian authorities to reconsider its decision. We also call upon them to stand by the Mauritanian Muslim People and to provide them with every kind of economic assistance in order not to remain an easy prey to the Zionist greediness.

We also call upon the Mauritanian authorities to reconsider its decision and to run in harmony with the ambitions of the Mauritanian, Arab and Muslim masses who reject any kind of relation with the Zionist Regime. We hope that the Mauritanian authorities will reconsider their decision, which deforms the image of the Mauritanian People from which famous Islamic scholars have emerged.

Islamic Resistance Movement - Hamas - Palestine

22 September 1999

An Open Message from
Khaled Mishaal to the Jordanian Monarch
(broadcasted by the Jazira Channel)

Your Majesty, the Islamic Resistance Movement, Hamas, did not change in a matter of few months and cannot change in years. The Hamas Movement that your father the late King Hussein, may Allah have mercy on his soul, knew quite well; is the same Hamas that is present today in Jordan. The late King knew Hamas and embraced a number of its leaders, hosted Dr. Abu Marzouq from his prison in America and received the Mujahid Sheikh Ahmed Yassin. He also adopted a manly stand, full of gallantry, firmness and wisdom, in resisting the Mossad agents on the land of dear Jordan and insisted on providing the antidote. This Hamas Movement did not change, so why is there a change in the stance towards it? What has changed? Mohammed Abu Seif, who repelled the Mossad agents' attack against Jordan's sovereignty and security and who was honoured a year ago by the Interior Minister, what has changed so that he would be in prison today?

Hamas did not change but regrettably stands towards it have changed. We hope that your Majesty would return things to normalcy. We also say to the Jordanian government and to all security and judicial apparatuses that those pressures on Hamas and those charges are not true and unjustifiable. It is not appropriate that Hamas would be prosecuted for the sake of non-Jordanian interests. This does not fall in line with dear Jordan's interest nor that of the Ummah. We say to the dear Jordanian people, who stood in support of us with its northern, central and southern areas, with its tribes and (refugee) camps, with all political trends, with all its parties, syndicates and nationalist and Islamic figures, we tell them that Hamas will remain loyal to its pledge and that Jordan's security and sovereignty will remain our concern and will remain untouchable.

Hamas will never target anyone from the Ummah and will never change its policy especially in dear Jordan. The Movement's pendulum will remain directed against the Zionist enemy. I say to those who think that pressures on Hamas along with harassment measures would lead to its deviation from its path and political belief, I tell them that they are wrong. No-one, insha'al-lah, will ever succeed in eliminating Hamas in this sensitive stage when the Palestine cause is passing through the most dangerous attempt for its liquidation under the pretext of final status talks. Hamas is not a thing that can be eliminated in a certain stage. We are going back to Jordan, and we say to all Hamas lovers and those afraid on its behalf, do not be afraid for there are loyal Hamas leaders and cadres within the occupied homeland and outside it. So, if some of Hamas leaders were absent or absented for one reason or another, the march of Hamas will persist by the will of Allah.

Your brother
Khaled Mishaal
Political Bureau Chairman of the Hamas Movement
22 Sep 1999

5 June 1999

In commemoration of the 32nd anniversary of June 1967 Defeat

Latent elements of victory waiting to be stirred

The 32nd anniversary of the 5 June 1967 defeat has come at a time when the Arab Nation is still overwhelmed with the psychological defeat caused by the peace process that has been signed now for several years. The anniversary, which was ignored by the media, re-focuses the light on the reasons for the defeat, which cannot be forgotten by our Nation, and on the potential elements of the victory waiting to be stirred.

The Arab Nation was defeated in 1967 because it did not possess the will of victory. Instead, their disability was concealed behind rhetoric and enthusiastic speeches. Although the results of this defeat were in the military field, its reasons were internal and referred to the deteriorating Arab political situation.

Unfortunately, after 32 years of this route, some Arabs still believe in co-existence with the Enemy, alleging they can convince it to abandon part of our occupied land. In the meantime, they do not give enough attention to strengthening the Arab ranks or to building the Arab power in order to force the occupation troops to withdraw from the Palestinian and Arab occupied lands. The practical outcome of this attitude is the feeble peace agreements which deepen the roots of the Zionist occupation after they recognized the Zionist usurpation of the majority of the Palestinian occupied land. It was a defeat of will in confrontation with the usurping enemy. Moreover, the Palestinian Authority accepted to play a part of the oppressive role of the Occupation against our people, believing this would convince the Zionists to introduce feeble relinquishments here and there!

The reasons for the June 1967 defeat still exist in the Arab Nation. But the Nation has not remained in the same condition since that date. It witnessed attempts to get rid of the consequences of this defeat and to confront and resist the Zionist Occupation by all means possible.

The great intifadah (uprising) triggered by the Palestinian People and their resistance and Jihad led by the Islamic Resistance Movement (Hamas) on the one hand, and the resistance of the occupation by the Lebanese People, especially the Hizbullah and the Lebanese Resistance on the other hand, are the most significant embodiment of the steadfast will and challenge which has never been shaken in the Arab People although it is weak at the Arab official level. The coming of this anniversary a few days after the escape of the Occupation troops and their agents from Jizzin area, south of Lebanon, is a good example to compare between the two cases.

The anniversary of the defeat carrying all these pains and misfortunes should be taken as an opportunity to learn from these lessons in order to achieve a comprehensive renaissance, including the people and the rulers alike. This renaissance should be based on the Arab and Islamic solidarity and on confronting the force with a similar force. We should use all means possible and available to confront the challenge posed by the Zionist Enemy, which tries to expand its rule in our region under the cover of peace and normalization.

While Hamas reminds the Palestinian People and the Nation of the necessity to learn from the lessons of the June 1967 defeat, it vows to continue its Jihad and resistance of the Occupation, and to abide by and defend the legitimate rights of our People and Nation. In this course, Hamas is supported by the Almighty Allah and by the Palestinian, Arab and Muslim people. It asserts that the victory's exultation experienced by our Enemy will not be long. The eventual victory is, God willing, for this people and for this Nation, by our faith and by the arms of our heroes, as well as by the unity and solidarity of our Nation.

The Islamic Resistance Movement
Hamas—Palestine
8 June 1999

18 May 1999

A new terrorist assumes power in the Zionist State

Electorates in the Zionist entity wrapped up a page in their political life and opened a new one with a new professional terrorist leader, who has exerted all efforts over many decades to chase, assassinate, or arrest our people and their leaders in and out of Palestine.

The victory of the terrorist Ehud Barak has never and will never change anything concerning the nature of the Zionist project which is based on expansion, hegemony, and oppression. This was asserted by Barak more than once during his election campaign which marketed a platform similar to the Likud's without any political differences. This platform does not change the hostile and aggressive nature of the Zionist society against our people and nation.

A view of Barak's electoral campaign, which concentrated on his role in the wars against the Arab States, the Palestinian Resistance, and against our people, proves that the Zionist General has assumed power in the Zionist State based on his military history and his platform which in turn is based on extremism and arrogance. This proves more that the Zionist Society is inclining more and more towards extremism.

Barak's success as Prime Minister in the Zionist State should not lead some to show too much optimism. It is true that there are some differences between him and Netanyahu in manner and tactics, but they have identical objectives and perspectives. Moreover, Barak stands on the far right of the Labour Party and he is an extremist hawk. His hands are stained with Palestinian blood. The platform he adopted concerning the Palestinian track was very clear. In his first speech he delivered after his winning, he asserted that the united Jerusalem is the eternal capital of the Zionist State. He also declared that the Occupation troops will never go back to the 1967 borders and that he will never allow the presence of any Arab army west of the Jordan River. He said that he would not dismantle the Jewish settlements, which will be kept under Zionist control. As for the Palestinian State, Barak and his Party reject a full supremacy of the State and reject our people's right of return. Barak, on whom the Palestinian Authority pins its hopes, had rejected the Oslo accords few years ago.

Therefore, there are no essential differences between Barak's and Netanyahu's positions regarding the basic issues that will be negotiated in the final status talks (the State, Jerusalem, the refugees and the Jewish settlements). This proves again that the failure of the peace process was not because of the arrogance and the hard-line policy of the defeated terrorist Netanyahu but because of the nature of the Zionist project and its real objectives which have not changed in essence but only in the means and tactics.

Relying on Barak's victory and cheering for his coming reflect the utmost disability and the desire to mislead our people. The reality that all of us should be aware of is that Barak's advent imposes a big challenge on our people and nation. It is the same challenge of that with the Zionist project but in a new way and tactic. The snake does not change its nature when it changes its skin. Therefore, the battle is still ongoing and the war has not ceased as yet. Our rights should be extracted, not waited for. They need more work, Jihad and resistance.

The Labour Party has come back to power carrying a long history of aggression, oppression and terrorism, not to mention Rabin's policy of breaking our people's bones or the Qana massacre perpetrated by the infamous terrorist Peres. Our people are well-aware that their salvation will never be in the hands of their new enemy, Barak, who boasts of receiving many medals for his role in the wars against the Arab people and in the special terrorist operations he carried out against the Palestinian Resistance and Palestinian leaders.

While we, in Hamas, warn from rushing towards the Zionist Enemy and the normalization of ties with it at the expense of the security and rights of our people, we reiterate that our people will not rely on empty promises and that they will continue in the resistance option until they are liberated and their rights are restored by the will of our Almighty God.

The Islamic Resistance Movement
Hamas—Palestine
18 May 1999

5 May 1999

The Zionist Enemy continues campaign of settlement and Judaization; The Palestinian Authority arrests the nobles

The Zionist Enemy continues its arbitrary measures against our People. These measures have escalated during the election campaign to appease the Zionist electorate. The conspiracy to Judaize occupied Jerusalem also continues through the demolition of Palestinian homes and the annexation of vast areas of the Bethlehem Municipality's land to occupied Jerusalem in order to expand its borders and to seize more of our 1967-occupied territories as part of the Jewish State.

The herds of Jewish settlers also continue on a daily basis in their attempt to Judaize the Palestinian usurped land and to seize more of our People's land. All this is continuously done publicly, without any Arab, Muslim or international counter-move to put an end to these atrocities.

All of the above is happening while the Palestinian Authority (PA) insists on abiding by its fragile agreements with the Zionist Enemy. The PA also submits to the Zionist dictates and threats, continuing its oppressive measures against our noble people who oppose its policies and rejects its submission to the Zionist arrogance.

The PA has re-arrested members and supporters of the Islamic Resistance Movement (Hamas) shortly after their release. This means that our People are subject to the moody decisions of the PA. They have become cards and tactical messages in the hands of the PA, using them according to its needs and objectives without giving any attention to the dignity, freedom and rights of our People.

Hamas condemns the PA's unchanged manner against our people, which aims to busy them with internal disputes and problems and which endangers our national unity. Meanwhile, it leaves the Zionist Enemy free to swallow more land and continue settlements throughout the Palestinian territories.

We call again upon the PA to stop traveling along this dawdling Oslo track and to side with its People, their concerns, and their sincere *Jihadi* forces who confront the Enemy's plots. We also call upon it to resist the Enemy's expansionist projects in order to rescue our land and holy places.

We also call upon the Arab and Islamic States to take practical steps to support our People and strengthen their resistance of the settlement and Judaization campaigns.

We appeal to all ranks of our Palestinian People to resist the settlement and Judaization campaigns with all means possible. We give a covenant to our People to remain in the trenches confronting the occupation Enemy, and to continue resistance of the occupation, settlement and Judaization activities. We also vow that Hamas will stand by all *Mujahideen* and honest people as an impenetrable and insurmountable barrier protecting our land and holy places.

Allahu Akbar and victory is to the faithful

The Islamic Resistance Movement
Hamas—Palestine
5 May 1999

2 February 1999

In the name of God, the Mercy-giving, the Merciful

Sparing the Palestinian blood is a responsibility of the Palestinian Authority

A communiqué issued by the Islamic Resistance Movement (Hamas)

"God defends those who believe; God does not love every thankless traitor"

Surat Al Haj: 38

Due to the unfortunate incident that occurred in Rafah on Monday, 1 February, during which Captain Rifaat Mohammad Judah and the infant Fadwa Jarwaneh were killed, we in the Islamic Resistance Movement (Hamas), based on our keenness to secure national unity and to suppress the sedition that Israel has always sought and which was made clear in the Israeli media following that unfortunate incident, and because of certain accusations, would like to stress the following:

1. Hamas reiterates its consistent policy that prohibits internal fighting and its continuous strategy of sparing and protecting Palestinian blood.

2. Our brothers—Usama Taha, Mohammed Abu Shamala and Raed Al Attar—whose names were mentioned in connection with this incident

by the local press, have never been wanted by the PA's security service since their employment in a PA security apparatus headed by Colonel Sami Abu Samhadaneh. Therefore, we wonder why they were being chased? And why their problem, if any, has not been solved by the security service in which they have been working? We condemn the policy of chasing people that is practised by the PA security, such as shooting live gunfire in the streets, raiding houses by armed men and damaging their contents, and generally terrifying the people. Such policies open the door widely for agents of Israel's special forces to implement their schemes against our People.

3.   Our People's blood is deposited in trust and is a responsibility of the PA's security services that should protect and guard them. The protection of the blood of Captain Rifaat Judah and the children Fadwa Jarwaneh and Mohammed Yaziji was the responsibility of the authority which should protect the citizens and enhance the security and stability among the people.

4.   The hasty attempts to link Hamas to this incident are rejected and baseless. They do not serve the interests and the unity of our People on which Hamas stresses in all its positions, especially during this critical stage being experienced by our People and Cause. Therefore, Hamas reiterates its rejection of these repeated attempts to deform its bright image and to destroy its Jihad and established position, which is based on the fact that our People's main conflict is with the Zionist Enemy.

5.   We in Hamas regrettably condemn the disgusting phrases mentioned in Fatah Movement's statement that was distributed in Rafah and which talk of a "misled and misleading category of people" with the aim of deforming the image of the Islamists, who proved their honesty and loyalty to their Nation and Homeland. Such a statement increases the tension instead of defusing it and instead of protecting the security and safety of our society.

6.   Hamas reiterates the necessity of making the Israelis and their conspirators miss the opportunity of waging an internal war by controlling ourselves and by fighting rumours that aim to destabilize the Palestinian arena. We should close the door in the face of those who want to spread sedition among our People. Hamas also reiterates its continued resistance of the Zionist occupation and usurpation. It also strongly rejects the attempts to transfer the conflict into our Palestinian arena.

Finally, we call upon our People to be cautious and to cling firmly by means of God's rope.

"God was Dominant in His affair, even though most men do not realize it"

Surat Yousuf: 21

The Islamic Resistance Movement (Hamas)—Palestine
2 February 1999

17 December 1998

Condemnation alone is not enough . . .
Giving up secondary differences and breaking the siege imposed on the Iraqi People should be the Arab reaction to the American brute aggression

After his failure to invest his recent tour in Occupied Palestine in covering his disgraceful scandals, the head of the U.S. "Zionized" Administration decided to launch cowardly raids on the Iraqi People and their children by using long-range missiles and air bombers. He justified his aggression by claiming that he wanted to protect the United Nations Security Council resolutions, although the Council was not consulted prior to the American aggression that was made in collusion with the United Kingdom.

The U.S. President had failed to exert any pressure on Netanyahu to force him into implementing the Wye River memorandum. Therefore, he rushed to cover up this failure and the humiliation he received from Netanyahu, as well as to disguise his fear of a likely Congress vote to oust him from his post, by shelling and bombing the Iraqi People.

This infamous crime that has been perpetrated by Clinton shows the real and ugly face of both him and his "Zionized" Administration. It also blatantly exposes how trifle and ridiculous are those who tried to market the false friendship of Clinton and the Americans among our Palestinian People, as well as those who applauded for him for a long time while they were slaughtering the Palestinian National Charter and the legitimate rights of our People.

We strongly condemn this cowardly and perfidious aggression. It is a serious threat to the Arab and Islamic security. It is a stupid decision made by a corrupt President, who is subservient to a lobby that is full of hatred against humanity. It is a decision that only serves Zionist goals and opens the door for attempts to partition an Arab State and an important regional power, which eventually makes the security of the region and the future of the Nation exposed to storms.

The perfidious aggression on the Iraqi People does not aim to defend the security of the Gulf States as alleged by Clinton, who is facing a vote that will force him to resign after he lied to his people. The massacres that are being carried out against the Iraqi people and their children are just a bloody bill paid by the Arab Nation for the cost of Clinton's mistakes and misconduct and of his submission to the Zionist blackmailers.

We, the Islamic Resistance Movement (Hamas), consider the criminal aggression against Iraq as a violation of all international laws, conventions and values. It shows how the White House Administration could care less about the Arab Nation, its values and feelings of its people. This requires an urgent Arab and Islamic decisive move to put an end to these crimes and atrocities against a dear part of this Nation, of whose people are being destroyed by an Administration that lacks in will and by bribed inspection committees which have connections with the Zionist State.

We call for an urgent Arab summit to discuss the tragedy of the Iraqi People and to take a serious and responsible position in which the Arab States put aside their secondary differences and disputes, which will also pave the road for the restoration of Arab solidarity, as a prelude to lift the infamous siege imposed on the Arab people of Iraq, Libya and Sudan. The Arab summit should put an end to the continuous American atrocities and abuses of the human rights of the Arabs everywhere and at all levels.

The Islamic Resistance Movement
Hamas-Palestine
17 December 1998

27 October 1998

Following is the full text of a memorandum by the Islamic Resistance Movement (Hamas) concerning the Wye River Memorandum signed on 23 October 1998 by the Israeli Prime Minister Netanyahu and the Palestinian Authority Chairman Yasser Arafat under the sponsorship of the U.S. President Clinton.

The Wye River Memorandum of 23 October 1998 Its Indications and Consequences

After eight days of negotiations between Netanyahu's Government and the Palestinian Authority at Wye River, Maryland, the United States of America, the two parties, under the direct sponsorship of the U.S. Administration, concluded an agreement pertaining to the application of the redeployment of the Israeli occupation troops in the West Bank as provided for in the former agreements. This agreement will be implemented in conjunction with a pledge by the PA to take strict and specific security measures against the forces of the Palestinian People that reject any relinquishments and that also resist the Occupation, in particular the Islamic Resistance Movement (Hamas). The agreement was signed on Friday, 23 October 1998 at the White House.

In view of the dangers of this agreement and its negative consequences to the Palestinian Cause and to the present and future conditions of the whole region, we, in the Islamic Resistance Movement (Hamas), would like to introduce this memorandum directly to our People and Nation as part of our duty to enlighten and warn them. In addition, we strongly encourage everyone to play their role in defending Palestine's Cause, its people and its holy places, as well as to work seriously to prevent the expansion of the Zionist project at the expense of the Nation's interests now and in the future.

First: The main comments on the agreement's provisions

The Wye River Memorandum tackles five subjects: the redeployment, security, economic issues, the final status talks and the unilateral activities. The agreement details the security issues making it, formally and practically, a non-political security accord.

The Wye River Memorandum considers the "Note for the Record" by the U.S. of 17 January 1997, which was annexed to the Hebron Agreement and the Interim Agreement on the West Bank and Gaza Strip of 28 September 1995, as an authority to the application of the agreement. One of the most serious ramifications of this Memorandum is the recognition of Israel's sole right to determine the percentage and time-schedule of the redeployment. As long as there are no maps attached with the new agreement, the Israeli enemy will, alone, determine the criteria for which the redeployment will be made.

Although the agreement talks about the reciprocity principle, it is free of any details or required guarantees from the Enemy. It was satisfied with what was mentioned in the prior agreements. However, the present agreement describes in detail a list of commitments and relinquishments that must be carried out by the PA.

The agreement states that the redeployment of the Occupation troops should be linked to the PA's commitment to the application of a time-schedule for the security measures that must be implemented in order to encounter the Palestinian forces that resist or call to resist the Occupation. While the provisions concerning the commitments by the PA are clear and specific, the commitments by the Enemy are vague and general. Examples of the provisions regarding the different security measures that should be implemented by the PA according to the agreement are as follows:

The ensuring of systematic and effective combat of "terrorist" organizations and their support structures along with the environment conducive to the support of "terror".

Combat should be continuous and constant over the long term, without pause in its implementation.

Security cooperation between "Israel" and the Palestinians as well as a continuous exchange of information, concepts and actions. The cooperation should be "bilateral, complete, continuous, intensive and comprehensive."

A U.S.-Palestinian committee will meet biweekly to review the steps being taken to eliminate "terrorism".

A U.S.-Palestinian committee will meet to review and evaluate information pertaining to the decisions on prosecution, punishment or other legal measures to be taken against suspects. The PA will abide by this condition.

There must be professional cooperation in investigations between the two parties along with an exchange of information.

A U.S.-Palestinian-Israeli committee will meet not less than biweekly to assess current threats and to deal with any impediments.

The Palestinian side will fully inform the members of the committee of the results of its investigation of suspects.

Instant apprehension of 30 Palestinians wanted by the "Israeli" Enemy to try them under CIA supervision.

The Palestinian side will prohibit the importation or smuggling of illegal weapons in areas under Palestinian jurisdiction.

The prohibition of all forms of incitement to violence or terror. A U.S.-Palestinian-Israeli committee will monitor cases of possible incitement to violence or terror and exchange information in this regard.

The Palestinians will provide the United States with a detailed security work plan after the first week of the implementation of this agreement.

The agreement does not give specific meanings for some terms such as terror, violence and its support structures, and the concept of incitement. Instead, it leaves this identification to the joint security committees between the PA and the "Israeli" Enemy or between the PA and the CIA, or to a trilateral committee; this means that their definitions will be varied because the Israeli Enemy and the CIA will be the ones who will impose their meanings.

The gist of the agreement concerning the land is the agreement of the Israeli Government on a conditional redeployment of its troops that will be in conjunction with the implementation of strict and specific security measures by the PA. The redeployment will be from 13% of the West Bank area, excluding Jerusalem: 1% will be transferred to area (A) and 12% to area (B); 3% of the latter will be allocated as Nature Reserves (the security of which will be controlled by the Occupation forces). In addition, 14.2% will be transferred from area (B) to area (A). If these redeployments are implemented according to the specified percentages, the situation of the West Bank would be as follows:

18.2% area (A) (under PA's security and administrative control)

21.8% area (B) (administration run by the PA but security by the Occupation)

60% area (C) (fully controlled by the Occupation).

In addition, the agreement mentions the operation of Gaza airport and the need to renew negotiations on the safe passage between Gaza and the West Bank. The parties also agreed to conclude an agreement to allow the construction and operation of Gaza port. Issues such as the settlement, the third phase of redeployment and other issues of the Interim Agreement were adjourned by referring them to negotiation committees.

According to the agreement, Netanyahu has obliged the Palestinian negotiators to nullify specific provisions of the Palestinian National Charter in a humiliating manner. The PLO's Executive Committee will start this work and the PLO's Central Council will ratify the nullification. Then a joint meeting will be held and attended by members of the Palestinian National Council, the Central Council and the Palestinian ministers to be addressed by President Clinton to reaffirm their support for the decisions of the Executive Committee and the Central Council regarding the nullification and the amendment of the Palestinian National Charter.

The agreement does not include any specific or clear provision that restricts the settlements or strips the settlers of their arms.

Although the media talk about an Israeli pledge to release 750 detainees out of 4,000 detainees presently in the Israeli jails in stages, the agreement does not include a clear and specific provision regarding this issue. Instead, it refers this issue to the "prior agreements".

Second: Analysis of the contents and meanings of the agreement

The agreement reaffirmed Netanyahu's approach, which is to renegotiate on what was already agreed upon with the aim of increasing the Palestinian commitments while at the same time reducing the Israeli ones. He agreed last August to the redeployment from 13% of the occupied territories, however, he took many Palestinian relinquishments at Wye Plantation using this as a bargaining chip.

The Palestinian Authority introduced new relinquishments, the most important of which are as follows:

Responding to Netanyahu's approach by accepting new negotiations on what was already agreed upon.

Accepting the 13% redeployment but with the added condition of using the formula of (10+3) that was imposed by Netanyahu even though the PA was initially demanding the redeployment from 40% of the West Bank as stated in the Interim Agreement, then only to turn around and agree on 13% as outlined by the American initiative.

The 4 May 1999 deadline for the end of the final status negotiations was left undecided, which denies the PA its negotiating card of declaring the independent State of Palestine before that date. The reference to that date in the agreement is general and not binding.

Retracting from the comprehensive solution of the Interim period and accepting a partial solution.

Accepting the CIA's partnership and supervision on the implementation of the required security measures against the Palestinian People and their forces that resist the Occupation. This puts the PA in a position unable to free itself from any commitments or room to maneuver, nor will it be able to declare the independent State.

The agreement would not be signed without efforts exerted by all of the U.S. Administration in general and President Clinton in particular. Also, it will not be implemented unless under the supervision of the U.S. Administration through the CIA. This makes the provisions of the agreement decidedly in favour of the Israeli concepts because of the strategic alliance between Israel and the United States.

The agreement gives the U.S. Administration represented by the CIA a big role in planning, implementing and supervising all provisions of the agreement, which means that the PA has accepted its lowered status of merely an administrative authority, which is already undermined, to be confiscated in favour of the American party. Playing this role requires the CIA to expand its activities, increase its cadres and to establish its own offices in the West Bank, Gaza Strip and perhaps in other countries.

Although the agreement puts an end to the freeze that has been dominating the Israeli-Palestinian negotiation track over the past 19 months, the victory achieved by Netanyahu's way of thinking and the generality of the provisions pertaining to Israel's commitments enable Netanyahu, who already does not believe in the Oslo Accords, to rid himself of the agreements under various pretexts such as his non-conviction that the PA would meet its commitments or that he would not be able to convince his partners in the Government of the agreement that has just been signed. Because there are no guarantees to implementing the agreement by Israel, and because there are many gaps that impede its implementation, this could be reason enough to aggravate the situation again.

The agreement includes a call to start the final status negotiations but it does not put any restrictions on the contents of these negotiations. This could make the Interim situation of the final status turn out the way Netanyahu's Government has already planned.

The Zionist negotiators persisted in the nullification of certain provisions of the Palestinian National Charter and in the way it is described in the agreement. This means that Israel was not satisfied with the PA's recognition of the occupation and that it wants it to condemn its history and past. It also wants to humiliate the Palestinians by obliging them to change their convictions and ideology.

The agreement ignores the issues of settlement and the settlers' arms, which is a serious mistake and is proof that the PA is unable to protect its people and to provide them with security. Or it could mean that the PA does not care, which subjects the civilian Palestinians to the savage acts and atrocities at the hands of the settlers. Is this the security and the stability that will be achieved by the agreement?

Third: Consequences and dangers to the Palestinian situation

The agreement transfers the Palestinian Cause from a national liberation question to an Arab demographic minority in a Zionist State. It also poses an authority on this minority with a function to preserving the security of the Zionist entity and to suppressing the Palestinian "minority" in order to prevent them from resisting the occupation and even from expressing their opinions regarding the resistance and removal of occupation.

Because the PA is committed to the provisions of the agreement and because there is a mechanism to supervise the implementation of this agreement in participation with the CIA, the PA will be involved in a direct struggle with the Palestinian People, whether from Hamas, the Islamic Jihad or others because they have adopted a programme to resist occupation. The PA will also suppress the forces that have views supporting the resistance under the pretext of incitement. It will even suppress the pro-PA forces when the PA starts collecting their weapons.

As a result of the PA's atrocities of combating the resistance programme; silencing the opposition forces; suppressing the journalists; arresting the Muslim scholars, notables, politicians and thinkers; breaking up the Zakat (alms) committees, social and charitable establishments under the pretext that they support the resistance; and destroying the mosques, media and cultural institutions under the pretext that they incite people to resist the occupation, the Palestinian society is facing a state of confusion and instability as well as internal conflicts that may develop into a civil war that in the end only benefits the Israeli Occupation, which has been working on that objective and knows that the agreement is pushing the Palestinian people in that direction.

The unilateral implementation of the agreement will enable Israel to establish its occupation and superiority over the whole of the Palestinian territories and to close the file of the Palestinian Cause under the pretext that the Palestinian People have obtained an authority of administration and services in the highly populated areas, while the majority of the West Bank remains under the control of the Israeli Occupation to build more settlements. The fate of the Palestinian People in the West Bank will become the same as the Palestinian People in the territories occupied in 1948.

The expanded role of the CIA in the agreement, which includes participating in investigations, the monitoring of the courts' sentences, adding details to the concept of incitement, collecting information and performing their own investigations, makes the U.S. Administration a direct enemy in the eyes of the Palestinian People and another tyrant that has developed its previous role in supporting the Zionist enemy into a direct role of suppressing our People and hatching plots against them. This will complicate the situation more and undermine the stability to which the peace process supposedly aims.

Fourth: Consequences and dangers to the Arab and Islamic situation

The implementation of the agreement will open the region to the Israeli Enemy, because it undermines the steadfastness of the Palestinian People and their ability to resist the occupation by involving them with internal disputes causing the dismantling of their national unity. Consequently, the Enemy will be in a position to confiscate more Palestinian land, erect more settlements and Judaize the region before shifting to the expected procedure of expelling more of the Palestinians to the neighbouring Arab countries. This agreement harms the Palestinian question and the Arab and Islamic interests as well.

The agreement encourages the isolation of the Palestinian question from its Arab and Islamic dimensions. It gives the American-Zionist alliance an additional card to separate the Palestinian track from the Syrian and Lebanese tracks while simultaneously pressuring Syria and other Arab countries to make similar agreements. The Israeli Enemy will be stronger in any future bilateral or regional negotiations, especially with their unlimited U.S. support.

The agreement helps the Israeli Enemy and the United States to continue imposing regional security plans to protect the Zionist entity and to dominate the region. These plans will also prevent the countries of the region from procuring advanced technology of weaponry and atomic energy. The Israeli-Turkish military alliance could be the beginning in this regard.

As a result of the partnership between the Israeli Government and the Palestinian Authority, which was boosted by the agreement, the PA, virtually and necessarily, will be involved in the alliances between Israel and some countries of the region. The Zionist enemy will also make use of the PA's relations with the Arab countries by making the PA an instrument for spying, pressuring or persuading them to achieve the Zionist interests, especially because the Zionist entity has already succeeded in planting its agents within the PA's services.

In view of the expanded role of the U.S. Administration in the implementation of the agreement, it will request, as it did before, the Arab and Islamic countries to stop the financial resources they give to the Palestinian People and their civil and social institutions under the pretext that they support what it calls "violence and terrorism". The U.S. Administration, encouraged by the PA itself, will pressure these countries to sever their relations with the Hamas Movement in particular, although we are sure that the Arab and Islamic attitude will not yield to these pressures that do not serve the interests of our cause and our Nation.

As a result of this hostile effort to isolate the Palestinian question from its Arab and Islamic dimension, Jerusalem and the holy mosque of Al Aqsa will be the victims in the final status negotiations. The Muslims' first Qibla will remain under the control of the Zionist enemy whose future plans include demolishing Al Aqsa and building the so-called "Third Temple" on its present site.

Fifth: Conclusions and the required attitude

The agreement is of a security nature and yields to the Zionist conditions and demands. It should be considered an instrument used to destroy the capabilities and potential of the Palestinian People, along with their civil society, institutions and national unity. It will cause instability in the region in a way that serves the Zionist-American interests at the expense of the interests of the Arab and Muslim people.

The combating of the agreement and its consequences is not exclusive to the Hamas Movement, the other Palestinian opposition forces, or even the Palestinian People in general. It is rather the duty of the Arab and Islamic governments and people.

The PA began the implementation of the security provisions of the agreement from the first moment after signing the agreement. It arrested the journalists who visited Sheikh Ahmed Yassin to interview him concerning the agreement. The PA's security forces also started an arrest campaign against members and supporters of Hamas and Islamic Jihad movements. They also arrested Sheikh Hamed Al Bitawi, the *khatib* of Al Aqsa Mosque and President of the Palestine Ulam' League, after he gave a statement to a TV channel via telephone, and Sheikh Nafez Azzam of the Islamic Jihad after his speech in a rally in Gaza. The Palestinian Military Intelligence raided Fateh Movement's office in Ramallah to confiscate weapons and opened fire at a peaceful demonstration organized by Fateh supporters, killing a young Palestinian supporter and injuring others, causing increased tension in the city.

In view of the dangerous situation that makes it impossible to wait or to give a chance to examine the agreement, we, the Islamic Resistance Movement (Hamas), call upon our Palestinian People to be aware of the reality of the agreement, which destroys the present and future of our Palestinian Cause, and which destroys the achievements and attainments over the past decades. We also appeal to all popular forces and activists to unite their ranks to defend the rights of their people, institutions, security and national unity.

We call upon all Arab and Islamic government and popular forces to take the initiative to voice their views about the agreement and its dangers, and to press the PA, using all means possible, to prevent it from cracking down on the Palestinian *Jihadi* forces and from igniting an internal war, which would put the Palestinian People at the mercy of the Zionist ghoul. If the Palestinian wall of unity collapses, the Zionist flood would sweep the whole Nation.

On this occasion, the Hamas Movement is fully confident that no part of the agreement, or the Zionist enemy, or the Palestinian Authority will be able to uproot the resistance of our People or to prevent them from continuing their resistance programme.

Finally, while we in Hamas condemn this agreement and warn of its dangers and consequences to our People, our cause and our Nation, if the PA insists on implementing its contents and playing the role of the servant and the instrument of the Occupation, we reiterate our stand prohibiting Palestinian-Palestinian fighting. We also reiterate our keenness to preserve National Unity. We shall be firm in rejecting oppression and the Occupation while at the same time very positive in maintaining Palestinian unity and directing our People towards the resistance of the Enemy in order to build their present and future. We shall remain, by the Will of God, beside our People and Nation, and defend our legitimate rights, land and holy places until we achieve victory, liberation and the return of our People to their homeland.

Everyone should learn that the Right will triumph and the falsehood will no doubt be removed, even if it is bristling with arms and supported by all earthly powers.

Hamas Military
Communiqués

Hamas Military Communiqués

16 February 2002

In the name of Allah the most Gracious the most Merciful

Military communiqué
Issued by the Qassam Brigades
Our Palestinian people . . . our Arab and Islamic Ummah:

With the grace of Allah the Qassam Brigades declare responsibility for the missile bombing with Qassam-2 missiles of the Zionist settlement complex in Palestinian lands occupied since 1948 to the east of steadfast Gaza city on Saturday 4th Thul Hijja 1422H—16/2/2002Ad at 6.15 am.

The Qassam Brigades declare responsibility for the missile bombing this morning and affirm the following:

1. Firing Qassam-2 missiles at early morning hours and not at noon and in open areas came as a retaliatory warning to the Zionist criminals over their criminal bombardment of our people with warplanes and tanks the latest of which was Friday night and this morning along with the constant insults, murder, destruction, displacement and detention of our people.

2. Zionist criminals should only blame themselves if they continue to commit crimes believing that no reprisal would be made. They know quite well what a missile could do amidst houses in the morning hours as they have seen for themselves today, a matter that we had avoided till now.

3. The Qassam-2 missile is a deterrent weapon and it is Palestinian made. We are proud of it and it is not mere fireworks as Zionist agents try to picture to discourage Palestinian resistance. The missile is intended to serve the Palestine cause and not a certain party.

*"And Allah hath full power and control over
His affairs; but most among mankind know it not."*

And it is a Jihad until either victory or martyrdom

Qassam Brigades
4th Thul Hijja 1422H
16/2/2002AD

12 February 2002

In the name of Allah the most Gracious the most Merciful

Military communiqué by the Qassam Brigades

*"It is not ye who slew them; it was Allah:
when thou threwest it was not thy act, but Allah's"*

One of our heroic units launched a commando operation in Beer Sheba in retaliation to the enemy's continued crimes against our people namely killing, slaughtering, dislodging, aerial bombing, demolishing of houses and spreading panic among children and women and in retaliation to the Zionist gangs' massacre against a group of our best men in Nablus: the group of four martyrs (Sheikh Yousef Sourkaji group) who were assassinated by Zionist gangs in cold blood.

The unit consisted of:

Martyr hero Khaled Khalil Jibril Al-Tal, 22.
Martyr hero Mohammed Misbah Al-Battat, 23.

The martyrs from Dhaheriya town, south of Khalil, launched a heroic and unique operation as the enemy admitted on Sunday 10th February 2002. The group members attacked the Israeli army command in the occupied city of Beer Sheba and showered it with bullets inflicting several casualties in enemy lines. The enemy acknowledged the death of two Zionist female conscripts and the injury of 24 other soldiers four of whom in serious condition.

Our Mujahid people:

We in the Qassam Brigades along with all honorable and free people in this Ummah vow before Allah then before you to remain loyal to blood of martyrs and to continue along the path of right until ejection of occupation from the land of Palestine and until it is purged from the Jewish occupiers' dirt.

And it is a Jihad until either victory or martyrdom

Wallaho Akbar Walillahi Al-Hamad

Qassam Brigades
Martyr Iyad Al-Battat Unit
Palestine—Al-Quds
30th Thul Qai'da 1422H
12/2/2002AD

7 February 2002

In the name of Allah the most Gracious the most Merciful

Military communiqué
By the Qassam Brigades

"Fight them, and Allah will punish them by your hands, cover them with shame, help you (to victory) over them, heal the breasts of Believers"

In retaliation to the heinous crime perpetrated by the Zionist enemy namely the assassination of martyr Yousef Al-Sourkaji and his three bothers in Nablus in addition to terrorizing our innocent people, one of the Jihad units of the Qassam Brigades affiliated with "Martyr Yousef Sourkaji" group on Wednesday night (6/2/2002) stormed the so-called "Hamra" settlement to the east of Nablus. The surprise night attack led to the death of four Zionist settlers and soldiers and the injury of four others. The settlement itself was in a state of terror and panic as Almighty Allah said, *"Assault them at the (proper) Gate: when once ye are in, victory will be yours."*

Enemy reinforcements were summoned and a clash took place between them and the attacking unit that later withdrew after one of them was martyred:

Ziyad Al-Khalili

We in the Qassam brigades vow to the martyr Hero that we will continue along the road of Jihad and martyrdom until ejection of the usurping occupier form our pure lands and the return of our Palestinian people to their country.

Let our mothers rejoice and the martyrs rest and we will continue living to our pledges.

And it is a Jihad until either victory or martyrdom

Qassam Brigades
Al-Quds-Palestine
25th Thul Qai'da 1422H
7/2/2002AD

31 January 2002

In the name of Allah the most Gracious the most Merciful

"It is not ye who slew them; it was Allah: when thou threwest, it was not thy act, but Allah's . . ."

Military communiqué by the Qassam Brigades

Our proud Palestinian people:

The Qassam Brigades declare responsibility fort the armed attack in the so-called Gush Qatif settlements complex this morning Thursday 16th Thul Qa'ida 1422H—31/1/2002Ad at 6.30 am.

The commandos who launched the operation were:

Martyr hero: Mohammed Abed Rabbo Emad from Jabaliya refugee camp

Martyr hero: Mazen Ribhi Badawi from Sheikh Radwan suburb—Gaza

Details of the operation:

1. The Mujahideen Mohammed and Mazen with the grace of Allah managed to penetrate all of the Zionist enemy's external and internal security fortifications in the so-called Gush Qatif settlements complex and planted a number of anti-armor guided explosives on the main road of the so-called Gush Qatif settlements.

2. At exactly 6.35 am the Mujahideen operated the guided explosives when a convoy of Zionist gangs was passing by then they threw hand grenades at them and opened machinegun fire after which smoke was seen rising form one of the Zionist buses.

Our Palestinian masses:

This daring operation affirms the brittle Zionist security and the continuation of the march of Jihad and resistance until ejection of occupation from our lands.

And it is a Jihad until either victory or martyrdom

Qassam Brigades
17th Thul Qa'ida 1422H
31/1/2002AD

15 January 2002

In the name of Allah the most Gracious the most Merciful

Military communiqué
The Qassam Brigades

"Fight them, and Allah will punish them by your hands, cover them with shame, help you (to victory) over them, heal the breasts of Believers,"

Allaho Akbar . . . Allaho Akbar . . . Allaho Akbar

We are the ones who vowed to strive in the right path as long as we lived

Blasting a bus carrying Zionist settlers

And attacking it with machineguns north of Jenin

Here they are the Qassam Brigades continue to fight the Zionists and revenge for the innocent souls the latest of whom was commander of Aqsa Brigades the Mujahid martyr Ra'ed Al-Karmi. The Qassam Brigades launched the operation in retaliation to the repressive measures against our people and the demolition of houses in steadfast Rafah, Eisawiya village in Al-Quds and all areas in Palestine. The operation also came in reprisal to the tightening siege laid to the city of Ramallah and all other brave Palestinian cities. The operation was launched by the Unit-19 specialized in killing Zionist settlers and attacking their terrorist groupings in the 1967 occupied areas of Palestine. The Unit members attacked a bus carrying Zionist settlers at the circular road to the north of Jenin after getting out from the so-called settlement of Kadim established on our people's lands in the West Bank, Jenin district causing direct and painful hit to the target.

We tell the Zionists there will be no security or safety for you on our land and you have to leave. We vow to our people in Rafah refugee camp, the patient Gaza Strip and the entire land of Palestine that we will persist in Jihad until the occupiers pack up and leave.

And it is a jihad until either victory or martyrdom

PS: The operation is videotaped and the film was sent to the media means.

Qassam Brigades
Tuesday 15/1/2002

9 January 2002

In the name of Allah the most Gracious the most Merciful

Military communiqué by Qassam Brigades

*"And slay them wherever ye catch them, and turn them out
from where they have turned you out;"*

Four Zionists killed, an officer and three soldiers, and two wounded

The Qassam Brigades, military wing of the Islamic Resistance Movement, Hamas, declare responsibility for the heroic operation that the two following heroic Mujahideen launched this morning:

Martyr: Mohammed Abdul Ghani Abu Jamoos and martyr Emad Etaiwi Abu Rizk

Who defended the holy Aqsa Mosque and the land of Arab-Islamic Palestine on behalf of the Arab and Islamic Nation.

We declare success of this operation and would like to affirm the following:

1. All praises to Allah for that success and we call on all Muslims to pray at night for the success of Mujahideen.

2. The Qassam Brigades affirm the pledge of keeping up operations in support of our country until its liberation.

3. The operation comes to expose the lie of Zionist security and to retaliate against the Zionist entity's arrogance namely storming our cities and villages, murder and displacement, demolition of houses and finally the Zionist act of piracy against the vessel in Arab territorial waters and steering it to the usurping entity.

4. The Qassam Brigades will not remain captive to Sharon's dictates in determining whatever he wished as days for calm, while continuing to strangle our people and to dismember their land.

5. Our option is that of Jihad and resistance, which is a heavenly option that no one can deviate from and we will live up to it God willing.

Our Mujahid people:

Your Brigades the Qassam Brigades offer this operation as a gift to all the oppressed captives and as a message to the Arab and Muslim people namely that the Qassam guns would remain directed at our enemy the usurping Jews only despite the numerous stabbings in our backs from those who sold themselves to the Americans.

We vow before Allah then before you to persist along that road until the usurped homeland is liberated from this evil occupation.

In conclusion we report what the Jewish radio broadcast in Hebrew when it said that two Mujahideen were able to penetrate the security fence and clashed with a number of Jewish army units using machineguns and explosive devices killing an officer and three soldiers while two others were wounded one of them seriously.

Finally we hope that the two martyrs' filmed will, would reach you soon Insha'allah.

And it is a Jihad until either victory or martyrdom

Allaho Akbar wa Lillah Al-Hamad

Qassam Brigades
Wednesday 25th Shawwal 1422H
9th January 2002AD

2 December 2001

In the name of Allah the most Gracious the most Merciful

Military communiqué by Qassam Brigades

"It is not ye who slew them; it was Allah: when thou threwest, it was not thy act, but Allah's"

Our proud Palestinian people . . . our Arab and Islamic Ummah:

With the grace of Allah the Qassam Brigades declare responsibility for the armed attack against a convoy of Zionist occupation vehicles grouping settlers and soldiers along the road between the so-called settlements of Ely Sinai and Nesanit to the north of Gaza Strip on Sunday 17th Ramadan 1422H—2/12/2001AD.

Those who launched the attach were the two heroes:

Martyr / Maslama Ibrahim Al-A'raj nicknamed
Abu Ibrahim, 20, from Gaza city

Martyr / Jihad Hamdy Al-Masri nicknamed Abu Ibrahim, 17, from village of Beit Lahya

Our Mujahid Palestinian masses:

Our Mujahideen have trodden on the false myth of Zionist security when they penetrated all Zionist security precautions and reached training trenches of the Zionist army inside the settlement and launched an attack from those trenches then they got out and stood in mid of the road with their machine-guns and started firing at the enemy vehicles that fled the scene.

Our proud Palestinian masses:
Our operation today affirms the following:

1. It was a natural retaliation by a people slaughtered day and night and whose dignity is being humiliated by the Zionist enemy's war machine.
2. This is not the revenge for martyr Mahmoud Abu Hannoud and the other martyrs and our Brigades will soon launch that revenge Insha'allah.
3. The American administration's General did not come to the region to ask the Zionists to evacuate our lands but rather came believing that our people will be satisfied with less than liberation of their usurped lands . . . he is only dreaming.

And it is a Jihad until either victory or martyrdom

Qassam Brigades
17th Ramadan 1422Ad
2/12/2001AD

27 November 2001

In the name of Allah the most Gracious the most Merciful

"It is not ye who slew them; it was Allah: when thou threwest, it was not thy act, but Allah's"

"And there is the type of man who gives his life to earn the pleasure of Allah"

Military communiqué by the Qassam Brigades

Our proud Palestinian masses . . . our Arab and Islamic Ummah:

With the help of Allah the Qassam Brigades declare responsibility for the armed attack using hand grenades and machineguns against a convoy of Zionist usurpers along the so-called road of the Gush Qatif settlements complex to the south of Gaza Strip inflicting a number of dead and wounded, which the enemy confessed.

Executor of the attack is the martyr hero:

Osama Hillis (from the steadfast suburb of Shija'ya)

He had purchased his Kalashnikov machinegun from his own money and had yearned for martyrdom for the past months.

The Qassam Brigades declare responsibility for the operation and affirm the following:

1. Jihad and resistance will continue until ejection of Zionist occupation.

2. Unity of Palestinian lines is a necessity for protection of the blessed intifada.

3. People should not to be deceived by western promises and Zionist withdrawal from lands which it destroyed and displaced its inhabitants.

And it is a Jihad until either victory or martyrdom

Qassam Brigades
12th Ramadan 1422H
27/11/2001AD

24 Nov 2001

In the name of Allah the most Gracious the most Merciful

"It is not ye who slew them; it was Allah: when thou threwest,
it was not thy act, but Allah's . . ."

Military communiqué by Qassam Brigades

We swear by Almighty Allah to avenge from you Zionists, the most mean of God's creatures, even if only one man was left of us

Our Palestinian masses and our Arab and Islamic Nation:

With the grace of Allah the Qassam Brigades declare responsibility for shelling the so-called Kfar Darum settlement in the center of Gaza Strip with mortar shells today Saturday 9th Ramadan 1422H—24/11/2001Ad spreading panic in lines of the Zionist cowards.

Our Palestinian masses:

The usurpers and settlers have fled after the first explosion in the heart of the settlement leaving behind their casualties the dead and wounded and how truthful is Allah's words: *"if they come out to fight you, they will show you their backs."*

And we in the Qassam Brigade would also like to affirm the following:

1. We have shelled today the so-called Aires area to the north of Gaza Strip with mortar shells and pounded the so-called Doget settlement with Qassam (1) missiles and the enemy admitted that shelling in addition to bombing Kfar Darum.

2. We affirm the continuation of armed intifada until ejection of occupation and we declare that Zionist murder and criminality would only boost our insistence on Jihad and resistance.

3. We call on our people to side by the Jihad and resistance option and not to heed the shuttle trips to and from America and Europe, which only aim at forcing our people to bow down.

And it is a Jihad until either victory or martyrdom

Qassam Brigades
9th Ramadan 1422H
24/11/2001AD

26 October 2001

In the name of Allah the most Gracious the most Merciful

*"It is not ye who slew them; it was Allah: when thou threwest . . .
it was not thy act, but Allah's . . ."*

Military communiqué by the Qassam Brigades
Karame Battle (2)

Attacking Zionist military outpost in northern Gaza

Our heroic Palestinian people . . . our Arab and Islamic Nation:

With the grace of Allah, the Qassam Brigades declare responsibility for attacking and storming the Zionist army post established on our Palestinian lands in the area called Doget settlement to the north of Gaza Strip on Friday 9th Sha'aban 1422H, 26/10/2001AD.

A fierce battle took place that started with our Mujahideen firing projectiles then hurling more than 20 grenades and engaging the enemy in a violent battle involving machineguns over almost half an hour. A helicopter landed to carry away their dead. We declare through this operation that our Mujahideen would persist in their Jihad until ejection of occupation.

Three Mujahideen from the Qassam Brigades were martyred in this operation:

Martyr hero: Othman Deeb Al-Razayna, 22, from Jabaliya refugee camp.

Martyr hero: Iyad Rabee Al-Batsh, 21, from the town of Jabaliya.

Martyr hero: Fuad Mustafa Al-Dahshan, 17, from Zaitun suburb, Gaza.

The Qassam Brigades, while declaring responsibility for storming the Zionist military position, pays no attention to enemy's allegations that no casualties were sustained in the lines of its soldiers. We vow before Allah then before you to continue along the road of Jihad and resistance until occupation is forced out of our lands.

And it is a Jihad until either victory or martyrdom

Qassam Brigades
Friday 9th Sha'aban 1422H
26/10/2001AD

24 October 2001

In the name of Allah the most Gracious the most Merciful

Massacre in Beit Reema . . . where is al-Mo'tasem?!

Our Arab and Islamic Nation:

A new massacre is committed by the Zionsit enemy this time in Beit Reema village, Ramallah district, scores of martyrs and wounded have fallen in the streets, squares and olive orchards of that village. The enemy has prevented paramedics from carrying away the bodies of martyrs or extending assistance to the wounded and has even fired at the doctors and medical teams. Such acts have been taking place today and last night in Beit Reema while scores of martyrs were falling in Tulkarm, Qalqilya and Bethlehem.

Our Arab and Islamic masses:

Our Mujahid, patient and steadfast people in Beit Reema and in the entire land of Palestine are asking today what is our Nation waiting for? What is our Nation's reaction while witnessing its sons in the holy land murdered, slaughtered and their houses and villages demolished and destroyed? Is such silence towards this pogrom permissible among brothers and holders of the same religion? Will Arab dignity and chivalry accept continuation of that silence? What is the Nation waiting for, if such daily shed blood did not make it act?

We ask the Nation's leaders and governments to shoulder their historic responsibility towards the Zionist enemy's massacres of our people. We urge them to embark on an urgent initiative and practical steps to save and defend our people and check the Zionist aggressions. We call on them to exercise real and serious pressure on the American administration to halt the enemy's massacre and end its protection of Sharon and his terrorist government.

We affirm that our people and Mujahid forces would remain loyal to their pledge of persisting in Jihad and resistance, defending their lands and holy shrines and remaining patient and steadfast for the sake of Allah. We also invite our Nations' masses to rescue their brothers in Palestine and beseech them to commence practical steps to end that carnage and check its possible spread into other areas.

Our Mujahid and patient people:

Our enemy is only deterred by force and only steadfastness and confrontation would halt its aggression. In such difficult moments, we call on all our people's forces and factions especially the resistance brigades in the Qassam, Aqsa Martyrs, Martyr Abu Ali Mustafa, Quds and elements of the Palestinian Authority police and national security to unite their efforts in confrontation of the Zionist enemy that is launching an open war. We urge them to retaliate to the atrocities in an open confrontation that would target all of its leaderships, soldiers and settlers in away that reaches the depth of its security.

"So lose not heart, nor fall into despair:
for ye must gain mastery if ye are true in Faith."

And it is a Jihad until either victory or martyrdom

The Islamic Resistance Movement
Hamas-Palestine
Wednesday 7th Sha'aban 1422H
24/10/2001AD

23 October 2001

In the name of Allah the most Gracious the most Merciful

"Among the Believers are men who have been true to their Covenant with Allah: of them some have completed their vow (to the extreme), and some (still) wait: but they have never changed (their determination) in the least."

Qassam Brigades military communiqué

All praises be to Allah the Supporter of Mujahideen, all praises be to Allah who honored His servants with Jihad, all praises be to Allah who bestowed martyrdom on His servants to reward them and peace be upon his Messenger, the leader of Mujahideen and his family and companions.

With all pride and confidence in Allah's victory and the destiny He has pre-determined, the Qassam Brigades bear the news of the martyrdom of the Qassam commander hero:

The engineer of martyrdom operations
Eng. Ayman Halawe
(Abu Adnan)

who was assassinated by Zionist treacherous hands in a cowardly operation on the land of Nablus, Jabal Al-Nar (Mountain of Fire) on Monday evening 22/10/2001 after spending a lifetime as a Mujahid for the cause of Allah along with his brothers in the Qassam Brigades. He was daily yearning for martyrdom . . . so we congratulate you Abu Adnan over the martyrdom, paradise, nearness to Allah and meeting previous martyrs, prophets and the virtuous who are the best of companions.

Our heroic Palestinian masses: the relatives of martyrs, wounded and detainees, family of martyr hero Ayman: all of you who have suffered at the hands of the usurping occupiers, we in the Qassam Brigades while bidding farewell to one martyr after the other, we affirm to villainous Sharon that his assassinations do not change the destiny that Allah has predetermined as martyrdom is one of the aims of the Mujahideen. Pre-destiny is befalling all of us and those assassinations would only boost our strength with the grace of Allah. But let the usurping occupier know that we in the Qassam Brigades never forget the blood of our martyrs and that our commandos will punish Zionists, God willing, chasing and burning them in all areas . . . in Al-Quds and Tel Aviv, in Netanya and Haifa, in Khadera and Afula to avenge for martyrs. We will not speak more but our actions will soon speak for us.

Allahu Akbar and our determination is as solid as ever

Allahu Akbar wa Lillah Al-Hamd

Qassam Brigades
Military wing of the Islamic Resistance Movement-Hamas
Tuesday 23/10/2001

2 October 2001

In the name of Allah the most Gracious the most Merciful

"It is not ye who slew them; it was Allah: when thou threwest . . ."

Military communiqué by Qassam Brigades

Attacking the so-called Ely Sinai settlement with mortars, grenades and machineguns

"Assault them at the (proper) Gate: when once ye are in, victory will be yours;"

Our Palestinian people, our Arab and Islamic Nation:

With the grace of Allah the Qassam Brigades declare responsibility for storming the so-called Ely Sinai settlement that was established on our Palestinian lands to the north of Gaza Strip on Tuesday night 15th Rajab 1422H, 2/10/2001.

Our operation tonight affirms the following:

1. Blood of our Palestinian people is not cheap and whoever sheds our blood we will shed his blood at the opportune time and place.
2. Zionist security is fragile and we are capable of reaching the Zionist terrorists even if they hid in the clouds as we have pledged in the previous communiqué.
3. Jihad and resistance will continue until ejection of occupation.

Our Palestinian people:

This is our second gift to our people in the second year of the holy Aqsa intifada. We promise you to avenge your blood regardless of the Zionist terrorists' ceasefire lie that attempt to deceive the entire world into believing it despite the fact that 20 of your sons were killed (during the alleged ceasefire).

We ask you to unite regardless of the different trends and currents in face of the Zionist offensive and we vow to launch other reprisals to Zionist crimes.

<u>We will declare names and photos of the martyrs later Insha'allah.</u>

And it is a Jihad until either victory or martyrdom

Qassam Brigades
15th Rajab 1422H
2 October 2001

26 September 2001

"It is not ye who slew them; it was Allah: when thou threwest . . ."

Military communiqué by Qassam Brigades
Anti-terrorist unit
Blows up a building of Zionist terrorists
Our Palestinian people . . . our Arab and Islamic Nation:

With the grace of Allah the Qassam Brigades declares responsibility for the destruction of a building used by Zionist terrorists to practice their terrorist activity: killing and assassinating our people and spreading corruption in the steadfast city of Rafah.

Today Wednesday 9th Rajab 1422H (26/9/2001AD) our Mujahideen planted a big quantity of explosives under the foundations of the Zionist terrorist den then blow it up on heads of its occupants. They resembled the Quranic verses: **". . . but Allah took their structures from their foundations, and the roof fell down on them from above; and the Wrath seized them from directions they did not perceive."**

Our proud Palestinian people:

Your enemy is weak and coward; so do not be afraid of its military war machine. Your belief in Allah, your solid determination and unity of lines are stronger than your enemy's military might. Keep up the determination to get that enemy out of our lands through Jihad and resistance and we are capable, with the help of Allah, to force that enemy out of our lands after a military defeat similar to the way its soldiers fled South Lebanon. Our operation is in response to occupation and its murders and terrorist practices. It also asserts our insistence on persisting along the road of Jihad and resistance until ejection of the enemy and to let it know we are capable of reaching its soldiers even if they hide in the clouds.

PS: <u>we affirm that the operation has been filmed.</u>

And it is a Jihad until either victory of martyrdom

**Qassam Brigades
9th Rajab 1422H
26/9/2001AD**

5 September 2001

"Fight them, and Allah will punish them by your hands, cover them with shame, help you (to victory) over them, heal the breasts of Believers."

Qassam Brigades military communiqué

With the grace of Allah the Qassam Mujahid hero:

**Ra'ed Nabil Al-Barguthi
From Abud village, Ramallah district**

launched a martyrdom operation on Tuesday 4/9/01 at Al-Anbiyaa street in the heart of occupied Al-Quds after penetrating all enemy security lines and smashing the myth of its security apparatuses that claim incessant successes. The operation led to the death of five Zionists and the injury of scores others, according to our own sources. Our Mujahideen, who shared in the attack, have returned safely to bases waiting for the next operation.

The act is a revenge to the blood of our martyrs and in retaliation to the cowardly assassination attempt against our Mujahideen the commanders Mohammed Daif and Adnan Al-Ghoul and the assassination of Abu Ali Mustafa. The reprisal is merely the first in a series of Qassam operations that would force terrorist Sharon and his General Mofaz to admit their defeat in face of the Jihad and resistance determination. We tell Mofaz that although he escaped from Qassam bullets near Al-Quds last week, next week he won't survive, God willing.

Finally, we present this operation as a special gift to Qassam Mujahid martyr Bilal Al-Ghoul who sacrificed himself to protect his father . . . wait for Qassam's next surprise.

Wallahu Akbar wa Lillah Al-Hamad

And it is a Jihad until either victory or martyrdom

Martyr Mohiuddeen Asharif Unit
Qassam Brigades
Al-Quds-Palestine
5/9/2001

9 August 2001

In the name of Allah the most Gracious the most Merciful

Military communiqué
Qassam Brigades

"It is not ye who slew them; it was Allah: when thou threwest . . . it was not thy act, but Allah's . . ."

With the grace of Allah the Qassam Mujahid:

Ezzeldin Shuhail Ahmed Al-Masri
From the village of Ekaba, Jenin district

this afternoon Thursday 9/8/2001, 19th Jumada Awal 1422 launched a martyrdom operation in a restaurant in the heart of occupied Al-Quds inflicting large number of casualties in Zionist lines. The operation came to avenge the blood of our children, women and old people and in defense of Al-Quds and Palestine. The operation is also a gift to souls of the martyrs in Jenin Mujahid Mahmoud Mousa (Abu Musaab), Jamal Daifallah and a loyal gesture to the Mujahideen leaders Jamal Mansour, Jamal Salim, Salah Darwaza and their brothers in Jabal Al-Nar and the Bethlehem martyrs Omar Saadeh, Taha Al-Urouj and their brothers in addition to Qassam martyrs Amer Hudeiri and Fawaz Badran from Tulkarm and Aqsa Brigades' martyrs in Fara and the Mujahideen martyrs Mohammed Basharat and their brothers.

This retaliation is the first in a series of Qassam strikes that will teach the Zionists an unforgettable lesson as a penalty for their cowardly act of liquidating Mujahideen and activists of the Palestinian people.

Allahu Akbar wa Lillah Al-Hamd

Wa Allahu Akbar and victory to Islam

And it is a Jihad until either victory or martyrdom

Qassam Brigades—Jenin District
Military wing of the Islamic Resistance Movement-Hamas
9-8-2001

13 July 2001

"Think not of those who are slain in Allah's Way as dead. Nay, they live, finding their sustenance in the Presence of their Lord;"

Military communiqué issued by:
The Qassam Brigades

To our proud Palestinian people:

The Qassam Brigades bear the glad tidings of the martyrdom of its martyr hero:

Atef Mohammed Tafesh

who martyred while planting explosive devices against occupation forces and herds of settlers along the road leading to the so-called "Nisanit" settlement that is located on our usurped land to the north of the Gaza Strip.

Our hero martyred after planting the devices. A Zionist armored force surrounded him. Our martyr managed to fire at the force and hurl a hand grenade at its members before rising to heaven as a martyr of Islam, Palestine and Qassam Brigades.

Our Mujahid Palestinian masses:

We in the Qassam Brigades while conveying the glad tidings about martyrdom of the hero Atef Tafesh, we vow before Allah then before you to continue along the road of Jihad and martyrdom until ejection of occupation, which will never rest on our Palestinian lands.

And its is a Jihad until either victory or martyrdom

Qassam Brigades
Friday 22nd Rabee Thani 1422H
13/7/2001AD

8 July 2001

"Fight them, and Allah will punish them by your hands, cover them with shame, help you (to victory) over them, heal the breasts of Believers,"

Military communiqué issued by the Qassam Brigades

The military wing of the Islamic Resistance Movement "Hamas" Retaliation to blood with blood

The Qassam Brigades declare their responsibility for the Jihad operation yesterday Saturday 7/7/2001 when an explosive device was blasted near a Zionist patrol along the ring road leading to Aibal mountain. The blast directly hit the patrol and its occupants and as usual the enemy only admitted the injury of two of its Zionist soldiers.

The operation affirms the continuation of resistance against the occupying enemy and comes in retaliation to the Zionist continued aggression and siege against the Palestinian people.

The Qassam Brigades would like to confirm that they would strongly retaliate to any assassination of Mujahideen and strugglers as planned by criminal Sharon. The Zionists would pay blood in return for each drop of blood of any Palestinian Mujahid. We remind terrorist Sharon and his criminal government that when the Brigades promise, they live up to their promise. And we will remain committed to our pledges.

Allahu Akbar wa Lillahu Al-Hamad

Note: There is videotape of the operation attached.
Qassam Brigades
17 Rabee Thani 1422H
8/7/2001AD

22 June 2001

In the name of Allah the most Gracious the most Merciful

"It is not ye who slew them; it was Allah: when thou threwest, it was not thy act, but Allah's . . ."

". . . they deemed that their strongholds would protect them from Allah. But Allah reached them from a place whereof they recked not . . ."

Qassam brigades military communiqué

To the Zionist terrorists

If you allow your army and settlers to wreak havoc then our Brigades will be on the watch and you will see rather than hear (our revenge).

To our Palestinian masses . . .
to the Arab and Islamic Nation

The Qassam Brigades declare responsibility with the grace of Allah for the heroic martyrdom operation that targeted a military convoy in the heart of the so-called Doget settlement that is colonizing part of the northern sector of our lands in the Gaza Strip.

Our Palestinian people: The Qassam Brigades also declare the name of the executor of that operation the hero martyr:

Mujahid Ismail Basheer Al-Mi'sawabi

who launched the operation on behalf of the Arab and Islamic Nation to retaliate to the Zionist occupation's policy of murder and repression.

Our proud masses:

If the Zionist enemy declares that it has a free hand to assassinate and kidnap anyone, we also declare that our hands are free in all areas of our occupied lands in Palestine against the Zionist terrorists. We vow before Allah then before you to continue along the road of Jihad and martyrdom until defeat of occupation.

And it is a Jihad until either victory or martyrdom

Qassam Brigades
Friday 30th Rabee Awal 1422H
22/6/2001AD

5 June 2001

In the name of Allah the most Gracious the most Merciful

Qassam Brigades have no connection to the joint truce statement

The Qassam Brigades, military wing of the Islamic Resistance Movement, Hamas, affirm the falsehood of the joint truce statement circulated with the signature of both the Qassam Brigades and the Aqsa Martyrs Brigades.

We consider that statement as an intrigue aimed at besmearing our heroic Brigades after the heroic Tel Aviv operation.

We in the Qassam Brigades did not previously issue any joint statement with any other party. Furthermore, such practice is not of our policy.

We are confident that our Mujahid, mindful Palestinian people would not be beguiled by such media deception. They know who spreads such statements and who benefits from them.

The Qassam Brigades vow before Allah then our Palestinian people and Nation to continue resistance, Jihad and strikes deep inside the occupation lines until it evacuates our lands Insha'allah.

Qassam Brigades
5/6/2001

4 June 2001

In the name of Allah the most Gracious the most Merciful

"Fight them, and Allah will punish them by your hands, cover them with shame, help you (to victory) over them, heal the breasts of Believers,"

Qassam Brigades by the grace of Allah strikes hard with precision

We carry the glad tidings of the tenth martyr The executor of the qualitative operation The martyr hero / Saeed Hassan Hussein Al-Hoteri

Our Palestinian patient and Mujahid people
Our Arab and Islamic Nation

The tenth martyr the hero Saeed Hassan Hussein Al-Hoteri, 20, approached his target confidently last Friday at 11.30 pm according to the plan. He carried out his qualitative martyrdom operation in the enemy's depth and heart then ascended to heavens to meet the prophets, the truthful and the martyrs in Allah's Jannah (paradise).

The qualitative operation healed the breasts of believers and humiliated Jews and their collaborators. The blast was made using a highly explosive material (Qassam-19), which was developed by Qassam Brigades' experts in their own factories. The enemy experienced its bitterness in the first test in Netanya at the hands of the martyr hero Mahmoud Marmash.

We tell our people and Nation to rest assured that the Brigades' reprisal, by the grace of Allah, would always be a pioneering retaliation in its implementation, quality and effect.

The Qassam Brigades hail our people and brothers the Mujahideen in Jordan who begot such a martyr hero who mastered the state of wait and see as a true Mujahid.

We tell Jews . . . you have to leave or perish . . . for the Qassam promise of ten martyrs had achieved its goals of realizing balance of deterrence and horror with the grace of Allah. Still wait for what is coming is stronger and more bitter.

A salutation to our lions behind bars . . . here are your brothers working with your guidance the way you wished. Soon relief will ensue. Jihad greetings to all honorable Mujahideen of our people in their various positions and a grateful greeting to all martyrs and their relatives and to all those wounded on the land of Aqsa.

And it is a Jihad until either victory or martyrdom

Qassam Brigades
Palestine—Al-Quds
4/6/2001AD

27 April 2001

In the name of Allah the most Gracious the most Merciful

"It is not ye who slew them; it was Allah: when thou threwest, it was not thy act, but Allah's . . ."

Qassam Brigades military communiqué

Blasting a remote-controlled device inside the Nitsar Hazani settlement

With the grace of Allah the Qassam Brigades declare responsibility for storming the settlement of Nistar Hazani and blasting a remote-controlled device, near the water tank that supplies the complex of Gush Qatif settlements with fresh water, as a Zionist foot patrol was passing by on Friday 27/4/2001.

The Zionist enemy's radio admitted the operation claiming that an officer and a Zionist settler were wounded in the operation.

Our Palestinian people:
Our Arab and Islamic Nation:

The explosion was remote controlled so that the occupiers would suffer from the same methods used against us.

We vow before Allah then before you to persist along the same road until defeat of occupation.

And it is a Jihad until either victory or martyrdom

Allahu Akbar wa Lillahi Al-Hamd

Qassam Brigades
Friday 4th Safar 1422H
27th April 2001AD

18 April 2001

In the name of Allah the most Gracious the most Merciful

*"It is not ye who slew them; it was Allah: when thou threwest,
it was not thy act, but Allah's . . ."*

Qassam Brigades' military communiqué

Gift to families of the Syrian martyrs at the Syrian radar position

The Qassam Brigades declares responsibility for the shelling of the Zionist Nisanit settlement, built on part of northern Gaza Strip, in a televised operation that took place on Wednesday 18/4/2001. Our shelling retaliates to the pounding of the Syrian radar position and the martyrdom and injury of a group of Syrian soldiers. It further comes in reprisal to the usurping Zionist entity's concerted bombardment of our steadfast people.

Our Palestinian people, our Arab and Islamic Nation:

We affirm our responsibility for the shelling and pledge before Allah then before you to continue Jihad and resistance. We vow never to leave the Zionists enjoy security as long as our Palestinian people lack security and freedom.

To the prime minister of Israeli occupation:

You must stop killing our kids and women. We are not interested in killing your kids and women, as the continuance in this policy will lead to destruction on your people.

It is a Jihad until victory or martyrdom

Allahu Akbar wa Lillahi Al-Hamd

Qassam Brigades
Wednesday 24th Muharram 1422H
18/4/2001AD

27 March 2001

In the name of Allah the most Gracious the most Merciful

"Fight them, and Allah will punish them by your hands, cover them with shame, help you (to victory) over them, heal the breasts of Believers,"

Qassam Brigades military communiqué

The Mujahid Hero Dia' Hussein Mohammed Al-Tawil, one of our martyrdom cells' heroes blasted a 15-kilogram explosive device in one of the Zionist enemy's buses at one of Jerusalem's crossings afternoon today Tuesday 27/3/2001. The blast inflicted 20 casualties in lines of the Zionist usurpers in retaliation to Zionist repression, siege and murder daily practiced by the government of criminal Sharon against our unarmed Palestinian people.

We warn the Zionist occupation government topped by Sharon that our Brigades will retaliate double fold and will defend our people and sanctities till the last drop in our blood.

It is a Jihad until either victory or martyrdom

Qassam Brigades
Al-Quds Al-Sharif
Palestine
27/3/2001

PS: the martyr is from the city of Ramallah and is one of the Birzeit University students

22 March 2001

In the name of Allah the most gracious the most Merciful

"It is not ye who slew them; it was Allah: when thou threwest, it was not thy act, but Allah's . . ."

Military communiqué issued by Qassam Brigades

Shelling for shelling . . . and Zionists will not go unpunished

The Qassam Brigades declare with the grace of Allah its responsibility for the shelling of the two settlements of Mirage and Nitsarim with mortar shells on the anniversary of the Karame battle on Wednesday 25 Thul Hijja, 1421 that is 21/3/2001 in a quick and direct reprisal to the Zionist gangs' bombardment of the position of the brothers in Froce-17 that led to martyrdom of the hero officer Kamal Al-Jamal and the serious wounding of four of his colleagues.

Our proud Palestinian people . . . our Arab Islamic Nation:

Our operation comes on the anniversary of assassinating our brothers the leaders in Fatah Movement Abu Yousef Al-Najjar, Kamal Edwan and Kamal Nasser in Firdana in Lebanon. The Zionists have exceeded all limits, they killed, displaced, imprisoned, destroyed houses and property even our grave-yards were not spared. We have no other choice but Jihad and developing its means until victory or martyrdom.

We in the Qassam Brigades vow before Allah to continue along the road of Jihad and martyrdom and affirm our responsibility for the following:

1. Bombing the settlement of Dobit in north of Gaza Strip with mortar shells on Friday evening 22/3/2001.

2. Shelling the settlement of Nahal Oz to the east of Gaza city on Sunday evening 18/3/2001 also using mortars.

Our proud masses: your Brigades, the Qassam Brigades, pledge to remain your faithful and strong arm with which you fight the arrogant occupiers until they are cleansed out of our usurped lands and sanctities.

And it is a Jihad until either victory or martyrdom

Allahu Akbar wa Lillahi Al-Hamad

Qassam Brigades
26 Thul Hijja 1421H
22/3/2001AD

28 January 2001

In the name of Allah the most gracious the most Merciful

"It is not ye who slew them; it was Allah: when thou threwest,
it was not thy act, but Allah's . . ."

Military communiqué by the Qassam Brigades
Unit (103)

"Retaliation to the killing of two of our people in Rafah"

We declare in the Qassam Brigades-unit (103) our responsibility for a series of explosions targeting a convoy of Israeli tanks along the road of Nitsarim-Karni completely destroying one of them and slightly damaging another. With the grace of Allah our commandos in the unit (103) were able to cross the failed Zionist security blocks, in spite of their big numbers, plant the devices, return to specified positions and blast the devices . . . thanks to almighty Allah.

We could not film the operation because the area was exposed with no enough security allowed for the fighters but we promise you that future operations will be documented God willing.

Our Mujahid people / our operation is in retaliation to the Zionist criminals' murder of two Rafah citizens and to coincide with the passing of 40 days on the death of Qassam element Nooruddin Safi, who executed the recent Aires operation.

Our modest operation is a simple reprisal to the massacres committed by the Zionist occupation against our unarmed people for our memory is full of tragedies. In this month only the Zionist enemy forces committed the following:

1. The Zionist Argon gangs blasted the big Yaffa mall killing 26 persons on 4/1/1948.

2. The Zionist Haganah blew up the Samiramis Hotel in Al-Quds killing 20 Palestinians on 5/1/1948.

3. On 7 January that same year, the Argon gangs exploded the Khalil gate in Al-Quds killing 20 Palestinians and wounding scores others.

4. On 26 January the Haganah gangs razed to the ground the Skreir village in Gaza district.

This is only a few of the massacres committed by the Zionist Nazis against our people. The blood of all Zionist occupiers is not enough to avenge for our spilt blood.

Allahu Akbar wa Lilahu Hamad

It is a Jihad until either victory or martyrdom

Qassam Brigades
Unit "103"
28/1/2001

21 January 2001

> *In the name of Allah the most gracious the most Merciful*
>
> *"It is not ye who slew them; it was Allah: when thou threwest,*
> *it was not thy act, but Allah's . . ."*

Military communiqué issued by Qassam Brigades unit "103"

Retaliation to kidnapping Palestinian girl
Our Mujahid people

We did not rest following our latest operation but rather launched a fresh painful one against the arrogant Zionists. We would never let the herds of settlers spread corruption with no punishment. Your unit that of revenge: "103" pledged to strike with force and to chose its targets accurately. The enemy's Generals and rats did not expect our operation this time at the same place of the former one with the simple difference of a more powerful explosion and heavier losses.

We were able, with the grace of Allah, this morning Monday 22/1/2001 at 7:7 am to blast a Zionist tank allocated to escorting Israeli army and settlers' convoys. Our Mujahideen, with the help of Allah, were able to plant a remote-controlled 40-kilogram explosive device less than one meter away from the tank leading to its complete destruction. We affirm that our Mujahideen were able for the second time to record the operation on videotape and we are surprised over the media blackout on our first operation, which came in retaliation to the assassinations and which was distributed then.

Our proud people

This operation falls in line with the series of reprisals to the Zionist entity's savage massacres against our stationed and unarmed people **especially the kidnapping of a Palestinian girl from Bir Nabala** and poses as a last warning to the herds of settlers who have escalated their offensive against our steadfast and stationed people in Khan Younis.

We in the Qassam Brigades / unit "103" only own our souls and bodies, along with the grace of Allah, that we would willingly sacrifice for the sake of our people without any partisan or political discrimination. We are your arm that strikes the usurping Zionist enemy.

Allahu Akbar wa Lilahu Hamad

It is a Jihad until either victory or martyrdom

Qassam Brigades
Unit "103"

Hamas Press Releases

Hamas Press Releases

4 February 2002

In the name of Allah the most Gracious the most Merciful

Press Release

Commenting on the article "Palestinian Vision of Peace" published in the American newspaper 'New York Times' on 3rd February 2002 and signed by Yasser Arafat, a responsible source in the Islamic Resistance Movement, Hamas, stated the following:

Our Palestinian people have met with absolute dismay and denunciation content of that article in which Yasser Arafat described resistance as terrorism that did not represent the Palestinian people and their legitimate aspirations for freedom and labeled the resistance movements as terrorist organizations. The denunciation was particularly vociferous because the statements came at a time of great steadfastness and resistance, which our people consider as their only option in retaliating to aggression and in liberating lands and holy shrines.

We in the Islamic Resistance Movement, Hamas, are astonished at content of that article and believe that Yasser Arafat was mistaken in voicing such statements that were meant for begging certain stands. He is mistaken when he describes our people's Mujahideen and martyrs as terrorists and when he describes Palestinian heroism as terrorism in harmony with the Israeli logic and American demands. He is also mistaken in his own right and history for he himself was involved in resistance along with the Fatah Movement, which he heads. Does Arafat want to consume this asset and eliminate what is left of it with such stands?

The dangerous thing in this article is also linking the return of refugees to demographic needs of the Zionist entity. He thus dropped the inalienable right of return, ignored the holy shrines and turned his back to the question of Al-Quds as the Arab capital of the state of Palestine.

This article, which is meant to beg for Israeli satisfaction and American sympathy, has failed similar to previous attempts that targeted achieving the same goal. All attempts pursuing the same method believing in the possibility of winning that satisfaction would fail. The clear proof was the American officials' declarations that called for outright quelling of the intifada and that said that Arafat knew what exactly was required of him. For their part, the Zionists affirmed that wiping out resistance was the required goal and not carefully worded articles. Moreover, the practical retaliation was shelling Jabaliya only few hours after publishing the article and the assassination of four popular resistance elements in Gaza on that same morning.

The question also arises about the timing of that article since it coincided with the suspicious meetings held between Palestinian Authority officials and each of Sharon and Peres as if they were racing to win Zionist and American satisfaction and aspiring for a role in the next stage even if that role was aboard an Israeli tank or under its protection.

The siege on PA chief and the continuous pressures by Zionists and Americans do not justify such a position since the entire Palestinian people were under siege and pressures in addition to being target of Zionist savage terrorism namely daily shelling, continuous assassinations, demolishing houses, damaging plantations, uprooting trees and destroying infrastructures.

We in the Hamas Movement refuse content of that article and we believe that ending such a state would not be through this method or a series of suspicious meetings but rather through more steadfastness, continuation of resistance and escalation of the intifada, endorsing national unity and boosting internal Palestinian ranks in addition to spurring an Arab role in confrontation of the Zionist aggression and American blackmail.

It is in the interest of Yasser Arafat to side by the Palestinian people's option that of intifada and resistance until ejection of occupation from our lands and holy shrines and he will find out that the Palestinian people are capable of shouldering such a responsibility.

The Islamic Resistance Movement
Hamas-Palestine
Monday 22nd Thul Qa'ida 1422H
4th February 2002AD

31 January 2002

In the name of Allah the most Gracious the most Merciful

Press Release

On American President Bush's Terrorism Charges against Hamas

A responsible source in the Islamic Resistance Movement, Hamas, stated the following:

The American administration's media declarations accusing the Movement of terrorism have escalated the latest of which was American president George Bush's statement on 29/1/2002AD before the Congress charging Hamas, Islamic Jihad, Hizbullah and other movements and countries with terrorism or sponsoring terrorism. He called for wiping out terrorists and affirmed that the USA would act in this direction if the concerned governments did not act on their own. In the light of all this and in response to it we in the Islamic Resistance Movement, Hamas, affirm the following:

1. Resistance against occupation is a legitimate and legal right and is a principle endorsed by UN charter. The Hamas Movement and other Palestinian forces exercise that right with the goal of ending Zionist occupation. This right of resisting occupation coincides with all heavenly and international norms in addition to the UN charter.

2. The American administration's definition of terrorism is linked to its interests and ambitions and not based on international law. The USA seeks to categorize the Palestinian resistance forces as terrorist organizations in a bid to weaken the Palestinian people, curb their anti-occupation resistance, enforce their surrender to the usurping Zionist enemy and endorse occupation in a serious international precedence.

3. The statement clearly reflect the degree of American bias in favor of the Zionist entity to the extent that the American administration was viewing the Palestinian people through Zionist eyes and deal with the Palestinian people's inalienable rights as mere requests that occupation might or might not grant. It also considers the Palestinian legitimate anti-occupation resistance as terrorism while ignoring the real terrorism practiced by occupation against the Palestinian people.

4. The American administration's hostility against Palestinian resistance movements is in reality a hostility against the Palestinian people and the entire Arab and Islamic Nation because the resistance program is a broad-based national program that enjoys sweeping support among our Palestinian people and is not limited to a specific Palestinian movement. It furthermore enjoys a large-scale Arab and Islamic backing in its capacity as the Nation's real choice. Hence America's antagonism of Hamas and Palestinian resistance movements put it in confrontation with all Arabs and Muslims.

5. Escalation of American hostility and provocation against Hamas and resistance movements in Palestine and Lebanon would mean waging an all-out war against the Nation and its creed. The Arab and Islamic Nation would not accept American courtesy statements of Islam and Muslims while declaring war against the Nation's resistance movements and practically besieging Muslims everywhere, which in fact meant that the American administration was practically fighting Islam and Muslims.

6. The USA shoulders responsibility of the occupation's crimes against the Palestinian people through its backing of Zionist occupation and its opposition to the Palestinian people's rights, interests and resistance and struggle movements.

7. The American administration has no right of appointing itself a ruler of the entire world. It is also not entitled to interfere in internal affairs of other countries without legal justification. It is not entitled to interfere in freedom of people to impose its hegemony since it is the party exercising aggression and violating human rights against many world peoples, which is blatant terrorism.

8. Occupation is downright terrorism and even the worst form of terrorism that should be eliminated. Accepting occupation and even supporting it pose as a shameful spot in records of the international community topped by the USA.

9. The Islamic Resistance Movement, Hamas, would not be terrorized or weakened by such threats and would continue alongside the Palestinian people in resisting occupation until it got out of our lands and holy shrines.

    America and all oppressive countries in the world would never impose security and stability in the region at the expense of our Palestinian people's rights. Moreover, they would never be able to protect the

Zionist entity's security and the only path towards achieving peace and stability in the region would be ejection of occupation.

10. We urge leaders of Arab and Islamic countries and their governments to adopt an Arab-Islamic definition of terrorism and to insist on differentiating it from resistance in confrontation of the American-Zionist attempts to mix things up. We also call on them to mobilize the Arab and Islamic Nation's potentials to repel American-Zionist terrorism and to reject American-Zionist concepts, stands and threats and not to surrender to them. On this occasion we hail the Arab and Muslim leaders and officials who rejected Bush' statements and defended our Palestinian people's right of resisting occupation.

The Islamic Resistance Movement
Hamas-Palestine
Thursday 18th Thul Qa'ida 1422H
31st January 2002AD

16 January 2002

In the name of Allah the most Gracious the most Merciful

Press Release

Commenting on the security apparatuses of the Palestinian self-rule Authority's arrest of brother Ahmed Sa'dat the secretary general of the Popular Front for the Liberation of Palestine, a responsible source in the Islamic Resistance Movement, Hamas, stated the following:

The PA has arrested the PFLP secretary general Ahmed Sa'dat at a time when the Zionist enemy's authorities were assassinating the intifada and resistance cadres, demolishing houses in Rafah, Gaza and Al-Quds and displacing our people.

We in the Islamic Resistance Movement (Hamas) denounce the PA's crime of arresting brother Ahmed Sa'dat the PFLP secretary general and declare our solidarity with our brothers in the PFLP in face of such measure that was rejected by our people as obvious in the spontaneous massive demonstrations.

This crime comes in submission to dictates of the Zionist enemy's government and a result of the security coordination with the enemy under American security apparatus' patronage. It posed as a treacherous stab in the back of national unity, which was endorsed and still protected by our people's blood, sacrifice and Jihad through the blessed intifada.

We believe that this condemned step tampers with our people's higher national interest while serving the Zionist enemy's interests with the hope of winning American illusionary promises to the Oslo team.

We call on the PA to immediately release brother Ahmed Sa'dat and all detainees in its jails to enable them shoulder their duty in confrontation of occupation.

The Islamic Resistance Movement
Hamas-Palestine
16/1/2002

11 December 2001

In the name of Allah the most Gracious the most Merciful

Press release by the Islamic Resistance Movement . . . Hamas

Retorting to the European foreign ministers' stand towards Palestinian resistance

We in the Islamic Resistance Movement—Hamas consider the European Community's foreign ministers demand in their joint communiqué issued in Brussels yesterday to the Palestinian Authority to dismantle what they called terrorist networks affiliated with Hamas and Islamic Jihad including arresting all suspects (according to their own words) and prosecuting them and issuing an Arabic language call for an end to the armed intifada as outright support to Zionist occupation and aggression against our unarmed Palestinian people.

We condemn this biased stand in favor of the Zionist aggression and affirm our rejection to describing our legitimate struggle against occupation as terrorism. We also absolutely refuse to end the intifada and anti-occupation resistance. We remind all that the cruelest form of terrorism is occupation and its practices represented in mass murders of our children, women, the elderly and youth in cold blood. Those massacres did not stir the European conscience, which is hostile to our people and their aspirations for liberation.

The Islamic Resistance Movement
Hamas-Palestine
11/12/2001AD

11 December 2001

In the name of Allah the most Gracious the most Merciful

"Hatred has already appeared from their mouths: what their hearts conceal is far worse."

Press release by the Islamic Resistance Movement—Hamas

Responding to American secretary of state Powell's statements

It is a shame to humanity to hear American secretary of state Collin Powell urging chairman Arafat to move against the Islamic Resistance Movement, Hamas, saying, "I believe that the Palestinian chairman is capable to exert more efforts than what he has done so far and he has to handle Hamas," pointing out that Arafat had thousands of armed elements capable of attacking Hamas.

We in the Islamic Resistance Movement, Hamas, strongly denounce such black hatred and declare the following:

1. Those statements reflect America's keenness on igniting a Palestinian civil war in service of the Zionists who are practicing the harshest form of murder, oppression and terrorism against our unarmed Palestinian people whose sole crime is seeking to win liberation and independ-

ence. We affirm that such a cheap attempt would not succeed and that the Hamas Movement would always remain keen on unity of our Palestinian people in face of the atrocious Zionist aggression.

2. Inviting the Palestinian Authority to attack Hamas is an evil call for killing members of the Islamic Movements. This clearly indicates that the current American campaign is a spiteful crusade against Islam. We affirm that this campaign against Islam will not achieve its mean goals. Islam will defeat the black spiteful crusade, God willing, and America will never rejoice for seeing Palestinian blood being shed by Palestinian hands.

3. Those statements point to America's partnership in the Zionist enemy's aggression against our people. They constitute a blatant backing of occupation and the policies of assassination and of murder of innocent children, the elderly and women. We would like to affirm that Muslim blood is not cheap and will never be so. The Islamic Resistance Movement will not remain arms folded in face of the Zionist aggression and it will not stop resistance until ejection of occupation and return of displaced Palestinians to their country to establish their own state on their national soil.

4. Such statements indicate that America wishes to ignite fires in each and every Islamic area and that Palestine tops the list of that criminal scheme with the aim of protecting the Zionist entity and its security at the expense of the Palestinian people and their freedom, future and holy shrines. The Hamas Movement calls on our Arab and Islamic Ummah to confront such a brutal campaign before it is too late through uniting their stands, shunning differences and drawing necessary plans to confront the hateful American scheme.

5. The Zionist entity is exploiting those statements to shed more Palestinian blood and to escalate its ferocious offensive against our unarmed people. Hamas realizes that America's statements give terrorist Sharon the green light to exercise the cruelest form of terrorism against our Palestinian people to force their acceptance of Zionist dictates. It also realizes that our people will never kneel down before Zionist dictates. We have great hopes that the PA would not respond to those detestable American calls and pressures out of keenness on our people's unity and strength in face of the American conspiracies to liquidate the Palestine cause and our people's future. Those conspiracies aim at consolidating the Zionist presence on the land of Islamic Palestine.

And it is a Jihad until either victory or martyrdom

The Islamic Resistance Movement
Hamas-Palestine
11/12/2001

24 July 2001

Press Release

Occupation crimes against our people continue

The Zionist terrorist authority committed yet another heinous crime when it arrested two Mujahideen from the Qassam Brigades on Sunday 1/7/2001 during an armed clash at the ring road to the east of the town of Qabatiya. Eyewitnesses said that the Mujahideen:

The commander hero Mahmoud Mousa Sulaiman Khalil (Abu Musa'ab)
And
The commander hero Jamal Daifallah Hassan Thulaiji (Abu Dia')

were arrested alive. The contradiction in the Zionist stories on the two martyrs affirmed the fact that they were detained alive. After the wide media coverage of the incident their bodies were referred to Abu Kabir clinic for autopsy, which was made with the participation of a Scot and a Palestinian doctors on Tuesday 24/7/2001. At a late night hour their bodies were handed over with the clear signs of torture visible on both that distorted their faces and that was proved in the preliminary autopsy reports. All available factors point without any reasonable doubt that the Zionist occupation was involved in liquidating both martyrs days after their arrest where they faced cruel investigation to extract any possible confessions from them.

We, in the Islamic Resistance Movement, Hamas, hold the Zionist entity fully responsible for liquidating the martyrs and affirm that their blood along with the blood of all Palestine martyrs will not be wasted. We pledge to the two martyrs and to all our people that the intifada will persist along the road of Jihad and resistance until liberation . . . God willing.

We also ask all legal and humanitarian institutions to embark on serious moves to expose the occupation forces' crimes and practices and to reveal the conditions and circumstances that engulfed past crimes against our people's Mujahideen and strugglers.

The Islamic Resistance Movement-Hamas
Jenin District
3rd Jamadi Awal 1422H
24/7/2001AD

3 July 2001

Press Release

On the failure of the smart sanctions package against Iraq and extending the work of the oil for food program, a responsible source in the Islamic Resistance Movement, Hamas, stated the following:

The failure of the project to impose smart sanctions on brotherly Iraq in the Security council voting yesterday and the failure of the American administration to win approval of the Arab countries surrounding Iraq to join that project did not mean an end to the attempts. The Americans and the British are still insisting on the programme, which calls for the Arab and Islamic Nation in particular to work for foiling such a project, the destructive repercussions of which are not limited to Iraq and its besieged people only but also affects the dignity of the whole Nation in its present and future.

Despite the Russian Federation's positive stand whose threats in using the veto contributed in withdrawing the British draft resolution, yet it linked lifting the siege to Iraq's acceptance of resuming the work of arms inspection teams. Consequently the Security Council agreed to extend work of the oil for food program for 150 days.

It is about time to lift the sanctions and siege on brotherly Iraq once and for all to be able to promote its potentials and boost its role alongside its Arab brothers in confrontation with the Zionist project and in support of the Palestinian people's steadfastness and resistance of the Zionist occupation, because it is terrorist Sharon's aggressive schemes that threaten the whole region rather than brotherly Iraq.

The Islamic Resistance Movement
Hamas-Palestine
10 Rabee Thani 1422H
3rd July 2001AD

2 July 2001

Press Release

Commenting on the Zionist aggression against Syria and Lebanon and the enemy's aerial bombardment of the Syrian Arab army's radar position in the Bekaa valley, a responsible source in the Islamic Resistance Movement, Hamas, stated the following:

The sinful Zionist aggression against a position for the Syrian Arab army in the Bekaa affirm the aggressive nature of the Zionist entity towards our Nation especially its steadfast and resistance forces.

We, in the Islamic Resistance Movement, Hamas, condemn this grave aggression on Syria and Lebanon and declare our siding, in addition to our people, alongside the two sisterly countries and our support to our brothers in the resistance in Lebanon.

We urge our Arab and Islamic Nation to adopt a decisive stand in support of our brothers in Syria and Lebanon and our people in Palestine that would develop from condemnation to practical measures. The expansion of the Zionist aggression, which falls in line with nature of that enemy, and execution of Sharon and his government's schemes would open the door wide open before similar aggressions against other Arab countries. Consequently our Nation is called upon to be prepared for such a possibility and to provide mechanisms of effective backing to resistance and steadfastness to confront such aggressions.

This attack puts the whole world before its responsibility namely to support our causes in face of Zionist occupation of our Arab lands in Palestine, Syria and Lebanon and its terrorist practices against us. It further sends a clear message to those concerned that continuation of support to that usurping, terrorist entity means more aggression the responsibility of which must be shouldered by those providing cover and backing to the Zionist entity.

The Islamic Resistance Movement
Hamas-Palestine
Monday 11 Rabee Thani 1422H
2nd July 2001AD

1 July 2001

In the name of Allah the most Gracious the most Merciful

Press Release

Commenting on the return of brother Ibrahim Ghoushe to his country Jordan safe and sound, all praise be to Allah, and the settlement of the crisis of his deportation and detention via direct contacts between the Jordanian authorities and the Movement and despite our reservations towards the unjustified method of executing that settlement: his travel to Bangkok then his return to Jordan, in violation of the agreement signed between the Jordanian authorities and the Movement, the Movement's political bureau affirms the following:

1. The return of brother Ghoushe to his country Jordan laid the foundation for a comprehensive solution to the crisis, which we hope would be soon Insha'allah in harmony with the constitution, law and citizenship rights in addition to uniting the Arab and Islamic ranks in confrontation of the Zionist enemy whose terrorist leader Sharon is waging a ferocious war against our Palestinian people.

2. Brother Ibrahim Ghoushe is still occupying his post in the Movement as member in its political bureau. The halt in his activity in the name of the Movement is limited to the Jordanian arena only.

3. The Movement's political bureau extends its thanks and appreciation to all of our Jordanian-Palestinian people, the parties, syndicates and national and Islamic figures for their stands and solidarity with the Movement and its deportees' issue. It also thanks and appreciates the official and popular Arab leaders and leaderships that exerted efforts and mediation bids to solve that crisis. We would like to mention specifically here the leaders of Yemen, Libya and the Sudan along with the Arab League's secretary general. We extend special thanks to the state of Qatar, its Emir, government and people, for their generous hospitality accorded to Eng. Ghoushe and his brothers.

The Islamic Resistance Movement
Hamas-Palestine
Sunday 1—Rabee Thani 1422H
1st July 2001AD

30 June 2001

Press Release

Mr. Ibrahim Ghoushe in Amman

Ghoushe: There is no change to my post in Hamas

Political bureau member of the Islamic Resistance Movement, Hamas, Mr. Ibrahim Ghoushe arrived in the Jordanian capital Amman at dawn today after spending 48 hours outside the country.

In the first statement after his return Mr. Ghoushe affirmed that there was no change in his position in the Hamas Movement or in his service of the Palestinian people and their just cause or in confronting the usurping Zionist entity.

Ghoushe said that his commitment not to practice any informational or political activity was limited to the Jordanian arena in accordance with the agreement signed between the Jordanian authorities and Hamas Movement. He explained that there would be no change to his political and informational work outside the Jordanian arena.

The Engineer thanked King Abdullah II for his initiative and intervention to put an end to the crisis and its repercussions. He appealed to the monarch to allow the remaining deported brothers to return to their country.

He also thanked the Emir of Qatar and the Qatari government and people for their hospitality and concern.

Ghoushe deeply appreciated the Jordanian people including all sectors: citizens, partisan leaders, organizations, syndicates and national figures, for their honorable stand and solidarity with him and Hamas leaders in the crisis.

The Islamic Resistance Movement-Hamas
30/6/2001

28 June 2001

Urgent Press Release

On developments of Mr. Ibrahim Ghoushe's case

A responsible source in the Islamic Resistance Movement, Hamas, has stated the following;

The Hamas' leadership is following up with great concern the situation of Mr. Ibrahim Ghoushe after receiving information from official Jordanian sources that he was deported to Bangkok at a late hour yesterday.

We condemn this step and hold the Jordanian government and its concerned apparatuses the full responsibility over life, security and safety of Mr. Ibrahim Ghoushe.

We demand the immediate disclosure of his situation and his whereabouts. We also demand his immediate return to his country Jordan, affirming our insistence on the right of Mr. Ibrahim Ghoushe and his brothers to return to Jordan.

The Islamic Resistance Movement
Hamas—Palestine
Thursday 7th Rabee Thani 1422H
28th June 2001AD

28 June 2001

Press Release

A responsible source in the Hamas Movement stated the following:

Two weeks after detention of Mr. Ibrahim Ghoushe in Amman airport while he was returning to his country Jordan after the Jordanian authorities' refusal to allow him enter the country; the Jordanian authorities contacted the Hamas Movement expressing willingness to end the crisis. They offered a solution based on the Movement's readiness not to allow any political or informational activity for brother Ghoushe in the name of the Hamas Movement in Jordan unless with approval of the Jordanian authorities.

They also asked the Movement to agree to his departure from Jordan for three days at the most after which he would be allowed back into Jordan enjoying full citizenship rights in accordance with that agreement.

We said that such a step could take place without Ghoushe having to leave Jordan even temporarily especially when the Jordanian authorities could announce acceptance of an Arab mediation to end the crisis. However, to facilitate the matter from our side, especially after those authorities' insistence on that condition, the Movement agreed after detailed dialogue that led to the written agreement signed by a representative of the Jordanian authorities and a representative of the Hamas Movement. The Movement retains a copy of the signed agreement. Brother Ghoushe was informed of the agreement in the presence of a representative of the Jordanian authorities and a representative of the Hamas Movement where he affirmed commitment to whatever the brothers in the political bureau deemed fit.

An agreement was also reached on implementation mechanism of that agreement. The Movement tabled Yemen as the country that would host Mr. Ghoushe for three days in appreciation of its mediation initiative and that country would guarantee the agreement. We started contacting our brothers in Yemen who welcomed the idea and affirmed their preparedness to start their mediation when they receive an official contact from the Jordanian leadership. We informed the Jordanian authorities' representative with that. However, we were surprised at a late hour last night that the Engineer was carried to Bangkok instead of Sana'a in mysterious circumstances. The Movement's contact with the Jordanian authorities was severed and the Engineer remained isolated from contacts with the Movement, his family or his lawyer until the present moment.

In such an atmosphere, the Jordanian government announced that it received a message from Mr. Ghoushe then declared its permission allowing him to return to Jordan from Bangkok in response to instructions of Jordanian monarch, King Abdullah. Consequently the return of Mr. Ghoushe is on the basis of not practicing any activity in the name of the Movement in the Jordanian arena in accordance with the position previously tabled with the Jordanian government by the Movement that was endorsed in the aforementioned agreement.

The Islamic Resistance Movement
Hamas-Palestine
Thursday 7 Rabee Thani 1422H
28th June 2001AD

The agreement signed between the Jordanian authorities and Hamas representative on settling Mr. Ibrahim Ghoushe's case

In the name of Allah the most Gracious the most Merciful

Brothers in the political bureau of the Hamas Movement have informed me of their agreement on the departure of brother Ibrahim Ghoushe to Sana'a for three days after which he would return to Jordan on condition that he would not practice any informational or political activity in the name of the Hamas Movement in Jordan.

On that the agreement was signed.

27/6/2001

on behalf of Hamas
signature
on behalf of Jordan
signature

23 June 2001

In the name of Allah the most Gracious the most Merciful

Press Release

Commenting on the brothers in Yemen's decision to withdraw their mediation, which they had launched to end the crisis resulting from the Jordanian authorities' measure denying Eng. Ibrahim Ghoushe to enter his country and detaining the Qatari plane, a responsible source in the Islamic Resistance Movement, Hamas, stated the following;

1. We, in Hamas, followed up with great appreciation the honorable mediation bid of our brothers in Yemen under the patronage of Yemeni president Ali Abdullah Saleh, which they tabled out of their keenness on unity of Arab ranks and to defuse the crisis between Jordan and Qatar and between Jordan and the Hamas Movement. We immediately welcomed the Yemeni mediation and positively responded to it out of our keenness to ensure its success but the Jordanian govern-

ment's stubbornness and insistence on its old stand and oppressive conditions that violated the constitution and the interests of both the Nation and the case led to halting the Yemeni mediation compelling the brothers in Yemen to declare its withdrawal.

2.   We affirm, on this occasion, that we in the Hamas Movement had displayed absolute keenness and extreme feeling of responsibility in dealing with the oppressive decision to deport the four brothers from their country Jordan. We gave all the appreciated mediation bids the opportunity to solve the crisis especially the sisterly state of Qatar and the dear Jordanian figures but the Jordanian government closed all doors before those mediations during the past year and seven months of deportation. We had no other alternative but to exercise our legal and constitutional right to return to Jordan. We informed the Jordanian government with our decision through a third party. We also postponed the date of our return more than once at the request of the Jordanian government itself so as to give it more time. We affirmed to that government our readiness to accept the condition of not practicing any political or informational activity in the name of the Movement in Jordan. Yet the Jordanian government remained insisting on its strange, oppressive and stubborn stance that the deported brothers should choose between giving up their Jordanian nationality and accept the two years temporary travel documents if they wished to continue in their role in service of their people and cause and links to the Jihad Movement Hamas or to retain the Jordanian nationality after severing all relations with the Hamas Movement. We categorically rejected that offer because it contravened the Jordanian constitution and because working for the Palestine cause through the Hamas Movement or any other was a duty on all those belonging to our Nation and did not contradict their right in the nationality they carried.

3.   In the light of all this Eng. Ibrahim Ghoushe decided to return to his country Jordan in a calm way so as to facilitate things for the Jordanian government but it regretfully did not absorb that meaning and chose a boisterous security handling of the matter that contradicted the constitution. It furthermore fabricated another unjustified crisis with the sisterly state of Qatar at a time when terrorist Sharon and his herds of settlers were waging a war on our people and at a time when the heroic Qassam Brigades were confronting the criminal Zionist enemy and the Qassam elements were launching martyrdom operations to defend their people and sanctities in addition to avenging for dignity

of the Arab and Islamic Nation. The Jordanian government is still insisting on detaining Eng. Ibrahim Ghoushe for the tenth consecutive day in the Amman airport in an inhuman was that does not befit an ordinary citizen let alone a Mujahid like him. That government is also exercising pressures on him to accept its oppressive conditions under threat and by force and insist at the same time to prevent doctors from seeing him or checking his health condition. It further barred his family members and lawyers from calling on him!

4. We salute our brother the Eng. Ibrahim Ghoushe for his steadfastness and patience and for his rejection of all bargaining on his national and religious role in service of the Nation's central cause and in defense of our Mujahid Palestinian people. We also greet and appreciate our Jordanian people with its various trends, parties, syndicate and national and Islamic figures for siding with our just case. That people expressed solidarity with Eng. Ghoushe and his deported brothers, expressed absolute refusal of the Jordanian government's step and affirmed backing to the Hamas Movement in its steadfastness and resistance of Zionist occupation. We call on them to express more such dignified stands for the interest of Jordan, the Palestine cause and the Nation in its struggle against the Zionist enemy. We repeat our thanks and appreciation to all Jordanian popular mediations and efforts along with Arab bids that sought to solve the unjustified crisis and end the detention of brother Ibrahim Ghoushe to enable him enter his country.

The Islamic Resistance Movement
Hamas-Palestine
2nd Rabee Thani 1422H
23rd June 2001AD

20 June 2001

Press Release

On the health condition of Eng. Ghoushe detained in Amman airport

Commenting on the reported deterioration of Eng. Ibrahim Ghoushe's health condition, who is detained in Amman Airport, a responsible source in the Hamas Movement stated the following:

We follow up with utmost concern in the Islamic Resistance Movement, Hamas, along with family of Eng. Ghoushe the information that recently pointed to the worsening of his health condition. This deterioration comes at a time when the Jordanian Authority is still insisting on detaining him in Amman Airport under inhuman circumstances for the sixth consecutive day and insisting on preventing him from entering his country while trying to deport him anew.

Eng. Ghoushe, 65, suffers from high blood pressure along with other diseases that necessitate constant health care and necessary treatment in fixed dates under doctors' supervision. Detaining him and refusing his admission into a hospital might pose a danger to his health and life.

In the light of the aforementioned and in the light of the Jordanian Authority's refusal to hospitalize Ghoushe and its rejection of numerous requests to see him, including demands by the chief of the Jordanian bar and the chief of the Jordanian doctors syndicate, we hold the Jordanian government and its security bodies the full responsibility over health, life and security of the Engineer. We demand his immediate release and an end to his oppressive detention to enable him enter his country Jordan.

20/6/2001

16 June 2001

Urgent

Press Release

Commenting on the announcement by certain Arab countries, such as Libya, their readiness to intervene by offering planes to carry Mr. Ibrahim Ghoushe from Amman airport to those countries or to Qatar, we, in the Islamic Resistance Movement, Hamas, would like to clearly declare that any mediation should be based on convincing the Jordanian government to allow Mr. Ghoushe to enter his country, for this is the natural situation and it will be welcomed on our side.

Any other mediation to transfer Mr. Ghoushe to any other country than Jordan is really unacceptable on our part and on the part of Mr. Ghoushe himself. It will in fact facilitate his deportation and displacement out of his country anew.

It is worth mentioning that he had no problem in finding a country to live in. He lived in Qatar amidst utmost welcome and hospitality but he, along with his deported brothers, insist on their right to return to their country Jordan, a right that is guaranteed by the constitution and the law.

16/6/2001AD

13 June 2001

In the name of Allah the most Gracious the most Merciful

Press statement on PA's acceptance of George Tenet's proposals

Commenting on the Palestinian Authority's acceptance of the American Central Intelligence Agency (CIA) chief George Tenet's proposals, even with certain reservations, a responsible source in the Islamic Resistance Movement, Hamas, said that the Movement would like to affirm the following stands:

1. Based on the Movement's previous declaration along with all Palestinian forces and factions on rejecting American and western pressures and initiatives, we reject the PA's acceptance of the CIA chief's proposals, which are in fact Israeli proposals in American guise. We affirm that the PA's approval came in response to feverish American and western pressures over the past few days and not in response to the Palestinian national position that was reflected in the popular and factional unanimity today on continuation of the intifada and resistance. Consequently we ask the PA to rescind its stand towards those proposals and side by our people's stands, rights.

2. The American and western moves, especially the recent George Tenet's efforts, were not active over the past eight months to stop Palestinian blood letting including hundreds of martyrs and thousands of

wounded or to halt destruction of houses and agricultural fields in addition other sabotage acts. They only acted when Sharon failed to restore Zionist security and quell our people's intifada, resistance and heroic operations, which had almost led to real changes in the Zionist entity's situation. Tenet's proposals and the western-American proposals were meant to save the Zionist entity from its ordeal in addition to saving mass murderer Sharon from his predicament. They do not care for our people's rights and sufferings; they even ignore and bypass them.

3. Mitchell's report, the American proposals and all political initiatives in the region blatantly ignore the core of the conflict and deal with the Palestinian people's cause and rights in accordance with wrong and oppressive equations, which we denounce. Once they call for reciprocal end of violence as if the clashes were between two neighboring and equal parties rather than an occupation and oppressive aggression against an unarmed people. On another occasion, they call for halting the construction of settlements in return for ending the intifada and resistance, which is the essence of Mitchell's report, in a way downgrading our people's demands of expelling occupation into merely ending settlement activity while endorsing occupation and its hegemony.

The American proposals then follow dealing with the issue from security point of view for the interest of the Zionist enemy and its priorities without any considerations to our people's rights and just demands. They impose on the PA certain security prerequisites that would lead in conclusion, according to the American-Zionist speculation, to Palestinian feudal fighting, halting the intifada and resistance and aborting their accomplishments.

This means that the political moves target more concessions and political retreat, which were originally oppressive and unfair and were rejected on our part and on the part of our people, so how would the situation be with such bias and quickening downfall.

4. We, in the Hamas Movement along with our people's masses and forces, affirm that the intifada will continue and the resistance will persist. We declare our absolute rejection to the return to security coordination and cooperation with the enemy, the policy of arrests and prosecution of Mujahideen and disarming them. This will entail a most serious impact on our people's national unity, interests, rights

and accomplishments of their intifada and resistance. They do not serve anyone on the Palestinian arena not even in the PA. Our people will not allow the return to such policies and measures and will remain insisting on their right in resisting occupation.

Islamic Resistance Movement
Hamas-Palestine
13/6/2001

5 June 2001

In the name of Allah the most Gracious the most Merciful

"Fight them, and Allah will punish them by your hands, cover them with shame, help you (to victory) over them, heal the breasts of Believers,"

Sharon is preparing for aggression . . . let us prepare for resistance and confronting the aggression

Our great Palestinian people . . . the people of sacrifice

In the light of recent developments . . . quickening events . . . and after the Zionists experienced the same bitterness they inflicted on us . . . escalation in the Israeli public opinion's demands for revenge . . . background of the Israeli cabinet members . . . the lust for murder and revenge controlling their minds . . . the bloody criminal history of Sharon . . . and his threats to halt the Aqsa intifada . . . and wiping out the dream of liberation and independence in implementation of his promise to safeguard the security of each Israeli individual through forcing submission on the Palestinian people and their forces . . .

In the light of the previously mentioned, Sharon started to prepare his terrorist schemes and mobilized his racist forces in an attempt to storm the Palestinian Authority areas thinking that it would be a picnic for his "invincible" army.

Our heroic people . . . the sons of Qassam, Salahuddin, Al-Wazir and Ayyash . . . your painful blows to that deformed entity had shocked its senile premier Sharon who is not capable of safe thinking and does not benefit from past lessons. His decisions are based on muscles of his arrogant chief of staff. They have forgotten your Qassam Brigades, Aqsa Brigades, Quds Brigades, armed popular resistance . . . you are Ayyash, Abayat and Hamran, your are Said Hoteri, Hamed Abu Hijle, Ibrahim Abdul Karim and Thabet Thabet. You are the ones who caused that enemy's worst nightmares; you love martyrdom as much as the Zionists love life.

Yes, Sharon might be able to enter our areas but could he get out of them? We believe that the Zionists will soon meet their end; their graves will be in our garbage dumps. Hundreds of commandos with explosive belts will chase them along with thousands of throwers of Molotov cocktails and hundreds of hunters of their insect soldiers along with thousands of women and children who pose as the logistic support of the courageous heroes. You Zionist women if you wish to mourn your sons, brothers and husbands and turn the Zionist society into one of only women send the soldiers to us.

Our heroic Palestinian people . . . the Mujahideen and strugglers:

To perform this duty and to be victorious in that war we invite you to the following:

First: on the resistance and confrontation level:

1. Estimate and expect the spots through which the Zionists might enter or storm the PA controlled areas in coordination with the PA apparatuses.

2. Based on the former point: choose strategic positions for the confrontations and deploy in them activists and all those wishing for martyrdom and known for distinctive performance to obstruct advance of the occupation army and to serve as the people and their institutions' protection shields. Commandos would be of benefit in those positions.

3. Ambushes: to be set near to target areas (houses of wanted activists), (premises of organizations) and to deal with foot patrols when they attempt to storm a certain position to arrest or assassinate certain elements.

4. Planting explosive devices along the roads that the occupation troops are expected to pass through that would be blasted via remote control (after taking necessary precautions, accuracy and preparedness).

5. Preparing a big number of Molotov cocktails mixed with sticking materials and gas cylinders.

6. Preparing explosive belts . . . the number to be estimated by experienced elements that would be available for any commando wishing for martyrdom amidst the enemies.

7. Installing barricades to hurdle the occupation army's movement.

Second: on the security level:

1. Monitoring the enemy's moves and collaborators.

2. Requesting officials of sensitive areas to evacuate all precious equipment and to clean their offices from sensitive information.

3. Establishing emergency clinics equipped with necessary needs to treat the wounded commandos and others in the event the army taking control of hospitals.

Third: on the mobilization and guidance levels:

1. Preparing statements for circulation in the street including the real facts on events and expectations.

2. Field mobilization: leaders and representatives of organizations and factions in the city would shoulder that responsibility after spreading in various affected areas . . . guiding and lifting the moral. It would be a good idea to use unified earphones.

Fourth: on the relief level:

1. Forming a relief committee in each area in the city grouping voluntary doctors, engineers and university professors the soonest.

2. Preparing relief material and securing telephone numbers of owners of tractors and trucks to contact them whenever necessary.

3. Providing medicines and medical equipment for first aid in various areas.

4. Providing certain foodstuffs and stocking them in stores far from expected strikes at the ground floors.

5. Counting the buildings that might be used as shelters in each area to distribute inhabitants of that area on those centers.

6. Publishing guidance publications that would deal with shelling, evacuation procedures, carrying wounded and first aid.

May Allah bless and aid you

The Islamic Resistance Movement
Hamas-Palestine
5/6/2001

5 June 2001

In the name of Allah the most Gracious the most Merciful

Press Clarification

The Islamic Resistance Movement, Hamas, leadership has followed up media coverage of a joint communiqué signed by Qassam Brigades and the Aqsa Brigades. On that issue we would like to clarify the following:

1. It is not true that Qassam Brigades and Aqsa Martyrs Brigades issued a joint communiqué on a truce with Zionist occupation.

2. The only party entrusted with expressing Hamas' political stands is the Movement's political leadership. On the other hand the military wing of the Movement is solely concerned with resistance operations and taking responsibility for them.

3. On this occasion we affirm the Hamas Movement's stable strategy based on continuation of the intifada and resistance until liberation of the lands and ejection of occupation.

The Islamic Resistance Movement
Hamas-Palestine
Tuesday 13 Rab'ee Awal 1422H
5th June 2001AD

27 March 2001

Press Release

Zionists commit a new of crime

In line with the Zionist enemy's terrorist schemes against our unarmed Mujahid people, the Zionists launched a new method in confronting our people and their blessed intifada, which is ever escalating.

The Zionists inundated the Shija'iah suburb in Gaza city with water, some of which was sewerage water, after opening huge water tanks that used to store water inside occupied Palestinian territories in 1948 and some of which are adjacent to the Gaza Strip leading to a humanitarian disaster that damaged houses, cattle and plantations in addition to paralyzing life activity of our people in the area.

The Zionists' use of such a method in confronting our people and intifada points to a serious escalation and a cowardly act that targets breaking the determination of our people and aborting their intifada and struggle. It further represents the start of a new aggression planned by terrorist Sharon's government and his gang, which stipulates using all means.

We, from the heart of Palestine, which is throbbing with Jihad and resistance, ask our Arab and Islamic Nation to boost its stands and solidarity with our besieged people and to support our people in face of that disaster that covered a whole region adjacent to the occupation forces and settlers.

Such a method displays the enemy's bankruptcy and failure in confronting our people and their intifada. It will never weaken our people's determination and insistence on persisting along the road of Jihad and struggle regardless of circumstances for the sake of realizing freedom, liberating Al-Quds and the Aqsa and returning our people to their homeland and property from which they were forcibly evacuated.

The Islamic Resistance Movement
Hamas-Palestine
2nd Muharram 1422H
27th March 2001AD

13 February 2001

In the name of Allah the most gracious the most Merciful

Press Release

On the escalation of terrorism and assassination against our Mujahid people

A new cycle of intensified terrorism is being waged against our Mujahid people along the confrontations arenas confronted by self-defense in face of the brutal Zionist enemy. A new and continuous terrorist scheme is being hatched aimed at quelling and stopping the intifada and to imposing conditions of an oppressive settlement on our people through agreement and coordination between symbols of Zionist terrorism Sharon and Barak and through understandings reached by the Likud in line with the formation of a coalition government.

The savage massacre perpetrated by the Zionist enemy in Khan Younis and the Mawasi area, in which more than 100 people were wounded, other than destroying houses and property then the terrorist assassination of martyr Masoud Ayyad from the force-17 furnished additional proof to savagery of the occupation and its aggressive plans against our people without any distinction.

The Islamic Resistance Movement, Hamas, affirms that the policy of indiscriminate torching and cowardly assassinations will not deter our people from persisting along the road of intifada and struggle with all forms. Our people that resisted all aggressive and terrorist campaigns over the past century on the land of Palestine and organized one revolution after the other and one uprising after the other smashing on their way oppressive and arrogant symbols, are capable of indulging in the battle until achieving the goals of defeating occupation and returning to their lands from which they were forcibly ejected.

This stage, where the usurping enemy is preparing to launch more murders and terrorism, calls on our people to be prepared to shoulder their great responsibility. It necessitates providing all requirements for steadfastness and resistance in addition to arming those capable of using arms within framework of continuous resistance.

We urge all Arab and Islamic peoples to act swiftly in support of our people in their Jihad and intifada. We ask them to form various pressure groups against the Zionist enemy so as to halt its terrorism and aggression. We also call on all world countries to end the conspiracy of keeping silent vis-à-vis the enemy crimes.

We are sure of Allah's victory for He is the One capable of annihilating our enemy and make us govern the land of Palestine . . . that of Islam and Muslims . . . occupation and tyranny will definitely end.

And it is a Jihad until either victory or martyrdom

The Islamic Resistance Movement
Hamas—Palestine
13 February 2001

7 January 2001

In the name of Allah the most gracious the most Merciful

Press Release

On the security coordination meeting Between the PA and the Zionist enemy in Cairo

Commenting on the security coordination meeting between security officials in the Palestinian Authority, the Zionist enemy and the American central intelligence agency that is held today in Cairo, a responsible source in the Islamic Resistance Movement, Hamas, said:

The Zionist aggression is continuing against our people along with the daily killing and cold-blooded assassinations of our men and women in addition to besieging and dismembering cities, villages and camps and starving our people and children. Terrorist Barak is renewing his refusal to surrender sovereignty over Al-Quds and the Haram Al-Sharif and his absolute rejection of the return of our people's refugees to their lands and country. At such a time, chairman of the Palestinian Authority agrees on holding such a serious meeting in submission to the Zionist enemy and the American administration's dictates. The Zionists had set the condition that the meeting should tackle the mean theme of ending what they call violence (i.e. the intifada) and fighting terrorism (i.e. resistance). This is the required sinful security price that the Palestinians must pay in preparation for continuing the absurd negotiations on Clinton's proposals that aim at liquidating our cause.

This dubious meeting has a clear goal namely to abort and end our people's intifada . . . the holy Aqsa intifada, in addition to persecuting and liquidating our people's Mujahideen to complement the role of the enemy's army and special units.

We denounce the PA's submission and approval to name our people's intifada as "acts of violence" and dealing with it on equal footing with Zionist terrorism and aggression. We condemn the PA's pledge in Washington to work for ending the intifada and repelling its heroes and resistance heroes and to accept to attend such a dubious meeting in service of occupation and to realize its security at the expense of our people's security and rights.

The resumption of security cooperation with the Zionist enemy and the American intelligence and under its patronage poses as a treacherous stab in the back of our people and the holy Aqsa intifada. Furthermore, it scorns the blood of more than 370 martyrs and 20,000 wounded who fell and still fall in the intifada for the sake of expelling occupation, purging the Aqsa and achieving our people's goals not for the sake of returning to the negotiations and the criminal security cooperation with the enemy. It also deals the cruelest blow to national unity that grouped our people around the intifada and struggle option and poses as a return to a joint security march with the enemy that lead to the death or detention of the cream of our people and Mujahideen.

We, in the Islamic Resistance Movement, Hamas, regret that Cairo is the venue that hosts and patronizes such a meeting. Egypt had always been the supporter of our cause and its people had taken to the streets out of anger and condemnation over what the Aqsa and the people of Palestine were suffering at the hands of the Zionist aggression. Our people always appreciated Egypt. How come it would then host such dubious meetings that harm its image and role? Especially when it knows that our people reject and condemn such meetings because they are directed against them!

We affirm to the whole world that the feverish attempts and efforts will end up in failure, God willing, and will not be able to deter our people from persisting in their Jihad, resistance, intifada and confrontation of the

Zionist enemy, its war machine and herds of settlers. Our people will never deviate from resistance in its capacity as the road leading to liberation and restoration of rights.

The Islamic Resistance Movement
(Hamas—Palestine)
7 January 2001

31 December 2000

In the name of Allah the most gracious the most Merciful

Press Release

On the assassination of Fatah official
And the heroic operation against Kach leader

Commenting on the assassination crime of the Fatah Movement's secretary in Tulkarem martyr Thabet Thabet and on the heroic operation that targeted the leader of the Zionist Kach movement, a responsible source in the Islamic Resistance Movement, Hamas, said:

The crime of assassinating secretary of the Fatah Movement in Tulkarem martyr Thabet Thabet falls in line with the ongoing campaign of terror and murder launched by gangsters of the Zionist enemy's army against our people's Mujahideen and strugglers. It also falls in line with the cold-blooded murders against our peoples in all Islamic and national factions and forces.

We condemn the assassination crime and affirm that blood of the martyr along with other martyrs of our people will not be wasted and that it will turn into fire burning the occupier. Our people's retaliation to the enemy's crimes will be more escalation of the intifada and resistance.

The heroic operation launched by our people's heroes and Mujahideen this morning against leader of the Zionist Kach movement Benjamin Meir Kahana son of the slain rabbi Meir Kahana is the appropriate answer to crimes of that enemy's army and its herds of settlers.

The Zionist enemy and settlers should pay a costly price in return for what their daily crimes of murder, terrorism, assassination and destruction against our people and their property and against Al-Quds, the Aqsa and the holy shrines. Our people should not remain the only one paying the price out of their unarmed sons' dear blood.

Such heroic operations are the best alternative to the infertile negotiations and the strong retaliation to Clinton's proposals that belittles our people and their full rights in Al-Quds, return and liberation.

We call on our people along with all forces and factions to escalate the intifada and intensify painful Jihad operations against occupation. We urge them to pressure the Authority to end once and for all the humiliating settlement process and to unite over a national program that concentrates on steadfastness and resistance.

The Islamic Resistance Movement
(Hamas—Palestine)
31 December 2000

16 December 2000

In the name of Allah the most gracious the most Merciful

Press Release

The declaration on resumption of negotiations Between the PA and the Zionist enemy

Commenting on the Palestinian Authority and the Zionist enemy's declaration on the resumption of their negotiations as of next week, a responsible source in the Islamic Resistance Movement, Hamas, stated the following:

This declaration coronates secret and declared meetings that did not cease one day with the Zionist entity. We have repeatedly warned against such meetings that were always denied by PA officials.

The return to the negotiating table with the criminal Zionist enemy does not in any way serve our people's goals and higher interests. It further snubs the holy Aqsa intifada and neglects the blood of more than 300 martyrs and 18,000 wounded other than our people's sufferings and sacrifices.

The settlement and negotiation option had taken its chance and had proven for more than seven meager years that it was a failure. Its result was more Zionist arrogance, terrorism and repression. The return to negotiating and speeding up the process at this particular time targets aborting the Aqsa intifada and helping the terrorist criminal Barak in winning the upcoming elections. It means they are betting on him anew, like in the first time, despite his past and ongoing crimes against our people. Martyrs still fall, our cities and villages are still shelled with missiles and many of our people are murdered in cold blood at the hands of Barak's soldiers and Special Forces.

Our people have defended Al-Quds (Jerusalem) and the Aqsa with dear blood and they are always ready to sacrifice their sons in defense of them and of each and every inch of our blessed land. Our people will never accept that the fruit of their sons' Jihad and blood of their martyrs be the return to the negotiating table to surrender our lands, rights and sanctities.

We urge the PA not to attend those talks and to end all forms of secret and open negotiations with the criminal enemy. We ask the Authority to halt all forms of security coordination that only serves the Zionist enemy and targets strugglers and Mujahideen groups and cadres in all Palestinian factions.

The return to negotiations with the criminal enemy will be met with anger and absolute dismay on the part of our people. Any result emanating from those negotiations would not represent our people or bind them.

The holy Aqsa intifada that united our people over the option of struggle and steadfastness calls on all to further enhance such national unity and unite the ranks in face of that criminal enemy in addition to escalating resistance and exhausting the enemy for the sake of defeating and deterring occupation along with defending our holy shrines and grabbing our rights with our own hands.

The Islamic Resistance Movement
(Hamas—Palestine)
Friday 19 Ramadan 1421 H
15 December 2000

23 November 2000

In the name of Allah the most Gracious the most Merciful

Press Release

On the Zionist assassination of Mujahid Ibrahim Abdul Karim One of the Qassam Brigades' commanders

The Zionist occupation forces, in consistency with their savage crimes against our steadfast people, today assassinated Mujahid Ibrahim Abdul Karim Bani Odeh from the town of Tammon, Nablus district. A missile that targeted his car led to the immediate martyrdom of Ibrahim, who was one of the commanders of the Qassam Brigades.

The martyr was released from the Palestinian Authority's Junaid prison last night along with seven others on temporary basis.

The cold-blooded murder of martyr Ibrahim Abdul Karim at the hands of occupation forces follows the same suit of yesterday's crime in the Gaza Strip when occupation soldiers murdered four Palestinians in broad daylight. It also falls in line with the occupation forces' series of daily crimes against our unarmed people, which will never dissuade our Mujahid people from continuing with the Aqsa intifada and brave struggle for the sake of liberating our lands and defeating the occupiers.

We, in the Islamic Resistance Movement, Hamas, affirm that blood of the heroic martyr and those of all Aqsa martyrs will turn into fire burning the usurpers.

The Islamic Resistance Movement
(Hamas—Palestine)
23 November 2000

16 December 2000

In the name of Allah the most gracious the most Merciful

"Among the Believers are men who have been true to their Covenant with Allah: of them some have completed their vow (to the extreme), and some (still) wait: but they have never changed (their determination) in the least:"

Press Release

Martyr hero Noor Mohammed Safi martyr of the Hamas anniversary

The Islamic Resistance Movement, Hamas, mourns with pride its heroic martyr Nooruddeen Mohammed Safi from the Shati' refugee camp who martyred in the industrial area at Beit Hanun while avenging for martyrs of the Aqsa and Palestine, defending Muslims' sanctities and honor and retaliating to the liquidation and assassination operations launched by the Zionist enemy against symbols of resistance and strugglers of the Palestinian people.

The martyr, who ascended to meet His Lord, had written a will reflecting his deep faith and wish for martyrdom. His martyrdom decorated the anniversary of Hamas' outbreak and proved continuation of its march of martyrdom, Jihad and resistance until liberation of the holy land of Palestine and Al-Quds (Jerusalem) the first Qibla and third holiest shrine in Islam.

The Islamic Resistance Movement, Hamas, while offering martyrs as lighthouses along the road of freedom and dignity including the martyr Noor who graduated this year from university to win the heavenly certificate only few months later, affirms that the offering of martyrs and sacrifices will boost its insistence on the road of Jihad. Hamas also declares that it will continue to reject all forms of oppressive settlements, which appear in the horizon through open and secret meetings. Hamas also affirms its insistence on continuation of the intifada, the holy Aqsa intifada until defeat of the occupation and liberation of the land of Palestine Insha'allah. May Allah have mercy on you.

And it is a Jihad until victory or martyrdom

The Islamic Resistance Movement
(Hamas—Palestine)
15 December 2000

13 December 2000

In the name of Allah the most Gracious the most Merciful

Press release

On the new massacre in Khan Younis

Zionist massacres are persisting in a show of spiteful Jewish terrorism against our unarmed people who are defending their lands and holy shrines with modest and simple potentials.

The enemy committed yet another carnage against our brothers in the Khan Younis refugee camp and Al-Amal suburb using tanks and heavy machine-guns in a savage and indiscriminate manner inflicting numerous martyrs and scores of wounded.

The Islamic Resistance Movement, Hamas, condemns that continuous terrorism and hails our heroic people who confronted the Zionist enemy and forced its troops to retreat despite the wounds that our people suffered in Khan Younis. Hamas further affirms that it would go ahead with its reprisal attacks against such massacres and that it would continue along the road of Jihad and resistance until defeat of that criminal occupation and liberation of the lands and sanctities.

We visualize the meanings of victory and Godly support to the few believers in the greater Badder battle on its anniversary, which we live today while facing that enemy and its supportive forces of oppression. We have big confidence in Allah's victory and support towards ending that suppression on us and on our Nation.

"And Allah hath full power and control over His affairs;
but most among mankind know it not."

The Islamic Resistance Movement
(Hamas—Palestine)
13 December 2000

13 December 2000

In the name of Allah the most gracious the most Merciful

Press release

The Mujahid Dr. Abdul Aziz Ranteesi declares a hunger strike

Dr. Abdul Aziz Ranteesi has declared a hunger strike last Sunday 14 Ramadan / 10 December to protest continuation of his detention in Palestinian Authority prisons.

The strike follows the failure of all mediation bids launched at all levels for the sake of ending his detention.

The Islamic Resistance Movement, Hamas, affirms the importance of releasing the Doctor along with all other political detainees since continuation of his detention contradicts the spirit of the intifada that spread and invigorated the Palestinian people.

The Palestinians in this intifada are the targets of the cruelest form of Zionist shelling and terrorism, the latest of which was what took place in Khan Younis the hometown of Dr. Ranteesi.

We appeal to all bodies, institutions and responsible people to exert efforts for the sake of releasing the Doctor along with other political detainees in the PA jails.

And Allah is the best Guide to the right path

The Islamic Resistance Movement
(Hamas—Palestine)
13 December 2000

9 December 2000

In the name of Allah the most Gracious the most Merciful

Press Release

"Among the Believers are men who have been true to their Covenant with Allah: of them some have completed their vow (to the extreme), and some (still) wait: but they have never changed (their determination) in the least:"

The Islamic Resistance Movement, Hamas, announces the martyrdom of Hamdy Arafat Ansyo commander of the Teyba operation and marine Rafah martyrdom operation

Martyrs fall one after the other and their blessed heroism mix together to form our Palestinian Muslim people's lives that are featured with Jihad, resistance, martyrdom and blood of heroic Mujahideen who are making glory of that Nation. They write its history with their pure blood and souls that are yearning to live in craws of the green birds that fly everywhere in paradise.

Today the Islamic Resistance Movement, Hamas, carries the glad tidings to our Mujahid Palestinian people and to our Arab and Islamic Nation on the martyrdom of one of the heroic Mujahideen who died in a heroic martyrdom operation, the first of its kind in history of the blessed intifada namely that of Rafah. The marine operation took place one month after outbreak of the intifada and targeted one of the naval vessels of the Zionist enemy off the coasts of Rafah. The enemy hid its losses after the heroic martyr's remains blasted in one of its vessels and his blood mixed with the roaring Palestine sea.

One of the Qassam Brigades' Mujahideen, who did not wish to disclose his name, told the Hamas Movement's office over the telephone, that the Mujahid Hamdy Arafat Ansyo, another Qassam member, was the one who launched the martyrdom operation off Rafah coasts against the Zionist enemy. He wished to meet his fate as a martyr in a qualitative operation to revenge martyrs of the Aqsa intifada and in retaliation to Zionist terrorism that escalated through missile and artillery bombardment of our steadfast and stationed people.

The Qassam martyr continued his blessed Jihad after taking part in the famous Teyba operation in March 2000 during which he penetrated, along with his brothers the Mujahideen, all barricades to strike deep into the enemy's lines. In that operation four Mujahideen were martyred namely Na'el Abu Awwad, Ammar Hassanein, Anwar Al-Bura'ee and Ihab Al-Hattab.

Our Mujahid people:

The Islamic Resistance Movement, Hamas, while bearing the glad tidings to our people and Nation along with news of famous operations launched along the march of the blessed intifada, it would like to affirm on the option of resistance and Jihad until liberty and dignity are achieved for our people and Nation.

This brave martyr, who loved Jihad and martyrdom, had his fingers cut off in the previous intifada in an explosion operation. However, he continued the march of Jihad launching the heroic Teyba operation then he was martyred in a qualitative operation that the enemy never before experienced. May Allah have mercy on his soul and rest his soul in peace alongside the prophets and martyrs.

Peace be upon you

It is a Jihad until victory or martyrdom

The Islamic Resistance Movement
(Hamas—Palestine)
9 December 2000

23 November 2000

In the name of Allah the most Gracious the most Merciful

Press Release

On the Zionist assassination of Mujahid Ibrahim Abdul Karim One of the Qassam Brigades' commanders

The Zionist occupation forces, in consistency with their savage crimes against our steadfast people, today assassinated Mujahid Ibrahim Abdul Karim Bani

Odeh from the town of Tammon, Nablus district. A missile that targeted his car led to the immediate martyrdom of Ibrahim, who was one of the commanders of the Qassam Brigades.

The martyr was released from the Palestinian Authority's Junaid prison last night along with seven others on temporary basis.

The cold-blooded murder of martyr Ibrahim Abdul Karim at the hands of occupation forces follows the same suit of yesterday's crime in the Gaza Strip when occupation soldiers murdered four Palestinians in broad daylight. It also falls in line with the occupation forces' series of daily crimes against our unarmed people, which will never dissuade our Mujahid people from continuing with the Aqsa intifada and brave struggle for the sake of liberating our lands and defeating the occupiers.

We, in the Islamic Resistance Movement, Hamas, affirm that blood of the heroic martyr and those of all Aqsa martyrs will turn into fire burning the usurpers.

The Islamic Resistance Movement
(Hamas—Palestine)
23 November 2000

2 November 2000

In the name of Allah the most Gracious the most Merciful

Press Release Issued by the Islamic Resistance Movement—Hamas

In the light of statements from the office of the enemy's premier about understandings reached during chairman Arafat's meeting with Shimon Peres, the Islamic Resistance Movement - Hamas would like to affirm the following:

1. At a time when martyrs and wounded are falling in defense of Al-Quds (Jerusalem) and while the terrorist aggression is continuing against our people, Hamas rejects such meetings with symbols of Zionist terrorism whose hands are smeared with blood of our unarmed Palestinian people and who are still threatening our people and their

Jihad. Such American-Zionist plots are only aimed at aborting the shining Intifadha, which lit the way for our people and Nation towards liberation of Palestine and the holy city of Al-Quds.

2. The blessed Aqsa Intifadha, which broke out for the sake of defeating occupation and ejecting the settlers and which was decorated with blood of thousands of martyrs and wounded and posed as a Jihad guide for our Arab and Islamic Nation, could not stop under any pretext without achieving its legitimate goals represented in defeating Zionist occupation on the land of Palestine and the holy city of Al-Quds the first Qibla, third holiest shrine in Islam and Isra' site of our prophet Mohammed, peace be upon him.

3. We call on all forces of our Palestinian people and their Mujahid masses to continue the Intifadha in retaliation to the barbaric aggression that is still being waged against our people. We urge our people to maintain their unity, which was evident in this blessed Intifadha and which was endorsed in the resistance and Jihad trench. We affirm our rejection of returning to the option of negotiations that divided our people and drove a wedge among its various sectors.

Here they are our virtuous martyrs ascending to the heavens even after the office of terrorist Barak declared that understandings were reached last night meaning that Zionist terrorism was ongoing necessitating continuation of the Intifadha with all its forms and means.

Allahu Akbar and Alhamdullilah

**The Islamic Resistance Movement
(Hamas—Palestine)
2 November 2000**

25 October 2000

Press release

Commenting on terrorist Barak's plan to segregate and isolate Palestinian areas, and Clinton's invitation to both Arafat and Barak to meet him, a responsible source in the Hamas Movement said:

1. Terrorist Barak's plan to segregate and isolate Palestinian cities and villages comes as a chain in a series of repressive measures against our Palestinian people and an attempt to halt their roaring popular

Intifadha. On the other hand the plan further targets pressuring the Palestinian and Arab parties that are still insisting on the settlement process to return to the negotiating table and accept the Zionist conditions and dictates. Despite the racial dimension of such a policy yet it is based on the de facto situation resulting from the Oslo A, B and C agreements, which endorsed retaining the settlements and constructing circular roads around them.

Today as terrorist Barak is continuing his declared war against our unarmed people using missiles, tanks, choppers and artillery to bombard our cities, camps and villages, our people assert with blood, martyrs and solid unity that there is no other road or option but Jihad, struggle and steadfastness to foil the enemy's measures and aggressive policies.

2. The reports of Clinton's invitation to both Arafat and terrorist Barak for separate meetings come as a new attempt to abort the Aqsa Intifadha following the Paris and Sharm Al-Sheikh meetings. Such meetings only target luring the Palestinian Authority chairman into accepting American and Zionist dictates and conditions. The American administration, which compelled the PA to attend the Paris and Sharm Al-Sheikh meetings, is rudely biased in favor of the Zionist enemy. It attempts to justify and conceal the enemy's suppression and terrorism and equals between our people's unarmed children who use stones and the enemy's criminal army that is armed to the teeth with all kinds of weapons and that is shelling our cities and unarmed people with missiles.

We warn the PA chairman against going to that meeting, which is considered by our people as a new conspiracy aimed at aborting the Aqsa Intifadha. And we affirm that our people who offered more than 140 martyrs and five thousand wounded would never accept that price of that blood would be the return of the PA chairman to the negotiating table or an improvement in his negotiating conditions!!!

We, along with our heroic people, wish to emphasize that Jihad, resistance; escalating the blessed Intifadha and the comprehensive popular confrontation against the Zionist enemy were the only means to defend the Aqsa and holy shrines, to grab our rights and to defeat occupation.

The Islamic Resistance Movement
(Hamas—Palestine)
25 October 2000

16 August 2000

In the name of Allah the most Gracious the most Merciful

Press release Commenting on the assassination of the (Mukhtar) mayor of Sarda village Mahmoud Abdullah at the hands of the Zionist occupation soldiers

Commenting on the assassination of the (Mukhtar) mayor of Sarda village Mahmoud Abdullah at the hands of the Zionist occupation soldiers, a responsible source in the Islamic Resistance Movement, Hamas, said:

A group of Zionist undercover soldiers, specialized in pursuing and assassinating Palestinian Muhajideen, has murdered the mayor of Sarda village in the Ramallah district. The occupation authority claimed that the unit was looking for one of the Hamas Movement's Mujahideen and started shooting killing the mayor of that village Mahmoud Abdullah, 73, who was standing on the rooftop of his house.

The occupation authority alleged that the martyr had fired at the soldiers. It was not requited with murdering him but also arrested his sons, one of whom is a correspondent for the French news agency (AFP) who was charged of belonging to Hizbullah. They were later released in a bid to justify and cover up the crime.

The fact is that the martyr's house was the target of repeated stealing attempts last year. At dawn today, he heard sounds outside his house so he went to the roof to discover the cause of such noise and immediately the undercover soldiers shot him.

The occupation authority issued perplexed statements to explain what happened; it accused the martyr of firing first and later said that the soldiers thought he was a Hamas cadre, as if the Hamas cadres' blood was permanently wasted. It then claimed that one of his sons was a member in Hizbullah but all those attempts could not conceal the abhorred crime.

The occupation authority's crime reflected the occupation's real ugly face and its aggressive and repressive practices against our unarmed people. It also exposed reality of that criminal enemy with which the Palestinian Authority was trying to make peace at the expense of our people's blood and our rights and sanctities.

It is regrettable that the Zionist crime had coincided with the official declaration of the resumption of negotiations between the PA and the arrogant Zionist enemy.

We demand the PA to halt is absurd negotiations with the occupation authority and to respect the will of our Palestinian people, who reject such negotiations and insist on their rights, Quds and holy shrines. We urge the PA to respect the blood of our people, including that of martyr Mahmoud Abdullah that would not be the last to be shed, and to halt all forms of security coordination with the enemy aimed at pursuing and liquidating the Mujahideen.

**The Islamic Resistance Movement
(Hamas—Palestine)
Information office
Wednesday 16 August 2000**

3 August 2000

In the name of Allah the most Gracious the most Merciful

Press Release

On Arafat's statements surrendering the Buraq Wall to the Jews

Commenting on Palestinian Authority chief Yasser Arafat's statements to the Yemeni News Agency 'Saba' and the Yemeni television last Sunday 30 July in which he said, <u>"As for the Israelis they have the Wailing Wall (Buraq Wall) and we respect that Wall and allow them to pray at it . . . but otherwise we never allow any tampering with Islamic or Christian holy shrines"</u> . . . a responsible source in the Hamas Movement said:

The serious statements delivered by chairman of the PA on an alleged right for the Jews in the Buraq Wall point to what took place in the Camp David summit and indicate that big concessions were made by the Palestinian party on our Islamic holy shrines in Al-Quds (Jerusalem) topped by the

Buraq Wall, as indicated in Arafat's statements. Such a development is a serious precedence that affects each and every Muslim on our planet and necessitates a decisive stance.

The Wall named by Arafat as the Wailing Wall, which is the Jewish name, is in fact the Buraq Wall that was given that name after the Buraq of prophet Mohammed, peace be upon him, that which was fastened to the Wall on the night of the Isra'. In Muslim creed it is part and parcel of the holy Aqsa Mosque and enjoys a great and sacred status with all Muslims in the east and west. For preserving its sanctity much blood were shed across history. It is really a painful coincidence that Arafat's statements had coincided with the anniversary of the Buraq revolution that swept Palestine in August 1929 and led to the martyrdom of 120 Palestinians and the injury of 232 others in addition to the death of 133 Zionists and the wounding of 339 others and which was followed by the execution of the three famous Mujahideen the martyrs Fuad Hijazi, Ata Al-Zeer and Mohammed Jamjoom.

It is regrettable that such statements be voiced by head of the PA ignoring the Muslims' right in the Buraq Wall, a right that was granted to them by the international committee formed by the League of Nations in 1930, which endorsed the Muslims' right in the Buraq Wall and issued a report that included: "The Muslims alone have the ownership of the western wall and they alone have the right of property because it constitutes an integrated part of Al-Haram Al-Sharif's yard, which in turn is a part of the Waqf property. Muslims also own the pavement in front of the Wall at the suburb known as Bab Al-Maghareba (which was razed to the ground by the Zionists after their occupation of eastern Jerusalem in 1967) since it is a Waqf land revenues of which go to charity according to Islamic Sharia. The Jewish attempt to install any worship tools or others whether according to that resolution or based on approval of both parties should not mean, under any circumstances, the founding of a property right for the Jews in the Wall or the pavement near to it."

We call on the Arab and Islamic Nation to move quickly and seriously to check the feverish Zionist attempts aimed at judaizing Al-Quds and sacrilege the Aqsa through the PA's capitulation. We, in the Islamic Resistance Movement, Hamas, affirm anew that the land of Palestine is an Islamic Waqf land for all Islamic generations until the Day of Judgment. It is religiously prohibited to give it up partially or wholly not by any King or president or all kings and presidents, not by any organization or all organizations whether Palestinian or Arab.

"And Allah hath full power and control over His affairs; but most among mankind know it not."

The Islamic Resistance Movement
(Hamas—Palestine)
Thursday 3 August 2000

30 July 2000

In the name of Allah the most Gracious the most Merciful

Press statement on the arrest of
Dr. Abdul Aziz Ranteesi by PA security men

Commenting on the Palestinian security apparatuses' detention of Dr. Abdul Aziz Ranteesi, one of Hamas leaders and spokesmen in Gaza Strip, a responsible source in the Hamas Movement said:

Palestinian Authority's security men stormed house of Dr. Abdul Aziz Ranteesi at 4 am today and arrested him. The detention followed Dr. Ranteesi's statement to Jazeera space channel in one of its programs that affirmed the Hamas Movement's stands in sticking to our lands and Palestinian national rights. He questioned the real PA positions regarding the issues of the refugees, borders and settlements and called on the PA to divulge the whole truth to the people. Such a statement embarrassed one of the PA officials who is well known for his corruption and strong relations with the Zionist enemy and who was sharing in the same program.

Dr. Ranteesi's arrest is an attempt by the PA to silence the opposition and prevent our people's vivid forces from declaring their stands and opinions vis-à-vis what took place in the Camp David summit or to reveal the Authority's concessions on the questions of the return of the refugees, settlements, borders and others.

The PA should have rather gone to the Palestinian people to re-arrange the Palestinian house and consolidate the internal ranks in face of Zionist and American arrogance instead of detaining the symbols of loyalty among our people, confiscating freedoms and quelling opposition.

We strongly condemn the arrest of Dr. Ranteesi and demand his immediate release along with other political detainees in PA prisons. We also affirm that repression and detention are the methods of the feeble and will not cover up the truth and what truly happened in the Camp David negotiations.

The Islamic Resistance Movement
(Hamas—Palestine)
Sunday 30 July 2000

4 July 2000

Press Release by Hamas
On results of the PLO Central Council meeting

A responsible source in the Islamic Resistance Movement, Hamas, commented on the meeting of the Palestinian Central council (PCC) in the period 2–3 July 2000 by saying:

Despite the fact that the establishment of a really sovereign Palestinian state on Palestinian lands was a national demand of all Palestinians, yet regretfully the Palestinian Authority (PA) has turned that demand into a mere slogan after the Oslo agreements. The PA maneuvers with that slogan in accordance with developments of the meager negotiations with the Zionist enemy whether in the transitional stage negotiations or the so-called final status talks.

Results of the latest PCC meeting came in harmony with that fact since the decision of declaring the state was left to the Palestinian leadership, in response to its pressures, so that it can use such a decision as a bargaining card to win the remaining bits and pieces of the transitional stage.

The apparent rigidity in statements of both the Palestinian and Zionist parties is apparently a mere fabrication to prepare the public opinion for future steps that include concessions and surrendering of our people's rights and sovereignty.

The American administration's total biased stand in favor of the Zionists, including the rejection of the declaration of the Palestinian state, affirms that the American administration cannot be depended upon in ensuring justice for our people or realizing their rights.

If the PA was really serious in not giving up Palestinian rights topped by Jerusalem, the refugees and establishment of the independent state, then it should announce its withdrawal from the absurd negotiations with the Zionist enemy. It also must return to the Palestinian people's option in resisting and defeating occupation. The PA ought to end its persecution of the Mujahideen and terminate its protection of the occupiers. Finally it should not rein in our people's potentials in resisting occupation.

The Hamas Movement re-affirms that Jihad, struggle, patience and sacrifice constitute the road towards liberating our lands and grabbing our rights. The experience, of the brave resistance and its victory, in South Lebanon is strong evidence that rights are only grabbed by Jihad and bloodletting and not begged at the negotiating and bargaining tables. We call on our Arab and Muslim Nation, on the official and popular levels, to support resistance on the land of Palestine in its capacity as the Nation's choice to realize liberation and victory similar to the Lebanese experience where the people along with the government and the whole country embraced the resistance option.

The Islamic Resistance Movement
(Hamas—Palestine)
Tuesday 4 July 2000

3 May 2000

Urgent

Press Release

A number of media means today circulated a news report on the deportation of Hamas leaders from Jordan, claiming that the Qatari foreign minister had carried to Jordan a proposal allowing the return of the Hamas deportees for a short period before leaving Amman on their own free will. They attributed that report to what they called sources close to the Hamas Movement.

We, in the Hamas Movement, affirm that this report is totally untrue and baseless. It is an attempt to smear the stands of the Hamas Movement and deceive the public opinion. We also affirm that Hamas did not table any proposals in this regard and that it was insisting on the return of its deported leaders because their deportation came in violation of the Jordanian constitution, in defiance of citizens' rights and an infringement of their citizenship.

We, in the Hamas Movement, realize the true intentions of those parties that try to leak such fabricated news in a bid to besmirch the image of the Hamas Movement and its steadfastness. We are confident, at the same time, of the awareness of our Arab and Islamic masses.

The Islamic Resistance Movement (Hamas—Palestine)
Informational Bureau
Wednesday 29th Moharram 1421
3rd May 2000

10 April 2000

In the name of God, the Merciful, the Mercy-giving

Press Statement concerning a fabricated news report carried by Reuters

Reuters news agency circulated a news item a few days ago by its correspondent in the West Bank city of Ramallah quoting an unnamed senior official in Hamas and another in the PLO who requested anonymity as claiming that Hamas had enhanced its presence in Damascus following collapse of the peace talks between Syria and "Israel". The report further alleged that the Syrian foreign minister had agreed that Hamas would develop its office during a meeting with Dr. Abu Marzouq last week. Reuters claimed that the Hamas official said the step was aimed at exploiting "extremist groups" to make trouble after "Israel" withdraws its forces from South Lebanon.

We in the Hamas Movement categorically deny the Reuters news report in toto and affirm that it is completely fabricated, for no Hamas official whether inside or outside Palestine delivered any statement neither to the Reuters news agency nor to its correspondent Wafaa Amr on that subject. This is not the first time that the abovementioned correspondent publicizes fabricated news leaked by officials in the Palestinian Authority to serve certain PA goals with which that correspondent maintains numerous interests and relations.

We regret that Reuters would publish such baseless news, a matter which affects its news credibility.

The PA circulates such news and press leakage in line with its role and feverish efforts in pursuing the resistance forces and in service of the Zionist goals to pressure Syria following the failure of the Geneva talks. For sure such practice is not in the interest of the Palestinian nor the Arab stands but rather serves the interests of the Zionist enemy.

Informational bureau
Islamic Resistance Movement—Hamas—Palestine

27 February 2000

Press statement concerning the Palestine Authority's campaign of arrests of Bir Zeit University students

In the name of God, the Merciful, the Mercy-giving

Commenting on the campaign of arrests of Bir Zeit University students that is being carried out by the Palestine Authority's security agencies; an official source in the Islamic Resistance Movement—Hamas—declared the following:

The Hamas Movement has followed with extreme indignation the campaign of arrests undertaken by the security agencies of the Palestine Authority of Bir Zeit University students in response to their protest demonstrations against statements by the French Prime Minister. In his remarks, the French Prime Minister described the heroic and legitimate resistance actions of the Islamic Resistance in south Lebanon as "terrorist acts."

The rage and protest of our students in Bir Zeit University yesterday and the protest demonstrations by students at al-Najah University today against the French Prime Minister are nothing but a spontaneous and natural expression of the conscience of our Palestinian people and of the Arab and Islamic world that rejects such provocative statements.

The French Prime Minister's description of the legitimate acts of resistance against the Zionist occupation and its military establishment as "terrorist acts" contradicts all international principles, conventions, documents, and laws. It is also blatant alignment with the Zionist position and support for its aggression and arrogance. It is something that demands the firm disapproval and condemnation by all sincere forces in our Arab nation.

We find it strange that the Palestine Authority would undertake a campaign of arrests against the students, making common apologies for their protests and spontaneous actions in defense of the honor of our nation, its rights, and its legitimate resistance activity, at a time when the statements of the French Prime Minister have elicited tremendous condemnation and rejection inside France itself on many levels.

The defiant students of Palestinian Universities who were and still are the first to defend their people and their national causes, of whom thousands have fallen martyrs or been imprisoned in confrontation with Zionist aggression, deserve to be highly praised and honored, not repressed, arrested, and hunted down!!

We demand that the Palestine Authority immediately release all the students it has arrested and apologize to our people and our students for their practices of repressing their rights.

Long live the defiant student movement as a true expression of the conscience of our people and our nation!

Islamic Resistance Movement—Hamas—Palestine

9 February 2000

In the name of God, the Merciful, the Mercy-giving

Press statement on the treacherous acts of Zionist aggression against Lebanon

Commenting on the acts of naked aggression committed by the aircraft of the Zionist enemy on civilian targets whose purpose is to provide utility services to Lebanon; an authorized spokesman for the Islamic Resistance Movement—Hamas—made the following statement:

The new acts of Zionist aggression reveal the true, ugly face of Ehud Barak's Zionist government, which has tried to market itself as a seeker of peace. The aggression exposes the impotence and bankruptcy to which the Zionist enemy has been reduced in its confrontation with the qualitative military operations of the Islamic Resistance against both its soldiers and puppet troops. The Resistance operations have deeply disturbed the ranks of its forces, dashing their morale. The Islamic Resistance Movement (Hamas) and with it the Palestinian people reaffirm their complete commitment to the Lebanese people, to their state, and their resistance, and stress their right to resist the Zionist occupation and to retaliate for the treacherous attacks to which their utility services were subjected.

In this context, the Hamas movement calls on the Arab and Islamic world to take a serious stand on the side of Lebanon and its heroic resistance, and to give them all forms of support until the enemy has been defeated and routed from Lebanese territory.

In light of this development the Arab political establishment must halt all contact and cooperation with the enemy state, now that it has confirmed its disdain for the feelings and scorn for the values and norms of the world community, after it has committed these criminal acts, intended to inflict comprehensive harm on civilians on the pretext of preserving the security of the Zionist settlers, in a vivid example of the racist practices unique to the Zionist enemy.

The Hamas movement hails the firm national unity that characterizes Lebanon in its confrontation with Zionist treachery, and hails the solidarity of the Lebanese people and government with the Resistance. The failure of the occupation forces to respond to the ability of the Resistance to penetrate its military strongholds proves clearly that the hour of the defeat and rout of the enemy has come, and that the liberation of Lebanese territory is, by the grace of God, imminent.

Islamic Resistance Movement—Hamas—Palestine

3 February 2000

Press statement by Hamas concerning the Stockholm Conference on the alleged Holocaust of the Jews

In the Name of God, the Merciful, the Mercy-giving.

Commenting on the international conference in Stockholm on the alleged Holocaust of the Jews during the Second World War, a responsible source in the Islamic Resistance Movement—Hamas—made the following statement:

The convening of this conference clearly serves the Zionist aim of falsifying history and obscuring the truth that the so-called Holocaust is nothing but a baseless, fictitious claim. This malicious conference seeks to reinforce a guilt complex vis-à-vis the Jews in Europe in general and in Germany in particular, to facilitate the continued fleecing of the world in support of the Zionist entity's expansionism and aggression. Creating great fantasies about an alleged "crime" that never happened while ignoring the millions of Europeans who died or suffered at the hands of the Nazis during the Second World War clearly exposes the face of racist Zionism with its belief in the superiority of the Jewish race over all other peoples.

The attempt to rouse concern over a baseless, fictitious story while overlooking the sufferings of our people, ignoring Zionist massacres such as Deir Yasin, Kufr Qasim, Tantoura, Jerusalem, the Ibrahimi Mosque, and Sabra and Shatila, not to mention the enemy's massacres of our Arab people in Bahr al-Baqar, and Qana, and the killing of thousands of Egyptian prisoners of war, etc., all of this confirms that many western states still are deluded by erroneous Zionist propaganda. As a result, their positions lack credibility and justice as regards our cause and our people and their ongoing suffering. This will never lead to stability in the Middle East region, nor will it obscure the fact that the Zionist entity was built upon racial discrimination, terrorism and repression.

By means of the Stockholm conference and the tale of the Nazi Holocaust, the Zionist entity practices psychological and intellectual terrorism. Meanwhile, in Palestine and Lebanon, it practices the bloody terrorism of which it accuses other peoples. We call upon the countries that took part in this conference to review their positions and not to submit to Zionist haughtiness or to its continued plunder. We call on free-minded thinkers and writers and the vital forces of the world to work to uncover the crimes of world Zionism against our people, our nation, and against humanity as a whole, to expose them and not to fear the assault of the Jews, their intellectual terrorism, and their efforts to stifle voices and keep fair thinkers and researchers from exposing the claims and lies of Zionism. For the Jews in the world oppose the scientific method of study and research whenever it contradicts their racist interests

God is Greatest! Praise be to God! For it is a struggle for victory or martyrdom!

Islamic Resistance Movement—Hamas—Palestine

30 November 1999

Press Statement

The arrest of several national figures by the Palestinian Authority

Commenting on the arrest campaign and the imposing of house arrest by the self-rule authority against a number of Palestinian national figures after they signed a statement condemning the tyranny and corruption in the PA and its various bodies, which also condemned the PA's political deception and misleading of our people regarding the final status negotiations, a responsible source in the Islamic Resistance Movement (Hamas) has stated the following:

Hamas condemns the arrest campaigns being implemented by the security bodies of the Palestinian Authority against a number of Palestinian national figures and the imposing of house arrest on the veteran Bassam al-Shakaa and others who signed the statement. It considers these arbitrary and suppressive measures a continuation of the PA's policy of dictatorship, oppression and confiscation of freedoms.

All Palestinians will readily agree on the questions raised by the national figures that signed the statement. Hamas and other national forces and figures used to expose the reality of the agreements signed with the Zionist Enemy and to reveal the relinquishments regarding their rights, land, holy places, and the dignity of our people.

We call upon the PA to reconsider its policies, to rectify perversities within its ranks, and to stop the series of relinquishments and abandonment of the rights of our people it introduces to the Zionist Enemy in every round of negotiations.

The status of tension and confusion being experienced within the PA and its bodies is a direct result of the PA's ongoing questionable practices and the stalemate in the peace process, which has failed to achieve the promises made by the PA to our people, and the expected introduction of serious relinquishments in the present negotiations regarding the issues of Jerusalem, the return of refugees, Jewish settlements, prisoners, Statehood, the borders, water issues and others.

We call upon the PA to promptly release the detainees and to lift the house arrest imposed on the national figures. We also call upon it to release from its jails Hamas and other prisoners who have been detained because of their political opinions and stands.

Islamic Resistance Movement—Hamas—Palestine

09 November 1999

Press Release

The Arrest of Ezzat Rasheq

Commenting on the arrest of Brother Ezzat Al-Rasheq by the Jordanian authorities, a responsible source from the Islamic Resistance Movement (Hamas) has stated the following:

In another escalation step, the Jordanian security authorities arrested on Monday night, 8 November 1999, Brother Ezzat Al-Rasheq (known as Abdel Aziz Omari), member of the Hamas Political Bureau.

While we in the Islamic Resistance Movement (Hamas) condemn and denounce this arbitrary and unjustified measure, we see it as contradictory to statements made by His Majesty King Abdullah II in which he hoped this crisis would be resolved very soon.

This sudden escalation of the crisis with the arrest of Brother Al-Rasheq threatens the current good offices that seek to find a political solution to the crisis. It also puts an end to hopes created by these good offices.

While we call upon the Jordanian government to promptly release Brother Al-Rasheq and the other brothers detained in the Jordanian jails, in particular Khalid Misha'al, head of the Hamas political bureau, and Ibrahim Ghousheh, the spokesman of Hamas, we call on the Jordanian government to listen to the voice of sense and logic and not to respond to calls of incitement that are hostile to our nation and that drive the Jordanian government to be involved in disputes that waste the nation's efforts and power. This does not serve anyone but the Zionist Entity.

We also call upon the Jordanian government to respond to the efforts that have been made to solve this crisis, and not to spoil the spirit of brotherhood and solidarity that dominate the relation between the Jordanians and the Palestinians in order to preserve the nation's efforts and to serve the causes of our people and nation.

Islamic Resistance Movement—Hamas—Palestine

22 September 1999

Press Release

On the arrest of the Movement's leaders: Khaled Mishaal, Ibrahim Ghoushe and deportation of Dr. Mousa Abu Marzouk

We, in the Islamic Resistance Movement—Hamas, declare our regret and denunciation of the Jordanian government's measures which led to escalation of the crisis at a time when benevolent efforts were being exerted to contain it and prevent its negative repercussions.

We consider the return of the brothers to their country and families as an evidence of their innocence of what has been held against them and of legitimacy of their presence (there).

We affirm that such measures affect the relationship between the Jordanian and Palestinian peoples and do not serve the interests of the Jordanian people, the majority of whom support the Islamic Resistance Movement, Hamas and reject the measures against its leaders.

We also affirm that deportation of Dr. Mousa Abu Marzouk contradicts with the residence right granted to him by the late King Hussein.

We renew the call on the Jordanian government to re-consider its measures, and we appeal to King Abdullah II to interfere in continuation of his late father's policy in boosting national unity within Jordan and unity of the two Jordanian and Palestinian peoples.

We confirm persistence of the Movement's stable policy of non-interference in internal affairs of the Arab and Muslim countries and its keenness on maintaining their security and stability.

We affirm that the pressures against the Movement only increase its insistence on pursuance of its Jihad march to restore our Palestinian people's right in their homeland and sanctities. The march will continue to prevent giving up any of them in addition to the return of the evicted Palestinian people to their country, lands and full sovereignty.

We appeal to the Kings, Presidents, Ameers and peoples of the Arab and Muslim Ummah, especially the intellectuals, political parties, organizations, syndicates and societies to intervene and seek the release of the detained leaders. We hope that they would also seek the return of Dr. Abu Marzouk, who was deported, so as things would return to normalcy in brotherly Jordan.

"And Allah hath full power and control over His affairs;
but most among mankind know it not." (Quran 12/21)

Islamic Resistance Movement—Hamas—Palestine

Saturday, 20 March 1999

The Islamic Resistance Movement (Hamas)

Press Release

A responsible source of the Political Bureau of the Islamic Resistance Movement (Hamas) has stated the following:

The allegation by some officials of the Palestinian Authority that some brothers in the jails of the Israeli Enemy had sent a letter to the Hamas leadership pertaining to contacts with the Enemy are absolutely baseless. Hamas leadership, whether in or out of the Occupied territories, did not receive such a letter from its heroes detained in the Occupation jails.

It is regrettable that the Palestinian Authority creates a crisis among our people and their active forces, especially Hamas, whenever the PA has a crisis with the Zionist Enemy. This is considered a desperate attempt by the PA to disturb Hamas, its positions, its Mujahideen and its detained heroes; and to distract the public opinion from the PA's crisis with the Occupation. This is one of the fabrications and calumnies which the PA used to spread and which have become known to all of our people.

Hamas reiterates its decisive and clear position that the resistance of the Zionist Occupation is a legitimate right of all our people as long as the Zionists occupy our land and our Jerusalem, and until our people achieve their goals of liberation, freedom and the right to return. Hamas also reiterates that the resistance option is not a question of bargaining at any time.

Saturday, 20 March 1999

Selected Bibliography

BOOKS

Abu 'Amr Ziyad, *Islamic fundamentalism in the West Bank and Gaza:* Muslim Brotherhood and Islamic Jihad, Bloomington: Indiana University Press, 1994

Ahmad, Hisam, H., *Hamas: from religious salvation to political transformation: the rise of Hamas in Palestinian society*, Jerusalem: Palestinian Academic Society for the Study of International Affairs, 1994

Alexander Yonah; Colbert, James, *Middle East terrorism:* selected group profiles, Washington DC: Jewish Institute for National Security Affairs, 1994

Alexander, Yonah; Sinai Joshua, *Terrorism: the PLO connection*, New York: Crane Russak, 1989

Appleby, R. Scott, *Spokesmen for the despised:* fundamentalist leaders of the Middle East, Chicago: University of Chicago Press, 1997

Aruri, Naseer, Hasan, *Palestinian refugees: the right of return*, London; Sterling VA: Pluto Press, 2001

Asia, Ilan, *The quest for Arab territorial continuity as a focus of the Middle East conflict*, Ariel, Israel: Ariel Center for Policy Research, 1998

Ateek, Naim Stifan; Prior Michael, *Holy land, hollow jubilee: God, justice, and the Palestinians*, London, England: Melisende, 1999

Bar, Shmuel, *The Muslim Brotherhood in Jordan*, Tel Aviv: Moshe Dayan Center, Tel Aviv University, 1998

Barghouti, Mustafa, *The post-Oslo impasse*, Washington DC: The Center for Policy Analysis on Palestine, 1998

Bar-Siman-Tov, Yaacov, *Israel and the Intifada:* adaptation and learning, Jerusalem: The Leonard Davis Institute for International Relations, The Hebrew University of Jerusalem, 2000

Becker, Jillian, *The PLO:* the rise and fall of the Palestinian Liberation Organization, New York: St. Martin's Press, 1984

Benvenisti, Meron, *Intimate enemies Jews and Arabs in a shared land.* Berkeley: University of California Press, 1995

Ben-Yehuda, Hemda; Sandler, Shmuel, *The Arab-Israeli conflict transformed:* fifty years of interstate and ethnic crises, Albany: State University of New York Press, 2002

Beres, Louis Rene, *Israel's survival imperatives: the Oslo agreements in international law and national strategy*, Ariel, Israel: Ariel Center for Policy Research, 1998

Binder, Leonard, *Ethnic conflict and international politics in the Middle East*, Gainsville, FA: University Press of Florida, 1999

Bishara, Marwan, *Palestine/Israel: peace or apartheid*, Halifax, N.S.: Fernwood, 2001

Bleving, Leonard C., *The PLO: a victory in terrorism?* Fort Leavenworth, Kan: US Army Command and General Staff College, 1991

Bornstein, Avram, *Crossing the green line between the West Bank and Israel*, Philadelphia, PA., Wantage: University of Pennsylvania Press; University Presses Marketing, 2001

Bregman, Ahron; El-Tahri, Jihad, *The fifty years' war: Israel and the Arabs*, New York: TV Books, 1999

Brown Michael Frederic, *Hamas's Development Efforts in the Gaza Strip:* Grass roots initiatives, democratic participation and the role of women, Annandale, VA: United Association for Studies and Research, 1997

Bryren, Rex, *Echoes of the Intifada:* regional repercussions of the Palestinian-Israeli conflict, Boulder: Westview Press, 1991

Bryren, Rex, *Sanctuary and Survival:* the PLO in Lebanon, Boulder; London: Westview Press, Pinter Publishers, 1990

Buchanan, Andrew S., *Peace with justice: a history of the Israeli-Palestinian Declaration of Principles on Interim Self-Government Arrangements*, Houndmills, Basingstoke, Hampshire: Macmillan Press, 2000

Buckley, Richard; King, John, *Middle East Stalemate:* What hopes for progress now?, Cheltenham: Understanding Global Issues, 1999

Burgat, Francois and William Dowell, *The Islamic Movement in North Africa*, Austin Center for Middle Eastern Studies, University of Texas, 1993

Cattan, Henry, *The Palestine question*, London: Saqi, 2000

Chirot, Daniel; Seligman, Martin E. P. *Ethnopolitical warfare: causes, consequences, and possible solutions*, Washington DC: American Psychological Association, 2001

Clay, Andreia, *Fundamentalism and secular nationalism:* the cases of Hamas and Gush Emunim, Thesis, 1991

Cohen, Stuart; Kanovsky, Eliyahu; Inbar, Efraim, *Military, economic and strategic aspects of the Middle East peace process*, Ramat Gan, Israel: Bar-Ilan University, 1995

Cordesman, Anthony H., *Peace and war: the Arab-Israeli military balance enters the 21st century*, Westport, Conn.: Praeger, 2002

Djerejian, Edward P., *Strategic equation of peace:* the negotiations between Israel, Syria and Lebanon, Tel Aviv: Tel Aviv University, Tami Steinmetz Center for Peace Research, 1999

Dolan, David, *Israel in crisis: what lies ahead?* Grand Rapids, Mich.: Fleming H. Revell, 2001

Drake, Laura, *Hegemony and its Discontents:* United States policy toward Iraq, Iran, Hamas, the Hezbollah and their responses, Annadale, VA: United Association for Studies and Research, 1997

El-Rewany, Hassan Ahmed, *The Ramadan war: end of illusion*, Carlisle Barracks, PA: US Army War College, 2001

Esposito, John, L., *Political Islam:* revolution, radicalism, or reform? Boulder, CO: Lynne Rienner Publishers, 1997

Finkelstein, Norman G., *Image and reality of the Israel-Palestine conflict*, London; New York: Verso, 2001

Frangi, Abdallah, *The PLO and Palestine*, London: Zed, 2001

Freedman, Robert Owen, *The Intifada:* its impact on Israel, the Arab World and the Superpowers, Miami: Florida International University Press, 1991

Freund, Wolfgang, *Palestinian Perspectives*, Frankfurt am Main; New York: Perer Lang 1999

Friedman, Thomas L., *From Beirut to Jerusalem*, New York: Anchor Books, 1995

Gazit, Mordechai, *Israeli diplomacy and the quest for peace*, Portland, OR: Franck Cass, 2002

Gefen, Aba, *Israel at a crossroads*, Jerusalem; New York: Gefen Pub. 2001

Gilboa, Amos, *The Threat of PLO Terrorism*, Jerusalem: Ministry of Foreign Affairs, 1985

Ginat, J; Perkins, Edward J., *The Palestinian refugees: old problems—new solutions*, Norman: University of Oklahoma Press, 2001

Gordon, Neve; Lopez, George A., *Terrorism in the Arab-Israeli conflict*, Notre Dame, IN: University of Notre Dame, Joan B. Kroc Institute for International Peace Studies, 1999

Gresh, Alain, *The PLO: the struggle within:* towards an independent Palestinian state, London; New Jersey: Zed Books, 1988

Gruen, George E., *The PLO and the Palestinian uprising:* their tactics and declared objectives, New York, NY: American Jewish Committee, 1988

Hamid, Rashid, *What is the PLO?*, London: PLO, 1981

Harakat al-Muqawamah al-Islamiyah, *Charter of Islamic Resistance Movement—* Hamas, Gaza, August 1988: selected translation and analysis, S.L.: Simon Wiesenthal Center, 1988

Harkema, Theodore Ray, *The changing security environment in the Middle East and the implications for Israeli defense*, Thesis, 2001

Harub, Khalid, *Hamas: Political Thought and Practice*, Washington DC:Institute for Palestine Studies, 2000

Hatina, Meir, *Islam and the Salvation of Palestine: the Islamic Jihad movement*, Tel Aviv: The Moshe Dayan Center for Middle Eastern and African Studies, Tel Aviv University, 2001

Hiro, Dilip, *Sharing the Promised Land: a tale of the Israelis and Palestinians*, New York: Olive Branch Press, 1999

Holliday, Laurel, *Why do they hate me: young lives caught in war and conflict*, New York, NY: Pocket Books, 1999

Hunter, Shireen, *The PLO after Tripoli*, Georgetown University Center for Strategic and International Studies, Middle East Program, Washington DC: Center for Strategic and International Studies, Georgetown University, 1984

Jamal Amal Ahmad, *Mobilization under control:* the PLO and the Palestinians in the West Bank and the Gaza Strip, Yarka, Israel: A.A. Jamal, 1996

Juergensmeyer, Mark, *Terror in the Mind of God:* the global rise of religious violence, Berkeley: University of California Press, 2001

Kanovsky, Eliyahu, *Arab-Israel peace agreements since Camp David:* a look backward and a look ahead, Ariel, Israel: Ariel Center for Policy Research, 1997

Karsh, Efraim, *Between war and peace:* dilemmas of Israeli security, Portland, OR: F. Cass, 1996

Katz, Samuel M., *The Hunt for the Engineer:* how Israeli agents tracked the Hamas master bomber, New York: Fromm International, 1999

Khatchadourian, Haig, *The quest for peace between Israel and the Palestinians*, New York: Peter Land Publishing, 2000

Kirisci, Kemal, *The PLO and World Politics:* a study of mobilization of support for the Palestinian cause, New York: St. Martin's Press, 1986

Klein, Yitzhak, *Israel's war with the Palestinians:* sources, political objectives, and operational means, Shaarei Tikva, Israel: The Ariel Center for Policy Research, 2001

Kurz, Anat; Tal, Nahman, *Hamas: radical Islam in a national struggle*, Tel Aviv: Jaffee Center for Strategic Studies, Tel Aviv University, 1997

La Guardia, Anton, *Holy Land, unholy war: Israelis and Palestinians*, London: John Murray, 2001

Laqueuer, Walter; Rubin Barry M., *The Israeli-Arab reader: a documentary history of the Middle East conflict*, New York: Penguin Books, 2001

Lewis J. Bernard, *The Palestinians and the PLO:* a historical approach, New York: American Jewish Committee, 1975

Litvak, Meir, *The Islamization of Palestinian identity:* the case of Hamas, Tel Aviv, Israel: Moshe Dayan Center for Middle Eastern and African Studies, 1996

Livingstone, Neil, C.; Halevy, David, *Inside the PLO:* covert units, secret funds, and the war against Israel and the United States, Washington DC, New York: Morrow, 1990

Lustick, Ian, *From the land and the Lord: Jewish fundamentalism in Israel*, New York: CIAO, 1998

Makovsky, David, *Making Peace with the PLO:* the Rabin government's road to the Oslo Accords, Boulder: Westview Press, 1999

Mark, Clyde R.; Katzman, Kenneth, *Hamas and Palestinian Islamic Jihad:* recent developments, sources of support, and implications for US policy, Washington DC: Congressional Research Service, Library of Congress, 1994

Masadeh, Mohamad Taisir, *The search for security in the Middle East between Israel and neighboring countries*, Carlisle Barracks, PA: US Army War College, 2000

Merari, Ariel, *PLO: core of world terror*, Jerusalem: Carta, 1983

Miller, Aaron David, *The PLO and the Politics of Survival*, Georgetown University Center for Strategic and International Studies, New York: Praeger, 1983

Mishal, Shaul, *Hamas: a behavioral profile*, Tel Aviv: Tel Aviv University, Tami Steinmetz Center for Peace Research, 1997

Mishal, Shaul, *The PLO under Arafat:* between gun and olive branch, New Haven:Yale University Press, 1986

Mishal, Shaul; Sela, Avraham, *The Palestinian Hamas Vision, Violence, and Coexistence*, New York: Columbia University Press, 2000

Mollen, Bjorn, *Three futures for Israel and Palestine*, Copenhagen: Copenhagen Peace Research Institute, 1999

Moses-Hrushovski, Rena; Moses Rafael, *Grief and grievance: the assassination of Yitzhak Rabin*, London: Minerva Press, 2000

Munayer, Salim J., *Seeking and pursuing peace:* the process, the pain, and the product, Jerusalem: Musalaha, Ministry of reconciliation, 1998

Mussalam, Sami, *The Palestinian Liberation Organization—its function and structure*, Brattleboro, VT: Amana Books, 1990

Naaz, Farah, *The road to peace: the Israeli-Palestinian conflict*, New Delhi, India: Institute for Defense Studies and Analyses, 2000

Norton, Augustus R.; Greenberg Martin Harry, *The International relations of the Palestinian Liberation Organization*, Carbondale: Southern Illinois University Press, 1989

Nusse, Andrea, *Muslim Palestine:* the ideology of Hamas, Amsterdam: Harwood Academic Publishers, 1998

Nusse, Andrea, *The Ideology of Hamas:* an example of contemporary Sunni Fundamentalist Thought, Thesis, 1991

O'balance, Edgar, *Islamic fundamentalist terrorism, 1979-1995:* The Iranian connection, Washington Square, NY: New York University Press, 1997

Olivier, Roy, *The failure of political Islam*, Cambridge, Mass: Harvard University Press, 1995

Oren, Michael, *PLO, nexus for international terror*, Jerusalem: Jerusalem Center for Public Affairs, Jerusalem Institute for Federal Studies, Center for Jewish Community Studies, 1983

Ovendale, Ritchie, *The origins of the Arab-Israeli wars*, London; New York: Longman, 1999

Paz, Re'uven, *"Sleeping with the Enemy":* a reconciliation process as part of counter-terrorism: is Hamas capable of "Hudna"?, Hertzelia: International Policy Institute for Counter-Terrorism, The Interdisciplinary Center, 1998

Pellestiere, Stephen C., *Hamas and Hizballah the radical challenge to Israel in the occupied territories*, Carlisle Barracks, PA: Strategic Studies Institute, US Army War College, 1994

Rabinovich, Itamar, *Waging peace: Israel and the Arabs at the end of the century*, New York: Farar, Straus and Giroux, 1999

Rashad, Ahmad, *Hamas: Palestinian politics with an Islamic hue*, Annandale, VA: United Association for Studies and Research, 1993

Reich, Bernard, *Arab-Israeli conflict and conciliation:* a documentary history, Westport, Conn.: Greenwood Press, 1995

Rosenthal, A.M., *Modern political myths of the Middle East:* a western journalist's view, Ramat Gan: Bar Ilan University, Faculty of Jewish Studies, Martin (Szusz) Department of Land of Israel Studies, 1999

Rubin, Barry M., *Inside the PLO: officials, notables, and revolutionaries*, Washington DC: Washington Institute for Near East Policy, 1989

Rubin, M., *Israel, the Palestinian Authority, and the Arab States*, Ramat Gan, Israel:

Begin-Sadat Center for Strategic Studies, Bar Ilan University 1998

Rubin, Barry M., *The PLO's new policy: evolution until victory?* Washington DC: Washington Institute for Near East Policy, 1989

Rubin Barry M., *Revolution until victory?:* the politics and history of the PLO, Cambridge, Mass: Harvard University Press, 1994

Ruebner, Joshua, *Israel national unity government and implications for the peace process,* Washington DC: Congressional Research Service, Library of Congress, 2001

Sacco, Joe; Said, Edward W. and others, *Palestine,* Seattle, WA.: Fantagraphic Books, 2001

Said, Edward W., *The end of the peace process: Oslo and after,* New York: Vintage Books, 2001

Savir, Uri, *The process: 1,100 days that changed the Middle East,* New York: Vintage Books, 1998

Schiff, Z., and Ya'ari E., *Intifada,* the Palestinian Uprising, Israel's Third Front, New York: Simon & Schuster, 1989

Schoenberg, Harris O., *A mandate for terror: the United Nations and the PLO,* New York: Shapolsky Publishers, 1989

Scott, Ivan, *Jew vs. Arab: sibling rivalry of the ages,* Fort Bragg, CA: Lost Coast Press, 2001

Sela, Avraham; Ma'oz Moshe, *The PLO and Israel:* From armed conflict to political solution, 1964–1994, New York: St. Martin's Press, 1997

Shabath, Yehezkel, *Hamas and the Peace Process,* Shaarei Tikva, Israel: ACPR Publishers, 2001

Shipler, David K., *Arab and Jew: wounded spirits in a promised land,* New York: Penguin Books, 2002

Shlaim, Avi, *The Iron wall: Israel and the Arab world,* New York: W.W. Norton, 2001

Shlaim, Avi; Rogan, Eugene L., *Rewriting the Palestine war:* 1948 and the history of the Arab-Israeli conflict, Cambridge: Cambridge University Press, 2001

Smith Charles P., *Palestine and the Arab-Israeli conflict,* Boston; Bedford: St. Martin's Press, 2001

Stav Arie, *Israel and a Palestinian state: zero sum game?* Tel Aviv: Zmora-Bitan; Ariel Center for Policy research, 2001

Stav, Arie, *Palestine will rise upon the ruins of the state of Israel,* Shaare Tikva, Israel: Ariel Center for Policy Research, 2000

Stein, Janice Gross, *The widening gyre of negotiation: from management to resolution in the Arab-Israeli conflict,* Jerusalem: The Leonard Davis Institute for International Relations, The Hebrew University of Jerusalem, 1999

Susser, Asher, *Double Jeopardy:* PLO strategy toward Israel and Jordan, Washington DC: Washington Institute for Near East Policy 1987

Susser, Asher, *The PLO and the Palestinian entity,* London: Anglo-Israel Association, 1989

Timmerman, Kenneth R., *In their own words: interviews with leaders of Hamas,*

Islamic Jihad and the Muslim Brotherhood: Damascus, Amman, and Gaza, Los Angeles, CA: Simon Weisenthal Center, 1994

Tsiddon-Chatto, Yoash, *Israel-Arabia:* eye to eye with the future, Israel: Ariel Center for Policy Research, 2001

Wagner, Heather Lehr, *Israel and the Arab World*, Philadelphia: Chelsea House Pub., 2002

Wallach, Janet; Wallach John, *Arafat: in the eyes of the beholder*, Secacy, NJ: Carol Publishers Group, 1990

Watson, Geoffrey R., *The Oslo Accords international law and the Israeli-Palestinian peace agreements*, Oxford; New York: Oxford University Press, 2000

Webman, Esther, *Anti-semitic motifs in the ideology of Hizballah and Hamas*, Tel Aviv: Tel Aviv University, Faculty of the Humanities, 1994

Wootten, James P., *Hamas: the organization, goals and tactics of a militant Palestinian organization*, Washington DC: Congressional Research Service, Library of Congress, 1993

ARTICLES

Abdallah-Shallah Ramadan; Al-Ayid-Khalid (interviewer), "The movement of Islamic Jihad and the Oslo process," *Journal of Palestine Studies*, 1999; XXXVIII 4 (112)

Abu-Amr, Ziad, "Hamas: A historical and political background," *Journal of Palestine Studies*. XXII, no.4, summer 1993: 5

Andromidas, Dean, "Israeli Roots of Hamas Are Being Exposed," *Executive Intelligence Review*, vol 29, no.2, January 18th, 2002

Ahmad, Hisham H., "Hamas," *PASSIA*, Jerusalem, 1994

Ahmad, Hisham H.; Robinson, Glenn E., "Hamas; from religious salvation to political transformation: the rise of Hamas in Palestinian Society," *International Journal of Middle East Studies*. 28, no. 2, 1996: 273

Bligh, Alexander, "The Intifada and the new political role of the Israeli-Arab leadership," *Middle Eastern Studies*, v.35, no.1, Jan.1999

Cubert, Harold M., "The PFLP's changing role in the Middle East," in *Peace Research Abstracts*. 37, no.5, 2000

Esposito, John L., and Piscatori, James P., "Democratization and Islam," *Middle East Journal* 45, no.3, summer 1991

Falah, Ghazi, "Intifadat Al-Aqsa and the bloody road to Palestinian independence," *Political Geography*, 2001 (February); 20:2

Fricsh, Hillel, "The Evolution of Palestinian Nationalist Islamic Doctrine: Territorializing a Universal Religion," *Canadian Review in Nationalism*, 21, nos. 1–2, 1994

Garfinkle, Adam, "Israel and Palestine: a precarious partnership," *Washington Quarterly*, v.20, summer 1997

Gee, John R., "Unequal conflict: the Palestinians and Israel," in *Peace Research Abstracts*. 38, no.1 (2001)

Glass, Charles, "The scene is set for another Lebanon," *New Statesman*, v.130, 2001

Hatina, Meir," Hamas and the Oslo Accords: religious dogma in a changing political reality," *Mediterranean Politics*, autumn 4:3, 1999

Hatina Meir; Pipes D., "Islam and salvation in Palestine: the Islamic Jihad movement," *Middle East Quarterly*, VIII4, fall 2000

Heller, Mark A., "Towards a Palestinian state," *Survival*, v.39, summer 1997

Honig, Parnass Tikva, "The Al-Aqsa intifada: taking off the masks," *New Politics*, 2001, winter, VIII:2

Al-Jarbawi, Ali, "The position of Palestinian Islamists on the Palestine-Israel Accord," *The Muslim World*, 83, nos. 1–2, January–April 1994

Karon, Tony "Hamas Explained," *Time, http://www.time.com/time/world/article/0,8599,188137,00.html*

Keller, Adam, "The Middle East: hope is a scarce commodity," *New Politics*, 2001 (summer), VIII:3

Kjorlien, M. L. "Hamas in Theory and Practice," *Arab Studies Journal*, I, no.2, 1993

Kodmani-Darwish Bassma, "Arafat and the Islamists: conflict or cooperation?," *Current History*, 1996 (January);95:597

Kramer, Martin, "Fundamentalist Islam at large: the drive for power," *Middle East Quarterly*, 3, no.2, June 1996

Kushner, Harvey W., "Suicide bombers: business as usual," *Studies in Conflict and Terrorism*, v.9 Oct/Dec1996

Lahman, Shay, "Sheikh 'Izz al-Din al-Qassam," in Elie Kedourie and Silvia Haim, eds., *Zionism and Arabism in Palestine and Israel*, London: Frank Cass, 1982

Legrain, J.F., "Hamas: Legitimate Heir of Palestinian Nationalism?" in John L. Esposito, ed. *Political Islam: Revolution or Reform*, Boulder, Colo: Lynne Rienner, 1997

Lewis, Bernard, "Rethinking the Middle East," *Foreign Affairs* 71, no.4, Fall 1992

Litani, Y., "The Militant Islam in the West Bank and Gaza Strip," *New Outlook* 32, nos.11–12, November–December 1989

Litvak, Meir, "The Islamization of the Palestinian-Israeli conflict: the case of Hamas," *Middle East Studies*. 34, no.1, 1998: 148

Luft Gal, "Who is winning the Intifada?" *Commentary*, v.112, no.1, July/Aug. 2001

Mayer, Tomas, "Pro-Iranian Fundamentalism in Gaza," in E. Sivan and M. Friedman, eds., *Religious Radicalism and Politics in the Middle East*, Albany: State University of New York Press, 1990

Monshipouri, Mahmood, "The PLO versus Hamas: Peace, Democratization and Islamic Radicalism," *Middle East Policy*. 4, no.3, 1996

Muslim, Muhammad, "The Foreign Policy of Hamas," *Council on Foreign Relations, http://www.cfr.org/public/pubs/Muslih2.pdf*

Muslin, Muhammad, "Palestinian civil society," *The Middle East Journal*, v.47, spring 1993

Newman, David, "From peace to war: relighting the flames of the Israel-Palestine conflict," *Boundary and Security Bulletin*, 2001 (autumn); 9: 3

Nirenstein, Fiamma, "How suicide bombers are made," *Commentary*, v.112. no.2, Sept. 2001

Norton, Augustus Richard; Telhami, Shibley; Robinson, Glenn E.; Peretz, Don; Alterman, Jon B.; Xavuz, M. Hahan; Gunter Michael M., "The Middle East: is the peace process dead?" *Current History*, 2001, (January); 100:642

Peled, Alisa Rubin, "Towards autonomy? The Islamic movement's quest for control of Islamic institutions in Israel," *The Middle East Journal*, v.55, no.3, Summer 2001

Perlmutter, Amos, "The Israel—PLO accord is dead," *Foreign Affairs*, v.74, May/June 1995

Pundak, Ron, "From Oslo to Taba: what went wrong?" *Survival*, (autumn), 4:3, 2001

Robinson, Glenn E., "Palestine after Arafat," *Washington Quarterly*, v.23, no.4, Autumn 2000

Rodman, David, "Israel, Hamas, and Islamic Jihad," *Midstream*; a monthly Jewish review. 42, no.5, June 1, 1996

Satloff, Robert, "Islam in the Palestinian Uprising," *Orbis*, 33, no3, summer 1989

Sayigh, Yezid, "Arafat and the anatomy of a revolt," *Survival*, v.43, no.3, autumn 2001

Sayigh, Yezid, "Palestine's prospects," *Survival*, v.42, no.4, winter 2000/2001

Schlze, Kirsten E., "Camp David and the Al-Aqsa Intifada: an assessment of the state of the Israeli-Palestinian peace process, July–December 2000," *Studies in Conflict and Terrorism*, v.24, no.3, May/June 2001

Seitz, Charmaine, "Hamas stands down?," *Middle East Report*. 31, no.4, 2001

Shanab, Ismail Abu "Interview; Founding Member of Hamas," *Middle East Policy*. 6, no.1, 1998

Shikaki, Khalil, "Peace now or Hamas later," *Foreign Affairs*.77, no.4, 1998: 29

Silverman, Johnathan, "The US view of Hamas: Then and Now," *Jewsweek*, *http://www.jewsweek.com/israel/078.htm*

Singer, Joel, "Mayday for Oslo," *National Interest*, no.55, spring 1999

Steinberg, Matti, "The PLO and Palestinian Islamic Fundamentalism," *Jerusalem Quarterly*, no.52, 1989

Tutunji, Jenab; Khaldi Kamal, "A binational state in Palestine: the national choice for Palestinians and the moral choice for Israelis," *International Affairs*, v.73, Jan. 1997

Usher, Graham, "Letter from Jerusalem: impact of Islamic suicide bombings on relations between Israel and the occupied territories," *New Statesman and Society*, v.9, 1996

Usher, Graham, "What kind of nation? The rise of Hamas in the occupied territories," *Race and Class*, v.37, Oct/Dec 1995

Viorst, Milton, "Middle East peace mirage on the horizon?," *Washington Quarterly*, v.23, no.1, Winter 2000

Zahhar, Mahmud, "Hamas: Waiting for Secular Nationalism to self-destruct," *Journal of Palestine Studies*. 24, no.3, 1995:81

"Arafat's choice," *The Economist*. 361, 2001

"Arafat's latest climb-down reflects a weakening domestic position. Watch out for Hamas resurgence." *Middle East International*, no.621, 2000: 9

"Group profiles report," 01-25-1995

"Hamas and Arafat's men," *The Economist*. 350, no.8101, 1999: 56

"Hamas in waiting," *The Economist*. 350, no.8101, 1999

"Hamas and the PLO," *The Economist*. 332, no.7879, September 3, 1994

"Hamas 1, PLO 0," *The New Republic*. 211, no.24, December 12, 1994

"Hate makes hate—an interview with Hamas: A top military leader talks," *Time*, November 13, 2000:56

Israeli military indictment against Nabil Abu Ucol, Case number:3442000, 3562000, Gaza court, 8-24-2000.

Israeli military indictment against Kitan Mahmid Handauwi, Case number:4745/00, 136/00, Hebron court, 2-23-2000.

Israeli military indictment against Basel Rashed Mechmad Daka, Case number: 40243/00, 194/00, Hebron court, 9-24-2001.

"International Affairs," FBIS-NES-94-182, 20 September, 1994

"International Affairs," FBIS-NES-94-182, 27 October, 1994

"International Affairs," FBIS-NES-94-182, 25 October, 1994

"International Affairs," FBIS-NES-94-182, 24 October, 1994

"International Affairs," FBIS-NES-94-182, 18 October, 1994

"International Affairs," FBIS-NES-94-182, 17 October, 1994

"International Affairs," FBIS-NES-94-182, 12 October, 1994

"International Affairs," FBIS-NES-94-182, 11 October, 1994

"Palestinians look to Lebanon's example," *The Economist*. 354, no. 8163, 2000

"Popular, extreme and an alternative to Arafat. Also why the suicide bombers keep dying, and the charity accused of terrorist links," *Time*, December 17, 2001: 50

"Sharon's strategy, if he has one," *The Economist*. 361, 2001

"The Palestinians and Hamas—Hamas has the people's heart," *The Economist*. 361, no.8250, 2001

"What's next for Hamas?," *http://www.janes.com/security/international_security/news/jid/jid011108_1_n.shtml*

"What is the Hamas up to?," *The Economist*.348, no.8082, 1998:46

PRIMARY SOURCES, PERIODICALS, AND NEWSPAPERS

al-Bayadir al-Siyasi (East Jerusalem)
Biladi—Jerusalem Times (East Jerusalem)
Filastin (Gaza)
Filastin-al Muslima (London)
Filastin al-Thawra
Ha'aretz (Tel Aviv)
Ha-Mizrah he-Hadash (Jerusalem)
al-Hayat (London)

al-Hayat al-Jadida (Gaza)
al-Istiqlal (Gaza)
Kol Ha'ir (Jerusalem)
Kol Yerushalayim (Jerusalem)
Majjallat al-Dirasat al-Filastiniyya
al-Manar (East Jerusalem)
Ma'ariv (Tel Aviv)
al-Mujtama` (Kuwait)
al-Nahar (East Jerusalem)
The New Republic (Washington DC)
News from Within (Jerusalem)
The Observer (London)
al-Quds (East Jerusalem)
Qira`at Siyasiyya (Florida)
al-Rasid (noncirculating internal Hamas report)
al-Risala (circulating internal Hamas report)
al-Sharq al-Awsat (Paris)
Sawt al-Haqq wal-Hurriyya (Umm Al-Fahm)
Shu'un Filastiniyya (Nicosia)
al-Tahlil al-Siyasi (circulating internal Hamas report)
al-Wasat (London)
al-Watan (Gaza)
al-Watan al-`Arabi (Paris)
Yediot Aharonot (Tel Aviv)

WEB SITES

Hamas:
http://I-cias.com/cgi-bin/eo-direct.pl?hamas.htm
http://www.terrorismfiles.org/organizations/hamas.html
http://megastories.com/islam/world/palestin.htm
Hamas Charter *http://terroristwatch.tripod.com/hamascharter.html*
http://encyclopedia.com/articlesnew/05593.html
http://www.ict.org.il/inter_ter/orgdet.cfm?orgid=13
http://web.nps.navy.mil/~library/typ/hamas.htm
http://www.terrorism.com/terrorism/HAMAS.shtml
http://www.fas.org/irp/crs/931014-hamas.htm
http://www.palestine-info.com/hamas
http://www.terrorismanswers.com/groups/hamas3.html
http://www.palestine-info.com/hamas/leaders/index.htm
http://www.ds-osac.org/globalnews/story.cfm?KEY=14741
http://www.pmo.gov.il/english/ts.exe?tsurl=0.22.2718.0.0
http://www.mapreport.com/countries/israel.html
http://world.std.com/~camera/docs/oncamera/ochezb.html

www.ict.org.il
http://www.cnn.com/WORLD
www.nytimes.com
http://news.bbc.co.uk/hi/english/world/middle_east/
http://dailynews.yahoo.com/h/abc/20010731/wl/mideast010731_1.html
http://www.jpost.com/
http://www.palestine-info.com/hamas/communiques/
http://israelemb.org/press/terror/homepage.html
www.adl.org/israel/hamas.html
http://www.iap.org/politics/misc/truth.html
Popular Front for the Liberation of Palestine (PFLP):
http://ict.org.il/inter_ter/orgdet.cfm?orgid=31
Palestinian Islamic Jihad (PIJ): *http://web.nps.navy.mil/~library/tsp/pij.htm*
http://news.bbc.co.uk/hi/english/in_depth/middle_east?2001?israel_and_the_pales-tinians/profiles/newsid_1658000/1658443.stm
History of Middle East Conflict: *http://news.bbc.co.uk/hi/english/in_depth/mid-dle_east/2000/mideast_peace_process/newsid_340000/340237.stn*
Middle East history and references *http://www.mideastweb.org/history.htm*
The Palestinian-Israeli conflict *http://www.usnewsclassroom.com/resources/activi-ties/act001023.html*
Camp David II: Assumptions and Consequences *http://www.brookings.edu/views/articles/telhami/Chjanuary2001.htm*
Israeli Foreign Ministry *http://www.israel.org/mfa*
Palestinian National Authority *www.pna.net*
Israeli-Palestinian Interim Agreement *http://www.israel.org/mfa/go.asp?MFAH00qa0*

AUDIO-VIDEO

Suicide bomber, New York: CBS Video, 1997
We are Allah's soldiers, East Jerusalem: Al-Quds Distributions, 1993

About the Author

A former director of the Terrorism Studies Program at The George Washington University, Prof. Yonah Alexander is currently Director, Inter-University Center for Terrorism Studies (affiliated with academic institutions around the world). In addition, he is a Senior Fellow and Director, International Center for Terrorism Studies, Potomac Institute for Policy Studies, as well as Co-Director, Inter-University Center for Legal Studies at International Law Institute.

Educated at Columbia University, the University of Chicago, and the University of Toronto, Professor Alexander taught at The George Washington University; American University; Columbus School of Law at Catholic University of America; Tel Aviv University; the City University of New York; and the State University of New York.

His research experience includes such appointments as Research Professor of International Affairs, The George Washington University; Senior Fellow, the Institute for Advanced Studies in Justice, School of Law, American University; Senior Staff Member, Center for Strategic and International Studies, Georgetown University; Director, Institute for Studies in International Terrorism, State University of New York; and Fellow, Institute for Social Behavior Pathology, the University of Chicago.

Dr. Alexander is Founding Editor of the *International Journal on Minorities and Group Rights*. He also founded and edited *Terrorism: An International Journal* and *Political Communication and Persuasion: An International Journal*. He has published over ninety books on the subjects of international affairs, terrorism, and psychological warfare.